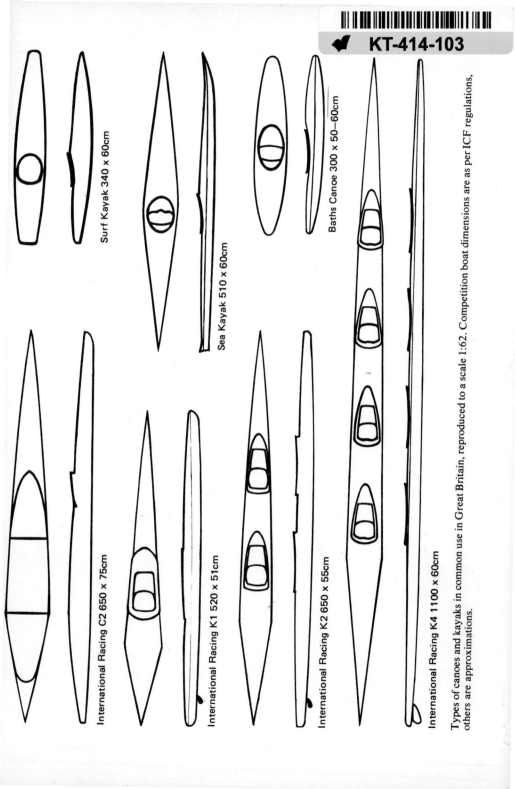

Surf Kayak 340 × 60cm

Sea Kayak 510 × 60cm

Baths Canoe 300 × 50—60cm

International Racing C2 650 × 75cm

International Racing K1 520 × 51cm

International Racing K2 650 × 55cm

International Racing K4 1100 × 60cm

Types of canoes and kayaks in common use in Great Britain, reproduced to a scale 1:62. Competition boat dimensions are as per ICF regulations, others are approximations.

'For I am the captain of my craft
My word is law from fore to aft,
I am the cook and the steward too,
I am the passenger and crew,
And though 'tis said I'm hard to please,
I'm not afraid of mutinies;
In fact my complement at sea
Is as perfect as it can be'.

From *Canoe Handling* by C. Bowyer Vaux,
Forest and Stream Publishing Co, New York
1885.

Canoeing Handbook

Edited by Geoff Good
Assisted by Bob Gray

with contributions by:
Frank Goodman, Jim Hargreaves, Graham Lyon, Derek Hutchinson,
Martyn Hedges, David Train, Ric Halsall, John Hermes, Ron Moore.

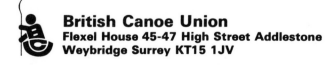

British Canoe Union
Flexel House 45-47 High Street Addlestone
Weybridge Surrey KT15 1JV

First Published 1981
Re-print with minor corrections 1982
Re-print with minor corrections 1983

ISBN 0 900082 03 8

Front Cover Picture: The late Dr Mike Jones on the river Chassezac, which flows into the Ardeche, in the Massif Central, France. Photo: Peter Midwood
Back Cover: River Alsek, Alaska. Photo: Peter Knowles

Printed in Great Britain by:
The Chameleon Press Limited
5-25 Burr Road, Wandsworth, London SW18 4SG.

Preface

Within the following terms and definitions this book sets out to be what its title claims – the 'Canoeing Handbook'. There is no area of canoeing activity which is knowingly unmentioned, though the work is not intended as a technical handbook for each of the separate disciplines that constitute the competitive elements of the sport.

It is successor to the BCU *Coaching Handbook*, and so it is written with the potential instructor in mind. A narrative form has been chosen, rather than that of a training manual, however, in order to make the book readable by, and useful to, all who wish to take up the pastime, exploring its full potential for simple enjoyment – or for challenge, excitement and adventure.

In Great Britain, the generic term 'canoeing' is used to describe any craft which is easily portable and is propelled by a paddle – the exception being the International 10 square metre Sailing Canoe. (The administration of this class, for historical reasons, is undertaken by the British Canoe Union. Nowadays, however, the International Canoe, for all practical purposes, is a sailing 'dinghy'.)

Due also to the traditions and natural evolution of the sport in the United Kingdom, it is 'kayaking' and not 'canoeing' that has flourished. There are signs that the canoe will come into its own, but the *Canoeing Handbook* is intended to show the present balance of interest, and stage of development of the whole pastime in this country.

Some sections are more detailed than others. This is a reflection, not of the relative importance of the subject, but of the purpose of the book. Even the comparatively explicit chapters deal with topics that really require a volume to themselves. The aim therefore has been to indicate the vital areas of knowledge, rather than to supply every last fact required for safe and successful canoeing within that realm.

The use of the pronoun 'he' or 'his' in the text is not sexist – it is used pending the invention of a new term that can be conveniently employed without the necessity to indulge in grammatical gymnastics.

Detailed syllabii of test and awards, BCU administration, and similar matter, subject to periodic review, have been deliberately omitted. All this is available in simple 'handout' form – as is information on any and every aspect of canoeing – from the British Canoe Union.

G. C. Good
Addlestone, Surrey 1981

Acknowledgements

It is with deep gratitude that I thank the following:

The individual contributors, whose standing is acknowledged at the outset of their work; the many who have advised, reviewed, suggested and commented, or whose competence and influence has led to the statements made, reflecting a consensus view among canoeists; Roger Lovesay, for being foolish enough to produce a comprehensive visual aid display on a course, say yes when asked if he would illustrate the Handbook, and who has answered every request with prompt efficiency; Bryn Hughes, Photographer of Kingsbury, London, who took most of the shots of different types of craft in chapter 8, the kayak rolling sequence, and various other pictures throughout the book – his technical guidance and his interest as a canoeist, have been helpful beyond measure; Ken Fidler, of Studio 69, Llanrwst, for the photographs in chapters 5 and 7; Mick and Vanda Powell, who spent many patient hours on the Canadian rolling drawings, which proved particularly difficult; Simon Maskell, for the canoe outlines, the polo training and certain other diagrams; the staff of the small BCU headquarters units, whose daily routine is always overfull, and yet who have managed to respond to urgent demands for copy typing – and re-typing; and those who have posed for pictures – willingly or unwittingly – or who have supplied them.

Thanks are due to the Commodore and members of the Richmond Canoe Club, the Leaside Young Mariners Youth Centre, and Plas y Brenin National Centre for Mountain Activities for providing facilities and equipment for the photographing of the various types of boat, and to the Welsh Harp Youth Sailing and Canoeing Base for opening the Centre for the pictures of clothing to be taken. The gear was kindly loaned by White Water Sports, Woking, and modelled by Helen Hughes and Richard Mullick.

A great number of people have commented, or contributed statements or ideas that have been incorporated, including Brian Barfoot (polo), John Drew, Keith Harrison, Randall Williams, Drew Delaney and Philip McKee (rolling) and many others, who I hope will not be offended if this list is not extended to include every name. The process of contribution and feedback is the lifeblood of coaching, and the part all have played in the whole, has been vital to our progress.

Roland Lawler and Colin Gray provided the technical information for the forward paddling sequence, and Chris Canham posed for the pictures.

Without the considerable practical help and professional guidance with the production, of my good friend Bob Gray, this work could not have been published by the BCU. To him, and our relieved wives, I say a special thank you.

Finally, my predecessor, Oliver Cock, MBE, deserves particular mention, for his *Coaching Handbook* formed a basis for much of the background material. Oliver's work over so many years on behalf of the sport, the Union as a whole, and the Coaching Scheme in particular, is deserved of a permanent tribute, and it is to him therefore that this book, and I would hope, its successors, is dedicated.

G C Good

Contents

Introduction

I read most of the books on canoeing as they are published. However having been a member of the Coaching Scheme for over fifteen years and a fairly active club canoeist I usually find little in them that is new to me. This Handbook is something of an exception and I should be very surprised to find anybody who having read it could honestly say that they had not learnt a great deal.

It is unique in the sense that it contains some of the very latest information and has been written by canoeists who are active in their specialised field. This has meant that a great deal of current thinking and practice has at last got into print and it is not just a re-write of what has gone before. There has also been a considerable effort to look at aspects of canoeing that have not been well covered in previous literature.

You will not be able to sit down and read this book from cover to cover in the same way that one might read a novel. Rather it has to be taken a chapter or even a few pages at a time and needs careful reading. It will be necessary to read certain sections several times with constant reference to the diagrams and illustrations before everything becomes clear. This is inevitable when you deal with a sport in book form and is particularly so in the case of a varied and complex sport like canoeing.

The Handbook has not set out to be a teach yourself canoeing, although in some cases it will be used in this way. The aim has been to provide a wealth of background knowledge to complement that already gained through instruction and experience. It should become the standard reference work that appears on almost all canoeists' bookcases.

Graham Lyon
Chairman of the Coaching Scheme

1 A Short History of Canoeing in Britain

Compiled by the Editor and Bob Gray, with acknowledgement to Oliver Cock, MBE for his booklet of the above title, published by the British Canoe Union.

INTRODUCTION

The modern canoeist or kayakist enjoys a primitive battle with a hostile environment, equipped only marginally better than his ancient forebears. For while the latest building materials give the advantage of greater strength, and allow for more sophisticated hydro-dynamic shapes, essentially the craft is still the simplest, most basic form of vessel on which it is possible, efficiently and successfully, to navigate the lakes, rivers, estuaries, coasts and oceans of the world.

Part of the attraction that canoeing holds must be that there is a sympathy with the past, when man first sat astride a log and drifted down-river. This may well have been before the invention of tools, although a branch would have made a crude paddle at an early stage. Logs tied together formed a more stable platform, and then the advantage of shaping points would have been discovered. Finally, the hollowing out of trunks by burning and chiselling, created the dug-out, which was the craft from which all other forms of water transport have evolved.

Still in use for hunting, fishing, trading and warring, in many parts of the world today, dugouts up to 60' in length, papyrus or balsa-wood rafts, outrigger canoes, all developed according to the raw materials available, and the type of water on which communities found it advantageous to travel. In North America, the dug-out was followed by the timber frame and birch bark river canoe of the Red Indian, while the Eskimos evolved the skin-covered sea-going kayak.

Victorians were exploring every corner of the globe, playing and refining all forms of games, and developing into recreational sports and pastimes ancient survival skills such as mountaineering and ski-ing when, in 1865, one such gentleman, John (Rob Roy) MacGregor, a London Scot who was a barrister by profession, after seeing canoes and kayaks in North America and the Kamschatka, persuaded Searle's of Lambeth to make him a craft based on his observations. Clinker-built (a form of construction whereby timber planks are overlaid, rather like a fence) the first 'Rob Roy' weighed around 90 lbs, compared to the 15-20 lbs of the present-day competition kayak. It was about 14' 6" in length, and decked in fore and aft, creating two bulk-headed compartments each end of an open 'well' or cockpit. The occupant sat on the floor and propelled the vessel with a double-bladed paddle, although a small lug-sail could be set to take advantage of a following or beam wind.

Rob Roy then began a series of remarkable journeys, covering over 1,000 miles of Continental waterways, later navigating on the Jordan and Nile, and paddling around the Baltic, besides other voyages. Lecture tours and books* of his journeys spread interest in

---

* Some books by MacGregor: *A Thousand Miles in the Rob Roy Canoe* (1867); *The Rob Roy on the Jordan* (1869); *The Rob Roy on the Baltic* (1872).

this new sport, besides raising many thousands of pounds, which he donated to charity – the plight of London's orphans in particular being of great concern to him.

The Canoe Club, the first in the world, was founded on the Thames at Twickenham in 1866, the Prince of Wales becoming Commodore in 1867 until his accession to the throne as Edward VII in 1901. By command of Queen Victoria, the name was changed to the Royal Canoe Club in 1873, and so it is known today. MacGregor's Jordan and Nile tour boat is still preserved there.

Many adherents began to cruise the rivers and coasts of Britain. *The Field, The Boys Own Paper,* other periodicals, and numerous books, attest the rapid growth in canoeing which occurred during that final quarter of the 19th century, spreading to Europe, and even to Australia. For instance, in 1879, using a 'Rob Roy' shipped to him by the designer, the Rev Fred C. B. Fairey paddled over 300 miles of the coast of Tasmania to visit outlying parishes, performing in the process the first recorded 'loop'.

Other types began to evolve as various boat-builders, some of whom had been making traditional punts and skiffs for 100 years, became interested in this fresh market. The 'Rob Roys' themselves were of varying lengths and beams, and open canoes were also popular. Much reliance was put on the expanding railway system for the transporting of equipment to the start and finish of watery explorations. A pictorial record of a trip by three elegantly dressed ladies on the Warwickshire Avon in 1885 is recorded in *The Field* at that time, culminating in a wait at the station, with all their gear, by the exhausted trio.

Interest in canoeing in Britain appears to have diminished following this first generation of intense activity however, and it is to Germany that we must look, with the invention by Klepper, before the first World War, of the folding canoe, for the further development of the sport in the early part of this century. It will be easier from then on to follow its evolution through the history of each section separately, for canoeing is a multi-faceted activity. No other form of water transport allows for quite the same feeling of being part of the element, and another of its great attractions is that once a person is equipped with the basic craft, and is in possession of the fundamental skills to operate it, the proponent of this ancient art can enter so many different realms. From paddling the peaceful solitude of a placid stream, to negotiating the roaring turbulence of raging rapids, or riding the mighty surge of savage surf, the canoeist is able to enjoy the whole spectrum of experiences that the sport has to offer, or to concentrate on that which gives him the greatest pleasure, as character or mood dictates.

GENERAL DEVELOPMENT AND ORGANISATION

The British Canoe Association was formed in 1887, primarily for touring canoeists, but quietly died in the 1920s, never having become the governing body for the sport. With the explosion of interest in canoeing on the Continent however, in spite of the set-back of the Great War, an international federation known as the Internationalen Representation for Kanusport (IRK) was formed by Austria, Germany, Denmark and Sweden in 1924.

It was an Austrian, H. W. Pawlata, who in 1927 performed the first Eskimo roll achieved by a European, having learned the art by studying papers about the Eskimos, particularly those by Rasmussen. Gino Watkins, an Englishman, dreamed of the Arctic Air Route over Greenland, and went there to explore its possibilities in 1930. Whereas Pawlata learnt to roll for the fun of it, Watkins did so to survive and obtain food for his expedition party. Film of Watkins' group in training for Greenland still exists in the BCU film library.

At that time travellers to Europe began to bring back news of the elegant folding canoes

Figure 1:1 *John MacGregor, MA, the founder of the sport of canoeing in Great Britain. From* Pictorial Chronicles of the Mighty Deep *about 1890.*

which were to be seen in thousands on German rivers. One of the first manufacturers in this country was Kissner, who started to make the 'Folbot' in London, about 1933. Another, F.O.D. Hirschfeld, a refugee from Hitler's Germany, started on Tyneside in 1935, creating the firm of Tyne Canoes Ltd.

The early '30s also saw the development of clubs, with Manchester Canoe Club, and the Canoe Camping Club being formed in 1933; so then it became important to establish a national governing body. After correspondence in the national press, the British Canoe Association (Mark II) was formed. It amalgamated with the Canoe section of the Camping Club, but remained as a section of the Camping Club of Great Britain, and affiliated to the IRK. As a national governing body needs to be entirely independent before it can affiliate other clubs to it, after much debate, a new national body was formed in March, 1936, called the British Canoe Union, and it was under the aegis of the BCU finally that Britain entered a team for the first Olympics to include canoe racing, in Berlin, later that same year.

When Frank Schulhof came to England as manager of the London branch of an Austrian company, significant developments were to take place, He was an experienced canoeist, with seven first descents of Alpine rapid rivers to his credit, and he had invented the 'Schulhof' or 'Put Across' method of rolling. In 1937 he took parties from the Royal Canoe Club to the French Alps and to the Hampshire and Sussex coasts, where films were made which were the foundation of the BCU library. Frank taught rolling, and in 1938 launched the first BCU Rolling Circus. He anglicised his name to Frank Sutton, and during the war distinguished himself as the first 'enemy alien' to gain a commission in HM Forces, being awarded the Military Cross. The first canoe slalom to be held in Britain, in 1939, was organised by Frank Sutton, assisted by Maurice Rothwell, among others.

The Second World War interrupted all development until in 1946 John Dudderidge represented Britain in the creation of the new International Canoe Federation (ICF) replacing the IRK, whose headquarters had been in Munich.

Kayak skills were dramatically improved in the early '50s by Milo Dufek, a Czechoslovakian canoe paddler who moved to Switzerland, and translated strokes used in the Canadian, to the kayak. Thus began the 'basic skills' defined later in this book. The British slalom team of 1953 were coached in these new techniques by the German champion, Erik Seidel, who also developed the shaped seat by sitting on a bag of sawdust.

The rapid growth of the sport required different levels of administration, and so technical committees were set up to cater for the needs of alternative disciplines. Paddle racing (sprint) and slalom were the first to be established, and now committees exist for marathon, wild water racing, sea canoeing, surf, canoe polo, touring, access, coaching, and the Corps of Canoe Lifeguards.

The establishment of the BCU Coaching Scheme owes much to the work of John Dudderidge, who travelled extensively in 1959 and 1960 selecting people to organise coaching on a regional basis. The scheme has developed into an effective network of organisers, and more recently part-time National Coaches have been appointed to train specialist competition coaches. Oliver Cock was appointed as the first full time National Coach in January 1962.

The initial signs of any form of standard qualification appeared in 1949 with the first Proficiency Tests. John Dudderidge produced a set of standards for the Duke of Edinburgh's Award, and later, the Advanced Tests were introduced. Thus the National Coaching Committee was given some groundwork upon which to develop its standards for teaching. After some years with John Dudderidge in the chair, he retired, and in 1966 Geoff Sanders, who had previously been its honorary secretary, took his place.

The Corps of Canoe Lifeguards was first conceived by Rear Admiral (then Captain) Hoare. The serious East Coast floods of 1953 gave him the idea that a properly trained

4

Figure 1:2 *'Crossing the Sound' from the book* Come Travelling *by Warrington Baden-Powell published in 1871.*

Figure 1:3 *'Somersault in the surf at Falmouth' (Tasmania) – surely the first loop. From the* Boy's Own Paper *of 1892.*

canoeist could render assistance. However, floods are occasional, and the Corps found itself drawn to lifeguard work on the beaches. It was difficult to convince the authorities that a canoe could be anything but a nuisance, and it was a long, hard battle before the Corps became an accepted part of the Life Saving services. Again, John Dudderidge was initially in the chair, until the scheme became established and could stand on its own.

Due to these developments the organisation of the sport by amateurs became impractical, and in 1962 the Union employed a professional secretary. Captain Alec Kennedy RN (Retired) was appointed, and offices were acquired in Central London.

The Scottish Canoe Association was formed in 1939 and became a 'division' of the BCU in 1944. Northern Ireland followed, with an independent association, the Canoe Association of Northern Ireland (1965). Both retained separate membership facilities and rights until 1978, when a move to create separate Associations for all four nations, with the BCU becoming the federal body to which all belonged, was defeated at a special general meeting. A compromise was reached, where the existing Associations, and the newly formed Welsh Canoeing Association, entered into an agreement with the BCU, which recognised them as the governing bodies within their countries. The BCU retained responsibility for federal (Great Britain) matters, and for England. Full reciprocal rights of membership exist between the Associations and the BCU. It was now essential for England to establish a regionally based structure. This was in keeping with the views of the Sports Council, and by the end of 1980 regional BCU committees had been established in accordance with the boundaries recognised by the Sports Council.

It will be noticeable within this chapter that one name persistently appears. The contribution that John Dudderidge has made to the sport, the Union, and the ICF, is immeasurable. His personal involvement in so many different aspects has been greatly responsible for the development of canoeing. Awarded the OBE in 1963, and in 1964 the Award of Honour of the ICF, in 1980, at the Moscow Olympics, he was presented by the ICF with a specially struck gold medal in recognition of his devotion and unique service which has led to the growth in strength and stature of the pastime founded in the 'pleasure of the paddle'.

SPRINT RACING

Sprint racing was the first type of organised canoe competition, with a formal regatta having taken place at The Canoe Club in 1867, when fifteen Rob Roys participated. In 1874 the, by then, Royal Canoe Club instituted the Paddling Challenge Cup, the oldest paddling trophy in the world. Races for this were competed in Rob Roys, which gradually became longer and narrower, and so faster. By the end of the century four-man kayaks had appeared, also clinker-built, known as Rob Roy Fours.

Following the Rob Roy, the 'Single Streak' evolved, constructed from two 'streaks', or planks, one on each side, of cedar less than ⅛" thick. The dimensions as to length and beam varied according to the weight of the paddler, but an average size would have been 20' by 22", decked fore and aft with a bulkheaded cockpit, or 'well', protected by narrow side decks and coaming. The paddler sat on the floorboards, bracing himself against a backboard and adjustable footrest, or 'stretcher'. The paddle was about 7'6" long, spoon-bladed, and unfeathered.

Paddle racing in Britain was carried on mainly in the spring and autumn meetings of the Royal Canoe Club and at a few local regattas on the Thames in the early 1900s, with the emphasis changing to single blade paddling. On the Continent, however, it grew from

Figure 1:4 *Franz Schulhof on the Bregenzer Ach, Western Austria in 1932.*

Figure 1:5 *A 'Senior Rob Roy Four' of 1926.*

7

strength to strength, until the President and Secretary of the IRK, both Germans, were influential in persuading the Olympic Organising Committee of the Berlin Games to put forward canoeing as a new sport for that programme. This led to a great leap forward in international canoe racing. The BCA immediately made a provisional entry for the 1936 Games, but with little or no idea how to implement it. John Dudderidge became involved in finding and preparing a team following the first British National Championships, at Chertsey, the previous year. In the autumn, canoeists were invited to take up intensive training, and a squad of twenty was gathered. Winter training began on the Tideway, but in the spring of 1936 the base was moved to the Royal Canoe Club, where a 10,000 metre course had been prepared. By this time the squad had fallen to about twelve. At Whitsuntide, with a move to Windermere to gain experience on water more like that which they were going to find in Berlin, the party numbered some half dozen.

The team were to concentrate on the 10,000 metre event. G. W. Lawton came 8th out of 13 in the Folding Singles, and A. R. Brearley and J. W. Dudderidge came 9th in the Folding Pairs. These Olympic Games were an important landmark, in that it was the first time a British team had taken part in an international event.

Although feathered blades were used for kayaks from early times, particularly in America, it was not until the late '20s that they were generally accepted in Europe. By the 1936 Olympics most nations had adopted them, apart from the Hungarians – who quickly followed suit.

In the spring of 1937, John Dudderidge organised a course at the RCC, and obtained the services of the leading German coach, Geerhard Quandt, who brought over with him the first K1 (international racing single kayak). The enthusiasm engendered was so great that the 'Royal' bought a fleet of racing kayaks from Austria, of three K1's and three K2's (doubles) which were supplied and delivered in London for £80 the lot!

The first Olympic Games after the war were staged in London, with the canoeing events at Henley-on-Thames. The BCU had no resources for purchasing boats, but Jicwood of Weybridge came to the rescue by building and donating twelve kayaks. Two racing Canadian Canoes were made by Austin Farrar of Wolverstone Shipyard, and these boats provided the basis for rebuilding British sprint canoeing. At Henley we were represented in all events, including, for the first time the Ladies' K1.

Eric Farnham took over the coaching of the team in 1950, and the Swedish coach, Hans Berglund, taught the first post-war racing course at Bisham Abbey. New boats, including modern K4s appeared. Altogether, the scene looked promising for the future, and there was great hope of achievement at Helsinki in 1952. But standards elsewhere had improved, and our placings were not as good as had been hoped. In 1953, we gained a second place in the first West European Championships in Duisburg, followed by a 1st in K4 at an international regatta at Namur. Also in 1953, the *News of the World* sponsored the first of the annual Sprint Championships on the Serpentine in London.

In their efforts to encourage others to join in sprint racing, the Paddling Racing Committee introduced the National Chine Kayak, but despite the fact that this exceptional canoe could be made easily and cheaply at home, the class did not flourish. By 1957 the number of competitors had dropped to a dangerously low figure, and in an effort to halt the decline Junior and Senior events were introduced. This decision produced a record number of junior entrants, and so the situation improved. By the time of the 1959 European Championships at Duisberg, Britain was able to enter the largest team yet. For the 1960 Olympic Games in Rome, we obtained better results than ever, and of the four events entered, only in one did our entrants not reach the semi-finals. In the K1 Men's event, Ron Rhodes not only reached the final – the first time in the Union's history – but by producing his best time, secured fifth place, thereby qualifying for an Olympic diploma.

1961 saw the birth of the British Open Youth Championships. It was hoped that, by building up a large group of enthusiastic young people in sprint racing, a sound pyramid of competitors, would develop, forming a broad base from which future world champions could be produced. However, due to lack of able administrators, the scheme foundered.

The creation of Holme Pierrepont National Water Sports Centre in 1972 was a significant factor in the development of British Racing, for this magnificent nine lane purpose built course has enabled world class events to be staged with pride and ease. The annual Nottinghamshire International Regatta, established in 1972, is now regarded world-wide as second to none, and attracts the top canoeing nations, with over 500 international athletes competing.

British interest in sprint Canadian racing was spasmodic until 1973, when Willy Reichenstein competed in the World Championships. Since then the sport has started to develop, particularly at Junior level. Steven Train and Alan Saunders, from Fladbury Canoe Club, reached the C2 finals at the 1979 Junior European Championships. A renewed attempt to maintain the C7 internationally at Junior level has arisen from Fladbury's interest. The first ever British crew was entered for the 1981 Junior Championships in Sofia, Bulgaria.

At the present time, the Eastern bloc nations have a virtual stanglehold on international racing competition, and only occasionally are medals won by others. Britain has still to achieve an Olympic medal, but British competitors have appeared regularly in finals at this level during the past decade. Leading the way have been Laurence Oliver and Doug Parnham. Doug, of Richmond CC, reached both mens' K1 finals in the 1976 Montreal Games and was placed 4th in the K1 10,000 metres World Championship final in 1977. At Junior level, progress has been even better, with Jeremy West, Royal CC, gaining the Silver Medal in the Mens' K1 500 metre event in the 1979 Junior Championships. The women too have made progress, culminating with both the K1 and K2 crews reaching their respective finals at the 1980 Moscow Olympics – the first time that this had been achieved at the same Games.

Considerable improvement was evident at the start of 1981, with gold, silver and bronze medals being won at international regattas in Amsterdam, Gent and Duisburg. In the highly successful World Championships staged at Holme Pierrepont, Britons not only reached the greatest number of finals ever – four – but our first World Championships medal was won by the 10,000 metre K4 crew of Williams, Canham, Brown and Jackson, who took the Bronze.

Strides have been made in the past decade with large increases in competitors, officials, national regattas, sponsorship and media coverage. Whilst like most of British sport we lack the sophisticated coaching system of the socialist countries, the potential, and the machinery to capitalise on it, now exists.

CANOE SAILING

In MacGregor's day, a small lug-sail could be set on the Rob Roy. Warrington Baden-Powell, brother of the famous 'BP', developed the canoe into a fully equipped sailing craft, and by the early 1870s the new sailing canoe possessed centre board (invented in the USA) yawl rig and outboard rudder, and could make a course against the wind. The canoeist stayed inside the cockpit, and from this position could operate all the controls. In 1874 the Royal Canoe Club put up the Sailing Challenge Cup, to match the Paddling Challenge Cup. This trophy, plus the New York Canoe Club (founded 1871) International Cup, are among the oldest in the world.

An early Baden-Powell design was exported to America, and international competition began when Warrington Baden-Powell and Guy Ellington challenged for the New York Canoe Club International Cup in 1886. They found that the Americans gained extra power by sitting up on the deck, using bodyweight to counteract the pressure of wind in the sails. Guy Ellington, on his return, designed *Charm,* a lightly-built craft in the American style, which crushed the opposition at home, but still could not beat the Americans. Soon after this, Paul Butler of the USA introduced the idea of sitting outside his canoe entirely, using a sliding seat.

By the early 1900's, the British had moved away from the original canoe concept of a craft 16' long by 30" beam, and in 1896, Baden-Powell sponsored a more powerful 'Cruising Canoe'. This was 16' × 42", and stubby, so the length was soon increased to 17'. The Cruising Canoe was raced, and became the 'B' Class, which quickly developed into a fast and effective sloop-rigged sailing vessel, beautifully fitted. The modern style of Bermudian rig appeared as early as 1911.

After the First World War there was a period of stagnation until in 1932 Uffa Fox designed and built two canoes which would with only a little bending of the rules, fit both the British 'B' Class, and the American specification. In company with Roger de Quincey, Uffa went to America in 1933 and won the New York Cup. Even more important than this, was the agreement between the Royal Canoe Club and the American Canoe Association, for new International Building Rules, which, with modification, form the basis of our present International Class.

On the continent a very different type of sailing canoe was in use. It carried 7½ square metres of sail, and was recognised by the IRK. A World Championships was held in Stockholm in 1938, and in 1939 the Swedes competed in their own canoes against the Royal Canoe Club. This demonstrated the overwhelming superiority of the 'Anglo-American' 10 square metre design, though it was not until 1946, when the ICF was constituted, that this vessel was adopted as the International 10 square metre Sailing Canoe under ICF Rules.

In 1955, the 'Ladder Slide' was produced, which allowed the helmsman to reach five feet out, with his feet firmly braced, and a ratchet block, which enabled him to lock or free the mainsheet at will. Again, the New York Cup stimulated action, and though in 1955 a strong British team failed to win, in 1959, with the new technique firmly established, Alan Emus and Bill Kemper brought the trophy to England where it has remained.

After a number of international regattas, the first World Championship in the IC class was held at Hayling Island in 1961, with Great Britain, USA, Sweden and West Germany competing. Britain swept the board, taking the first six places. Others were learning fast however, and although Britain still took the gold and bronze medal at the 1965 World Championship at Lake Constance, the silver went to Sweden. Sweden took the first four places in the 1967 European Championship, held on their home water, and just failed to take the gold from Alan Emus in the 1969 World Championship again in England, at Grafham Water.

During this time many technical changes had come about through the introduction of new materials, namely cold moulded, hot moulded veneers, GRP for hulls, aluminium alloy for masts and spars, synthetic fibres for sails and rope; and the complicated development of fully battened sails. Increasing international competition in Europe has raised sailing standards and improved techniques, with Denmark, and now Spain, joining the Canoe Sailing nations.

From 1971 the ICF adopted the Nethercot design as a 'one-design hull'. Regretfully the last decade has seen a decline in the popularity of International Canoe Sailing in Britain, but recent moves to promote this class have convincingly turned this trend into one of positive rejuvenation.

Figure 1:6 *A Modern International 10 sq metre Sailing Canoe*

SLALOM

Slalom first appeared on the continent in the late 1920's, where it was linked with skiing. One can imagine the skiers suggesting the hanging of poles over rapid water for a simple, timed run down between them. The first British slalom at Trevor Rocks on the Welsh Dee, in 1939, was followed by one at Ludlow on the Teme, in 1940. Due to the war, the next event was not until 1948, at Taymain Islands, again on the Dee.

A World Championships was held at Geneva in 1949, where British results indicated we were well behind the rest of Europe. The next World Championships were in 1951 at Steyr, Austria, where the 'Steyr' roll was first seen. Although doing somewhat better, it was not until 1953 at Merano in Italy, that the British were sufficiently depressed to consider remedial action. There was a meeting of interested people at the Chalfont Park Canoe Club at Hambledon that autumn, and Oliver Cock took on the job of coaching the British team. Improvements were gradual, until in 1959, once more at Geneva, Paul Farrant won the coveted F1 (folding single) World Championship. Tragically, he died in a road accident the following Easter. It is of interest to note that Paul had to fit his own footrest and knee grips as these were not then universally accepted.

At the end of 1961, having seen the British team win the Bronze Medal at Spittal-auf-dem-Drau in Austria, Oliver retired as the team coach and became the first National Coach for canoeing. British results were not as successful again until 1967, when Dave Mitchell won the World Silver Medal. Two years later, the mens kayak team of John MacLeod, Ray Calverley and Ken Langford took the Silver at Bourg St Maurice. These three names were at the forefront during the decade since the mid-60s, and the success achieved in the 1981 World Championships is in large measure attributable to their expertise and dedication subsequently in the coaching field.

By 1963 the folding and rigid canvas canoes had disappeared from championship events, replaced by glass reinforced plastic boats, first brought over from the Continent. The skills which Milo Dufek had introduced in the early 50s, allied to the new designs that were now possible, opened up a new and wonderful field of white water canoeing, although discussion was still enjoined as to whether curved blades could be successfully mastered in moving water! With the introduction of GRP, the kayak, with its deck already in existence, could be rounded off in cross-section, and it was found that this was an advantage for its performance in rough water, since there was no sharp angle at the gunwale for the water to catch and capsize the craft. In the case of the Canadian there was no big traditional deck, so the craft was decked in, making what looked crudely like a mis-shapen banana with round holes for cockpits.

Slalom kayaks have gradually become lower in profile. In 1965, Klepper introduced the SL5, which was the first designed to turn more efficiently in an upright position than when leaned. This seemed to be ahead of its time for it was not until about 1975 that a totally new concept and set of skills came into being, with boats being built to allow the ends to be 'dipped' or 'ducked' under the poles. This technique had, however, been observed in the late '60s and early '70s, used by such masters as Dave Mitchell, seven times British Champion besides World Silver Medallist, and Jorgen Bremmer, the East German who was twice World Champion and Olympic Gold Medallist.

Canadian canoes have moved in the same direction – it is now difficult for a non-slalomist to know whether he is looking at a single kayak or a canoe, and for doubles, the seating has moved to a central position, allowing for faster turning, as well as facilitating dipping techniques. A milestone was reached in the Canadian classes when in 1980, Martyn Hedges became the European champion, and in 1981 Britain won the World C2 Team Gold Medal at Bala, North Wales.

For the 1972 Olympic Games in Munich, a purpose-built slalom course had been

Figure 1:7 *Paul Farrant, Britain's first World Kayak Slalom Champion.*

designed at Augsburg, which is still used for international competition and is available for general practice. Victoria Brown (Vicky) was the best placed British competitor, coming 6th in the Ladies' K1.

The Welsh Water Authority had made available for canoeing events the River Tryweryn, which flowed into Lake Bala, but was now controlled by the Celyn Dam, allowing for metered water releases to be made. Through the generous sponsorship of the Sports Council, this was developed for international competition, and was the site of the 1981 World Slalom and Wild Water Championships which, together with the Racing Championships at Nottingham meant that Britain was unique in being the first nation to stage all three canoeing events with World Championships status in the same country in the same year.

In the 1977 World Championships in Austria, Albert Kerr had won the Gold Medal in the mens' K1, thus becoming our first World Champion since 1959, and taking the coveted 'Paul Farrant Trophy'. Two years later, the British mens' team took the Gold Medal at Jonquiere, in Canada, and successfully defended their title at Bala where Richard Fox also became the men's K1 individual World Champion. With the ladies winning the team Silver Medal, the past decade has seen growing success internationally, with a fundamental change in attitude to the importance of training and coaching in order to maintain our position in world rankings.

The Slalom Committee, faced with a continuing annual increase in demand, and a limit on suitable resources, are looking to purpose-built sites, and in particular to a proposed course at Holme Pierrepont National Water Sports Centre. This was first mooted in 1967, and a working model produced under the auspices of Frank Goodman, funded by the Sports Council, in 1974.

Regretfully, with canoe slalom subsequently being dropped from the Olympic Games mainly due to the high cost of providing sites, the pressure came off the provision at Holme Pierrepont. With the continued increase in demand, however, and the likelihood of canoe slalom being re-introduced into the Games, an action group has been formed to pursue the project to a satisfactory conclusion.

WILD WATER RACING

Meanwhile, the idea of just racing straight down rapid rivers had not escaped the minds of many. Here, skill in reading water was just as necessary as in slalom, and stamina became even more important. Several miles down rapids needs nerves of iron as well, and it is not surprising to find rapid river racing on the increase. The first World Championship White Water Race was held on the Vezere in France in 1959, and a British team consisting of most of the World Slalom team from Geneva was entered.

The terms 'white water' and 'wild water' are synonymous, 'wild water' being favoured internationally. In Britain, since the separation of slalom and racing, it has become accepted that 'white water' is used to denote all activities on rapids. Hence, there are two forms of competition held on 'white water' – slalom, and wild water racing.

Although the developments have not been so dramatic in wild water racing as for slalom, there has been a continual evolution of boat designs, which now, whilst being very buoyant, are almost as 'tender' for the novice as is a racing K1. The tradition of slalomists doubling as wild water racers continued until about 1977, when increasing specialisation and competition led to the BCU agreeing to a separate Committee being formed to concentrate on Wild Water Racing. Internationally, there is still a single Slalom and Wild Water Racing Committee governing the two sports.

Outstanding success came in the late 1970s when in 1979, Robert Campbell won the Silver Medal at Jonquiere, and in 1980, Britain took the first two places in men's kayak at the Bala pre-Worlds International. In 1981 Ann Plant became the World Bronze Medallist for ladies K1, and the British men's kayak team obtained the Silver.

When the difficulty of obtaining access to white water is considered against the fact that Britain has no *continuous* stretch of grade III rapids, at which level wild water racing is pursued, the world class standing of many of our competitors is all the more remarkable.

MARATHON RACING

It may seem somewhat absurd to find the foundations of Marathon Racing laid in a bet and a double sculling skiff! Owing to a threatened public transport strike in 1920, a group of friends in the Greyhound Public House at Pewsey, fell to discussing other means of conveyance, and ended up with a bet of £5 that they could travel with their skiff via the River Avon from Pewsey to the sea at Mudeford, near Christchurch, in less than three days. They won their bet with twelve hours to spare. Twenty seven years later, three RAF men and a local farmer met a member of the original crew in the same pub. They decided to try their luck, got to Christchurch in 51 hours, and so won a further £5.

Roy Cooke, a member of that 1947 crew, then planned a boat trip from Devizes to Westminster in 100 hours, and although his project fell through, the idea was taken up by the Devizes Rover Scouts. Their object was to reach the sea by way of the Kennet and Avon Canal to Reading, and thence down the Thames to Westminster. The townspeople of Devizes responded to the idea and put up money to be donated to the Unit in the event of a successful attempt. Thus it was, that at Easter 1948, with news of their progress interrupting cinema programmes in their home town, the first two crews from the Devizes Rovers, paddling cumbersome home-built double kayaks, completed the course with ten hours to spare. At Whitsun that same year, two doubles of the Chippenham Sea Cadet Unit covered the same course in just under 77 hours, and the competition was on.

Without any formal rules, except the broad stipulation that competitors should carry all their food and equipment from the start, and receive no assistance en route, twenty crews set off from Devizes at Easter 1949. The best time that year was 49 hours 32 minutes. Prompted by the growing interest, Frank Luzmore of the Richmond Canoe Club, set up an organising committee, and Easter 1950 saw the first formal race. From these modest beginnings, the event has continued to grow, so that now more than 300 crews regularly take part, and the winning time for the gruelling 125 miles and 76 portages has been cut down to the present record of 15 hrs 35 m – established by Brian Greenham and Tim Cornish in 1979.

Others became inspired by the concept of Long Distance Racing, as it was then called. At first, the Sprint Racing Committee took charge of this new form of competition, and set up a sub-committee in 1955 to administer it. Later, in 1958, when LD had developed further, this sub-committee became an independent technical committee of the BCU, racing being held in England, Scotland, Ireland, Europe, and now many other parts of the world. Renamed Marathon Racing, and thanks largely to the efforts of John Dudderidge, it was recognised by the ICF in 1979, where it is still under the control of the Paddle Racing Committee.

In the early days, any type of canoe could be raced by anyone in an 'open' class, but the impracticalities of this were soon recognised. Various handicap systems were tried, with varying degrees of success. In 1956 a junior class was set up for those between the ages of 15 and 19, and the canoes were also divided into four classes – singles under 15' and over 15'; and doubles under and over 17'.

The one-design National Chine Kayak was added in 1959. Ladies were given separate status, and 1960 saw further developments when classes included K1, K2 and NCK1 for seniors only, while others provided for seniors, juniors and ladies, making fifteen in all. Hard skin and soft skin canoes were put into different categories, the soft skin group still providing for folding and home built lath and canvas canoes. Hence there was an apparent anomaly between the maximum length for a soft skin double at 17'6'' (many folding doubles were of this length) and that of its hard skin counterpart at 17'. In 1964, junior K1 and K2 events were added to the list, and ladies' NCK1 in 1966.

With the increasingly improved standards in paddling it became apparent that newcomers were discouraged by having to compete against the country's leading competitors and so in 1971, a separate grouping was approved for the top paddlers. The other senior paddlers were included in an open class, with a third for juniors under 18. The Espada Youth K1 was introduced, with competitors racing in three age groups: 12 to 14; 14 to 16; and 16 to 18 – which was also agreed for sprint racing.

Previously, in 1957 Lloyds of London presented the Royal Marines with a beautiful trophy in memory of their raid on Bordeaux by canoe during the Second World War. This, the Hasler Trophy, named after Major 'Blondie' Hasler, the leader of the raid, was handed over by the Royal Marines to the BCU for administration. It is competed for annually by clubs on a points system.

The first National Championships in Long Distance Racing was held at Bradford-on-Avon in 1965. From 1971 to 1980 this event was held annually on the Severn at Worcester.

The name 'marathon racing' was adopted in 1978, and a re-appraisal of the class arrangement took place. There is now a 'divisional' system, which allows for all ages and all types of boat to be raced together, promotion from the lower divisions taking place on an ability basis. Once a certain level has been reached, paddlers naturally gravitate to a racing kayak or canoe if they wish to progress, or they can enjoy good competition in that division in a slower type of craft.

CANOE POLO

This game was first mentioned in two books: Noel McNaught's *Canoeing Manual,* and Oliver Cock's *You and Your Canoe,* both published in the mid 1950s. Although the rules differed, the basic objects of the game were to release people from their inhibitions and fears in their canoes. The idea of having fun was dominant, and rules were kept to the barest minimum for safety.

The origins of Polo must lie in the event at Hunter's Quay in Scotland (Figure 1:8) whilst in Germany games were played on football-size pitches on lakes, attracting great numbers of spectators, before the second World War. Today, a one-design small kayak is used there, and a regular national league is operated.

Polo in Britain was first demonstrated at the National Canoe Exhibition at Crystal Palace in 1970. This was met with enthusiasm, a competitive structure was soon formed, the first National Championships were held at the next Exhibition, and have taken place annually ever since. In 1979 a national league was formed.

The special boats for use in swimming pools had been developed as early as 1966, when Bert Keeble produced a wooden canoe, short, with rounded ends. Alan Byde designed a similar boat in GRP, which he dubbed the 'Baths Advanced Trainer' – BAT for short. Canoe Polo is therefore often referred to nowadays as 'Bat Polo'.

CANOE SURFING

Whilst an early film made by Schulhof prior to the Second World War depicted surfing at Cuckmere Haven, the sport did not become properly established until 1952. Oliver Cock took a small party to Polzeath in Cornwall and initiated an annual event. In 1964 the BCU surfing week moved to Bude, and it was here in 1967 that the first National Championships in Canoe Surfing took place. The early competitions used mainly slalom or general purpose kayaks, and the rules were adapted from those used for competitive Malibu board riding.

In 1970, a new type of canoe appeared on the scene from California, specially designed for surfing. It had a flat hull, and considerable rocker, which enabled many more manoeuvres to be carried out. At the same time however, it cut out some of the other tricks which were popular. Therefore a second class had to be allowed in the competitions, as the two craft could not fairly compete against each other. 1970 also saw the idea of competition in surf spread to the North East, when the first local championships were held. With the advent of the specialisation that the new surf kayaks brought, pressure built up for a separate governing body. A compromise was reached, however, and the BCU Surf Committee came into being in 1974. Since then, surf techniques and skill levels have improved considerably, and whilst there are still open classes for mainly slalom boats, the trend is to the specialist surf kayaks, and now skis.

The Surf Committee are currently pursuing an active policy of promoting the sport internationally and seeking ICF recognition. In 1980 a British team entered an unofficial World Championships in the USA, competing with merit.

Figure 1:8 *Water Polo at Hunter's Quay, Scotland. From* The Graphic *of 18 September 1880*

CANOE ORIENTEERING

This is a form of competition in canoeing which has got off to a slow start. It first appeared in print in the 'Know the Game' series, *Orienteering,* published in 1965, and has taken place perfunctorily all over the United Kingdom since then. Perhaps one of its strongest centres is at Martham Ferry in Norfolk, where an annual event has been held since 1970. The sport is well suited to almost any piece of water, but especially old wet gravel pit workings, which have been allowed to run to nature. It is a pity, therefore, that more have not been attracted to what can be a very exciting activity.

TOURING AND EXPEDITIONING

Rob Roy MacGregor undoubtedly undertook expeditions as well as tours, as did many of the pioneer canoeists. The illustrations from some of the early books demonstrate that many outstanding journeys were made. Rob Roy's voyages, and those of the Rev Fred C. B. Fairey have been mentioned. In 1885, T. H. Holding, founder Chairman of the Canoe Camping Club, led a group of four in three canoes from the Clyde, through the Kyles of Bute, past Corryvreken into Loch Fyne, and by land to Loch Lomond, paddling its length and back into the Clyde. He makes the interesting observation, 20 years after the beginning of the sport, that 'there had been a sad decline of interest in sea touring'!

Before and immediately after the second World War, there are matter-of-fact accounts of some very enterprising passages, both sea and inland. Frank Sutton, mentioned earlier, paddled the Upper Inn in Switzerland, in the 1930s, not officially recorded since until the descent in 1969 covered by the *Sunday Telegraph Magazine* which included the late Dr Mike Jones – then a 16 year-old. J. L. Henderson, a Scottish Sprint Champion, describes a voyage around Cape Wrath in 1950 in *Kayak to Cape Wrath*, and a number of unassuming Scottish paddlers undertook totally committing passages around the coasts, and out to the Western Isles in the '50s and '60s, often in PBKs (Percy Blandford designed Kayaks – these were mainly large-cockpit canvas covered boats, designed for the Scout Movement).

It is not always recognised that the Marine Commandos, using mainly folding canvas doubles, would have to paddle up to 60 miles when carrying out raids on enemy coasts and shipping during World War II, while a notable expedition was the crossing of the Atlantic by the German, Dr Lindeman, in a Klepper folding double, from Las Palmas to the Leeward Islands in 1956.

In more recent times, and probably the commencement of the present interest in major expeditioning, was the 1966 crossing of the Pentland Firth by Joe Reid and Andy Carnduff. This was followed in 1969 by the first crossing of the Irish Sea from Dun Laoghaire to Holyhead.

In 1971 the first British expedition to conquer the Colorado, the mighty river of the Grand Canyon, took place. This included Mike Jones who, the following year, with Mick Hopkinson, paddled down 220 miles of the Blue Nile. He followed this in 1976 with the 'descent of Everest' – canoeing down the Dudh Khosi from 17,500', and in 1977 successfully ran the Maipure Rapids on the Orinocco in South America, reputed to be the world's biggest cataract. As Dr Mike Jones, he was tragically drowned when trying to effect a rescue at the outset of the attempt in 1978 on the Braldu River, flowing from the Karakoram (K2) in Pakistan.

Meanwhile, the trend developed on the sea when Chris Hare expeditioned in Greenland in 1966, and brought back some Greenland kayaks. In 1969 Geoff Blackford designed the Anas Acuta, a complete glassfibre boat based on these traditional Eskimo types. With interest reawakened in this type of vessel, a number of individuals and manufacturers began to produce other designs, and major voyages followed.

The first attempt on the North Sea failed, and then a successful crossing was completed in 1976. A pinnacle was achieved when, in 1979, Cape Horn was rounded by a group of kayakists totally independent of either land or sea support. Although the entire coast of Britain has been canoed, in sections, with unrecordable frequency for more than a century it was not until 1980 that Paul Caffyn, a New Zealander, in company with Nigel Dennis, an auxiliary Coastguard, achieved a continuous circumnavigation of the whole of mainland Britain. Paul had previously circumnavigated both North and South Island of New Zealand, mainly solo.

Such is the interest and numbers now involved, that the Long River Canoeists Club has come into being, which exists to exchange information internationally on tours and expeditions, and the BCU has established an 'Expedition Committee' to monitor and vet British expeditions for grant aid and patronage purposes.

ACCESS TO WATER

During recent years the problem of maintaining and improving access to water, particularly the majority of our rivers, has occupied a considerable amount of voluntary and paid officers' time, besides columns of type in the canoeing, angling and the general press. Rivers are created and kept constantly changing by elemental forces over which man has no control. They have been used as natural highways since the stone age. Many people

Figure 1:9 *The River Usk near Gliffaes above Crickhowell. From* Rapid Rivers *by William Bliss, published in 1935.*

find it difficult to comprehend, therefore, how this part of man's natural heritage can be privately owned. Yet such appears to be the case in the UK, and the legal situation is outlined in chapter eight – Inland Canoeing.

A part-time National Access Officer was appointed in 1979 when Oliver Cock, MBE having been honoured for his services to the sport in 1977, retired as Director of Coaching to take up that position. The Access Committee was separated from the Touring Committee in order to give full attention to the problems, and a network of river advisers and regional access officers has been established.

Speak, however, to those characters mentioned in this history and their peers. They paddled all the presently disputed waterways in days gone by and will tell of courtesy, friendliness and interest, in the main, from those anglers they passed en route.

What has happened? An obvious factor is the sheer pressure of numbers. There are claimed to be 3 million anglers in Great Britain. At least 4.5 million canoeing days take place annually. This, allied to the extortionate sums of money involved in the buying and selling of 'fishing rights', has led to the present unhappy climate. Let us consider then, the words of John Dudderidge OBE, the BCU President of Honour: 'Canoeing is one of the few sports in which pure amateurism prevails. There are no great vested interests: canoes are quiet, and do not pollute the environment, nor do they have any adverse effect on the ecology of the river. *They pass down and away and leave no evidence of their passing.* Let us cling to this reputation for sportsmanship in competition, courage in face of danger, oneness with all other creatures living in, on, or by our waterways. Through courtesy, we may even win the tolerance of the angling bodies, for we already have many friends amongst individual anglers.

We hope that in these few pages canoeists and others will have learned something about the beginnings of our sport, one of the oldest, one which brings the participant near to nature, and brings pain and fear to no other living creature.'

2 Design and Selection of Equipment

Frank R. Goodman

Frank Goodman began to canoe in 1965 and designed his first kayak a year later while working as a Senior Lecturer in Art at Clifton College of Education, Nottingham. After twenty years as a teacher and lecturer he started the company of Valley Canoe Products, and was joined by his brother in 1970 and devoted himself to full-time canoe designing and building.

He was a Division I slalomist in 1969-70. Slalom, surf and sea have been his main interests. He began slaloming again in 1977 and rose to the dizzy heights of 3rd division before declaring himself a veteran. He has slalomed in the USA, Australia and Tasmania, and canoed many white-water rivers in these countries, as well as rivers in New Zealand, Europe and the UK.

He equalled the world record for surfing with a four mile run on the Severn Bore in 1974, and crossed the Irish Sea from Wicklow to Aberdaron in the same year. He was a member of the four-man team who first rounded Cape Horn by kayak in 1977.

In 1979 he organised a kayak-building course with the Inuit (Eskimo) in Baffin Island to introduce them to modern kayak building materials, and returned in the summer of 1980 to paddle with the Inuit from Frobisher Bay to Allen Island in Baffin.

THE CANOE

Introduction

Travel on the surface of water is extremely difficult. Even nature, by and large, avoids it. A few unintelligent birds swim on the surface, but the more sensible marine mammals who must come up to breathe do so as quickly as possible, and then continue their travels at depth, thus avoiding the unpleasant consequences of travelling half submerged.

Man has been clever enough to overcome partially some of the intractable problems associated with travel on the water. He started many thousands of years ago and is still learning. The unknown genius who first sharpened the ends of his floating log should have his place in history alongside his colleague who pierced its centre and added an axle.

The Problem

The fundamental problem is that waves created on the surface by any moving object create a resistance that grows very rapidly indeed with increasing speed. Other problems are created because design features that enhance one aspect of a canoe's performance may hinder another. For example, speed and manoeuvrability are mutually incompatible, as are other more subtle aspects of performance; thus a canoe must, of necessity, be a compromise.

Varying Conditions

Further, canoes are asked to perform under a wide spectrum of water and weather conditions, and worse, these are often of a very turbulent nature. This means that the normal mathematics that can be applied to problems of performance will often give unsatisfactory results. Most canoe designs therefore, are the result of experience and intuition – not necessarily any the worse for that, but very often the canoe's stated performance becomes a matter of extravagant subjective claims rather than objective reality. *Caveat emptor!*

Performance and Hydraulics

Luckily, many of the fundamentals of the underlying mathematics of motion reveal themselves in either the 'feel' of the craft or its effect upon the water surface. This chapter deliberately avoids the use of mathematics, but wherever possible basic principles will be related to phenomena that a canoeist can experience for himself.

'Performance' is an expression of the total resistance a canoe has to the hydrodynamic forces acting upon it. This resistance depends on the size, shape, contour, weight and surface finish. To select a canoe sensibly these attributes must be assessed in relation to the resistance they will create, so that an idea of its potential performance can be obtained. The canoe's resistances to hydrodynamic forces implies resistance to motion and can be conveniently divided into two main components – 'static' and 'dynamic resistance'.

Basic Resistances of a Canoe			
Static Resistance		Dynamic Resistance	
Inherent Buoyancy	Inherent Stability	Frictional Resistance	Residual Resistance

All static resistances to motion are dependent upon:

1   The magnitude and position of the centre of gravity.
2   The magnitude and position of the centre of buoyancy.
3   The relationship between them.

In other words they are dependent on the size, shape and weight of a canoe.

Inherent Buoyancy

The size of the canoe determines its ability to support weight. More precisely, the volume of the submerged portion of the canoe is a measure of the weight it is supporting. A grounded canoe, floating after the paddler gets out, is a reminder that a floating body displaces its own weight of water. Obviously a canoe must have enough buoyancy to float its occupants and their equipment. Too much buoyancy which may allow a high freeboard to catch the wind may be just as detrimental to performance as a canoe lacking in buoyancy, where the gunwales easily submerge, with consequent lack of stability. It is easy to see that an open Canadian canoe will be of little value in strong winds, and for completely opposite reasons, a low-profile slalom canoe is also difficult to control in heavy weather. Thus neither craft is effective for journeys on the sea, although both of course, perform extremely well in the correct situation.

Inherent Stability

A change in position of the centre of gravity within a craft may cause a change in the centre of buoyancy. If this change helps to return the canoe to its original position the canoe has some measure of stability. The form of inherent stability most obvious to the canoeist is lateral stability – the 'tippiness' felt by beginners in a canoe. It is clear that the wider the

Generally, a broad beam gives a stable canoe, but the hull shape in cross-section is important.

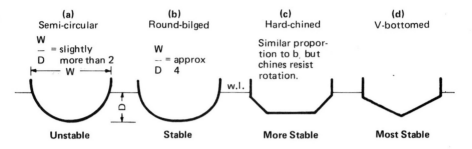

Figure 2:1a *(Lateral stability)*

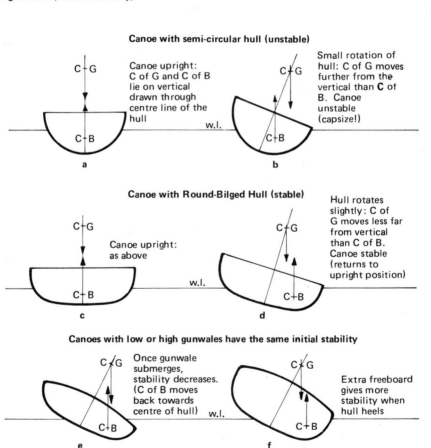

Figure 2:1b *(Lateral stability)*

beam, the more stable the canoe, but the actual cross-section shape of the hull is very important also (Figure 2:1a). More detail of the consequences of hull cross-sections are shown in Figure 2:1b, and it should be noted that freeboard, which does not affect the initial stability of the canoe (when it is upright) becomes important as the boat is progressively heeled over. Once the gunwale is submerged, stability decreases rapidly.

Generally speaking, for a single-seat kayak, any beam-width of more than about 60 cms starts to make the boat a bit of a barge. However, no hard and fast rules can be laid down, and as Figure 2:1c shows, varying conditions can alter the 'feel' of a canoe considerably.

Longitudinal Stability

The support given by a canoe at different points along its length will vary. This variation will correlate with the 'aspect ratio' of the canoe. Aspect ratio is the relationship between the length and beam of the craft. 'High' aspect ratio is long and thin, and will support weight at the ends better than a 'low' aspect boat. The fineness of the bow and stern, and the rocker of the hull, will also affect the longitudinal stability. Because canoes are often used in turbulent conditions, where bow and stern are submerged, the buoyancy of the deck and hull – the whole canoe – must be taken into account.

A low-profile slalom canoe can be looped easily because of its lack of buoyancy, which is so extreme, that the bow and stern can be forced under water deliberately by the slalomist himself. (Figure 2:2 drawings a and b).

Generally, fine-bowed canoes with rocker will be very wet boats in a sea-way, but in some lengths of wave a straight-keeled kayak can be worse, especially when it has a buoyant stern, since the stern may be lifted just as the bow is plunging into the face of the next wave. This is, of course, a contrary indication from the norm, and further shows that there are no simple answers to canoe design! (Figure 2:2 drawing c).

Although the stability of a craft is the relationship between the centre of gravity and the centre of buoyancy, in a dynamic situation the distribution of the component weights making up the centre of gravity is important. For example, in double canoes, the farther apart the crew sit, the fuller the bow and stern must be to counteract any pitching movements. (Figure 2:3).

Directional Stability

A canoe cannot travel in a straight line when the driving force, of necessity, is applied on either side of the centre line. It will yaw slightly from side to side, the amount depending on the resistance to turning of bow and stern. A deep section at the hull extremities will help to keep the canoe running true. Conversely, an increase in the amount of rocker will increase manoeuvrability (Figure 2:4b). This is not the only significant contour, however.

A high aspect ratio hull will be more directional than a beamy boat; but the shape in plan will also be important. If the widest section is behind the centre, this will allow the centre of gravity to be moved aft also. In this case, once a turn commences it will continue to grow in magnitude. Boats of this shape are known as 'Swedish Form' craft. The reverse is true if the centre of gravity is in front of centre – any change of direction will lessen, until the canoe continues on a straight line again. This type of craft has the name 'Fish Form' configuration (Figure 2:4a).

Leaning the canoe onto its gunwale will alter the under-water contours and produce a turning effect. Usually round bilge canoes will turn away from the lean, but hard chine will normally, but not always, turn into the lean. Obviously it follows that waves will alter the water-line contour and may affect the directional stability of the canoe.

Ease of turning is also a function of weight distribution in relation to the centre of gravity.

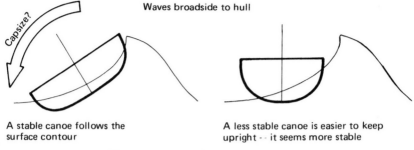

Waves broadside to hull

A stable canoe follows the
surface contour

A less stable canoe is easier to keep
upright -- it seems more stable

The wave can be surf, sea or stopper

Figure 2:1c *Wave effects on lateral stability*

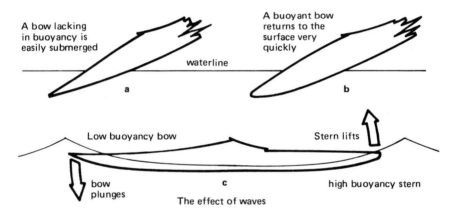

A bow lacking
in buoyancy is
easily submerged

A buoyant bow
returns to the
surface very
quickly

waterline

a

b

Low buoyancy bow

Stern lifts

bow
plunges

c

high buoyancy stern

The effect of waves

Figure 2:2 *(Longitudinal stability)*

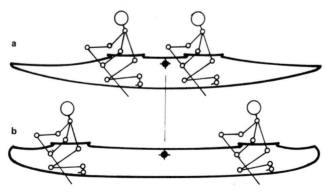

a

b

Figure 2:3 *(Longitudinal stability) Both centres of gravity are central, but the effect of the weight distribution in 'b' means that the bows here must be fuller in a dynamic situation*

25

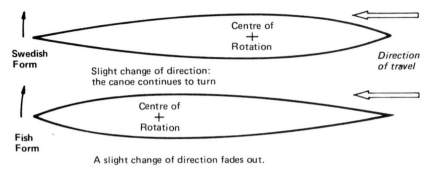

Swedish Form

Centre of
+
Rotation

Direction of travel

Slight change of direction:
the canoe continues to turn

Fish Form

Centre of
+
Rotation

A slight change of direction fades out.

Figure 2:4a *The effect of shape on directional stability*

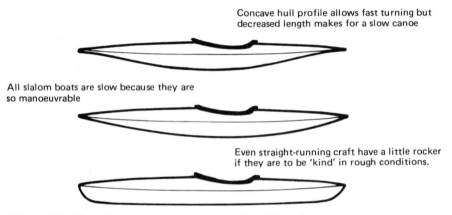

Concave hull profile allows fast turning but
decreased length makes for a slow canoe

All slalom boats are slow because they are
so manoeuvrable

Even straight-running craft have a little rocker
if they are to be 'kind' in rough conditions.

Figure 2:4b *The effects of rocker on directional stability. Increased rocker means more manoeuvreability but also more drag*

Weight near the ends will have a much more deleterious effect than weight near the centre. One pint of water in a bottle, pushed to the end of a canoe, has roughly the same effect as a gallon of water in the cockpit area. For the same reason, a C1 slalom canoe will always turn faster than a K1 slalom kayak, simply because the paddler's weight is more compact when kneeling, than when his legs are stretched out in the sitting position.

The static resistance of a canoe can be summarised as its resistance to rotation in three planes. Canoeists and other water users have many expressions to describe the phenomena! (Figure 2:5).

Dynamic Resistance

These resistances are the result of water flowing past the hull of the canoe. They are the same, whether the craft is moving through still water, or whether a current of water is flowing past a stationary canoe.

Frictional Resistance

As a canoe moves through water, molecules adhere to the hull, and move along with it, however fast it goes. Because of viscosity, the hull becomes surrounded by a thin layer of

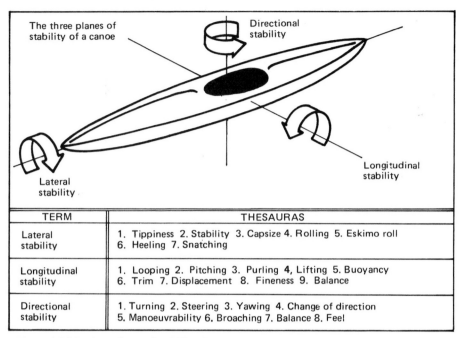

TERM	THESAURAS
Lateral stability	1. Tippiness 2. Stability 3. Capsize 4. Rolling 5. Eskimo roll 6. Heeling 7. Snatching
Longitudinal stability	1. Looping 2. Pitching 3. Purling 4, Lifting 5. Buoyancy 6. Trim 7. Displacement 8. Fineness 9. Balance
Directional stability	1. Turning 2. Steering 3. Yawing 4. Change of direction 5. Manoeuvrability 6. Broaching 7. Balance 8. Feel

Figure 2:5 *The three planes of stability of a canoe*

water being dragged along by the canoe. The outside of the layer is at rest, the inside (in contact with the hull) travels at the speed of the canoe. This is the boundary layer, and within it the forces of friction act to slow the canoe down.

Within the boundary layer the water molecules can move in two ways:

1   *Laminar Flow*
     The molecules slide past one another in orderly fashion, parallel to the hull. The thickness of the boundary layer is in the order of .1mm. Frictional losses are small.

2   *Turbulent Flow*
     The molecules cease to flow parallel to the hull, and jostle one another at random. The thickness of this boundary layer depends on the length of the craft, but can be as much as 4 cms on a 4m canoe. Frictional losses are large. Do not confuse turbulent flow within the boundary layer with the large eddies seen within the wake of a canoe. To keep frictional losses low we need to:

     (a) keep the boundary layer flow laminar,
     (b) keep the boundary layer itself as small as possible.

Point 2 is the easy one. The least wetted area for a hull is when its shape is hemispherical. Problems! The best compromise is a semicircular hull tapering at each end. Point 1 *seems* easy. A good surface finish, with imperfections not bigger than .1mm (the thickness of a human hair) is easily achieved. At very low speeds the boundary layer will remain laminar over virtually the whole of a hull made as smooth as this; friction is minimal, and the canoe will glide forward almost effortlessly. However, as speed increases, flow within the boundary layer becomes turbulent. At best, only about one fifth

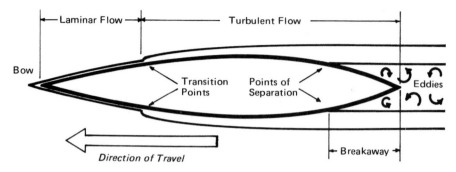

Figure 2:6 *Skin friction: the boundary layer*

of the total boundary layer, that part near the bows, retains its laminar flow, however smooth the surface.

To achieve the optimum situation as shown in Figure 2:6, you need:

1   Fine bows to part the water as gently as possible

2   No imperfections, particularly at the bow, to set up premature turbulence

3   A smooth surface finish with no imperfections bigger than .1mm

4   The surface may be polished (buffed) but not waxed. Wax will increase friction.

Frictional resistance increases steadily with speed. Up to about 2 mph it accounts for 90% of the total drag on the canoe. Above this speed, although frictional resistance continues to increase, residual resistance becomes more important.

Residual Resistance

Residual resistance causes the formation of waves and eddies. Eddies are so complicated and unpredictable that we shall have to ignore them, but waves are simpler, and knowledge of them will help us to assess a canoe's performance. Certain facts about waves should be remembered. They are listed here without any proof, but many books on oceanography or ship performance will give the mathematics behind these statements.

1   A wave is an oscilation upon the water surface. The water does not move with the wave but traces out an orbit as the wave passes. (We are talking about green waves in deep water, not breaking waves). The orbits are circular. It follows that the water molecules move forward at the crest, but backwards in the trough. (Figure 2:7).

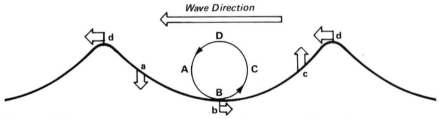

Figure 2:7 *The circular orbit ABCD shows the actual movement of the surface water molecules shown on the waves a. b. c. d.*

28

2   In deep water, the speed of the wave depends on its length only. The longer the wave, the faster it travels: speed is proportional to length. It is worth noting that the wavelength of a series of standing waves in a deep pool at the tail of a rapid, will give a rough indication of the speed of the water. To be 'deep' the depth must be more than half a wave-length.

3   In shallow water, the speed of the waves depends on depth only. All waves in a given depth of water travel at the same speed; the shallower the water the slower the waves travel. Speed is proportional to depth. To be 'shallow', the water must be less than half a wave-length deep.

4   The height and length together give an indicator of the energy contained in a wave. Energy is proportional to length times height. (A long low wave in deep water slows as it reaches shallows. The contained energy is the same (nearly). Since the wave-length gets shorter, the wave must get higher until eventually it breaks. Result – surf!).

5   The energy within a group of waves travels at half the speed of the individual waves. (If you 'surf' upon wind-blown waves in deep water, you will notice that if you start on a big wave it soon decreases in height, and the one behind it grows larger, and so on. This is a measure of the energy contained within a group of waves, and underlies the fact that you can only get intermittent surf-rides in a following sea).

How does wave formation, due to residual resistance, affect the canoe in motion? Above about 2 mph waves begin to develop, and form the distinct pattern we call the 'wake'. Eventually, the energy drained from the canoe to form the wake accounts for 60% of the total drag. The most conspicuous feature of the wake is the straight-armed V that spreads out from the bow. In deep water its angle is always 39° regardless of the speed of the canoe. Conspicuous though it is, the energy lost in this divergent wave-pattern is not great, but within its arms, another transverse wave-pattern is created, and it is these transverse waves that create drag (Figure 2:8).

The wavelength of transverse waves depends upon the speed of the canoe. Thus a canoe travelling at 3½ mph will generate a wave five feet long, while at 7 mph the wave will be 20 feet long. (Notice that when the speed is doubled the wave length is quadrupled).

Now let us see how this applies to a canoe of known length – say, a slalom canoe of 4m. At 2.75 mph it must generate a wave 3.25' long, so there will be four waves passing down the length of the hull at this speed. At twice this speed, the wave must be four times as long. In other words, the kayak is now sitting in the trough of a wave exactly the length of the hull – strictly speaking, the water-line length. (Figure 2:9).

How can the poor canoeist ever escape from this trough of his own making? The simple answer is that he cannot. As he paddles faster the wave created must lengthen; the bow of the canoe remains at the crest of the bow wave, but the centre of the trough moves towards the stern as the wave-length increases, and the kayak 'squats'. Not only has the paddler to overcome increasing skin, eddy and wave resistance, but he must literally climb up and out, off the back of the wave. Alas, the best athletes in the world cannot generate the power required for this. How near a paddler can approach the impossible, depends on several factors. The wave-making resistance of a canoe will depend on its shape. A blunt bow offers more resistance than a fine one, and therefore builds higher waves, as does a rockered hull and a broad beam. Higher waves of similar length mean steeper crests, so the paddler loses twice over; first because the energy needed to create the high wave has come from him originally; and second, because more energy is needed to climb up the steeper angle of slope.

Now another factor must obviously become important. Since the paddler is climbing a slope, the weight that he must pull upwards will determine how successful he is.

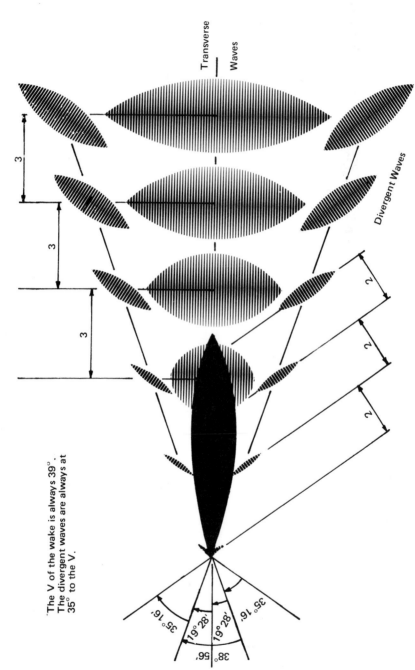

The V of the wake is always 39°.
The divergent waves are always at 35° to the V.

Transverse Waves

Divergent Waves

35° 16′
19° 28′
19° 28′
35° 16′
38° 56′

Figure 2:8 *The canoe wake formed in deep water. The transverse waves always have a wavelength one and a half times the wave length of the divergent train of waves. If this canoe is five metres long at what speed is it travelling?*

(a) SPEED 2.75 m.p.h. WAVELENGTH 1 metre
(EASY PADDLING)

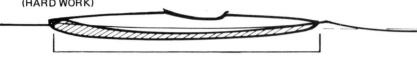

(b) SPEED 5.5 m.p.h. (twice diag. a) WAVELENGTH 4 metres (4 times a)
(HARD WORK)

(c) SPEED 7 m.p.h. WAVELENGTH 6.25 metres
(VIRTUALLY UNATTAINABLE)

Figure 2:9 *Waves formed by a slalom canoe at different speeds. At (a) canoe displaces its own weight of water. At (b) canoe 'sucks' itself deep into the water, thus displacement increases. (c) The stern lies in the trough and the canoe can never escape the wave*

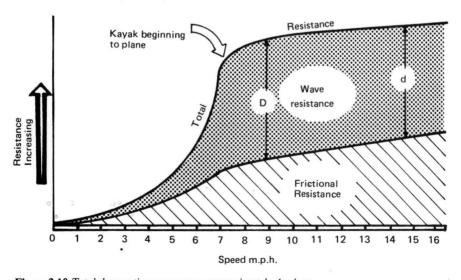

Figure 2:10 *Total drag acting on a canoe approximately 4m long*

31

Displacement is a factor of weight. Therefore, of two canoes with similar shape, the one with the least displacement will make most progress up the back of the wave, and be the fastest. Obviously the paddler's weight is the most important item here, and it is paramount that the canoeist's own power/weight ratio is high. Now we can see the intractable problem of travel at the water surface.

In a slalom canoe 4m (13.125') long, speeds up to 2.75 mph create skin-friction drag. This drag increases relatively slowly, roughly the square of the speed. (You must paddle four times harder at 2 mph than at 1 mph). Once fewer than about four waves are flowing along the length of the hull, wave-making drag becomes increasingly important, and resistance begins to increase at a higher rate. When there are less than two waves along the hull, wave drag gets really big, and by this time the canoeist is trying to claw his way out of his own trough. A 10% increase in speed may need a 100% increase in power. It cannot be done, and indeed it is this dramatic increase in power needed to increase top speed, that makes the finish of sprint canoe races so much less dramatic than track events. There can be no 'kick off the bend' or sudden explosion of speed. At best the canoeist will only edge forward to victory. (Figure 2:10).

Notice that of two canoes of identical proportions and weight, but different lengths, the longest one would always win, since a long canoe makes a longer wave to 'sit' in, and a longer wave is necessarily travelling faster. This does *not* mean that the longest canoe is always faster – there are other factors to take into account as we have seen. However, another point may be answered here: if the canoe sits in its own wave, which is travelling at the same speed as the canoe, why cannot the canoe surf on its own wake? The answer is found when it is remembered that the canoe generates a *series* of transverse waves and their group energy is only travelling at half the speed of the waves in the canoe's wake.

Notice, too, that in shallow water, the wake and wave-forms change. The wave must travel at a speed related to depth of water, not wavelength. The canoe 'feels the bottom' and slows down to the speed of these waves.

As we have seen, while solely under paddle power, a canoe can never reach the point where it begins to plane. In fact, when paddled at speed a canoe displaces *more* than its own weight, as the flow beneath the canoe actually sucks it down. (The ends of a slalom canoe are often at water-level when paddled at speed, yet when stationary they are well clear of the surface. Also, the effectiveness of self-balers indicate that there is reduced pressure below the hull).

If the speed of a canoe can be increased beyond the limits already indicated, for instance by sliding down the face of a steep wave, the pressure of water hitting the hull may be sufficient to raise the craft bodily almost clear of the surface. This dynamic lift is called 'planing', and the boat ceases to displace its own weight of water. Wave resistance decreases, but skin friction increases. Since there is considerable reduction in wetted area, this increase is much less than might be expected. However, a great deal of energy is needed to keep the canoe planing. Contrary to popular belief, there is no *fall* in resistance when on the plane, only a less rapid rise with speed. (Figure 2:11).

While most canoe hulls will plane, a completely flat hull, especially at the stern, will obviously help to force the canoe out of the water and onto the plane.

High velocities, and high drag owing to friction, suggest that a blemish-free hull is very important for maximum speed. Another major factor with planing hulls is the drag created when the water leaves the hull. Because the hull is flat, and the gunwale line is below the water-line, it is re-named the 'rail'. If the rail is rounded, or 'soft', the water tries to flow the curve, and high drag is the result. If, however, the rail is 'hard', meeting the hull at a very sharp angle, the water leaves the hull surface with minimum drag.

The rail is also important in preventing the stern of the kayak slipping sideways down the wave front. This is a job often shared by the canoeist's paddle and a skeg. The harder the rail, the better 'grip' the stern has on the wave. To increase this grip the stern of some boats are bifurcated. While this will increase the grip, the increased length of rail edge will create extra drag, which must have its effect on speed.

In practice, the rail usually has some rounding to give what can only be called 'feel' to the canoe, and, of course, a very sharp edge is vulnerable to chipping.

We have looked at the forces affecting the canoe when moving forward, and it must be remembered that these forces are also generated when the canoe is moved sideways through the water, as when a canoeist uses a draw stroke. The canoe can now be considered as having a length equal to the beam, and a beam equal to its length. Similarly, when a canoe is rotated horizontally by, say, an alternate forward and reverse sweep stroke, the bow and stern halves can be considered separately as hulls of very wide beam, and very short length, moving in opposite directions.

A canoe with forward motion, which is also being turned horizontally, will create forces that lie between two extremes of forward motion and stationary horizontal rotation.

It must now be clear that there is no simple answer to the best design for a canoe. Compromise is needed between all the different possibilities, and for some competition boats design restrictions are added, too. Not only are water conditions tremendously varied, but windage can become important and must be allowed for.

Probably the design of a sprint canoe needs to have the least compromise built in, since its sole purpose is to go as fast as possible on calm water. Indeed sprint canoes resemble

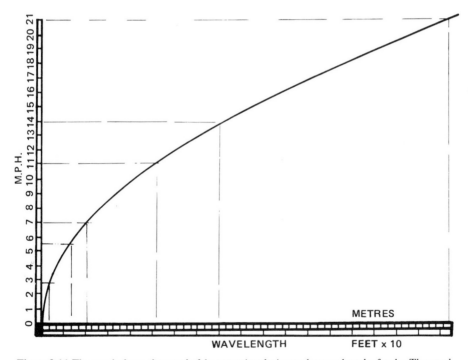

Figure 2:11 *The graph shows the speed of the canoe in relation to the wavelength of wake. The graph holds true for waves in deep water only. Deep water means water deeper than half a wavelength ie 'depth' varies with wavelength and therefore speed. Use this graph to solve the problem in Figure 2:8*

each other closely, and all have fine bows, non-rockered hulls, a forward cockpit position to keep the centre of gravity well forward, preventing squatting, and a minimum wetted surface to the hull by means of extremely narrow beam, and a semi-circular cross-section.

The design restriction, of a minimum beamsize, and convex curves only, creates the typical diamond shape of the gunwale in plan. This leaves the water-line contour as narrow as possible, and moves the widest point of the gunwale to the rear of the cockpit, allowing the paddler to place his paddle in the water as close to the centre-line of the canoe as possible. Even so, the hull section in the water gives a little stability to the paddler, by being very slightly elliptical rather than semi-circular.

The increase in paddle power due to this added stability, overcomes the slight increase in drag thus created, so even here some compromise must be built in. All very fast canoes have such poor turning characteristics that rudders are a necessity, and it is surprising what little thought has gone into these. Generally a flat plate of alloy is used. In fact there is ample evidence that to create the least drag the front section of the rudder should be parabolic. Sharp edges, or even circular leading surfaces, create turbulence, particularly when the rudder is angled. If you want to go faster – look to your rudder!

At the other end of the scale we can look at slalom canoes. Here we need good control in turbulent water, high manoeuvrability, but, if possible, fast forward speed. Within the design restriction on length and beam there is tremendous variety of form, as each designer tries yet another set of compromises. A large amount of rocker in the hull means a shorter water-line and quicker turning ability. A concave section in the rocker contour near bow and stern shortens the water-line even further. Add a very flat cross-section to the hull, and a highly manoeuvrable canoe is the result. To give such a canoe even a modicum of speed these design features must not be overdone, they must be modified – but by how much?

Low profile slalom canoes have such low decks that they can pass beneath slalom poles, and the extremities of the canoe have so little buoyancy that they can be pulled below the surface by weight shift and paddle stroke. Although sinking the ends of a slalom canoe was originated to avoid hitting the slalom pole, theoretical evidence shows that there is some advantage in sinking bow or stern. Firstly, since part of the canoe is completely submerged, wave-making, and therefore friction is reduced, and secondly, since the canoe is inclined to the horizontal, its total weight moves towards the centre of gravity, and resistance to the rotation is reduced. Thirdly, although energy is used to sink the stern, this energy is in fact stored (water is in-compressible), and the submerged section receives an acceleration which can help the canoeist. It would seem that the forward speed of the canoe through the water when dipping, and the final direction after re-surfacing, would play an important part in deciding whether a sink is advantageous. Certainly, in order to sink the canoe, the gunwales must be lowered to such an extent that lateral stability at high angles is drastically reduced. 'Gunwale snatch' is the observed result. This reduction in water-worthiness seems to be acceptable to slalomists, but it must be remembered that slalom is not conducted on the heaviest of water.

These points underline the fact that canoe design may follow fashions in paddling style, and, in the case of slalom, trends in slalom course design. This is not really surprising when it is realized that turbulent water allows little room for serious analysis, and the financial aspects of canoeing don't provide the necessary money anyway! The empirical approach is fine, but it must always be borne in mind that it cannot divorce performance from the current paddling fashion.

Let us look at one more case where varying conditions alter the design dramatically. Consider a wild-water racing kayak, and a sea-going kayak. Both need to move easily through large waves, but speed is paramount to the racer, which works in conditions where wind is of no importance. Speed is not essential for the sea-boat, but windage can be a problem.

For a wild water racer to achieve maximum speed, the bows must be kept fine, but they will then plow deep into an approaching wave. To counteract this, the bow section can be extended vertically, so that its buoyancy is increased when submerged, with very little loss of forward speed. The bow will now lift through a wave efficiently. If the same principle is applied to sea-boats, the deep bow will catch any cross-wind with dire consequences. How can the sea-boat have a fine bow for easy paddling, yet resist ploughing into waves without increasing its windage? One answer is to use 'shape' to resist immersion, rather than 'volume'.

An equilateral triangle with its apex as bow, and base as stern, creates a deal of resistance to water flow. If this shape is incorporated into the bow above the water level, and at the correct angle, it can be used to resist sinking as the bows bury in a steep wave. There need be little increase in volume, and therefore windage, to achieve this, but of course there will be somewhat more resistance to forward motion, than in the case of the wild water racer. This time, however, it is acceptable.

With the wild water racer, extra buoyancy provides the answer. For the sea-boat, form-drag solves the problem, and of course there are a dozen compromises in between.

It is possible to continue in this vein quoting how canoe design problems can be solved, but the main point to remember is that there is no simple answer or single solution. A subtle blending of many features that will give an acceptable compromise is needed. Among the many hundred of different canoe designs available it is clear that certain basic shapes give certain performance characteristics, and this enables canoes to be grouped into families. (Figure 2:12).

Obviously the design of competition canoes receives a great deal of attention to achieve the best possible performance, and the general purpose and touring canoe try to combine many traits, of necessity in conflict with each other, in order to produce characteristics that will tolerate many varying conditions.

Within each category listed in Figure 2:12 an infinite number of design compromises are possible. Even so there is no such thing as a genuine 'all purpose' canoe, and even within the specialist fields it is not easy to discover which set of compromises works best. Whether they are the result of thoughtful design, happy chance, or copying with utter lack of understanding other designs in the field, is even harder to judge!

It has already been noted that there is very little canoe design that has any serious scientific back up. As far as can be determined only one designer in the world, Jorgan Samson, actually has his designs tank-tested.

If the canoe designer must rely largely on his own experience and intuition, a novice canoeist must indeed be hard-pressed to make a sensible choice of craft. Even if it were possible to try out a variety of boats in varying conditions the canoeist himself may have insufficient skill to assess their performance successfully, and as we have already noted the interaction between skilled paddler and canoe will depend on individual style.

A chapter such as this, outlining just some of the basic principles of canoe design, cannot possibly take the place of actual canoeing experience, but an understanding of the forces affecting the canoe should help a canoeist to predict more accurately the canoe's performance.

The following table lists basic features and relates them to performance. They only apply if all other things are equal! For instance, although we have seen from the speed/length ratio principle that all similar canoes of a given water-line length have the same theoretical top speed, this will not apply to canoes of the same length but of different proportions. The beam, fineness of bow, cross-section, rocker, wetted area, surface finish and so forth, will affect the final performance.

FACTORS AFFECTING CANOE DESIGN

LATERAL STABILITY

INCREASED BY
Wide beam
Flat curves on hull cross-section
V-shaped hull sections
Hard chine hull
Low centre of gravity (seat close to hull)
Rounded gunwale
Extra freebord

DECREASED BY
Narrow beam
Semi-circular cross-sections

Multiple chine hull
High centre of gravity (high seat)

Sharp gunwale
Tumblehome amidships

LONGITUDINAL STABILITY

INCREASED BY
High aspect ratio hull
Full bow and stern
Deep bow and stern
Hogged hull
Weight in centre
Tumblehome at bow and stern

DECREASED BY
Low aspect ratio hull
Fine bow and stern
Shallow bow and stern
Rockered hull
Weight at bow and stern

DIRECTIONAL STABILITY

INCREASED BY
Narrow beam
V cross-sections to hull
Deep hull
Fish form waterline plan
Straight hull profile
Skeg
Weight at bow and stern

DECREASED BY
Wide beam
Flat cross-sections to hull
Shallow hull
Swedish form waterline plan
Rockered hull profile
Rudder
Weight in middle

SPEED

INCREASED BY
Longer waterline length
Semi-circular cross-sections
Straight hull
Narrow beam
Fine bows
Tapering stern
Smooth surface finish
Parabolic leading edges to rudder and skeg
Low weight
Weight near centre

DECREASED BY
Shorter waterline length
Increase in total wetted area
Rockered hull
Broad beam
Blunt bows
Blunt stern (except planing canoes)
Poor finish especially at bows
Flat-plate rudders and skegs

Heavy weight
Weight near bow and stern

When selecting a canoe for performance:-

1   Decide what type of canoeing you wish to do.

2   Study as many different canoes as possible and in particular the family to which your choice of craft belongs.

3   Paddle it in varying conditions if possible.

4   Assess the performance of the canoe in relation to its shape, contour, weight and finish.

5   Talk to as many canoeists as possible about the canoe. (Visit the local canoe club). Avoid individual canoeists who may have a bee in their bonnets!

6   Beware of canoes that are 'way out' in design. They are seldom satisfactory.

7   Check prices with reputable manufacturers.

Performance is not the only criterion by which you must judge, however. The price of a canoe is often the overriding factor in selection, and it can be a good indicator of quality, too. While it is true that the brand name of a product can inflate the price of a commodity, it is also true that you get what you pay for.

The cost of a canoe depends upon:-

1   Cost of development,

2   Cost of materials,

3   Cost of labour,

4   Cost of overheads.

These can be reduced by:-

1   Stealing the original design,

2   (a) Using a smaller quantity of materials

(b) Using materials of inferior quality,

3   Inferior quality labour rushing the job, and not finishing off properly

4   Overheads can be kept low by working in small premises that escape normal costs and the attention of the Factory Inspector!

It is fair to say that a successful canoe cannot be made cheaply simply because, if it is successful, the large numbers needed will preclude low overheads. Canoe-building is a cottage industry, and 50 hand-made canoes take fifty times as long to make, as one canoe. Of course it is possible to make canoes very quickly by injection moulding, rotational moulding or vacuum forming, but there are problems of storage, distribution, and of course the initial tooling costs. Maybe in ten years the canoe market will be large enough to sustain a mass-produced canoe, cheaply made. But the time is not yet.

With practical experience, some knowledge of hydraulics and current costs in mind, a canoeist can begin to make his selection. He will learn a lot, too, by looking closely at the details of the canoe. Are there 'fancy' shapes that cannot be explained? Do all the separate parts of the boat flow together into a rational whole? Unfortunately the truism 'If it *looks* right it *is* right' is true, but only experience will tell the canoeist what looks right!

Check the quality of construction with particular reference to the seat, buoyancy and footrest. The British Standards Institution Code of Practice for Canoe-Building and the British Canoe Manufacturers Association standards of construction are worth studying, and a knowledgeable friend looking at a possible purchase will help too. The neatness of the interior of the canoe is a good indicator of quality, and will tell you something about the laminate that you cannot see directly.

Go to a reputable dealer or manufacturer. The non-specialist sports shop is not the best place to purchase.

Although the use to which the canoe is put, dictates the shape, the material from which it is made also determines form. Since the introduction of glass re-inforced plastics in the '60s, this has been less true than previously. Obviously shapes in lath and canvas, or marine ply, are very much limited by the material. Today, the shape of a canoe is almost totally free from restrictions imposed by the material, and although this has allowed more

CANOES									
	KAYAKS – ORIGINATING FROM THE ESKIMO					CANOES – FROM THE BIRCH-BARK CANOE			
	TYPE	SINGLE	DOUBLE			TYPE	SINGLE	DOUBLE
RECREATION	Sea Expedition Sea Touring GP* Touring GP Slalom	X X X X	X X	TOURING SEA	RECREATION	NOT USED		
RECREATION	GP Touring GP Slalom	X X	X	TOURING INLAND (including flat & white water)	RECREATION	Open Cockpit Also many open cockpit canoes seating from one to four plus	X X	X X Plus
RECREATION	Surf Kayak Surf Ski	X X		SURFING	RECREATION	NOT USED		
RECREATION	GP Slalom GP Touring Baths Boats Competition Boats	X X X X	X X	TRAINING	RECREATION	ALL TYPES	X	X
COMPETITION	K1, K2, K4	X	X	SPRINT RACING	COMPETITION	OPEN COCKPIT C1, C2, C7	X	X
COMPETITION	† K1, K2,	X	X	MARATHON RACING	COMPETITION	‡ C1, C2	X	X
COMPETITION	K1	X		WILD WATER RACING	COMPETITION	CLOSED COCKPIT C1, C2	X	X
COMPETITION	K1	X		SLALOM	COMPETITION	CLOSED COCKPIT C1, C2	X	X
COMPETITION	K1 SKI	X		SURFING	COMPETITION	NOT USED		
COMPETITION	BATHS BOATS	X		POLO	COMPETITION	NOT USED		

* GP = general purposes. † Any type of Kayak or Canoe may be used, but above certain levels only Racing or Wild Water Racing Boats are likely to be successful. ‡ Consideration of the 'class rules' still underway at the time of publication.

Figure 2:12 *Families of Canoes. In the UK the generic noun 'Canoe' means 'any craft capable of being portaged by its crew'; 'kayak' and 'open Canadian canoe' naming the sub-species. In most other countries, the name 'canoe' is reserved for craft paddled with a single blade, and the term 'kayak' applied to boats propelled with a double paddle* efficient shapes to be developed, some designs bear little relation to any of the known facts about efficient motion across the surface of water, which all makes the selection of a canoe extremely difficult.

PADDLES

Fashion in canoe design changes, and as a consequence, or because of it, paddling styles alter. For instance, over the years paddles have become shorter, in line with the trend for less beamy canoes.

Few single kayaks have a beam of more than 60 cms, and the average paddle length has been reduced from 'Height of paddler with arm raised and fingers outstretched' to 'height of paddler with arm raised and fingers curled over paddle blade'. This means that paddle length lies roughly within the range of 210 cms for slalom to 230 cms for sea-canoeing, with something in between the two for sprint racing.

Since the paddle does not touch the canoe during the normal paddling stroke, there is no fixed fulcrum for the paddle to work against. The arms and body of the paddler form a very complicated series of levers and moving fulcrum which are beyond the scope of this chapter to analyse.

For the most efficient propulsion, it is important that the blade of the paddle must move along a line parallel to and as near to the centre line of the canoe as possible. This produces the 'high paddling' style of the competition canoeist. The touring paddler has other problems besides making his canoe move as fast as possible.

Apart from the water, windage becomes important, and a low paddling style, to keep the upper blade close to the surface where wind speeds are dramatically reduced, is the hallmark of the sea-canoeist in very windy conditions. (Figure 2:13).

An analysis of the function of the paddle blade will give some indication of good paddle design. The blade must perform three functions efficiently. It must:-

1   Enter the water

2   Grip the water

3   Exit from the water

On entry, any splashing or wave-making is wasteful of energy. Immediately, it becomes clear why curved blades are so much more efficient than flat. They can enter the water almost without disturbing the surface, and asymmetrical curved blades will do this even more smoothly. Once the paddle is in the water, any air around the blade will reduce its efficiency. As the paddle enters the water, air is dragged down with it, particularly at the back of the blade. Again the smooth entry of the curved blade is a sign that the minimum amount of air has been taken below the surface. 'Cavitation' is at a minimum. (Figure 2:14).

Once in the water, the paddle blade must create drag. All the rules that apply to the motion of a canoe also apply to the blade of a paddle. It is clear that 'form drag' is most important, and that the surface area of the blade is the most important factor here. Spooned blades are most efficient but the amount of curve that gives most effective propulsion is too great to allow the blade to slide in and out of the water without splash. Therefore a compromise must be reached, reducing these curves so that both functions are reasonably well catered for.

The eddies behind the paddle blade moving through the water form a distinct pattern. Vortices break away from the edges alternately, and it is these that cause pressures on the blade that can result in 'flutter'. Preventing flutter may require considerable effort from the

39

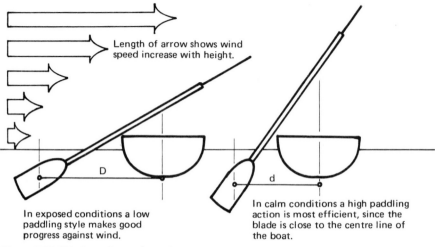

Length of arrow shows wind speed increase with height.

In exposed conditions a low paddling style makes good progress against wind.

In calm conditions a high paddling action is most efficient, since the blade is close to the centre line of the boat.

Figure 2:13 *Wind speed may determine the paddle action*

water surface

surface

Flat blade causes large cavitation on entry.

Curved blade reduces cavitation to a minimum.

Figure 2:14 *The entry of the paddle through the water surface*

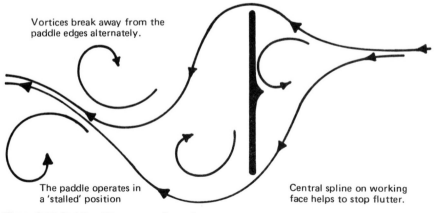

Vortices break away from the paddle edges alternately.

The paddle operates in a 'stalled' position

Central spline on working face helps to stop flutter.

Figure 2:15 *Paddle eddies as seen from above*

40

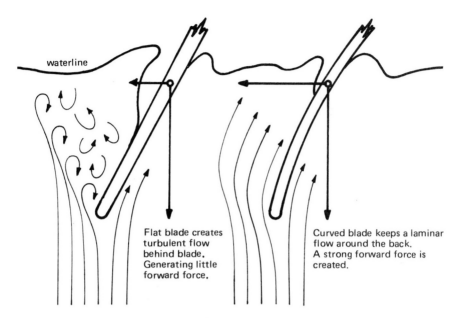

waterline

Flat blade creates
turbulent flow
behind blade.
Generating little
forward force.

Curved blade keeps a laminar
flow around the back.
A strong forward force is
created.

Figure 2:16 *As paddle blades submerge, their downward movement creates 'lift' which pulls the canoe forward. The figure illustrates the fundamental difference between flat and curved blades*

paddler, albeit he is unaware of it. If the face of the blade is divided vertically by a rib to part the flow of water, flutter producing forces can be reduced considerably. (Figure 2:15).

Although for most of the time during its travel through the water, the blade is working in a 'stalled' position, there is a short period as it plunges into the water vertically, when the blade acts much like an aircraft wing, creating 'lift' by virtue of its thin section and angle of incidence. Again the curved blade will be most efficient at creating 'lift' acting in a forward direction, and it may well be that parabolic sections at the tip of the blade could add to the propelling power. As far as can be ascertained little thought has been given to this aspect of blade design. (Figure 2:16).

Getting the paddle out of the water without loss of energy is such a huge problem that it is achieved by taking it out prematurely, while the blade is still close to vertical as it passes the canoeist's body. In this way, energy loss is kept to a minimum, in spite of the fact that some of the possible propulsive power from the tail end of the stroke is wasted.

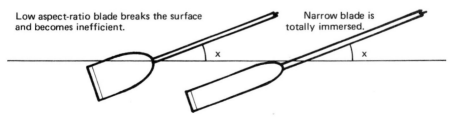

Low aspect-ratio blade breaks the surface
and becomes inefficient.

Narrow blade is
totally immersed.

x

x

Angle x is the same in both cases, and both paddle blades have similar areas.

Figure 2:17 *Paddle action may determine the blade shape*

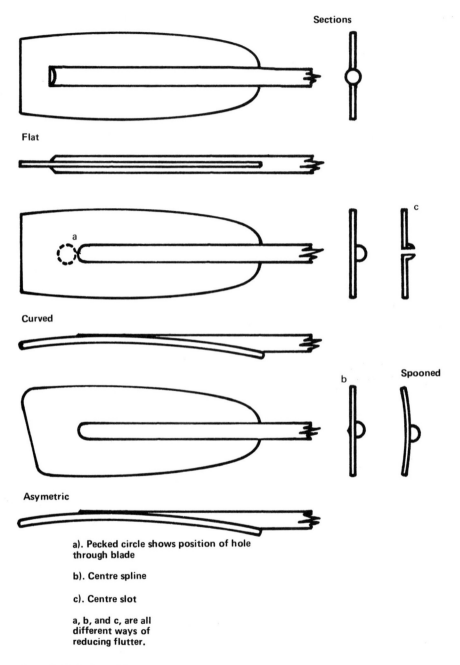

Sections

Flat

Curved

Spooned

a

b

c

Asymmetric

a). Pecked circle shows position of hole through blade

b). Centre spline

c). Centre slot

a, b, and c, are all different ways of reducing flutter.

Figure 2:18 *Basic paddle blades*

42

It is clear that on several counts the superiority of the curved blade is overwhelming. The correct aspect ratio of the blade is related to the angle at which the blade is used. When used vertically as in a racing stroke the aspect ratio is low, but if a blade is to be used in strong winds where it is beneficial to keep the angle of the loom closer to the horizontal, a high aspect ratio blade is helpful. This is because at a low angle the whole blade can be immersed more easily if it is long and thin. (Figure 2:17).

Present paddling style dictates that paddles shall be feathered. There is evidence that windage is reduced when paddling forward, but a feathered paddle may be more severely affected by cross winds. Paddlers prone to tino synovitis in the wrist have found that unfeathered paddles can give relief, and of course many of the traditional Eskimo paddles are unfeathered.

Once paddles are feathered, then the set of the blades for either left and right hand control becomes a factor. Flat blades avoid this issue, and the convenience factor offered by flat blades when a mixed group of paddlers share a set of paddles is, of course, considerable. This fact, together with the point that a flat blade is cheap to produce, are the only points in its favour. The idea that flat blades catch the wind less or are more efficient at a low angle of paddle, is unfounded.

Basic types of blades – flat, curved, spooned and asymmetric are shown in Figure 2:18.

The Paddle Loom

The action of the blade through the water suggests that the stiffer the loom the more efficient the stroke will be. While it is true that a springy shaft stores the paddler's energy and then releases it later during the stroke it can be shown that this has no advantageous effects. However, most paddlers feel that a slight spring in the paddle loom produces better results, and it may well be that there are physiological benefits from a springy loom. Diameter of loom is important. When grasped, the thumb nail should be level with, or overlap the line of the finger nails. A bigger loom than this can cause unnecessary fatigue and even 'tennis elbow'. The ovalling of the loom, at least under the control hand, is important to give the paddle 'feel', particularly so for performing Eskimo rolls.

Weight

Since a paddle is entirely supported in the hands, its weight is important. Clearly this must be related to strength, and it must be remembered that the strain placed upon a blade during a sprint start or a rocky slalom run, is tremendous. The strength of any material has an upper limit, and if sections are reduced for lightness, then these limits can be approached quite easily.

All the factors that were noted in relation to the selection of a canoe earlier, apply to the selection of paddles. Shape, size, weight, finish, feel, balance, and, of course, the specific use to which the paddle will be put, and price must be considered. However, the material used for paddle construction is of paramount importance, and plays a very large part in the strength and performance characteristics.

Any combination of loom and blade material is possible.

Loom	Blade
Alloy tubing	Wood
*Glassfibre tubing	Glassfibre
Wood	Cored glassfibre (sandwich construction)
	ABS plastic
*Glass reinforced plastic (GRP)	Glass reinforced polypropalene.

Wooden paddles

Wood is an underrated material and can still hold its own against the best artificial material man can devise. Generally, wood for paddles must be laminated to give homogeneous strength. This means that the quality of the waterproof glue is also very important.

Type of timber

Spruce, though soft, is very strong for its weight, and combined with Ash in the loom for added toughness, is probably the best combination possible. Beech is sometimes used as a substitute for Ash, but it is definitely inferior, especially when wet, which means the varnishing is particularly important. Waterproof plywoods of various timbers can be used with success. Birch ply with thin laminations seems strongest. Coarse grained timbers are less satisfactory. Points to look for:-

1   The thinner the glue-line between laminates, the stronger the join

2   The more laminations the stronger

3   Check for defects such as knots, resin pockets, short grain, shakes and warping

4   Look for a well-made, long-tapering splice on the loom

5   Check quality of varnish.

Alloy Looms

These are very cold unless sheathed in plastic – usually PVC. Alloy gives very good service and it is reasonable in price. Points to look for:

1   Wall thickness not below 18 SWG

2   Diameter not above 32mm (1¼")

3   Unblemished PVC sheath

Where there is an inserted blade, a belled end to the alloy tube allows the blade to be fitted without a sharp shoulder, which increases the strength of the neck considerably. This is an expensive operation, and cannot be expected on low-priced paddles, where the chief virtue of the paddles is the price.

Glassfibre looms

These are very strong, have a nice 'feel' and are light-weight. They need the addition of a fairing to oval them for the control hand.

Points to look for: The ends of the glassfibre tubing are liable to split. There must be some type of collar here to prevent this. Check.

Glassfibre blades

Strong, if made thick enough, but rather heavy and easily abraided. Points to look for:

1   Thickness of laminate

2   Use of woven roving cloth is important to give tensile strength

3   Check for air bubbles, dry mat

4   Alloy tips are needed for general purpose use

Cored Glassfibre blades

Many blades are now available where a core is sandwiched between two layers of glassfibre. The core can be:-

1   A sheet of non-woven fabric impregnated with minute hollow spheres of polypropylene.

2   High density polyurethane foam.

Both materials have drawbacks! The non-woven fabric absorbs up to 50% of resin, which makes it reasonably strong, but if the core is starved of resin, it will be very weak. It is difficult to detect dry regions within the core, but small sunken areas on the blade area are an indicator and should be looked for. Polyurethane foam will absorb some water if exposed. Unless the edges of the blade are protected with alloy they can wear away to the core quite quickly and allow water to add weight to the blade. Both these materials produce a light-weight paddle-blade, but there is a limit to the strength/weight ratio, and the paddler cannot expect to get the impossible!

ABS blades

These give a robust long-lasting blade. They are usually black to prevent deterioration by ultra-violet light. Their main drawback is that they are flexible. They are, however, durable and inexpensive.

Reinforced Polypropylene blades

These blades are stiffer than ABS, and are robust, but somewhat heavy.

Paddle Kits

These usually consist of an alloy loom and wooden blades that can be varnished and inserted into the tube by the canoeist himself. They are the cheapest form of paddle and can give good service and performance. Points to look for:

1   The more laminations in the ply the stronger

2   Check quality of timber, especially the piece that inserts into the loom

In general, a well-balanced paddle with a little 'give' in the ovalled loom, but with a stiff, curved blade, and a weight and length in line with its use, is the ideal. Remember that the paddle with the least splash is likely to be most efficient.

Paddle design can be just as controversial as canoe design. Most of it is based on personal paddling style, personal opinion, and prejudice. There is very little scientific fact to support any statement, and intuitive remarks are sometimes cloaked in pseudo-scientific theory. Very often the group prejudice dictates to the individual when informed opinion would be more helpful.

The twin subjects of canoe and paddle design cannot be thoroughly dealt with in one chapter. Much has been left out and only the surface of the subject has been explored – which is not surprising, since it was recognised at the beginning that travel on the surface of water is difficult!

Hot doggin' in Canada. Photo Ottowa River Kayak and Canoe School.

3 Canoe Construction and Maintenance

Frank R. Goodman

INTRODUCTION

Although canoes can be built from lath and canvas, marine ply, or even concrete, the popularity of glass reinforced plastic (GRP) canoes has continued to grow since their introduction in the early sixties. GRP (Glass fibre) canoes must account for well over 90% of the market, and the building method is so quick, that very few amateur builders would tackle other, more long-winded methods.

To build in glassfibre means hiring, borrowing or buying a mould, but they are readily available from canoe builders and resin suppliers. There are several books and leaflets on canoe-building available. These notes refer in general to the building of a general purpose slalom canoe. The same basic principles apply to most glass fibre work.

Since the advent of the Health and Safety At Work Act, strict controls have been applied to the standards required for workshops where glassfibre construction is taking place. The Act is enforceable in factories and schools, but not to private individuals or voluntary organisations. Common sense needs to be used, however, as the materials involved are both toxic and flammable.

TYPES OF MATERIAL USED FOR CANOE BUILDING

Glass Reinforcement

Chopped strand mat consists of 2″ long fibres of glass filaments, bonded together in random direction to form a mat which can be cut by knife or scissors. The bonding agent dissolves in resin, thus allowing the mat to 'drape' into a mould. The weight, or reference, refers to grams per square metre, ie $300gm^2$, $450gm^2$.

Woven roving has parallel glass threads, which are not twisted, woven into cloth form. This has a far better tensile strength than chopped strand mat, but is not so rigid when used in a laminate, and is also more expensive, does not soak up as much resin, and is used for lightweight canoes, or to make canoes stronger. The weight refers to ounces per square yard, ie 8 oz.

Surface Tissue is similar in form to chopped strand mat but is very thin and light. Not of much interest to the canoe builder but can be used to give a smooth finish to the inside of a laminate.

Diolen. This woven roving is not glass at all, but a surface-treated polyester fabric. It has high tensile strength but is somewhat flexible. Use as for glass woven roving. It needs a sharp knife to trim it.

Kevlar. Is a yellow woven roving that is a type of nylon. It is extremely tough and can only be trimmed and cut with difficulty. Kevlar delaminates rather easily, and is possibly beyond normal amateur use.

For the purpose of canoe building, the minimum requirement on a hull is a layer of $300gm^2$ chopped strand mat and a layer of 8 oz cloth. This will need to be strengthened by a full-length, longitudinal rib. For the deck, a minimum of a layer of $300gm^2$ chopped strand mat is needed, plus an extra layer around the cockpit, and longitudinal strengthening ribs. The seat will need at least three layers of $450gm^2$ mat. This will only be suitable for a lightweight competition canoe, which will need to be handled with care.

A good general purpose lay-up for the amateur builder, is: two layers of 450 gm^2 chopped strand mat (CSM) on the hull, with an extra layer in the centre section. The deck will need one layer of 450 gm^2 CSM, plus an extra layer around the cockpit area. The seat needs four or five layers of 450 gm^2 mat. For most purposes, strengthening ribs would not be necessary.

Resin – Lay-up resin and gelcoat

Gelcoat is a thick, viscous resin that is used to provide a pleasant exterior to a canoe. It can be given a high polish from the mould surface. Apart from aesthetic considerations, the gelcoat prevents the glassfibres within the laminate protruding from the surface and absorbing water.

Lay-up resin is a much thinner resin, that is used in conjunction with glass reinforcing to form the main body of the laminate.

Mixing Resins for Use

Resins and gelcoats have a storage life of several months, provided they are protected from light, and are kept in a cool place. Polyester resins need the addition of both accelerator and catalyst before they will begin to gel and cure. Most resins have the accelerator ready mixed in (hence the suffix PA, or Pre-Accelerated) and this is also an added safety precaution, as a mixture of neat catalyst and accelerator can be explosive.

Never work at a temperature of less than 16°C (62°F) as, below this, the resin will not begin to cure. The addition of 1% catalyst to resin, and 2% to gelcoat will give a pot life at normal temperatures, of about 25 minutes. When mixing, always add the pigment before the catalyst, stir very thoroughly and allow to stand for a minute or two to allow air to escape. You will find it easier to work in grams, as percentages are easier to calculate. One kilogram (1000 gms) resin will need 10 gms (or cc's) catalyst to give a 1% addition rate. Five cc's per pint, or per pound weight, is also equivalent to a 1% rate. When mixing gelcoat, particular care is needed as a badly catalysed batch can lead to wrinkling. Never wipe the mixing stick onto the side of the bucket, as this may not be properly catalysed.

Solid pigments should be used at a maximum of 5% in the gelcoat, and this should be reduced to a maximum of 2½% in the back-up resin. With translucent pigments, 1% is a maximum and ¼% is the normal rate.

Caution. *Catalyst is a powerful oxidizing agent. Protect your hands and wash off any splashes with water. Be particularly careful of splashes in the eyes, wash out with a weak sodium bicarbonate solution, or water, and rush to the nearest hospital immediately!* Lock catalyst away when not in use, but do not tighten the cap as pressure can build up. Do not leave rags soaked in resin or catalyst lying about, as spontaneous combustion can occur. Wash brushes out in acetone, or, use a detergent washing powder and very hot water. When brushes are clean, scrub bristles onto a bar of soap and store until required. (Don't forget to wash and dry out before using again!).

CANOE BUILDING

Preliminary preparations

Check that the room is clean, large enough (at least 18′ x 8′), ventilated and sufficiently warm – in the high sixties Fahrenheit and well lighted. See that the mould is safely mounted at a convenient working height (top of mould about waist high) and that there is access all round. Have a table or bench with a disposable cover for the resin materials and for mixing and cleaning purposes. Have another table or bench (clean or covered with clean ply hardboard or paper) for the glass materials and for cutting out. Check that all materials and

Table One   Materials used in the manufacture of one canoe

Material	Hull	Deck	Seat	Joining etc	Total
Release agent Wax					40 gms
Release agent PVA					75 gms
Resin: Gelcoat	gms 1300	gms 1200	gms 100		gms 2600
Resin: Main lay-up ML 864 PA	gms 3500	gms 2500	gms 1000	gms 2000	kgs 9.00
Catalyst: @ 2% Gel 1% Resin					142 gms
Pigment: Never more than 10% Subsidiary – for seat etc.					1 lb as required
Glass reinforcing: 1½oz Chopped strand mat	sq yds 7	sq yds 6½	sq yds 1½	sq yds 1	sq yds 6 kg 16
Alloy tube: 1¾″D X 16 swg Footrest	1 off 18″				18″
H-section PVC	If required				27′
Buoyancy:	Choose system to suit				min 30 lbs
Painter: min 6mm dia	Bow and stern loops only Deck lines also				3′ 30′
Acetone:	as required				2 kgs
Wing-nuts and bolts: ¾″ X ¼″ dia	For footrest				2 pr

The amounts shown above are those used by the amateur builder with little experience, who is making a heavy canoe. These quantities can be reduced slightly when experience is gained or if a lightweight canoe is required.

tools are clean and readily available and that there is a bucket of clean water for douching of skin accidentally splashed with chemicals. Unless splashes on the floor are unimportant, it should be covered with board, cloths or brown paper. Make sure all old resin is thoroughly emulsified before pouring away down a sink. Glassfibre casts of the sewage system are not required!

Method of Working

1 *Preparation of the mould*
    (a) Remove all traces of old glassfibre – this should only be present on the mould lips, and is best scraped away with the side of a chisel. Inside the mould, any small remnants can be removed by scraping with the thumbnail, and stubborn bits with wet and dry carborundum paper grade 360, finishing with at least 800 grit (careful polishing with metal-polish will restore the surface lustre). All this must be done very carefully so that no damage is occasioned to the mould.
    (b) Thoroughly wash out the mould with warm water, using soap if necessary, drying thoroughly with soft cloths.
    (c) Apply Silicone-free wax polish with a cloth, spread whilst moist, then polish thoroughly with clean fluff-free cloths.
    (d) Apply mould release agent (polyvinyl alcohol–PVA) solution with a small sponge. Make sure that the surface is completely covered (including edges) and that there are no bare patches – examining against the light helps here. A colleague is useful to search for 'misses'. Great care at this stage is vital. Careless work leads not only to a damaged shell, but also to a damaged mould. The separator must be thoroughly dry, ie to a hard cellophane-like full cover, before further work can proceed, and the surface must not be touched during or after the drying process.

Danger: Wet release agent will stick mould and canoe together. It *must* be thoroughly dry everywhere. Check any corners or grooves particularly bow and stern, where release agent may still remain wet. Sorry to go on, but it is important, and I won't mention it again! Wax release, plus PVA release agent, is the safest way to ensure release of the canoe. However, there are waxes that can be used alone, without PVA. The use of these waxes gives a more highly polished surface to the canoe than using PVA and it is only necessary to wax about once for every half dozen canoes taken from the mould. There are snags in preparation, however, and the notes below should be followed carefully!
    (a) New moulds must first be broken-in with PVA as detailed above, for at least the first two canoes taken from the mould.
    (b) After thoroughly washing out the mould, use a power buff with a good polishing compound, and thoroughly buff out the mould. (Do not use T-cut polishing compound as it contains ammonia, which can affect the mould).
    (c) Apply the special mould wax, and polish off by hand (on no account use a power mop).
    (d) Leave for at least 8 hours (this is essential).
    (e) Apply and polish off wax by hand again.
    (f) Leave another 8 hours.
    (g) Apply and polish off wax a third time. By hand only.

The mould is now ready. Remember that only moulds with a really good surface, carefully prepared, will release with these waxes. After many releases (you need to re-wax about every six canoes made, or when they start to get difficult to remove from the mould) you may get some wax build-up, which tends to dull the surface of the mould.

Buff out with a power-buff to remove this wax, and then re-wax at least twice, with an eight hour gap between before continuing.

2 *Applying the Gelcoat*

Measure out a reasonable quantity (see table one) of pre-accelerated gelcoat resin into a clean dry tin or bucket. Add catalyst at the rate of 2% and pigment if required. Stir thoroughly. With a brush, this is then 'laved' onto the inside of the prepared mould. It is best to do a section at a time, starting at the gunwale, and working down to the keel. The coat must be applied evenly, not too thickly, and should not be 'brushed out' too much, or the release agent may be damaged underneath.

Paint a 'touching spot' on a piece of spare card, and touch after about 30 mins. When fingerprint is left on the gel it is ready for the next stage. Remember that thick gel goes off faster than thin, and that the mould holds the heavy resin fumes that may extend the gelling time. Tipping the mould on its side helps here.

3 *Laying the main coat*

It is a good idea to have a set of templates, so that all the glass material can be cut to size and shape before the laying up is started. Make sure the mat is cut so that it only protrudes a fraction of an inch beyond the mould edge. This prevents the mat from flopping over the edge and allowing air-bubbles to form along the gunwale. Use brown paper or hardboard. Lay-up resin should be mixed with pigment and catalyst, and stirred. Amounts will vary with the size and experience of the group – 3 kgs is reasonable for experienced groups; about 2 kgs is safer for the inexperienced. The resin is applied carefully, but generously as in step 2, and the pieces of mat (glassfibre) laid on. The resin is then brought up to the surface of the layer of mat by a vigorous stippling action with the brush. Again, careful attention should be paid to the narrow corners of the mould. The upstanding mat at the mould edge should not protrude more than 1″. Don't bend it down onto the rim of the mould. Resin should not be over applied – it will drain down into the keel, and allowance for this should be made, since excess resin means a more costly job, as well as an unnecessarily heavy one. Patches of white mean insufficient 'wetting out', which calls for more resin. There is no reason why more resin cannot be added on top of the mat, so long as it is wet underneath too.

As the resin impregnates the mat, the binder holding the fibres together dissolves, allowing the mat to 'drape' to the shape of the mould. As soon as this happens, begin rolling the mat with the rollers, getting rid of all the air-pockets under the mat. Particular attention is needed again at the gunwale edges, as this is where most air-bubbles are likely to occur. When the mat looks curly, instead of the fibres lying straight, it is usually a sign that the rolling is satisfactory.

A second lamination can then be laid immediately, without waiting for the first to gel. If a heavy lay-up is used, say two layers of 450g chopped strand mat, then strengthening ribs may be dispensed with, but lighter lay-ups may need a rib down the centre of the hull and the deck. A ⅝″ × ⅝″ lath of wood as a former, covered with a layer of glass fibre tape cut from 450g CSM about 3″ wide, is adequate.

If you use woven roving cloth in your lay-up, note the following points: The cloth does not need very much resin to wet it out, and often the layer of CSM underneath will provide sufficient resin to impregnate the cloth. It does not drape as well as CSM and care is needed to remove all underlying air, and smooth the cloth to shape. A brush is more use on cloth than a roller. Keep all cut edges out of the boat, as fraying strands can be very messy. Cut the cloth so that only the selvedges run across the boat. Use a pattern!

51

Table Two   Time table for canoe building for a team of five people

Many instructions give no indication of the time involved and one line of type can mean days of work. The following is an attempt to give some idea of the time needed for each stage.

Note the following points.

1   Room temperature and humidity affects resin setting time.

2   Generally, at least two people must lay-up.

An ideal team would be:

1 resin painter
2 stipplers
3 rollers
_____
5 in all
_____

Others can be employed as resin mixers and glass cutters when available. Up to say twelve people can safely be employed.

3   Times given are for experienced people and experience saves time. Four adults have made four canoes in four days, but they were long days, and they were experienced canoe builders.

Handling number	Process	Working Time in mins	Waiting time in mins. Use this time for other jobs	Remarks
1	Preparation of moulds			
	Wash	10		
	Wax	10		
	Release agent	10		Wash out
	Release agent drying		30	sponge
2	Applying Gelcoat			
	Mixing	5		
	Laying on	10		Cut mat
			45	(under 3)
3	Laying up Main Coat			
	Cut glass mat	15		
	Mix resin	5		
	Lay-up. 2 layers			
	Paint on resin			
	Stipplers	30		Mat cut while
	Rollers			gelcoat is
	Laying-up gelling		30	drying
4	Trimming	5		Only if caught at the right moment. Watch it carefully and save time.
5	Cleaning up brushes rollers, etc.	5		Make sure this is done meticulously.
		105	105	Waiting time equals work time.

52

6	Deck lay-up	As above	As above	This can be completed in the waiting time above. Therefore total for deck and hull is approx 3 hrs 30 mins.
7	Cockpit–to complete	105	105	This is pessimistic
8	Hull deck cockpit leave in mould		Overnight	
	Releasing shells from mould	15		All three
	Joining cockpit to deck			
	Filing & cleaning up	40		
	Fitting	10		
	Sealing	20		
	Gelling		30	
	Fitting knee bars	15		
	Gelling		30	
	Joining hull & deck			
	Filing gunwales	20		
	Fitting H-section to hull	10		
	Fitting deck to H-section	30		
	Pulling all snug	10		
	Sealing hull & deck			
	Each quarter of canoe 20	80		
	Gelling time		30	
	Making footrest supports			
	Laying-up	15		
	Gell-time		30	
	Trimming	10		
	Fitting Footrest supports			Can be irritating as they sometimes dislodge before sealing
	Wedging in position	10		
	Sealing	20		
	Gel-time		30	
	Making footrest	15		
	Cleaning up	60		Depends on the individual
	Buoyancy			Depends on system
	Painter holes	5		
	TOTAL	595	360	

A group of 5 people should complete a canoe in 595 + 360 = 955 mins
16 hrs
2 days

4 *Trimming*

The work must be examined at short intervals. It should be caught when the gelling stage is well advanced, but not too far so, ie when a sharp knife will cut the laminations easily but without tearing up the glass fibres. A trimming knife or a chisel can be used - push it through from the inside of the laminate and cut with a shearing action, the mould edge guiding the blade. The edge can be quickly and efficiently trimmed in this way in about one minute. If the trimming has to be left for some time, remove the shell from the mould and saw off the excess mat with a coping saw (much quicker than a hacksaw, but still tedious). Watch it like a hawk so you can catch it just right with the knife. If you are joining in the mould it is *essential* to trim with a knife, and bolt hull and deck together *at once*. If you have to saw off the excess, you must join with H-section.

5 *Cleaning up*

All equipment should be cleaned immediately in detergent or acetone. For storage, many washings in soapy water are best, and then leave the soap between the bristles. Unless old tins are in short supply it is not worthwhile cleaning them for re-use. Hands should be cleaned with Kerrocleanse, or similar – put out small quantities at a time or it disappears fast.

6 *Laying up the cockpit*

In many ways this is the most difficult lay-up. Rollers can only be used sparsely, because of the shape, and the mat has a tendency to slide off the cockpit rim unless all stippling is absolutely square to the job. The amount of 'edge' in relation to the amount of the cockpit is great, and these edges are always the places where air bubbles can creep in.

Three layers of 450 gm^2 mat, plus a layer of woven roving cloth on the base of the seat, is usually rigid enough. Trim the cockpit when 'leather' hard. Failure to do this will mean that the seat will not come off the mould.

7 *Releasing the laminations from the moulds*

Leave overnight before attempting this step. On no account must any metal object be pushed between the laminate and the mould. It is usually unnecessary to even push wooden slats between, and this should only be done as a last resort.

Release all round the edge of the mould by pushing back the edge of the lay-up with a sharp chisel. (Figure 3:1). *The chisel must only touch the rim of the mould.* Using the fingers, push the lay-up away from the mould, and pull up the laminate, to allow air to enter between the laminate and the mould. Be careful if lifting out a shell, or half a canoe, as it will be floppy, and could easily break if lifted by nose and stern only. If you have joined the canoe in the mould, proceed as follows:

(a) Unbolt the flanges of the mould.

(b) Run a big screwdriver all round the mould, between the two flanges, forcing them apart and thus releasing the gunwales of the canoe.

(c) Release the cockpit edge with a chisel as above (Figure 3:1).

(d) Pull flanges at bow and stern apart until either deck or hull releases completely. Place released half of mould on one side, and put the half containing the canoe on the floor, mould side down, after placing something soft underneath (polystyrene, folded cardboard or similar).

(e) Press down on mould flange at bow and stern and the canoe will spring free.

(f) On no account may hammers, rubber or otherwise, be used to hammer the mould to induce a release. This will very definitely cause star cracks in the gelcoat, ruining the mould surface and, thus, your next canoe.

54

The cockpit is sometimes more difficult to part from the mould. First release the edges with a chisel, pull the front rim away from the mould, and wedge with two sticks as in Figure 3:2. Edge these sticks an inch at a time towards the seat, checking that the edges are releasing, and that too much strain is not cracking the rim at point X (shown in diagram) – this is the danger spot. Considerable pressure is built up in this way and the seat will suddenly release itself from the mould.

8   *Joining hull and deck with H-section*
Clean up gunwale edges with a coarse file, removing any pimps of resin and filing away any thick spots.

Push H-section onto hull, finishing with a butt-joint where the ends meet. It is best to start about a yard from the stern of the canoe. To navigate the sharp ends of the canoe, the inside wall of the H-section has to be pared away with a sharp chisel for about two inches each end. Start at one end of the canoe by placing bow end of deck into the H-section, and binding the two halves together with masking tape. Use the special joining tools, or any suitable piece of metal, and open up the H-section, thus allowing the deck to drop into the section. Work back from each side about nine inches at a time and then stick a piece of tape across the two halves to keep them in position (the use of the tools requires a knack which is learned only by experiment.) Local warming of the H-section, by a fan heater or electric fire, often helps if a particular section is being difficult. This is usually caused by not cleaning off the gunwale edges properly, before starting. Remember that as temperature drops, the H-section will

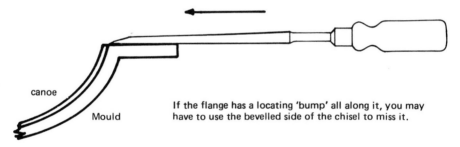

canoe

Mould

If the flange has a locating 'bump' all along it, you may have to use the bevelled side of the chisel to miss it.

Figure 3:1 *Releasing lamination from mould*

Sometimes just one stick can be used successfully. Use soft wood.

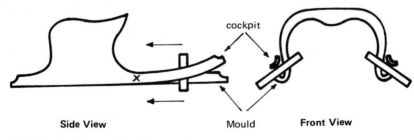

cockpit

Side View   Mould   Front View

Figure 3:2 *Releasing the seat from the mould*

stiffen. Don't attempt to put this H-section on if working below normal lay-up temperature (high 60'sF) otherwise you will find the PVC becomes too stiff and unwieldly. When all the edges are secure, go along the gunwales again, tightening up the strips of tape, and generally pushing the gunwales into shape.

9 *Joining hull and deck – solid join*
Immediately, but *immediately* after trimming, bolt the hull and deck mould together. Failure to do this will result in the canoe releasing from the mould as the two halves are bolted up. Consequently, when joining, the resin will run between the laminate and the mould, spoiling the finish on the canoe, and ruining the mould. Resin in the mould is extremely difficult to remove without damaging the mould surface.

10 *Sealing deck and hull*
Turn the canoe on it's side, place one end on the floor, and hold cockpit 4' high by tieing to a bench, post, or some other way to suit. If joining in the mould, hold the mould in a similar way. Cut strips of 3" wide 450g mat and place these on a 'wetting out' board close to the canoe. A strip of blockboard 4' X 8" X 12mm is a suitable 'wetting out' board.

Place a lighted bulb in the canoe so you can see what you are doing, and pour about 200 gms of resin down the inside of the gunwale join. Partially wet out a 3" strip of mat, and place it along your joining brush, as in Figure 3:5. If you wet out with too much resin, the mat will disintegrate before you can lift it into the canoe. Care and judgement are needed. Slide the loaded brush into the canoe and, with a twist of the wrist, drop the mat along the gunwale line, as close to the end of the canoe as possible. This is not as difficult as it sounds! Stipple the mat into place. Continue towards the cockpit until one quarter of the canoe is sealed.

The most difficult part is about 6" from the end of the canoe, as it is too narrow here to allow the brush to stipple properly. Seal the very end with a ball of resin and glass, tamped into position with a suitable rod, or pour a small quantity of neat resin into the ends while the canoe is held vertically.

Turn the canoe, so that all four quarters can be sealed. Some people like a double layer each side of the cockpit.

11 *Joining cockpit to deck*
This process may have to be varied to suit the particular canoe that is being made.
Clean up the cockpit edges with files and wet-or-dry paper. File vertically round the cockpit hole in the deck until a feather edge is produced on this rim (Figure 3:3).

Push cockpit into position and hold in place with ¾" PVC self-adhesive tape, sealing all round the outside under the rim. This tape can be left on the canoe permanently.

Seal back and sides of seat with 2" strips of CSM and wipe off unwanted splashes of resin with acetone. Seal the front rim with resin only, first making a barrier of masking tape to hold in the resin at the front (Figure 3:4).

All these operations are best performed with the canoe upside down and suspended about 4½' from the floor, so that you can stand comfortably under the canoe with your head in the cockpit. Slings from hooks in the ceiling are ideal. Wear a beret to keep resin out of your hair. File off all rough edges when all has gelled, especially on the front of the cockpit where the barrier of masking tape will leave a sharp edge to the resin.

Normally, the seat holds into the deck without any trouble, but sometimes it is awkward and will not stay in place. If this happens, a piece of wood 4' long X 3" X ⅝" can be laid across the seat and wedged between the deck and the ends of the batten (Figure 3:6).

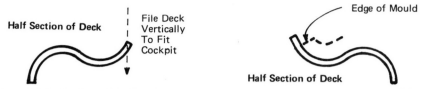

Half Section of Deck

File Deck
Vertically
To Fit
Cockpit

Edge of Mould

Half Section of Deck

Figure 3:3 *Fitting the cockpit. Sometimes the deck-hole is worn (too large for the cockpit). Trim it* away *from the mould edge, then file to suit*

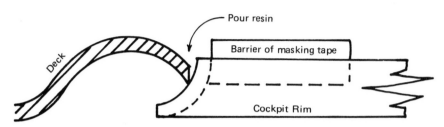

Pour resin

Deck

Barrier of masking tape

Cockpit Rim

Section: canoe is upside down.

Figure 3:4 *Joining the cockpit to the deck*

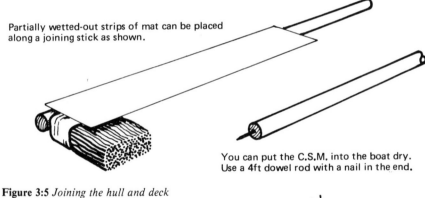

Partially wetted-out strips of mat can be placed along a joining stick as shown.

You can put the C.S.M. into the boat dry. Use a 4ft dowel rod with a nail in the end.

Figure 3:5 *Joining the hull and deck*

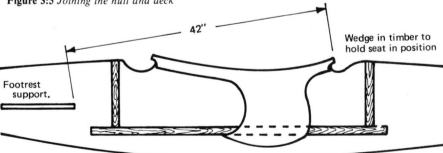

42"

Wedge in timber to hold seat in position

Footrest support.

Figure 3:6 *Holding the seat in place. The distance of footrest support to cockpit is approximate only. Check your own leg length in an existing kayak*

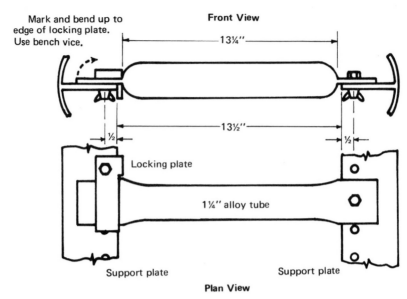

Mark and bend up to
edge of locking plate.
Use bench vice.

Front View

—13¼"—

—13½"—

½

½

Locking plate

1¼" alloy tube

Support plate   Support plate

Plan View

Figure 3:7 *The Failsafe footrest*

12 *Making the footrest supports*

Two supports are made by laying 4 layers of 1½ oz mat to the template in Figure 3:10. Lay-up on an old mirror and cut to shape when leather hard, with a sharp knife. If making several canoes, make a hardboard copy of the template. When fully hard, drill ¼" clearance holes as indicated (use the footrest support jig for this). If you are making a fail-safe footrest, make sure that the holes are exactly ½" back from the edge of the support.

13 *Fitting the footrest supports*

Make a support jig as shown in Figure 3:8, 15½" × 12" × ½" with hole spacings as on the support plate template (Figure 3:10). Chipboard, thickish ply, or blockboard is suitable. Hardboard is too thin! Bolt the footrest supports to this jig as shown in Figure 3:8, and keep resin out of holes by covering them with a strip of masking tape. Slide the whole assembly into the canoe until the back of the support is about 3' 6" from the rear of the cockpit rim (Figure 3:6). The supports should now be jammed against the gunwales and can be glassed into position with 2" strips of mat. This is fiddly, as the job is done at arms length down the canoe. Make sure you put the footrest supports in the bow of the canoe! Some time ago, a chap glassed his supports into the stern end – made a really good job too. We didn't stop laughing for a week, but he had no sense of humour – never even smiled once!

14a *Making the footrest*

(Fail-safe Footrest) Saw off a length of 1¼" dia. alloy tubing 17" long. Squeeze one end in a metal-work vice to form a flat, 1¼" long, at the end. Drill ¼" clearance hole in the centre of this flat, say ⅝" from end. Flatten the other end of the tube in the vice for a distance of 2½" from the end, making sure that the flats are lying in the same plane. Do not drill the second end. When the footrest supports are glassed into the canoe,

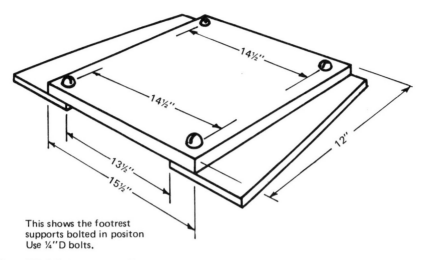

This shows the footrest
supports bolted in positon
Use ¼"D bolts.

Figure 3:8 *A footrest support jig*

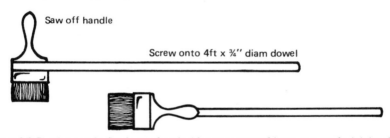

Saw off handle

Screw onto 4ft x ¾" diam dowel

Figure 3:9 *Brushes can be fixed onto dowel with screws or masking tape to make joining the canoe easier*

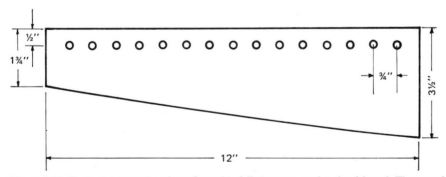

Figure 3:10 *Footrest support template. Copy this full-size onto card or hard board. The curved surface will have to be modified to fit the particular canoe being made. The holes are ¼" D. clearance. (17/64" is about right). The holes are ¾" apart so that when a fail-safe locking clip is fitted, the bar footrest remains at 90° to the centre-line of the canoe. If you look at diagram 3:7 you will see that the clip is bolted to the support, one hole behind the bar at the other side. Thus, a spacing of ¾" brings the bar end in the slot to the correct position.*

bolt one end of the footrest onto one support using a ¾" × ¼" dia. Whitworth brass bolt and nut, and bolt a nylon locking plate onto the other support opposite. (Nylon locking plates are available from canoe retailers and from most canoe-builders). Push the long flat end of the footrest into the slot formed by the locking plate and the footrest support, see Figure 3:7. Mark the position of the outside edge of the locking plate onto the flat of the footrest. Remove the footrest, and bend at right-angles in the vice, at the position marked (Figure 3:7). Remove all but about ½" of the bent-up flat with a hacksaw, and clean up both ends with a file. The footrest will now provide a firm foot-support in the canoe. It will release a trapped foot by pivoting about one end, and it will prevent the gunwales of the canoe from spreading, by hooking behind the edge of the locking plate.

14b *Platform footrest*
A platform footrest can be made by glassing the platform onto an alloy bar. The following points should be noted:
(a) Make up a bar as detailed in 14a but make *both* ends to slide into a nylon locking plate. Use two locking plates, one on each support. (Some clips are 'handed' left or right).
(b) Drill holes in the bar to 'key' the glassfibre onto the alloy.
(c) Cut a template for the platform from thick card, and make sure it completly fills the cross-section of the canoe when the footrest is at its furthest extent.
(d) By adding layers of glassfibre direct to the pattern both sides, a suitable platform can be made. Use at least 6 layers of 1½oz mat.
(e) Glass this platform onto the alloy tube with more layers of mat. The platform can come in front of the alloy bar and suitable slots to slide over the footrest support can be cut with a hacksaw and file.

Platform footrests are best reserved for flat-water touring canoes where little strain is placed on the platform. Competition kayaks and canoes subjected to heavy strain normally have bar-footrests.

15 *Cleaning up*
Wet-and-dry paper on the gelcoat tends to remove the lustre, and should be used with discretion. Fingernails, or a sharp chisel at worst, should be used to remove the odd splashes of resin. A final polish with metal polish will remove any smears, and a good wax will make it immaculate.

16 *Buoyancy*
Rigid polyurethane foam can be poured into the ends of the canoe. Equal parts of the two components are mixed with a mechanical mixer and poured as soon as foaming commences – about 30 seconds.

Polystyrene blocks can be cut to form pillars between hull and deck, but they need fastening in carefully. Unfortunately resin dissolves polystyrene (but not polyurethane) so if you want to hold the blocks in with glassfibre, you must use a barrier of masking tape round the end of the polystyrene. Better still, make a small wooden mould to lay up a channel of glassfibre that will then clip onto the end of the buoyancy. This can then be glassed into the canoe with a small piece of mat. See Figures 3:11a and 3:11b.

Old polyurethane bottles and containers can often be obtained for nothing, and can be jammed into the canoe. They are always liable to come out unless they are tied in. A ring of ⅛" alloy and about 2" in diameter glassed into the hull makes a good fastening ring for buoyancy or kit. Fibreglass is heavier than water and will sink when waterlogged. Its specific gravity is about 1.2 which means that a 36lb canoe will sink with a force of around 6lb weight pulling it under. Much more buoyancy than this is needed to keep the canoe afloat *and visible* in turbulent or choppy water. Don't neglect your buoyancy.

17 *Painter or loop fastenings*

Glassfibre is very slippery when wet and therefore toggles, or at least loops are essential. Drill holes for these through the thick wad of resin at bow and stern. Check the holes for leaks by blowing in them. While loops are the minimum requirement for the bow and stern of a canoe, they have been known to trap the fingers when the canoe has spun around in turbulent water. The addition of a toggle to the loop will prevent this unpleasant situation. Choose a toggle that will not deteriorate in use.

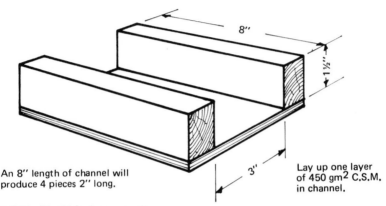

An 8" length of channel will produce 4 pieces 2" long.

Lay up one layer of 450 gm² C.S.M. in channel.

Figure 3:11a *Mould for buoyancy clip*

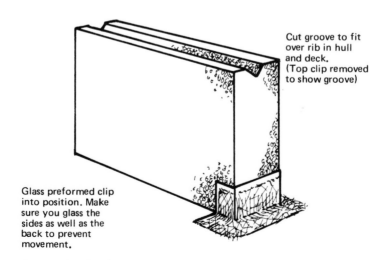

Cut groove to fit over rib in hull and deck. (Top clip removed to show groove)

Glass preformed clip into position. Make sure you glass the sides as well as the back to prevent movement.

Figure 3:11b *Holding the polystyrene block in position*

Some general points

A   Old clothes (including footwear) should be worn – particularly when your are newcomes to the game. The processes involved can be messy.

B   On activation, fumes are given off by the resin. Some people, particularly when working inside the mould, find them irritating. Do not rub the eyes or skin – get out into the fresh air. Though they often make themselves noticeable, fumes are not dangerous if the room is well ventilated and you do not work in heavy concentrations for hours at a time.

C   Some people find barrier-cream or gloves a useful protection of hands against irritation by glass and resin. Since there is the possibility of dermatitis unless all remnants of resin and other chemicals are removed, it is worthwhile taking precautions.

D   It is advisable to join the parts of the canoe as soon as possible after making them, and certainly within a week. The resin continues to cure for about two months and will become progressively harder and more difficult to manage. Fresh resin does not stick very firmly to fully cured resin.

Keep the canoes off the water as long as possible after completion to let the resin 'cure'. Strictly speaking, the completed canoe should cure for at least a fortnight in the 'ambient temperature' – the temperature at which it is made. I've never managed to keep my personal boats off for more than a week before trying them out, however!

E   Any group undertaking a wet lay-up job must maintain a sense of urgency. Once mixed, the resin will 'set' and nothing will stop it. Once the shells are started they must be finished in one go. Stopping work between laminations leads to weakness. Unless subsequent laminations are applied to 'green' laminations, separation at a later stage is likely.

F   Use only PA (pre-accelerated) resin, then only a catalyst is required. No accelerator is needed.

If you do use a non PA resin, an accelerator is needed as well as a catalyst. These two must never come into contact, as they may explode.

G   Catalyst is dangerous. Splashes must be washed off the skin immediately. If you get any in the eyes, flush with water, or better still a weak sodium bi-carbonate solution. (Keep a bottle of it made up handy). Go to a hospital at once.

H   Glassfibring needs a temperature of about 68°F (20°C) for best results. No draughts, and low humidity help too. Therefore electric heaters are good. Paraffin and gas flames produce water and are not to be recommended. Think of the fire risk too.

I   Cleaning materials for brushes etc.
   (i)   Acetone is the best substance but is quite expensive and is very flammable.
   (ii) Use a powder washing-up detergent as a substitute for acetone. Rub into brushes, wash in hot water, rinse and rub into soap block, leaving soap in the bristles.

J   Protect floors and benches with old opened-out cardboard boxes – much better than newspapers.

BASIC TOOLS AND EQUIPMENT NEEDED TO BUILD A CANOE

1   *Brushes:* Several 2½" brushes preferably with no polish on the handles for applying resin, stippling etc.

2   *Rollers:* Metal washer Rollers for rolling mat and elimination of air bubbles.

3   *Containers:* For mixing resins, old buckets, tins or wax cartons are useful. Also bucket for washing out the mould.

4   *Measures:* Mix resin and catalyst by either weight or volume.
    (a) Plastic Cook's measure approx. 1 litre size.
    (b) Set of cooking scales to weigh to at least 3lbs (or 2kg)
    (c) Accurate small measure for catalyst. Either a syringe or measuring cylinder marked in grams or millilitres.
    (d) If you don't measure pigments by weight you've just got to guess, as too much sticks to things, for volume to be accurate. Old teaspoons are as good as anything.

5   *Sponge:* Small sponge (synthetic type is best) for applying release agent.

6   *Rag:* Polishing cloths that are lint free, and preferably of open weave for wax polishing are best.

7   *Trimming Knife:* Sharp knife for trimming gelled lay-up, cutting glass mat etc.

8   *H-section Tools:* If you use an H-section join, these left and right hand tools are essential for fitting the H-section quickly and easily.

9   *Hand-brace and Twist-drill:* a 5/16" dia. drill will give ¼" clearance holes for footrest bolts and painter holes.

10   *Hacksaw and File:* For sawing alloy tube and general cleaning up of gelled lay-up edges.

11   *Wet and Dry:* Grit numbers 180 and 360 are medium and fine grains, suitable for cleaning up the edges of the cockpit etc.

12   *Joining Brush:* For stippling the joining strip inside the gunwale of the canoe. This can be made from a stippling brush – see figure 3.9 for details.

13   *Masking Tape:* For holding hull and deck together while joining, masking holes on footrest supports, holding seat while glassing in place, etc.

14   *T-cut Polish:* Better than metal polish for giving that final buff to the surface of the canoe.

15   *Jigs and Patterns:*
    (a) For footrest supports and fixing same see figures 3.8 and 3.9.
    (b) For fixing polystyrene pillar buoyancy see figure 3.11.
    (c) For glass reinforcing materials cut your own by placing brown paper in the moulds – copy in hardboard.

16   *Scissors:* For cutting glass mat are useful. They soon blunt however.

17   *Barrier Cream:* A good precaution to prevent any problem arising from resin and chemicals on the hands.

18   *Hand cleansers:* An antiseptic cream that emulsifies resins. Very useful where water for washing hands is not readily available.

MAINTENANCE

Glassfibre canoes need surprisingly little maintenance, but of course wind, water and sunlight will cause almost any material to deteriorate. Store in a cool dry place after wiping out the interior. If the canoe is left in the sun for long periods, the pigments will fade slightly. An occasional rub with T-cut polishing compound will restore surface lustre, and the deck can be wax polished. If you wax the hull, it will detract slightly from the canoe's performance. Abrasion and scratches are best left alone, as it is almost impossible to fill a scratch permanently.

Over the years, as scratches penetrate the gelcoat, and water percolates into the interior surface of the canoe, the glass fibres within the laminate will retain thin layers of water molecules over their surface. Eventually this layer of water will separate each fibre from the surrounding resin, and the laminate becomes 'mushy' and eventually disintegrates. It is important that a very old canoe in this condition is not allowed to freeze, as the expanding ice within the laminate will literally blow it apart. Keep the canoe as dry as possible and let it dry out between trips. A dry old canoe can be left out in the frost, and a new one, with no deterioration in the laminate, will come to no harm even if water freezes in it. It is best to support lightweight boats so that they do not 'sag' or distort. This usually only happens when the canoe is not fully cured. Do not store a canoe with a lot of heavy gear inside it.

Repairs to Glassfibre

Glass reinforced plastic cures over a period of several weeks. Repairs to cured resin are not always satisfactory unless care is taken. The following notes outline the necessary steps for making a satisfactory job.

1   *Drying out the damaged area*
    This is essential to a permanent repair. Unless the whole area of broken glassfibre is thoroughly dried and cracks prised open to allow evaporation, the repair is always liable to open up again. Several days in a dry room, or several hours with a fan-heater or similar, are required to dry out a canoe satisfactorily. Half an hour 'cooking' a boat over a primus stove is not usually satisfactory. If you have an accident, and need to do a running repair on the river bank or beach during a trip, it is best to strap up the canoe with PVC tape, carpet tape, or even masking tape, and leave the permanent repair until you can thoroughly dry out the canoe.

2   *Preparation of damaged area*
    Using a file or very course emery paper, clean down the whole area, even threading the emery paper through any cracks, until you have exposed the glass reinforcing and removed all trace of polished resin surface. You cannot afford to skimp this stage.

3   *Applying resin*
    If there is an actual hole in the skin of the canoe, stick some 2″ wide PVC tape over the hole on the outside to act as a barrier, then work from the inside of the boat. Cut pieces of CSM reinforcing (1 oz or 300 gm²), one piece the size of the hole plus 1″ overlap all round, and others increasing in size by 1″ all round. Three pieces will usually be enough. Add a piece of woven roving cloth if you wish, but don't use all woven roving cloth as it is too porous.
    Thoroughly wet out the area of the repair with resin, using a brush on the end of a stick if necessary. Wet out the smallest piece of CSM with resin by stippling it with the brush on a disposable 'wetting out board' (a suitable piece of wood or cardboard). Use the brush to place the CSM over the hole. Stipple! Repeat with the next larger piece of CSM and so on.

When the resin has set, remove the tape from the outside of the canoe. On an old boat, where surface finish is not important, it is enough to leave the repair at this stage – a little cleaning up on the outside with file or emery will suffice. Sometimes it is impossible to repair from the inside and the patching will have to be done on the external surface. External patches are never as satisfactory as internal ones, as they are keying to gelcoat and not to the main laminate.

4 *Repairing the gelcoat*
If an 'invisible' repair is needed on the outside, it is necessary to proceed from stage 3. First clean off the outside of the repair with a file, leaving the surface rough and lower than its surrounding. Cover the whole area with gelcoat. Gelcoat is an air-inhibited resin. This means that surfaces that cure exposed to air will remain sticky. It is necessary, therefore, to overfill with gelcoat and clean off when set, to remove the outer sticky surface. Another way, only suitable on small areas, is to fill the hole with gel and then stick adhesive tape over the repair. Often, when the tape is removed, it will be seen that no further cleaning up is necessary as the finished surface will be as smooth as the underside of the tape. Small blemishes, such as air-bubbles under existing gelcoat can be repaired in this way.

5 *Finishing the repair*
Where the gelcoat repair has been left proud, reduce with a file and as the final shape is reached use wet and dry paper. Use it wet and wrap it around a cork, rubber, or small piece of wood. Start with a grit number of approximately 80 and work through to a really fine grade, say 120, 280, 360, 600, 800, 1,000, 1,200. There is no substitute for this rather laborious process you'll be sorry to learn. However, a final finish to the surface with cutting-paste (metal polish will do) will give you a perfect finish.

6 *Colour matching the repair*
It is very difficult to match the colour of a repair to the job. Even if you get the pigment addition just right, the catalyst addition can sometimes affect the colour slightly. Judge as carefully as you can.

7 *Major repairs*
Occasionally the ends of a canoe are broken off completely, or canoes are broken in half. Repairs are not always out of the question although they may take a long time. If the separate pieces appear to fit reasonably well, stick the edges together with PVC tape. Impacted cracks can often be levered out with a screwdriver or chisel. When all is made as fair as possible, glass over on the inside as already described.

8 *Temporary repairs*
Often a repair must be made on a wet canoe, and the only way this can be done is with one of the weatherproofing tapes available from builders' merchants. There are various trade names for the tape, Denso Tape is one. Evostik make another. They are all essentially a hessian tape impregnated with a non-oxydising paste. It can be pressed over a crack or bound over a large hole. It is a nasty, messy material, but is invaluable for instant repairs, and can be used even at sea. A knife or scissors will cut it and petrol, paraffin or white spirit will clean and dissolve it.

There are rolls of sticky tape available for repair too. They vary in strength and adhesion, but all of them will only stick to a dry surface. If it is possible to get ashore and dry out the damage, this tape makes a very good temporary repair with no mess. A 2″ wide tape is ideal for most jobs.

9 *Permanent repairs outdoors*
If the canoe can be taken to a temporary campsite it is possible to make a more

permanent repair using normal resin and glass mat as detailed under sections 2 and 3. The problem is to dry out the damaged area quickly. It can be done by warming over a fire or cooking stove, but wash off sea-water with fresh water first.

The practice of wiping acetone or meths over the damage and putting a match to it is *extremely* dangerous and could lead to extensive repairs having to be done on the person perpetrating this silly method.

After drying, the repair can be made, and then another session of warming over the fire will cure the resin in a few minutes. Care must be taken not to blister the resin, by heating too much.

It must be said that repairs done like this seldom last very long. They will tide you over for the event or the holiday, but don't be surprised to find that the repair loosens after a few weeks.

10 *Paddle repairs*

Although it may be possible to make a temporary repair on a paddle with tape, glassfibre or glue, the necessary strength/weight ratio of the paddle makes it extremely difficult to make a satisfactory job. It is necessary to remove any varnish first, and if you spill resin it will dissolve the varnish, leaving a sticky mess.

Sometimes a broken wooden loom can be spokeshaved down and fitted into a short length of alloy tubing, but this needs a workshop really, and is not usually entirely successful. The best advice is to carry a spare.

MAKING A PADDLE

If you have lots of time to spare there is no reason why a competent woodworker shouldn't make a spruce/ash laminate paddle himself. He will need aircraft quality spruce which is very expensive. Each lamination will need to be planed with a sharp trying plane and glued with a good quality waterproof glue. Shaping will be done with spokeshave, for the loom, but the blades will need to be dealt with by using small block-planes. Use templates to check the shapes of two identical blades, each with a loom 3' long. When these are completed, except for the finishing off of the looms, scarf the looms together, glue up and clean up.

It can be very satisfying, working in wood to make your own paddle, but don't think you will get one on the cheap! Without machinery it is a very long-winded process, and only a skillful woodworker will succeed. Even turning up splines for flat ply blades can pose problems for the wood-turner as the thin diameter of the spline compared to its length causes a lot of 'chatter' which is difficult to eliminate.

4 Safety

Compiled by the Editor

INTRODUCTION

Safety should be a positive, not a negative, concept. It is a matter of adopting a realistic attitude to the inherent risks of the activity, rather than listing a series of 'dont's'. There must be an interaction of sound **knowledge,** good **equipment** and adequate **training and technique.**

When this is properly done, the canoeist can finally enter situations which challenge and thrill, and be having fun, where the untrained person may drown, and where few other vessels can operate.

Although not all canoeing is undertaken on raging rapids or pounding surf, even placid water can drown, and drowning can damage one's health! It is necessary therefore at all times to take the common sense precautions which experience and statistics demonstrate, reduces the risk of fatality in a canoe, to almost nil.

KNOWLEDGE

The Golden Rules

1   *The ability to swim.* Every person who sits in a canoe should be able to swim at least 50 metres in light clothing. The ability to swim vast distances is not essential, but basic confidence in and *under* the water without panic are fundamental to safe canoeing.

2   *Personal flotation aids.* A Life jacket or buoyancy aid should always be worn when afloat.

3   *Stay with the boat.* In the event of a capsize, stay with the boat, and if necessary tie yourself on. A canoe is more easily spotted than an individual swimmer's head in the water. On a river, it may be necessary to abandon the boat and swim as swiftly as possible across the current to the bank, if you are being carried into danger.

   Should you ever have to abandon a boat, inform the authorities immediately. Inland, this will be the police; at sea, inform the Coastguard. The Coastguard service is on the 999 emergency system also, but for routine matters the number of the nearest station can be obtained from the directory.

4   *Less than three there should never be.* Three trained paddlers, working within their experience, should be able to cope with most situations. With three persons available, one can always summon help while one deals with a casualty.

One can of course add other rules. If they are needed you can construct them from the material in this chapter and the safety aspects which appear in the relevent chapters related to specific activities. Appendix III lists sample safety regulations.

The group

The particular areas of knowledge required for the organisation of inland or sea journeys are highlighted within the relevant sections. If one factor is important above all others, it is the necessity to know the limits of one's personal ability, and that of every member of the group. The ability to identify situations which are apparently, but not inherently, dangerous, and will thus excite and challenge the novice, yet remain within manageable safety limits, is the basic art of the instructor.

Moving Water

Moving water is a powerful and relentless force. A simple 2-3 mph current can pin a canoe or a person against an obstacle, overcome a 6 kg buoyancy aid and hold the paddler under water. Obstacles in moving water must therefore be avoided. Rocks, bridges, posts, buoys, moored boats, and especially trees.

If you must hit, immediately throw your body weight onto the obstruction – see chapter 8.

Weirs

Three types of weir commonly exist in Great Britain: sharp crested; broad crested (also known as long-base) and triangular profile (or 'crump'). A variation on the triangular profile weir, but not usable on large rivers is the flat-V, or measuring weir. (Figures 4:1, 4:2, 4:3). Weirs exist in order to control levels between various sections of river; to divert water; to create a hydraulic head for power generation; to provide storage; or to facilitate flow measurement.

The main concern of water authorities, is to dissipate the energy created by water accelerating over a weir, as efficiently as possible. This means that the bigger the hydraulic jump (stopper), and the more it can be contained, the less the speed of the flow downstream of the weir, and consequently less erosion to the banks will occur.

A 'stopper' is, in fact, a vertical eddy current. Whenever moving water passes an

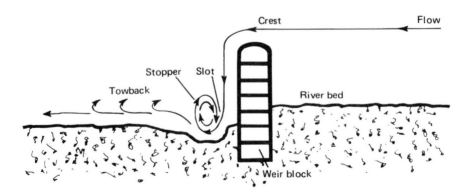

Figure 4:1 *Broad crested weir.*

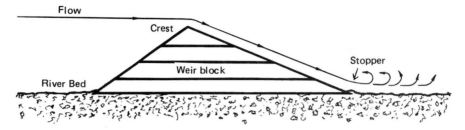

Figure 4:2 *Triangular profile or 'crump' weir.*

obstruction, there is a low-pressure area created on the down-stream side of that obstruction. This should appear as a hole, but as water must find its own level, and 'nature abhors a vacuum', this hole is filled by water coming back upstream. Therefore, behind any rock, or wherever water flows faster in one place than another, 'eddy' currents will form. (Figure 4:4).

In the case of a stopper, water has accelerated over a drop. This may be only a couple of inches, or the Victoria Falls, but the principle is the same. Because the water has accelerated, it does not just stop at river level below the fall, but in fact continues down and gradually rises as the velocity diminishes. The 'hole' that is thus left immediately downstream of the drop, is filled by water breaking away from the surface, and pouring down into it in the form of tumbling foam. An object failing to break through this foaming wave, is therefore pushed down by it, taken under by the water dropping over the fall, and

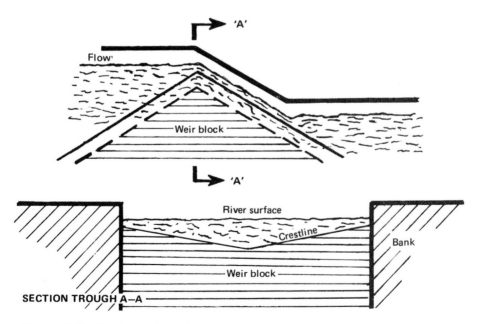

Figure 4:3 *Flat-V or 'measuring' weir.*

69

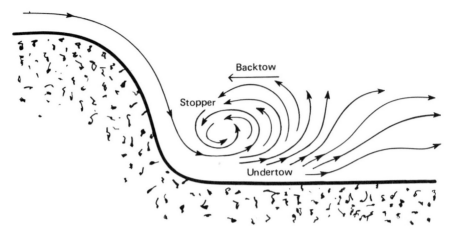

Figure 4:4 *Behaviour of water in a 'stopper' wave.*

provided it is buoyant, brought back up again. If this occurs too near the fall, the surface water moving upstream will take it (or him) back into the stopper, and the cycle will be repeated ... and repeated ... and repeated.

The greatest erosion problem is to the river bed, and in order to overcome this, an undesirable trend has been to build 'anti-scour' weirs, with a concrete step at the bottom. (Figure 4:5). This creates a continuous large area of 'back-tow'. The likelihood of anyone escaping from this situation is slight, and this type of weir must be avoided at all costs. The BCU is currently objecting to the building of these on the grounds of the lethal nature of the hazard which they create.

Other methods of dissipating energy include the planting of metal stakes, or the construction of concrete 'dragon's teeth'. Some weirs have wire baskets full of rocks, known as 'gabions' placed on the bed of the river. When the wire breaks, or becomes loose through the stones being moved by the force of the water, bows of canoes can become entrapped.

On natural weirs, and some man-made, there is an erosion problem under the fall. Here, the water can be circulating two ways, and anyone trapped in this situation is probably in an irretrievable position. (Figure 4:6).

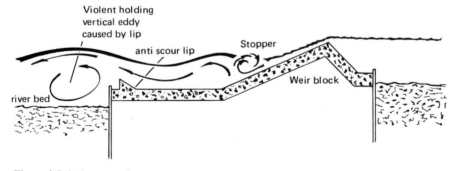

Figure 4:5 *Anti-scour weir.*

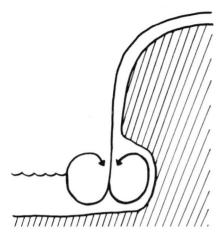

Figure 4:6 *Two-way stopper caused by erosion under-cutting a fall.*

Novices should never be encouraged to shoot a weir that the instructor does not know from practical experience. Factors that determine whether or not a weir is 'shootable' are: depth of water; vertical drop; amount of 'back-tow'; size of stopper; whether there is a natural break in the stopper; whether the stopper ends in a natural flow, or is sealed in by walls; the shape of the weir – a 'horseshoe' shape could mean that everything works into the middle and there is no escape; the power of the 'back-tow' – a large vertical drop into a deep pool, or a lot of water over a small drop, could produce a giant vertical eddy from which escape may be impossible. Careful study is required by experts for any unknown weir, before an attempt is made to shoot it. If in doubt, portage.

Cold and hypothermia

A body loses its heat to water 26 times as fast as it does to air at the same temperature. Survival time in water at $10° – 15°C (50° – 60°F) – maximum$ summer temperature around Britain – is one to six hours. Even a fit person can become unconscious in 30-60 minutes, particularly if energy has been used up, as when paddling hard for a period of time. A personal flotation aid is essential, but attention to suitable clothing is also vital.

Hypothermia (exposure) occurs when the body loses heat faster than it can replace it. In defence, the peripheral blood vessels are constricted, to reduce the heat loss, but eventually the core temperature of the body drops. A person is in hypothermia when it reaches $35°C (95°F)$. Unless the situation is remedied, the core temperature then drops dramatically, and death follows quite quickly – minutes, rather than hours. Violent shivering is a sign that the body is needing to create heat. Shivering however, uses up energy, and if the cause is not remedied, hypothermia is the consequence. The signs to watch for are:

Abnormal or irrational behaviour.

Uncontrollable shivering.

Vague, slow, slurred speech.

Memory lapses, incoherence.

Slowing down, stumbling.

Drowsiness.

The remedy is to remove the victim from the hostile environment. If wet, and it is

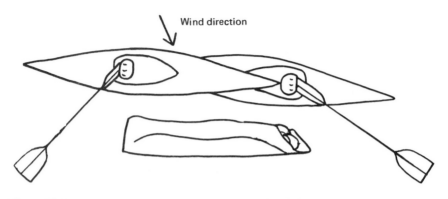

Figure 4:7 *Protecting a victim in an exposure bag from the wind.*

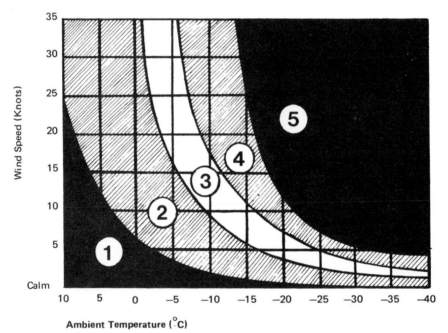

1 Comfort with normal precautions
2 Very cold, travel becomes uncomfortable on overcast days
3 Bitterly cold, travel becomes uncomfortable even on clear sunny days
4 Freezing of human flesh begins. Travel and life in temporary shelter becomes disagreeable
5 Exposed flesh will freeze in less than one minute

Figure 4:8 *Affect of wind on temperature – the 'wind-chill factor'.*

possible, change him into dry clothes. Place in an exposure bag, ideally also in a sleeping bag, or in company with a fit person, to provide warmth. It is vital to shelter the exposure bag from the wind – canoes can be propped up to act as wind-breaks. (Figure 4:7). Obtain help (i.e. ambulance). An exposure victim must be seen by a doctor, as complications can set in. If it can be done, immerse the patient in a hot bath. The water temperature is critical – 40-44°C. Keep him there, maintaining the temperature, until shivering stops. Then remove to warmed bed and await a doctor. Hot, sweet drinks may be given to a conscious patient.

Any situation where body heat continues to be removed more quickly than the body is able to replace it will lead to hypothermia. Correct clothing will increase survival time, even in water, and prevent loss of body heat in wind. A person can stand naked for a time in still air at -15°C. A wind of 25 mph at the same air temperature, will freeze the flesh. This is known as the 'wind chill factor'. (Figure 4:8). A combination of wind and wet, it will be seen, is therefore very serious indeed. Vital to survival in canoeing is the windproof anorak, which must always be worn over a warm under-garment.

Wet-suits are made of a closed-cell foam (ie. the material does not absorb water) called neoprene, and work by trapping a layer of water between the suit and the body. This is warmed by the body, and provides insulation. Obviously, the better fitting the wet suit is, the more effective. Where immersion in cold water is a risk a wet-suit should be seriously considered.

Lifesaving

All canoeists should be able to carry out a canoe to canoe rescue. There is also training available through the Corps of Canoe Lifeguards, and tests at elementary, intermediate and advanced standard in lifesaving techniques, and outlined in their training manual. See chapter 9 – *Sea Canoeing* – for information on the basic methods of supporting and transporting a swimmer with a canoe.

Expired Air Resuscitation (EAR) must be started directly a drowned person is reached. A canoe can be used for support, enabling EAR to commence while the victim is being towed ashore. The partially drowned person will be still breathing, although with much difficulty. Should his breathing become very slow, irregular or deeply sighing in nature, then EAR should commence at once. Cardiac arrest is always a possibility – absence of neck pulse and dilated (enlarged) pupils, in someone apparently dead, are signs. External Cardiac Compression (ECC) is then vital.

Some victims may appear to recover rapidly and show no sign of ill effect from their immersion. They must be treated for shock, however, and it is quite possible for secondary drowning to occur at any time from a few minutes to several days later. This can come on quite suddenly and prove fatal. All 'drowned' victims – even when a small quantity of water only has been inhaled – must therefore be seen at a local hospital as soon as possible.

Instances have been documented where drowned persons have been revived after long periods under water (30 minutes or more) and have recovered without apparent brain damage. The colder the water – around 20°C (70°F) and below – and the younger the victim, the better are the chances of recovery. It is incumbent upon lifesavers to 'have a go' every time with EAR and/or ECC until a qualified medical practitioner says otherwise.

Hydrocution is the name given to the cause of sudden death, which occasionally occurs when a person is immersed in very cold water – around 10°C (50°F) or below. It is thought that a reflex action includes involuntary inhalation, which in certain circumstances could lead to immediate drowning. The heart can be slowed through a reflex induced by cold, involving the vagus nerve, although there is no evidence of this causing complete arrest of the heart for the 5-15 minutes necessary to cause death.

First aid

First aid is largely a matter of common-sense, but it needs to be enlightened common-sense. Total competence is only achieved through pursuing a course of training, and studying the manual of one of the first aid services. The basic principles should be known by all:

1 Keep calm.

2 Do not move the patient unless absolutely essential.

3 Seek professional help.

4 Deal with priorities.

5 Do not give food or drink.

6 Be firm but gentle – reassure the patient.

Minor accidents that require professional assistance should be dealt with by the nearest hospital with an accident and emergency department. For a serious accident dial 999. Speak slowly, clearly and briefly. Give your location, name and address, the type of accident, and the number of casualties.

Dealing with priorities

In an emergency situation it is vital to establish the correct order of priorities. These are:

1 Breathing/heart stopped.

2 Bleeding.

3 Injuries.

4 Shock.

Expired Air Resuscitation (EAR)

The RLSS recommend the following: Place casualty on his back with head slightly raised to minimise risk of vomiting. Lift jaw and tilt head back by pressure on chin as far as reasonably possible. Clear mouth of any debris, damaged teeth or dentures. Jaw lift and head tilt must be maintained. *Keeping casualty's mouth closed, breathe steadily into nose.* Turn head to see whether casualty's chest has inflated. If not, try increasing neck extension and lifting jaw further before repeating the blowing, or trying alternative mouth-to-mouth technique.

The full sequence is: give a total of four breaths to partially inflate the chest (this helps subsequent inflation to be more effective); continue with a breath every five seconds, giving about half of this time to the actual inflation stage, until casualty regains consciousness or further help arrives; if breathing re-starts, place casualty in recovery position.

If the mouth to nose technique does not result in adequate inflation: pinch nose shut; maintain head extension and jaw lift; seal your mouth over casualty's, and start mouth-to-mouth inflation.

For a baby, technique should be modified to: place mouth over infant's mouth and nose, puff air gently from cheeks instead of deep breaths from lungs. Repeat about 20-25 times a minute.

Air may be breathed into casualty's stomach, particularly if head is inadequately extended to help open the air passages. Where this is suspected, casualty should be turned on his side, and stomach gently pressed to expel air through mouth and nose. Restart EAR immediately. Casualty may vomit. If so, turn on side to ensure stomach contents are carefully expelled and not inhaled. Clear residual debris promptly from mouth and immediately turn on back and restart resuscitation. The Holger-Nielsen or Sylvester methods should also be learned for cases where the face is too badly damaged, or poison burns or gasing is involved.

External Cardiac Compression

ECC must not be resorted to without reasonable certainty that the heart has stopped. There are three checks:

1 No pulse at carotid artery

2 Widely dilated pupils (both) which do not contract when exposed to light.

3 Skin and lips remain bluish despite effective EAR.

EAR must always be used in conjunction with cardiac compression, but ECC is not always required with EAR. The correct method and pressure to be applied needs learning, and courses are readily available through the RLSS or similar body.

Treatment of Wounds

In any case of external haemorrhage cover the wound with a dressing, **apply pressure,** pressing directly on to it for at least 10 minutes. Do not remove the original dressing, but add further ones if necessary. Tie with a tight bandage, but do *not* tourniquet. The limb below the bandage should be warm and pink. Reduce blood flow by raising the limb and/or keeping it cool.

If there is a foreign body in the wound, do not use direct pressure, but stop the flow of blood at a pressure point between the heart and the wound, as close to the latter as possible. Do not attempt to remove large foreign bodies as a massive haemorrhage may ensue.

Treatment for shock

Shock is a factor in all cases of injury or sudden collapse. An unconscious casualty, or one at all likely to become so, should be turned onto his side, with the limbs flexed in the uppermost position (ie a person lying on his left side will have the right limbs flexed), so that he cannot roll over onto his back or chest. Turn the head to the side. This is known as the recovery position.

If you cannot move the casualty (eg if spinal injury is suspected) watch his respiration carefully. Close the mouth and hold the jaw closed. Pull very slightly on the lower jaw to keep the tongue held forward. Do not leave a casualty alone in this position. Patients in shock should be covered with a light blanket, but not over-heated. Do not give food or drinks in case surgery is required.

Other and Minor Accidents

Bites

From *animals* – clean the wound, stop the bleeding, visit the doctor or casualty unit. From *snakes* – do not make an incision; kill the snake so it can be identified, make the casualty lie down, keep him cool and raise the limb to slow down the blood-flow to the heart; remove to a doctor or hospital, but do not exert the patient. From *insects*, apply a soothing cream or calamine lotion.

Burns and Scalds

Do not remove clothing adhering to the burn, or cover with ointment or spirits, or burst the blisters. For superficial burns wash immediately under cold, running water. Dry without rubbing. Cover with a dry sterile dressing. For extensive burns roll the casualty very gently, still clothed, into a clean sheet. Medical help must be obtained directly.

Foreign bodies

In the *nose* – do not meddle with tweezers or pointed objects; ask casualty to take a deep breath, block the other nostril, and breathe out hard; do not try this with small children – get to a doctor. In the *ear* – a live insect can be rendered harmless with a few drops of castor oil; do not use tweezers or similar; let the doctor remove the foreign body. In the *eye* – do not let casualty rub the eye; keep the eye protected, preferably closed and free from movement, and get to an accident and emergency department.

Fractures

Immobilise the joint. Legs can be tied together with triangular bandages, ties, belts or scarves. Tie the knots on the unaffected side, padded with handkerchiefs or similar.

Hyperthermia (Heatstroke)

Victims usually have a pale face with a pinched and worried expression, and a high temperature (but maybe not sweating) a racing pulse, and shallow breathing. Cool the casualty by uncovering him; sponge him and give lots of cool fluids. Keep in the shade and give well salted crisps to eat if he feels like it.

A death occurred in France due to a paddler climbing out of a gorge after losing his canoe, on a hot day, still wearing his wet suit. It is advisable to remove wet suits or excessive clothing in such situations.

Cramp

Cramp and Pins and Needles are often confused. Cramp is a painful spasm of the muscle, the exact cause of which is unknown. It tends to occur in tired muscles, especially when the circulation is impaired such as in cold conditions. The pain may be so severe as to completely immobilise the victim. Normal treatment is to stretch the muscle out, against its contracting spasm, and to pummel or massage it firmly towards the heart. Cramp usually occurs in the sole of the foot or the calf muscle, but any muscle of the body may suffer.

Pins and needles

These are caused by pressure on a nerve causing its temporary 'death' and the consequent loss of any feeling or control of the part of the body normally controlled by that nerve. The commonest form of pins and needles amongst canoeists is in the legs, nearly always caused through faulty design in the seat of the canoe, when pressure on the pelvic bone will cause the nerves of the legs to 'die'. The sensation is an aching limb, but is nothing like as painful as cramp. The cure is movement.

Head injuries

Anyone suffering a severe blow on the head, whether or not they go unconscious, should be seen by a doctor because of the danger of haemorrhage. Signs to watch for are drowsiness, vomiting and unequal dilation of pupils.

Anti-tetanus protection

Canoeists, due to the nature of their activity, should consider maintaining the anti-tetanus course of injections. See your own doctor.

Figure 4:9a *(Left) buoyancy aid; (right) BSI approved lifejacket with cover and expedition pouch.*

Figure 4:9b *Basic sea-going kit. Exposure bag, rocket and hand-held flare, repair kit and first aid kit, and clothing and food containers.*

Figure 4:9c *Basic river expedition kit. Exposure bag, crash helmet, duffle bag, repair and first aid kits, food and clothing containers, and a throw line. Also featured are a pair of purpose made neoprene lined boots.*

EQUIPMENT

The term 'equipment' does not imply 'lucky charm'. Criticism has been levelled at the departure of kayaks from our coasts, festooned like the proverbial Christmas tree, but with a consequential increased call upon the rescue services! Safety is a total concept. It is only when the right gear is used by the trained person, that risk is minimised.

Personal flotation aid

As will be deduced from the facts surrounding hypothermia, apart from preventing drowning, a buoyancy aid or lifejacket prolongs survival time in water by allowing the victim to conserve body heat through not expending energy in the effort to stay afloat.

Buoyancy aids

Some aids are made to no particular standard, and are therefore to be avoided. Buoyancy aids particularly suitable for canoeing are made to the specification agreed jointly between the British Canoe Union and the British Canoe Manufacturers Association: BCU/BCMA BA 83. This ensures a standard of production and a minimum inherent buoyancy of 6 kgs, which conforms to the International Canoe Federation (ICF) rule for competition. Other aids which may be suitable, depending upon the design of the particular model, are those which are produced to the specification of the Ship and Boat Builders National Federation (SBBNF/79).

In so far as it adds to one's own buoyancy, a buoyancy aid helps a person to remain on the surface and facilitate working whilst there. It will not, however, float the wearer face uppermost and support him in that position, should the victim become unconscious.

Good buoyancy aids are particularly applicable to competition, surfing (for competent canoeists) and rapid rivers. The types most popular for canoeing are either the one-piece, or zipped waistcoat variety. Some are available with pockets for touring canoeists.

Lifejackets

Lifejackets made to British Standards Institution (BSI) specification 3595/81 are made to guaranteed standards of manufacture, and are also designed to do their best to save wearer's life should the victim become incapacitated. They are particularly applicable to sea or open water touring.

The BSI has recommended different types of lifejacket for different uses. The BCU considers that only one of the six types available is suitable for canoeing. This is the one with two stages of buoyancy: an 'inherent' stage, which brings the wearer to the surface and has all the advantages of the buoyancy aid; and an inflatable stage which will do its best to keep the wearer afloat, on his back, at the correct angle, and turning to meet the waves, even if the victim becomes unconscious.

The inherent stage gives 13.2 lbs (6 kgs) buoyancy. When fully inflated (orally) the lifejacket has 35 lbs buoyancy. 'Inherent buoyancy' comprises closed cell plastic foam.

The current BCU recommendation on the wearing of personal flotation aids is:

1   Lifejackets to BSI 3595/81 with inherent buoyancy (min 6 kg inflating to 16 kg) are recommended for sea and open water expeditioning.

2   Buoyancy aids to SBBNF/79 Standards, with a minimum of 6 kg inherent buoyancy, are suitable for river canoeing, and other situations under close supervision.

3   Buoyancy aids to the above standard are recommended for rapid river work, surfing, canoe polo, and other situations where a risk of collision is involved.

When river canoeing, a safety factor can be the ability to swim as swiftly as possible to the bank. For this reason, and because of the greater body protection afforded, buoyancy

Figure 4:10a (top left) *Shortie wet suit with neoprene socks protected by polythene sandals; long john wet suit with soled neoprene boots.*

Figure 4:10b (top right) *Thermal jersey with chest high over-trousers; canoe cag (anorak).*

Figure 4:10 (left) *Neoprene spray deck with vest incorporated, and paddle gloves (pogys); nylon spray deck, neoprene open-palm mits, and crash helmet.*

aids are recommended rather than lifejackets. Make sure the buoyancy aid is not too long, preventing the wearing of an efficient spraydeck, and that it cannot 'ride up' in an emergency. A buoyancy aid combined in a spray deck is available, designed specifically for competition purposes.

Many experienced sea canoeists prefer to wear a buoyancy aid for comfort of paddling, but extensive research over a number of years has shown that a minimum of 35 lbs (16 kg) of buoyancy, correctly distributed, is necessary to keep an unconscious person's head clear in wave conditions of open water. Only a BSI approved lifejacket, when fully inflated, is capable of doing this. The inflationary capacity of a lifejacket is for emergency only, however. For all normal purposes they are worn uninflated, relying only on the inherent buoyancy.

Whatever type of flotation aid is worn, it will be useless unless properly fitted. Careful attention must always be paid to the manufacturers' instructions, and a leader must check those under his supervision.

Clothing

Upper Body
A number of firms now produce garments, known as 'thermal wear' from man-made fibre, which is specially designed to trap body heat, and not to absorb water. For most canoeing activities, a jacket made of fibre-pile, together with the availability of a wind and waterproof anorak, will be sufficient on the top body.

The legs
Many canoeists, particularly when expeditioning, wear wet-suit trousers, although in summer conditions shorts are adequate. Ordinary trousers are better than jeans, which absorb water. Chest-high waterproof over-trousers are very useful.

The feet
These should always be protected, but beware the training shoes which have the sole extended up over the toe, as friction can cause the feet to jam against the deck, particularly in low-volume slalom kayaks. Wellington boots have traditionally been taboo for canoeing, but the modern sailing boots, especially when wet suit trousers are worn, can be suitable, provided a lifejacket or buoyancy aid is used. Purpose made wet-suit boots are available, or a pair of neoprene socks, protected by polythene sandals, or an old pair of large plimsolls, will suffice.

Crash helmets

A number of serious and potentially serious accidents have been recorded to canoeists, in spite of the wearing of safety helmets. For those pursuing white water canoeing, careful consideration should be given to the protection afforded. Once capsized in fast flowing water, there is a tendency for the helmet to pull back, exposing the temple. It should therefore be worn and secured well down on the forehead. Protection should be given to the ears, and the lower part of the base of the skull. The inner adjustable padding must be capable of absorbing a hard shock, and the helmet itself made from a material that will not split on impact. The fastenings must be capable of remaining secure when under stress.

Canoeist's knife

No self-respecting seaman goes afloat without a sharp knife, and this is advocated by American white water canoeists, but seldom mentioned in the UK. There are many instances, however, where the immediate availability of a knife can make a difference, and the carrying of a stainless steel sailor's knife, in a handy pocket, or a diver's knife, should be considered for wild water and sea touring in particular.

Flares

These are dealt with in chapter 9 – *Sea Canoeing.*

Canoes

The British Standards Institution has approved a Code of Practice for Canoe Construction, and a Recommendation for Safety Features in Canoes. The Code states: 'There is no such thing as a "safe" canoe. There can only be a safe canoeist. And his or her safety is only ensured by good training and experience and the avoidance of unnecessary risks.'

Canoes should bear the manufacturer's declaration that they are made in accordance with the BSI Code (BS MA 91: Parts 1 & 2: 1981). The specific safety recommendations are:

Buoyancy
Each canoe should be fitted with at least 25 kg positive buoyancy, so placed that, when full of water, the canoe will float horizontally and will support a weight of 12.5 kg placed at either end of the canoe, or both ends simultaneously. Closed-cell foam buoyancy should be securely fixed so as not to become free. It may be placed so as to add to the structural strength of the canoe.

Water exclusion buoyancy of the sealed compartment type is not recommended unless sufficient closed cell foam is included to meet the buoyancy requirements above, or unless drainage plugs or caps are fitted to allow removal of any water seepage that may occur.

Provision should be made on any air-bags which may be used for buoyancy to allow them to be tied in position so that they cannot float out of a capsized canoe.

Footrests
Platform footrests in closed cockpit canoes should not, in any position, permit the canoeists' feet to pass forward of the footrest. They should be rigidly fixed and be incapable of rotation on their mountings.

Bar type footrests in closed cockpit canoes should be so designed as to allow canoeists to withdraw their feet or legs if they pass the bar. In practice this means that the bar must be of 'fail safe' design, ie rigid when the canoeists' feet are pressed against it in the normal paddling position, but capable of swinging or falling clear of the canoeists' feet if they pass beyond the bar.

Painters and Deck-lines
Where fitted, painters and deck-lines must be firmly secured in such a way as to hold them away from the cockpit area. They should be made of rot-proof line of one of the materials specified in BS MA 29 and should be of 6 mm diameter.

Spraydecks
When provided, a spray cover should be fitted with a release becket or strap to enable the canoeist, in an emergency, to remove the spray cover quickly from the cockpit rim. The spray cover should also permit the occupant to leave the canoe in an emergency without using the becket.

Colour
To assist in detection, the deck and hull of sea canoes should be predominently finished in opaque red, orange or yellow.

Figure 4:11 *A double-line figure-of-eight knot, leaving a loop. For use as a stopper-knot on a toggle, do not double the line.*

Toggles, deck lines and painters

Open Canadian Canoes require painters, but their use has virtually died out for kayaks. A tow-line, carried separately, can double as a painter, by being attached to the bow, if necessary. To fit toggles and deck lines it is necessary to drill holes through the gunnels about 1½" and 2½" from the bow and stern. For this, the ends must be solid fibreglass, and that should have been done at the time of manufacture. It would be possible to achieve this by mixing up resin, tearing up chopped strand mat and making a wad. Stand the dried canoe on end and ram this home with a long stick. After about 30 minutes it should be sufficiently set to do the same to the other end. The following day this could be drilled out to provide 12 mm diameter holes.

Feed about 20" of 4 mm diameter terylene or nylon line through one hole of a toggle, and out through the end. Tie a figure-of-eight knot (Figure 4:11) and pull the line so that the knot ends up inside the toggle. Double the line, feed the doubled line through the hole nearest the end of the canoe, and take the toggle and spare end of line through the loop thus formed. Then feed the spare end of the line through the other hole in the toggle and out through the mouth. Starting from the end that is anchored inside the toggle, pull the line taut until the toggle is held up close against the deck of the canoe and there is no slack anywhere in the line. Tie a figure-of-eight knot in the end of the line that is coming out through the mouth of the toggle. The knot can then be worked along so that it is as near the mouth as possible. Cut off the spare end and pull the toggle so that the figure-of-eight knot ends up inside. You will now have the toggle on a short, neat line.

Toggles can be made of short lengths of ¾" heavy duty hose.

For deck lines use unstretched 6 mm diameter nylon or terylene line. Feed the line through the second holes so that it forms a continuous loop. Work one end so that it is just behind the stern cockpit, form a small loop with this end, and tie a figure-of-eight knot with the doubled line, leaving a small loop. Take the other end of the line up through this small loop and pull the line as taut as you can get it, so that it is stretched in a narrow skein in the middle of the boat. Then secure the skein with two or three half-hitches, trim the ends, and finish by burning them to prevent fraying. Using the smallest fairleads you can obtain (from a dinghy chandler) pull the line to the sides of the deck, so that it is well clear of the cockpit,

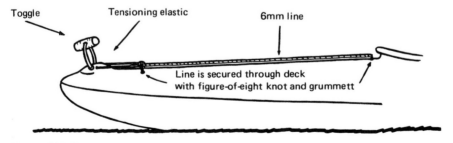

Toggle · Tensioning elastic · 6mm line

Line is secured through deck with figure-of-eight knot and grummett

Figure 4:12 *Single rope deck line.*

and keep it there by screwing the fairleads home. Brass or stainless steel nuts and bolts should be used. Make sure the fairleads are positioned so that knuckles will not catch on them.

Another method, probably better for white water use is to fit a single rope along the centre of the front deck of the boat and also along the back. It is held taut by elastic so it is less likely to be snagged, and for portages or rescues, lifejacket or paddle, can be tucked under it. (Figure 4:12).

There are differences of opinion as to whether the decks should carry equipment or be 'uncluttered' for expedition purposes. Certainly inland, with the danger of snagging on trees and so forth in moving water, nothing should be strapped to the decks. Whilst deck lines are insisted upon by some, they must, when fitted, be taut and unable to foul the cockpit area. The second system described above reduces the risk of the line entangling the paddler, should the canoe break up on an obstruction.

On the sea, the ability to swiftly hand out a paddle to a capsized canoeist who has let go of his in heavy seas, can be a significant factor in preventing a situation from worsening, and for this reason it is recommended that the leader and his competent helpers carry split paddles strapped to the stern decks of their boats. There is no particular advantage in having any other items, apart from flares, on deck, although personal preference will hold sway.

Fitting buoyancy

For sea canoeing and white water touring, buoyancy should fill all available space, but the cockpit must be unobstructed at all times.

A cheap means of providing extra buoyancy is to use such items as gallon polythene containers, with the lids firmly on, and by tieing them together, and stuffing them into each end, with a means of ensuring that they cannot work loose, a good degree of buoyancy can be obtained.

Two main methods of fitting the standard buoyancy exist. One is to pour into each end of the canoe, the chemicals which form polyurethane foam. The other is to purchase and fit either air bags or blocks of polystyrene or polyethylene foam.

In the first instance, the chemicals are purchased – sufficient to provide the recommended amount of buoyancy at each end. The canoe is stood on end, the chemicals mixed according to the instructions, and poured in. Ensure that the chemical arrives at the end of the boat. Expansion takes place, and care must be exercised to ensure that the kayak is not split open by this expansion. A draw-back of expanded polyurethane foam is that there is some absorption of water over a period of time – estimated as up to 16%.

The chemicals can be purchased from a number of canoe manufacturers and suppliers, as can expanded polystyrene or polyethylene blocks. Polystyrene needs to be fixed by making a bracket from fibreglass and bonding it in, whereas polyethylene can be simply 'glued' into place with fibreglass resin. The latter is more expensive, but it is more resilient, does not crumble, and is recommended. Where blocks are shaped and fitted to run centrally down the canoe, they assist with strengthening the boat by supporting the deck.

Two types of air bags are available. Tailored air bags, as their name implies, are shaped to fit the contours of the kayak, and provide a considerable amount of buoyancy. They can be supplied with polystyrene foam blocks inserted, so that some buoyancy remains if the bag becomes punctured. Straight-forward air bags as supplied for dinghies can also be used. Care must be taken to ensure always that bags are sound, and inflated. Always check thoroughly the inside of a fibreglass kayak to ensure that it is smooth, and that no splinters are around to cause punctures.

A recent innovation is a rigid plastic cockpit liner, or pod, which makes the cockpit into a sealed capsule. Insufficient water to affect balance can enter, and self rescue is simplified. The potential of these devices has yet to be fully explored.

Paddle park

In any situation where the canoeist is likely to have to carry out rescues, especially in difficult conditions, a paddle park is necessary. This can be a 5 or 7 mm diameter marine elastic stretched across the fore- or stern-deck, but ideally should be a means of retaining the paddle(s) when left floating alongside the canoe. Commercially produced systems are available. A short length of 3 mm line, or marine elastic, attached to the canoe, is adequate. This can have either a loop through which a paddle blade will just pass, or a plastic hook on the end, which clips on to the line after it has been taken round the shaft.

Repair kit

A minimum repair kit is a roll of good quality 2″ insulating tape and a knife. For open water canoeing, however, where it may be necessary to apply a patch to a wet boat, a quantity of mastic tape, available from hardware stores, is advised. This is very 'gooey', and a small portion of hand cleanser will be required for use after it has been applied. A product designed for application on wet surfaces is obtainable.

A means of drying the area to be mended is advised however, and a small blow-torch is favoured for this nowadays. In this instance, many prefer to carry a small quantity of glass-fibre mat, resin and hardener, particularly where the journey is for a longer duration than a single day tour.

First aid kit

Basic items would include: one triangular bandage, two medium wound dressings; a crepe bandage; six large plasters (or a strip); antiseptic cream; box of matches; pair of fine tweezers; pencil and paper; small pair of pliers; pair of scissors. This list would obviously need to be enlarged upon depending upon the size of the party, the duration of the journey and the particular hazards of the country involved.

TRAINING

A programme for learning canoeing skills is outlined elsewhere. If 'wild' or open water canoeing is the aim, be it sea or inland, then a gradual progression, learning to cope with increasingly difficult conditions, but in controlled situations, is vital.

When things do go wrong, however, remember first principles. It is the maintenance of the safety of those who are not yet in trouble, that must normally be given priority. There is no point in rushing to perform a heroic rescue on one person, only to discover, having effected it, that six others are now in jeopardy. This is easy to say, but not so easy to carry out in an emergency. Those who lead must cultivate a habit of thinking ahead, and delegating to other competent paddlers initial responsibility to rescue or tow when incidents occur, ensuring that someone is always giving consideration to the total safety of the group.

Capsize drill

Statistics show that an ability to swim, allied to the wearing of a personal flotation aid, and undertaking a basic course, virtually preclude any likelihood of drowning from a canoe in normal circumstances. Most 'canoeing' fatalities occur to non-swimmers, or poor swimmers who are invariably not wearing a bouyancy aid or lifejacket. Whatever type of

Figure 4:13 *Short tow.*   **Figure 4:14** *Rafted tow.*

canoeing is being pursued, the ability to cope with a capsize should be part of basic training. This does not mean that capsize drill must be carried out at the beginning of the first session, or even necessarily during that session, but must be practised at some stage. Where small cockpit, decked kayaks or canoes are involved, this should be earlier, rather than later, in a course.

Not everyone enjoys constantly falling out of boats, particularly in mid-winter, and the degree of emphasis put on capsize and rescue drills should be adapted to the type of canoeing that the individual wishes to pursue. It is a far more vital factor for the white water and surf paddler, or the sea tourist, than for others. Where a swimming pool is used for initial training, great emphasis must be put on immediately grabbing and maintaining a hold on the canoe when surfacing, and the routine practised out of doors at the first suitable opportunity.

Towing

The ability to attach a tow-line swiftly can play a significant part in preventing any 'incident' from developing into an 'epic'. In any situation, apart from the most sheltered of conditions, where beginners are involved, a leader needs to be able to efficiently pull a canoeist to safety, either away from danger out of the path of an oncoming vessel, or back to the edge if the group is drifting too far away from the bank or shore. The one student who cannot control his or her direction at this time, is a potential disaster. Once a group is journeying down river or on the sea, then the ability to tow one another is vital.

There is no single 'right' way of towing, but there are some basic principles that can be stated, and some ideas that can be incorporated. For simple situations, a small loop just aft of the cockpit allows a toggle to be threaded through, and a quick, efficient tow effected. (Figure 4:13).

It is possible also to 'tow' by the paddler in difficulties merely rafting on, facing the rescuer by leaning across his boat and holding on, keeping the bow of his own canoe in close to the rescuer, and assisting the steering by pulling with the knees. (Figure 4:14).

There is then the simple device of assisting a beginner who cannot control his or her own direction, by nudging the stern with your bow. This will apply where there is a beam or quartering wind, and the novice is constantly letting the boat turn up into the wind. (All kayaks have this tendency once they are being propelled forwards). The experienced paddler merely has to sit down-wind, at the beginner's stern, and prevent it from skating away. (Figure 4:15).

In this situation, unless conditions have deteriorated beyond the ability of the whole group, the individual who is having difficulty with steering needs help with technique. The most common cause of a sweep stroke failing to correct a boat that is turning off course because of the wind, is that the paddle blade is taken from the water too soon. It needs to drive in close to the stern, to correct the 'skating' movement that occurs with slalom-type hulls. The use of a detachable 'skeg' is advised for the person in a general purpose or slalom

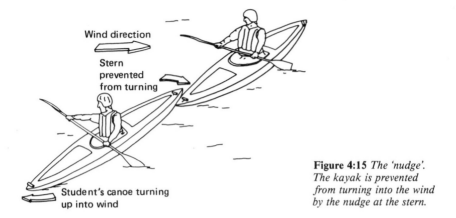

Wind direction

Stern
prevented
from turning

Student's canoe turning
up into wind

Figure 4:15 *The 'nudge'.*
The kayak is prevented
from turning into the wind
by the nudge at the stern.

boat who really cannot cope, and two types are illustrated. (Figure 4:16). These can be carried by the leader and fitted as necessary.

A full-length tow-line should permit another canoe to be pulled about 2'-3' astern of the rescuer. If this distance is too great, a considerable amount of 'veering' will occur to the boat being towed. Too short, and there will be constant collisions. For long craft, such as the eskimo kayak, the line can pass through the stern loop, which avoids it 'sweeping' the rear deck, and keeps the distance between towing point and casualty short, minimising the 'veering off' effect. Most prefer to tow from a point just behind the cockpit, or from the body. A 'cam cleat', available from dinghy chandlers, is most suitable as a towing point. A bridge (metal hoop through which the line passes) is necessary to avoid the rope jerking free. (Figure 4:17). 'Funnel cleats', 'jamming cleats' and similar, are best avoided as stones can become wedged in them.

The cleat does not need to be fixed exactly in the middle of the canoe, and is best not so positioned, as this makes for very tricky attachment and release – especially in difficult conditions with cold fingers! About a hand's width in from the gunnel on the control-hand side, is a useful position.

Some do not not like to have fixtures and fittings on the boat unless absolutely necessary and consequently prefer to tow with the line attached around the waist. This is an efficient system, and allows the body to act as an additional 'shock absorber'. When towing at sea, for instance, there will be times when the rescuer is 'surfing' down a wave, and the casualty is climbing up the back of another one. It is then that a 'shock-cord' incorporated into the tow-line comes into effect, and when using the body as the towing point can also have an advantage. It is obviously vital that there is a foolproof quick release system if the line is attached around the waist. A method of achieving this is shown, or a belt, to which the tow line is attached in the middle at the back, and which secures with a velcro strip, or other quick-release mechanism, on the stomach side, is favoured by some (Figure 4:18).

Whilst for sea canoeing the line may be worn around the waist or attached to the lifejacket, for rapid river touring many would prefer not to be tied on, in case of the line becoming 'snagged' in an emergency. Thought therefore needs to be given to a method of carrying the tow-line which allows for quick attachment and release, preferably with one hand. For small distances in moderate conditions, a 'short tow' is satisfactory, with the victim's bow 2'-3' from the rescuer's body. The paddler being towed can, in this situation, raft, holding on to the rescuer's stern deck if necessary.

Tyre bands: skeg can be fitted securely to different shaped boats

Fibre-glass skeg plate

Retaining cord

Figure 4:16 *Two designs of skeg.*

Shock-absorption has been mentioned, and it is worthwhile incorporating a short length of 5 or 7 mm marine shock-cord into the system. Keep the line intact, so that should the shock-cord break, the tow-line does not part (Figure 4:19).

The final piece of equipment for efficient towing, is the 'dog-clip'. There are a number on the market. Again, visit your local friendly canoe supplier or dinghy chandler. Climbing Karabiners are popular. Beware of 'fiddly' fittings, such as small brass shackles which need two fingernails to lift a tiny 'sprung' head. The shackle should be of stainless steel, and a reliable type for the job is shown in Figure 4:20. 4-6 mm diameter polypropylene line, which floats, is ideal for tow-lines. If terylene or nylon is used, then a small float needs to be attached near the shackle.

Rafting

Forming a group of canoeists into a raft can make an ideal platform to effect repairs or rescues, to gather together for instructional purposes, to have tea, or to have fun. Choose an anchor man, and build the raft up from both sides, all facing in the same direction. Each person holding onto both partners' cockpit coaming is probably the most effective way of keeping the raft together, with paddles captured under lifejackets. A three-man raft can rescue an unconscious patient from the water. Assuming the patient is on the left, the middle man grabs the patient's arms and pulls up, while the man next to the patient capsizes to his right. The middle man hands the patient's arms to the right man who pulls the patient across the deck, while the middle man pulls up the left man in a clockwise eskimo rescue.

Figure 4:17 *A cam cleat.*

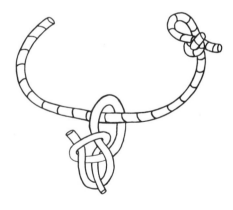

Figure 4:18 *A quick-release waist-line. Attach the main line to the waist line with a bowline.*

Figure 4:19 *Tow-line shock-cord system.*

Figure 4:20 *A suitable shackle.*

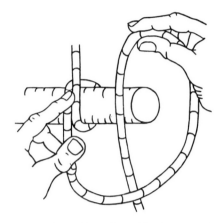

Figure 4:21 *Clove-hitch. Tension can be easily maintained while the locking loop is threaded.*

Canoeists will generally need to raft should a helicopter rescue be necessary, because of the considerable down-draught from the rotor blades. Do not touch the cable or winchman until he has earthed – static electricity can give quite a shock. Should the victim be in an exposure bag on a raft, it is vital that the bag is tightly secured. If it flies free as the casualty is winched away, it could cause the helicopter to crash.

Capsizes can occur when breaking from a raft in rough conditions, so practice needs to have taken place, and care exercised. Each end paddler can draw stroke out and paddle directly away, or every other paddler can place his paddle across the backs of his neighbours and shove hard backwards. It is worth turning the raft to face into the oncoming waves, by the outside paddlers using alternate forward and back sweeps, before breaking.

SAFETY ON THE ROAD

Boats must be secured with a final rope at bow and stern and onto the bumper of the car, for insurance purposes, and out of responsibility for the well-being of other road users, rather than reliance being placed on elastic straps alone. Where elastics are used on trailers, a rope through the toggle lines should be standard practice. A useful knot for securing canoes is the clove-hitch (Figure 4:21). The line can be held tight while the locking loop is applied. There are certain requirements concerning loads which overhang vehicles:

Permitted projections:
Up to .305m (1') on either side – max load width 2.9m (9'6")
Up to 1.07m (3'6") forward or rearward.

Distinctive flags at ends are required for:
Forward or rearward projection more than 1.07m (3' 6") but less than 3.05m (10'). (This is a dispensation for 'racing boats propelled solely by oars'. The normal load limit is 6', and between 6' and 10' red and white striped triangular boards are required, plus a light at night). For projections over 10' to front or rear prior notice to the police is required.

The AA publish *The Law and Vehicle Loads, The Law and Trailers* and *The Law and Dual Purpose Vehicles.* It is an offence to tow a trailer in the outside lane of a 3-lane motorway.

5 Kayaking – the Basic Skills

Jim Hargreaves

Jim Hargreaves is a BCU coach and an accomplished personal performer. He holds all three Advanced Proficiency Awards for Inland Kayak, Sea Kayak and Canadian Canoeing and is an experienced climber. He was a member of the first British expedition to descend the Colorado by canoe in 1971, where he met up with the late Dr Mike Jones. In 1977 he participated in the expedition that successfully rounded Cape Horn.

Initially, Jim pursued a career in the army and was at one stage British Inter-Services kayak and C1 slalom champion. In 1972, he took part in an army ascent of Mount Kenya and has also climbed and canoed extensively in the Alps and the Canadian Rockies.

In 1976 he left the army to become head of canoeing at Plas y Brenin – the Sports Council's Centre for Mountain Activities – a position he held for three years. He then became self employed, setting up a garage and canoeing retail business at Capel Curig, North Wales. Jim has recently been co-author of A Guide to North Wales White Water.

INTRODUCTION

The kayakist gains satisfaction from mastery of the skills which enable him to take his craft into virtually any situation that nature provides on river, lake or sea. Apart from the limits of technical feasibility, the only bounds to the trained paddler are those of his individual physical capacity and mental attitude.

This chapter concerns itself with identifying the basic strokes and skills, the development and application of which, with practise and experience, lead to the canoeist's special kind of freedom. These tools of the trade were first catalogued in the early 60's, following the development of kayak technique brought about by the influence of Milo Duffek. Since that time, little has been done to keep the written record up to date with the evolution that has occurred, influenced by the development of boat design, and increased knowledge and awareness of the acquisition and application of motor skills.

In consequence, there is no universally accepted terminology, learning sequence or method of teaching a particular art. Some would argue that it would be undesirable to have a too-rigid system, and they are probably right. Agreement on definitions, and general methods of approach, are however, to the advantage of everyone, if only to avoid the necessity of explaining what is meant every time a technical term is used. An attempt has therefore been made to bring some order to this area, without seeking to provide a rigid formula.

A good coach, with the aid of a stop watch, and perhaps a video camera, can help a top canoeist to improve a given routine – eg a particular sequence of gates in a slalom, the 'start' of a sprint race, or portaging on a marathon. He can do comparatively little, however, to enhance the paddler's established skills. It is of vital importance therefore that juniors are taught correctly. Sound basic technique must be established, and worked on, so that bad habits, or inefficient movements, do not become ingrained. It is no excuse to say that not everyone wants to be a world champion, or even to compete at all. Regardless of the type of canoeing involved, anyone pursuing the sport as a lifetime's hobby needs to be able to paddle efficiently in order to get where he or she wants to go with the minimum of effort, and to be able to handle their canoe in the chosen environment to their greatest personal potential. This can only be achieved through the laying of a solid foundation. The basic instructor therefore has a tremendous responsibility to those whom he introduces to the sport.

The ability to break a skill down into its constituent parts, perfect each part and then reassemble the whole, is a proven system of teaching sport technique – the Whole-Part-Whole method. There is, though, the premise that the whole is greater than the sum of the parts, and factors such as speed, rhythm, timing and style are involved. The coach needs to be able, through close observation, to identify the parts, recognising and isolating the components. Through imagination and resourcefulness he must develop exercises which pressurise a minor skill to its optimum level, before re-introducing it into the whole, and then achieve a fluidity and kinaesthetic awareness in the successful application of the complete skill to achieve its purpose.

An analytical and critical mind is necessary. It is an in depth study of teaching method, skills, progressions, mechanics, and the anatomy and physiology appropriate to the activity, that ensures that a coach becomes thoroughly familiar with techniques and their coaching requirements. The gladiator in the sport does not necessarily become the best coach.

A basic understanding of anatomy and physiology can only enhance ability to analyse technique. To know the muscle groups, and the joints involved in the execution of a skill, their limitations, ranges of movement, and flexibility, *must* help to improve the teaching of the skill being taught. A fundamental grasp of body mechanics will also assist when analysing the efficiency of a movement or position.

More than canoeing skill is required, therefore, to make a good coach. An open mind, flexibility of approach, the improvisation of methods of teaching when others fail, all rolled into one, help to make the complete instructor. Like the very skills he is trying to identify and perfect, so he must analyse the requirements of his own task, and develop the ability to meet them.

Both basic strokes and advanced techniques have been tackled so that each skill is approached as follows:

1   Description of Skill

2   Progressions

3   Coaching Points

4   General Observations

A careful analysis has been made, and where possible constituent parts identified. Some simple anatomic terms have been used and a basic understanding of body mechanics is assumed. Methods of introducing skills, where suggested, may be only one of many, and certainly no dogma is intended. The sequence in which the skills are listed is one which has proven satisfactory over a number of years, and seems to have general agreement, but is not necessarily the only good progression. Remember that the priorities for teaching and learning are:

1   Safety

2   Enjoyment

3   Learning

Without safety, we will have no canoeist; without enjoyment we will not have a recreational sport; and with both of these we will stimulate the learning of skills.

A logical sequence of instruction of basic skills, apart from getting in and out and capsize drill is:

1   Forward paddling
2   Backward paddling
3   Sweep stroke
4   Draw stroke
5   Recovery stroke
6   Stern rudder
7   Low brace turn
8   Sculling strokes
9   Bow rudder
10 Tilting the canoe to assist turning.

Terminology

Drive face
This is the face of the blade(s) that would pull against the water when the paddle is used for *normal forward propulsion*. The opposite side of each blade is called the back. For curved or spooned paddles, the concave side is the drive face, and the convex, the back. Where flat-bladed paddles are used, it is a good idea to paint one face of one blade a different colour, to help identify the drive face.

Controlling wrist
It is important at an early stage in a canoeist's career to ensure that a 'controlling wrist' is established. The controlling wrist does the rotating of the paddle shaft, with that hand holding firmly. The opposite hand allows the shaft – also called 'loom' – to rotate backwards and forwards as the paddle is feathered. Right handed people will normally favour a right controlling wrist, and vice versa, but this is by no means mandatory.

In all the descriptions of skills which follow, it is assumed that blade angles will be set by the controlling wrist, and that both hands will retain their normal position and hold on the paddle.

Low, High and Hanging Strokes
A low stroke is performed using the back – non-drive face – of the blade, with the wrists uppermost. A high stroke, or high version of a stroke, involves the drive face of the blade, with the wrists under the shaft. The hanging strokes, or versions of strokes, are when the paddle is used with the arms in an extended position.

Brace
The term brace can be applied to any stroke which involves the movement of water against the blade, or the action of opposing forces, rather than the working of the paddle itself, to effect movement, or give support. It is most commonly used to describe the action of supporting oneself on a surf wave or stopper, by leaning on, or hanging from, a relatively stationary blade which is placed flat on the upsurge of water.

PRE PADDLING PREPARATION

Length of Paddle

The best general guide to paddle length is still to stand upright with the tip of one blade placed on the ground by your feet, and reach one hand up and over the other end. The knuckles should curl comfortably over the tip. Very tall people will need shorter paddles, and very short people, longer. Paddles generally vary between 210 and 235 cms in length.

Holding the Paddle

With the shaft held at shoulder height ahead of you, the hands equi-distance from each end, the elbows should form right angles. The blade on the controlling wrist side should be perpendicular, when the paddle is held thus, the knuckles in line with the top edge of the blade. Curved blades are feathered for *either* right hand or left hand control.

Dry Land Drill

It is worth developing some basic feel for the use of the paddle by practising the feathering action for the forward paddling stroke, backward paddling, and forward sweeping, for a few minutes at this stage.

Figure 5:1 *Holding the paddle.*

Capsize drill

Every canoeist should be acquainted with what to do in the event of capsize, before venturing afloat for the first time. This does not mean, however, that the drill should necessarily be practised immediately. See chapter 12.

Where large cockpit kayaks are involved, the occupant will normally fall out as the boat inverts, and find him or herself bobbing in the water alongside. *It is essential immediately to grab hold of the boat,* but not to roll it upright again. A minimum amount of water will usually have entered, and so move the canoe along until one end can be grasped, and then swim the boat to the edge, or await rescue. It is easier to swim the canoe using a back stroke, particularly when a lifejacket is worn.

For small cockpit kayaks, it will be necessary to adopt a forward leaning position under water, reach forward to release the spray deck by use of the handle, and then exit with a forward roll.

If the hands are placed on the gunnels just behind the hips, evacuation can be aided by pushing with the arms. The legs should be relaxed and allowed to trail out naturally.

Spray decks on small cockpit boats should be loose fitting, or perhaps left off, until after an initial capsize drill has been practised.

Complete confidence under water needs to be achieved. Deliberately staying in the boat, banging the bottom three times with the hands, releasing the spray deck, and then banging again three times before coming out in a relaxed manner, is a good exercise, but only to be practised under supervision or when other canoeists are close by.

Banging on the bottom alerts others in the group to the fact that a capsize has occurred, and could mean later that an eskimo rescue may be administered, avoiding the necessity of a swim.

A great deal of anxiety is often aroused when a person capsizes a canoe. This is totally unnecessary, and there is no accident on record where a person has drowned through being unable to get out, in normal circumstances. The possibility of capsize is always present, however, and whilst some canoeists enjoy a lifetime of paddling without ever going over, it is an eventuality that must be allowed and trained for.

Carrying and emptying a kayak

Bend the knees and grasp the near coaming with both hands. Straighten your legs and balance the kayak on a thigh. Move the same hand as thigh across under the far coaming – palm uppermost. Then lift the canoe until it rests on your shoulder. Don't forget the paddle!

When a boat is lying upside down on the surface of the water it will be necessary to tilt it slightly to break the vacuum, lift it clear of the water, and then raise one end, ensuring the boat is kept level in an upside down position. Once the water has drained from that end, the boat is see-sawed, again ensuring it stays completely level, until the water has drained from the other end. This may need to be repeated. Where two people are involved, the process is very easy. One person can empty a boat by lifting it upside down across a thigh.

If the boat is waterlogged, it should be left in the water, tilted onto its side, and lifted very gradually and evenly at each end, allowing the water to drain from the cockpit. There is never any point in lifting water, and so only sufficient lift to ensure that the cockpit continues to drain, is necessary.

Slalom and general purpose glassfibre boats can be emptied by one person, by turning them the right way up on the water, pushing one end down so that the water rushes to that end, and then with a swift, smooth movement bring that end up to shoulder height, inverting the boat at the same time, so that the water pours out of the cockpit. This is repeated until the boat is empty.

Never drag a waterlogged boat ashore, as this puts considerable strain on the craft. There is absolutely no point in doing so, for a canoe is always easier to empty when it is afloat. Pulling one end of a capsized kayak ashore, or onto a boat, and then levering down will almost certainly break its back. Canoe to canoe rescues are explained in chapter 10.

Getting in

Racing and other boats with large cockpits should be entered as follows. Ensure the boat is floating, and pointing into any current. Hold the apex of the coaming firmly with the seaward hand, and maintain a grip of the bank with the other hand. Alternatively, where circumstances allow, the paddle may be held across the front of the cockpit, and this is grasped, together with the apex of the coaming, with the greater part of its length resting on the bank. The outside foot is placed near the keel-line, but on the far side of the canoe. The other leg is next brought in, sitting straight down onto it. The first leg is then adjusted. If the

Figure 5:2a (top left) *Hold bank and front of cockpit.*

Figure 5:2b (top right) *Put far foot in.*

Figure 5:2c (left) *Bring other leg in and sit straight down, then adjust first leg.*

paddle is not being used for support always ensure it is close enough at hand to be reached easily when seated.

For small-cockpit boats, the back of the coaming, in the centre, may be grasped, or the paddle held there firmly, by the seaward hand. Adopt a crouching position and place the outside foot in the canoe, next to the far side of the keel line. Grasp the bank with the other hand, or reach behind and take hold of the paddle loom above the gunnel. Do not push on the paddle shaft outside the gunnel line, as this may bend or break it. Total support is given by this method as the other leg is brought across, and both legs straightened in order to slide forward into the cockpit. Keep a firm hold with both hands until seated.

In all cases, if curved paddles are being used, the drive face of the blade on the shore should face downwards to avoid damage.

Seal launching is sometimes necessary, in order to slide down muddy banks, or where waves are breaking onshore on lake or sea. See chapter 16 – Surfing.

Spray decks are usually fitted most easily by stretching the elastic over the rear of the cockpit coaming first and leaning back against it. Slip the front over next, and then the sides. Always ensure that the release handle is free, and sound.

FORWARD PADDLING

Small-cockpit, slalom and general purpose kayaks, need to be *worn* by the lower part of the body, with a firm seat and footrest. The feet should be able to relax, but be pressed hard against the footrest when necessary, with the knees gripping the deck out to each side. Racing and large-cockpit kayaks need to have a comfortable seat, and firm footrest, with the hips just above the cockpit coaming. The knees are held lightly together, not too high or low. Sit fairly upright, with chin up, and relaxed shoulders.

The sequence which follows, commences before the left hand blade enters the water: With the paddler in a confident but relaxed position the blade is held above the water. The left arm and shoulder are fully extended, with the body straight, but inclined slightly forward and turned outward a few degrees from the waist. The right hand is held at shoulder height with the elbow low. In this attitude a paddler is positioned for maximum exploitation of his strength.

1   *The 'catch'.* The blade should be placed cleanly into the water at boat speed, as near the boat as possible, by dropping the leading arm.

2   *The 'pull'.* As the left forearm is smoothly drawn back parallel to the water, the body is turned from the waist, the boat being drawn to the paddle until the left elbow reaches the hip. At this point the stroke is at minimum efficiency, and should finish. Make sure the paddle blade remains at 90° to the keel line, and equi-distant from it, throughout the stroke. The right arm and shoulder have balanced this movement by moving forward in a line parallel to the centre line of the kayak, and as the left elbow reaches the hip, the right arm and shoulder are extended in a similar manner to that of the left at the beginning of the stroke.

3   *The 'lift'.* The cycle is continued by the left hand clipping the blade from the water, at right angles to the boat, taking the hand close to the shoulder and just above it, leaving the elbow low. This lifting action automatically dips the right blade down into the water. From there on the cycle is continuous. The co-ordination of the movements being smoothly produced, will result in a continuous flowing action with the arms, shoulders and body making their maximum contributions.

Figure 5:3a *Starting position. Leading arm straight and level with the shoulder. Hand open. Trunk fully rotated. Other hand at shoulder height.*

Figure 5:3b *Drop leading arm to water and move rear arm forward. The forward movement of the top arm brings the paddle up to the boat speed and puts it vertically into the water.*

Figure 5:3c *Pull initially with rotation and then with arm until elbow touches your side. Move top arm forward at shoulder level, and with the top hand open, or loosely gripping the shaft.*

Figure 5:3d *Clip paddle from water and return to position (a) fully extending forward arm with minimal cross over. The top arm straightening helps ensure that the paddle leaves the water in the correct position.*

Additional Comment

The top arm does not *push*, but obviously does have to resist the pressure on it, and extend smoothly forward with a straight wrist, the hand relaxed, and the fingers opening. The correct position of the top arm is a most important factor in the early teaching of technique.

The main concentration at first should be on ensuring that the lower, pulling arm, is fully extended before the blade is dropped into the water. Trunk rotation should develop naturally from this.

It is impossible to over-emphasize the importance and effectiveness of the body rotation movement. Lack of attention to this means that the powerful muscles in the back are not fully utilised, with a consequent reduction in performance. Concentration is necessary, therefore, to ensure that this body rotation movement is timed to take its most advantageous phase in the cycle – at the moment the blade is fully immersed in the water, and not before. Leaning forward in an attempt to lengthen the stroke prevents the use of body rotation.

The movement is supported by corresponding leg work. The leg on the same side as the pulling arm is braced by the foot being pressed against the footrest in rhythm with the stroke. Avoid all semi-circular movement which is usually caused when the arms are held too low, the stroke continues beyond the hip, or the top hand swings beyond the centre line of the kayak. Once the pulling elbow has reached the hip, any further pulling on the blade will merely lift water.

Remember that, within the limits of technical and mechanical efficiency, the stroke will be adapted to the physical quality possessed by the paddler. The adoption of the various paddling styles that may be observed at all levels of competition have resulted from the mechanically efficient stroke being adjusted to the individual physiological makeup of the paddler. They are not necessarily in themselves wrong. It is vital, however, that the correct ingredients and principles are establised at the outset, otherwise an individual will be developing the habits which will form his personal style, to compensate for poor technique, rather than to adapt that which is good to his advantage. Without the inculcation of sound basic technique at the early learning stage, a paddler is likely never to achieve his true potential.

To summarise

1　The paddle must be fully in the water when the back muscles are in their strongest position for pulling.

2　The paddle should present its maximum area to the direction of pull at this point.

3　The paddle should be pulled straight back as close to the side of the boat as possible.

4　The leg on the same side as the pulling arm should push against the footrest to impart the pull onto the boat.

5　The bottom hand pulls, the top hand guides.

6　The head must be quiet.

7　The paddler must sit comfortably and fairly upright.

Common Faults

1　The top hand is not straightened.

2　The top hand grips too tightly.

3　The top hand drops below shoulder level towards the end of the stroke.

4　The hand pushes forward above the line of the shoulder.

5　The top hand wrist is bent.

6　The trunk is 'unwound' before the paddle is fully immersed.

7　The paddle is angled to the direction of pull.

8　The paddle is pulled wide of the boat.

9　The top hand 'crosses over' at the end of the stroke.

10　The legs are contracted towards the body and the reaction goes through the seat only.

11 Possibly due to 10, the canoe wobbles.

12 Knees too high or too low.

13 The head is held on one side, or forward.

14 The head is constantly moved.

15 The canoe is not evenly balanced.

16 The paddle is pulled through too far.

Points for observation

Study the technique described. These notes are intended to help observers to identify the important ingredients of the skill, and suggest ways in which improvement can be achieved.

1 Is the blade entering cleanly, as far forward as is comfortably possible, with the body upright (or a slight forward lean), the paddle held correctly, the lower arm fully extended, and the trunk fully rotated? If not:
(a) *Is the paddle the right length?* The paddle is the correct length when the blade can be just fully immersed as close to the boat as comfortably possible.
(b) *Is the paddler unwinding before the 'catch'?* Get the canoeist to concentrate on entering the blade into the water by his feet. A piece of tape stuck on the deck as an aiming mark may be useful in some cases. Make sure this does not lead to the body pivoting forwards and backwards. The paddler should concentrate on the blade entering the water cleanly.

2 As the boat is pulled past the paddle as closely as possible, does the blade keep 90° and remain the same distance from the keel line throughout? If not:
(a) *Check body/arm action to ascertain reason.* Is the grip of the upper hand too tight, causing the top arm to be forced unnecessarily across? Persuade the paddler to concentrate on paddling with a relaxed grip, opening the fingers of the top hand and *keeping the wrist straight.*
(b) *Is the paddle the right length?*
(c) *Is the top, guiding hand, moving forward at shoulder height?*

3 Is the blade entering the water, without splashing, at boat speed? *Concentrate on the 'catch'.*

4 Is the blade exiting cleanly when the drawing elbow is level with the waist? The blade should be lifted out *at right angles* by the hand, leaving the elbow as low as possible.

5 Is the canoe running level? – it should not rock unduly from side to side. If it does, it is most probably caused by the trunk unwinding before the paddle has been dropped into the water

6 Is the same foot as pulling arm, moving against the footrest? There should be a cycling action with the legs – the knees should move up and down $1'' - 2''$.

7 Is the head quiet? When paddling, the head should remain relatively still.

8 Is the canoe upright? Ensure the paddler is not sitting to one side.

General remarks

Do not attempt to improve or emphasise more than one factor at a time, and don't pursue any concentration on technique to the point of boredom. Involve work on a particular aspect of paddling style at various stages throughout a trip or session. It may be helpful to make a paddler concentrate on a particular movement with his eyes closed.

Some dry land work – a few minutes – at the start of each session, should reinforce these points. Sit the learners on a bench or similar in a natural paddling position. A plank on a float over the water is a useful paddling practice aid.

When slalom or general purpose boats are being used, it can be helpful for the instructor to raft across the stern of the student's boat, who can then 'drag' him along. This allows the instructor to monitor technique, and give quiet advice. The rafted kayak removes the need for the paddler to steer, and so all the concentration can be on the forward paddling skill. It must be stressed, however, that the candidate should relax, and not fight to pull the instructor fast through the water. Or, by rafting across the bow, the instructor (whose boat must remain upright to avoid drag) can control direction.

BACKWARD PADDLING

Although it is unlikely that it will ever be necessary to travel long distances backwards, the development of a strong, accurate reverse paddling ability is important. The main problem experienced whilst paddling backwards is not the actual execution of the stroke, but the lack of vision whilst performing it. A big effort must therefore be made to twist the trunk so that it is possible to watch the directional stability of the boat.

To commence, the paddler should turn at the waist, bringing the shoulders parallel to the gunnel, and look over the same shoulder as the side on which the stroke is being performed. It should be possible to see the stern clearly. The back of the paddle blade is inserted into the water as close to the stern as possible, with the forward hand across the body, so that the loom is almost parallel to the keel-line and not following the curve of the gunnel. The most effective part is when the paddle is level with the hips, and the stroke can be very strongly applied at this point, as the paddler's body weight is directly above it. The blade continues alongside the boat until it is no longer effective – this is at a point approximately level with the knees. The paddle then is withdrawn, and a stroke performed on the opposite side.

Most people find they are more supple in one direction than in the other, and it makes sense to look over the shoulder on the side which is found to be the more comfortable. It is not essential to look over the shoulder on every stroke – every other is adequate – but it should be borne in mind that slight alterations in direction, spotted early, are simple to correct, and have a less damaging effect on momentum.

Progressions
Start very slowly, and practise paddling between slalom gates, buoys, or similar targets to develop accuracy. It is possible for the instructor to raft up in a T position, holding on to the

Figure 5:4 *Backward paddling. Pivot at waist. Look over shoulder (!)*

bow of the pupil's boat, when close quarter coaching can be given. Set 'stopping' goals, and work the skill to the point where the canoeist can stop from full ahead, and be reversing within three paddle strokes.

Coaching points
The intrinsic problem in paddling backwards, particularly in the old slalom-type kayaks in which most people are taught, is that these boats are basically designed to go forwards. The bow normally has a deeper section than the stern, as they are designed to hold the slack water in eddies, whilst the flatter stern section skims around in a fast turn. This means that when paddled backwards, there is little shape to the stern to aid directional stability, making life difficult.

It is simply a question of practise, and perhaps an effort on behalf of the coach to find a boat with more advantageous lines to help those experiencing a lot of difficulty.

General Comment
The skill of paddling backwards takes a long time to develop in the boats that are generally used for instructional purposes. Pupils must be encouraged to practise until they have a degree of skill and accuracy. Travelling down river backwards, and shooting small falls backwards, help to develop the paddler's ability.

THE SWEEP STROKE

The sweep stroke is a very simple, yet highly efficient turning stroke, which can be used to great effect by beginners and experts alike. It gives valuable assistance to those who may be frustrated by their craft's apparent desire to go in ever decreasing circles. The expert can use it with equal effectiveness to alter direction at a moment's notice.

Forward Sweep Stroke

The paddler leans as far forward as is comfortable, and inserts the blade close to the bow. With the paddle loom as near horizontal as the deck of the craft will allow, and the paddling arm extended, but not stiff, the upright blade is swept around until it reaches the stern, thus completing a semi circular arc.

Although this is good practice, and lengthens the stroke so that the novice can feel it for a longer period, in reality, for white water canoeing, it is more efficient to do two or three rapid strokes close to the bow. This can be borne out by observing an expert white water paddler preparing his boat for a break out. Several fast sweeps close to the bow will be used to push the boat towards the eddy.

The longer form of sweep can be used to good effect where a more leisurely turn is required on flat water, on the sea, or wherever the boat is being turned by the wind. It is vital then to ensure that the blade is driven well into the stern, by pushing the opposite arm across in front of the body.

Reverse Sweep Stroke

As in the case of the forward stroke the reverse sweep should be started as close to the end of the boat as possible. This is achieved by rotating the trunk through 90° so that the shoulder line is parallel with the gunnel. The back of the blade is inserted very near the stern, and swept with a near horizontal loom around past the hips, to the bow. In reality, the blade will probably be withdrawn when it is at right angles to the body, as before.

The reverse sweep is a very powerful stroke, which utilises stronger muscle groups and

100

Figure 5:5 Forward sweep stroke sequence. *The progression onto a slightly tilted blade is shown.*

positions, as well as having the weight of the canoeist directly above it, to add power. In the forward sweep, the paddler extends his levers more.

When applied to a moving craft, the opposing sweep has an arresting affect upon momentum. Thus it is useful in sudden changes of direction, where braking is also needed.

Progressions
A useful exercise is to have the beginner place the paddle blade near the bow as described, and then move the bow to and fro by appropriate short movements of the paddle. This should be repeated for all four stations.

The paddle can be held as an extended lever, with one hand on a blade tip, and the other on the neck about a foot from the blade. This gives a very long lever which, whilst requiring more strength to sweep, gives greater stability, and boosts confidence.

Once competent sweeps are being achieved as desribed, the stroke should be practised with the blade slightly tilted, so that the top edge is leading. This allows body weight to be put on the blade, and the reach extended.

Students should practise turning the canoe in its own length with alternate forward and reverse sweeps.

Coaching Points
Forward Sweep. The paddler should be encouraged to tilt the boat *slightly* towards the side on which he is executing the stroke. This has two effects:

1   Lowers the centre of gravity.

2   Enables the paddler to perform a wider sweep. This lengthens the lever of the stroke, giving it more power, and greater stability. If the boat is leaned too far, however, it

spoils the hydrodynamics of the hull, and causes drag. Throughout the stroke the forward arm should be slightly bent so that all the muscles in the arm can be brought into play. Although it is possible to reach further forward with a straight arm, this is more than countered by the fact that the arm is very weak in this position, as the bicep and associated muscles are fully extended and thus redundant.

Reverse Sweep The body should be rotated strongly to facilitate the paddle being inserted close to the stern. This can be awkward for the less supple, but should be encouraged, as the efficiency of the stroke is considerably impaired if the blade enters the water close to the hips – as is commonly observed. Because the back of the blade is used, and the canoeist is above it with a higher centre of gravity, the reverse sweep is not so stable as the forward stroke. If the canoeist leans over too far, and loses stability, it is easy to regain balance by swiftly turning the paddle over onto the drive face and performing a recovery stroke.

Common Faults

1   Arms straight.

2   Leaning the boat too much, causing the ends to drag.

3   Blade angle too acute in relation to the surface, causing the paddle to skim across the water with little turning effect.

4   Blade angle insufficient, causing too much resistance to allow the stroke to be performed efficiently, and detract from the stability of the stroke by reducing the blade area below the paddlers' weight.

5   Loom not horizontal enough. The more vertical the loom, the more unstable the stroke becomes, as leverage is reduced and centre of gravity raised.

General Comment
Although the sweep stroke is fundamentally a very simple skill it is also a very important one as it is regularly used in most aspects of canoeing where a positive turn is required. Fast, powerful turns can be achieved by combining forward sweeps with reverse sweeps on the opposite side.

THE DRAW STROKE

This is one of the most useful of all the basic skills. It is important that it is coached carefully, as the body, paddle and arm positions, form the foundation for the more advanced high combination strokes taught later. The skill is useful to the beginner for moving away from, and towards, the bank, or rafting up with other canoes. For the expert it is a vital stroke which should be mastered thoroughly, so that it may be used in any conditions.

From the normal paddling position, the canoeist turns his head through 90°, brings his shoulders round to about 45° and reaches out with the drive face of the blade towards the gunnel. The paddle is inserted as perpendicular as possible. The action of drawing the near vertical blade through the water towards the boat, pulls the canoe towards the paddle, resulting in a sideways movement.

The optimum position for the paddle is completely upright with the blade fully immersed, for in this position the working blade area being presented to the water is at its maximum. Both arms should work hard in levering the paddle. The top arm pushes away from the boat, with the back of the arm crossing the forehead, while the lower arm draws the blade towards the gunnel. The sooner the blade is rendered vertical the more effective the stroke will be.

Figure 5:6a *Just after the commencement of the pull.*

Figure 5:6b *The blade has been feathered through 90° and is being returned to the starting position.*

This is controlled by the top arm. Unless the upper arm reaches well across to the other side of the boat, so that it is almost directly above the lower arm, the working blade area will be ineffectively small.

When the stroke is complete, the paddle will be alongside the gunnel. Before it touches, the blade should be deftly twisted through 90°, with the drive face towards the stern, and feathered out at right angles to the boat, ready to repeat the draw.

Progressions
Initially, the blade can simply be lifted out of the water, or withdrawn by slicing it towards the stern, at right angles to the direction to the stroke. Ultimately the aim is to recover the paddle, or start the stroke again, by slicing it out into position through the water. Practising slicing the blade directly out and directly in without resistance, helps the student to achieve a full 90° feather.

The skill of working the paddle blade under water out of sight, is a very important one. An awareness of the blade angle by 'feel', rather than having to look at it to ensure that the angle is correct, is a necessary art to master. The sooner the student treats the paddle blade as an extention to his arms, the better. Just as most of us need not actually observe our hands to know what they are doing, so also should the canoeist be able to manipulate his paddle blade under the water, around the boat, through every conceivable position and movement, without needing to look at it. Eventually the aim should be to judge and adjust the blade and loom angle, and their positions in relation to the body and the canoe without thinking, just as a tennis or squash player adjusts his racket angle and position automatically to attack a ball.

Coaching Points

The stroke should ideally be performed at right angles to the Centre of Lateral Resistance (CLR) – that is, the point along the gunnel line where, if you attached a rope and pulled the canoe sideways, it would move symmetrically towards the direction of pull. This normally, but not always, is alongside the hips of the paddler. Observe closely the effect that the stroke is having upon the craft. If the bow or stern begins to gain, the paddle is not in line with the CLR, and will need to be moved to counteract this.

As emphasised earlier, the arm positions are most important during the execution of this skill. The upper arm, because of the range of movement of the shoulder joint (which incidentally sacrifices stability for mobility, which is why it sometimes dislocates) must remain fairly high in front of the face when pushing the paddle away from the boat. The lower the upper arm drops, the less efficient the range of movement becomes. It is the upper arm which causes the paddle loom to be vertical, and thus effective. This vertical position can be enhanced by a positive effort to curve the spine laterally, when reaching out to perform the stroke. This is an unnatural movement, but when employed, greatly improves the stroke. The task of the lower hand, as it is the closest, is to set and maintain the angle of the blade, as well as to draw it towards the boat in opposition to the action of the top hand.

Common Faults

1   Loom not vertical during middle part of stroke.

2   Blade not fully immersed.

3   Blade not moving towards CLR, resulting in uneven movement of canoe.

4   Top arm inactive, resulting in poor paddle presentation.

5   Top arm across body or neck, instead of high above face/forehead.

6   Failing to reach well out from boat with effort to arch spine laterally.

7   Poor recovery after stroke.

8   Top hand changed to under-grasp instead of normal paddling grip.

9   Leaning the boat too much, causing drag.

General Comment

The style that a canoeist adopts to perform the draw stroke, once established, will be his style also for the bow rudder and other high strokes. Try and ensure that the pupil sees success – this applies to all strokes – by making him practise with the current, or wind, using the conditions to help, rather than hinder, him.

RECOVERY STROKE

The recovery stroke is used to regain stability after loss of balance. It is useful to beginners, as it may help to prevent too many uncomfortable capsizes. Apart from the obvious advantage of being able to counteract a loss of balance, the act of deliberately tipping the boat into an unstable position, whilst learning this technique, boosts the beginner's confidence, and helps him to become familiar with the fact that the boat is not going to turn upside down the minute it leans a fraction off the vertical. It is vital that the paddler finds out where the point of no return actually is, as soon as possible. Practising this stroke will encourage him to experiment with his own sense of balance, or lack of it, and the stability of his craft.

Figure 5:7a *Low recovery stroke, using the back of the blade.*

Figure 5:7b *High recovery stroke, using the drive face of the blade.*

Upon losing balance the paddler reaches out to the side towards which he is capsizing with his paddle held as low as possible, and the flat of the blade presented to the surface, at right angles to the boat. The blade is pressed firmly on to the surface, and this provides a platform of resistance from which support is gained whilst the canoe is levered upright with legs and hips. The further out the paddler places the blade, the more support is obtained, as the lever of the stroke is lengthened. However, the leg/hip action must be correspondingly more efficient, and the body kept low to reduce the centre of gravity.

The beginner, of course, assumes that it is the act of pressing the blade on the water which rights the canoe. In fact, the slap arrests the capsizing movement, and a combination of continued pressure on the blade, and a co-ordinated hip flick actually initiates rotation in the opposite direction. It is whilst executing this skill, even in the early stages, that the pupil, quite unknowingly, is educating his legs and hips in the same action that will later complete an eskimo roll. Emphasis should be placed therefore, once confidence has been gained, on developing this 'hip flick' action. By leaning back slightly as the stroke is performed, the centre of gravity (C of G) is lowered to a minimum making success more likely. See chapter 11 (Rolling) for clarification of 'hip flick'.

After the paddle has been pressed on to the surface during the initial loss of balance, it will begin to sink with the weight of the paddler upon it. This is why it is most important that the loom is kept very low, presenting the flattest blade surface possible to the water. Equally important to maintaining a flat blade, and thus the widest possible radius to the stroke, is ensuring that the loom of the paddle is at right angles to the fore/aft line, or longitudinal axis, to obtain maximum leverage. The body should also be kept low.

Once the blade begins to sink it loses its efficiency, as the radius of the stroke is reduced. This can be counteracted by turning the blade through 90° and slicing it quickly back up to the surface for more support. This right angle twist at the end of the stroke also facilitates the withdrawal of the blade after recovery has been successfully executed.

Progressions

1 Raft up two canoes facing in opposite directions. One paddler at a time places his paddle blade on the other cockpit, and supports his body weight while alternately taking the canoe off balance and recovering it by rotating the boat from the hips. The knees must grip firmly, and the body remains comparatively still.

2 As for the sweep stroke, the paddle may be held by the end to provide a very long lever, which will give a lot of support. Gradually reduce the length of the lever until the stroke is being performed with the hands in the normal paddling position.

3 In warm conditions, or in a pool, stand in the water holding the student's canoe just behind the cockpit. By tipping him first one way then the other the skill can be put under considerable pressure.

4 Once some confidence is gained, make students keep their eyes closed whilst practising on both sides.

Coaching Points

The stroke initially will be performed most easily by the student using the drive face of the blade on his controlling wrist side, and the back of the blade on the other side. This is because the blade needs only to be rotated through 90° in the one case, whilst on the other side it must be rotated through 180° and the elbows tucked under the loom.

Both forms of the stroke need finally to be learned on both sides, the 'low' version being more applicable in practice, to racing craft.

Common Faults

1 Loom not horizontal, thus blade not flat to the surface.

2 Blade not at right angles to the boat.

3 Leaning away from the water. The opposite and equal reaction to this is for the hips to rotate the canoe towards the direction of capsize.

4 Not leaning back to decrease the centre of gravity.

5 Failing to rotate the blade through 90° to facilitate removal after the stroke is complete.

STERN RUDDER

This technique is most often used in surfing to steer the boat on the face of a wave, or when 'surfing' a stopper or standing wave. Another useful application is when negotiating narrow caves, or between rocks, usually on the sea. If the paddler is faced with a narrow gap which is not wide enough to allow normal paddling, he can accelerate up to it and use the stern rudder as he enters. This will enable him to neatly steer his way very accurately between the obstacles. It is useful for beginners when experiencing steering difficulty, as it controls direction without slowing the boat.

The stern rudder, as its name suggests, is a simple steering stroke applied at the back of the boat. Although the position of the paddle can be practised from a static position, the stroke requires forward movement to actually function. The paddle needs to be placed well back at the stern, with the drive face towards the canoe, and the blade upright. The loom should be almost parallel to the gunnel line, and held low to allow the maximum amount of blade surface to be presented to the water. The forward hand is approximately at stomach

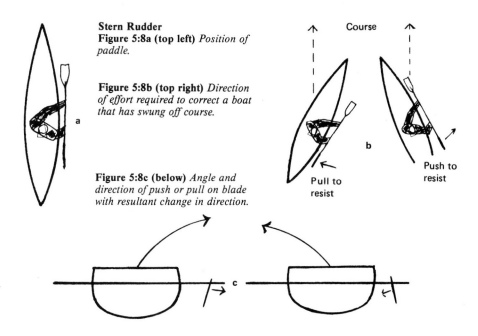

Stern Rudder
Figure 5:8a (top left) *Position of paddle.*

Figure 5:8b (top right) *Direction of effort required to correct a boat that has swung off course.*

a

Course

b

Push to resist

Pull to resist

Figure 5:8c (below) *Angle and direction of push or pull on blade with resultant change in direction.*

c

height, so that the paddle shaft, if viewed from the side, would be at around 30° to the surface of the water.

The boat is paddled forward – preferably down current or down wind, whichever is having most influence. When travelling at a reasonable speed the paddle blade is placed in the water at the stern as far back as is comfortable to reach. A pushing resistance – *not* a 'sweep' – with the top edge of the blade slightly tilted away from the kayak, will cause the boat to turn towards the side on which the paddle is operating. A pulling resistance – *not* a 'sweep' – with the top edge of the blade tilted towards the boat, will cause it to turn away from the side on which the paddle is placed. It follows therefore, that if the forces working on the boat are causing it to turn away from the paddle, the kayak can be brought back onto a straight course by a 'pushing resistance'. If the tendency is for the boat to turn towards the paddle, recovery is occasioned by using a 'pulling resistance'.

Considerable turning moment is possible with the push action – rather less with the pull. Once the canoe has passed a certain point, it will be necessary to move the paddle across and apply a push on the opposite side. With practise, however, it is possible, and in fact necessary, to maintain a straight course on a large surf wave without ending up like a windmill, having to frantically change the rudder from side to side.

Progression
Practise the paddle position statically, and then gradually apply it at faster speeds. Once mastered, the stroke will soon be found to be effective and simple to use.

Coaching Points
The edge of the paddle should be inserted so that the blade is parallel with the direction of travel. Reach well across the body with the forward arm, and insert the blade as deeply as possible. Although the boat can be leant slightly, generally speaking it is best to keep it upright. On the face of a surf wave during a diagonal run, the stroke will usually be applied

on the shore side, with the boat being tilted by the hips away from the stroke, to enable the uphill gunnel to act as a rail, gripping the wave, and assisting steering.

General Comments
A much neglected and ill taught skill in the past, the stern rudder is a very useful stroke, although it has fewer uses in river work. It is quite surprising how often good paddlers continue a forward paddling stroke to the back end of the boat and slip in a subtle steering stroke to pull the boat back on line. Essentially they are using the stern rudder technique, but preceding it with a forward stroke. When travelling backwards, the paddler leans forward and places the edge of his paddle close to the bow, and operates it as before – drive face towards the canoe.

LOW BRACE TURN

The low brace turn is a static stroke which requires momentum for it to function, and is used as a basic turning stroke when support is also required. The low telemark was the predecessor of this skill, and the name that has evolved to replace it, may be unfamiliar to some. However, it admirably describes the manoeuvre.

In the low brace turn, the paddler adopts a similar position to the start of a reverse sweep stroke, except that the flat of the blade is held close to the water, nearer right angles to the body.

The main point to remember is that, when used for real, the kayak should be positioned so that it can be driven well into the eddy by use of a powerful sweep stroke on the opposite side. As it enters the eddy, a strong lean upstream is necessary. This is where the paddle blade may come into play, to provide stability, but the turning is mainly caused by the combination of the sweep, the lean, and the bow entering the eddy while the stern is still in the current. If a lean is not applied, the sudden contrast in speed between the slack water you are entering, and the moving water you are leaving, can cause a capsize. When practised on still water, emphasis should be given to the sweep, and the lean, to create the turn. The paddle is used for stability if necessary. For most people it is the basic method used to learn breaking in and out in simple currents, as it provides greater stability than the bow rudder. In complete contrast, but for exactly the same reason, it is often used to break into very fast, very turbulent water, as it gives that extra little bit of comforting stability, when a capsize could be disastrous.

Figure 5:9a *Commencement of low brace turn.*

Figure 5:9b *Paddle sweeping forwards.*

Progressions
The stroke is not a technically difficult one to perform, and can be practised on flat or easy water until the paddler is confident enough to lean well onto the paddle blade and sweep it forward confidently.

Coaching Points
The stroke position should be taught statically at first, and once mastered can be applied to a moving craft on flat water. The faster the boat moves, the more lean the stroke will support. If the paddler is encouraged to commit himself from very early on it will make life a lot easier when he is introduced to a fast moving piece of water.

Common Faults

1   Blade placed driving face down.

2   Blade too flat. Thus leading edge cannot keep the paddle on the surface.

3   Blade not flat enough, providing little support during the turn.

4   Stroke applied out to the side like an outrigger. This is stable, but only acts as a support, and does not initiate any turning movement.

SCULLING DRAW

The sculling draw is another stroke which moves the canoe sideways. It may be used in much the same way as the ordinary draw stroke, for coming alongside the bank, or rafting up with other canoeists. It is of limited use in difficult conditions, as a well executed draw stroke is much more powerful. However, sculling is a valuable skill to master, as it teaches smooth and efficient handling of the blade under the water. It is an excellent exercise for developing blade awareness and co-ordination. For this reason alone, it is worthy of inclusion in the repertoire of basic skills.

The stroke is performed at a uniform distance from the gunnel, level with the CLR, with the paddle loom as near vertical as possible. Start with the blade ahead of you, parallel with, and about 12" away from, the gunnel, and fully immersed. The arms are in a similar position at this stage to the draw stroke, although the top arm is best arched over the head, as opposed to being in front of the forehead, in order to lock the shoulder joint in position. This enables the arm to act as a firm support rather like a rollock. From this basic starting position the drive face of the blade is opened towards the stern at an angle of about 30°. The paddle is then taken towards the stern of the boat, keeping the loom vertical in the process, and an equal distance from the keel-line, throughout. The blade travels for approximately three feet, and then the angle is switched, so that the blade is opened to the bow of the canoe, and sculled back the other way. This alternate pressure on the paddle face draws the boat towards it, resulting in a sideways movement. It can also be performed at the bow or stern quarter, resulting in a diagonal, crab-like movement.

Progression
Hold the lower paddle blade in a similar way to that employed by the Japanese when holding a table tennis bat – that is, four fingers down one side of the blade, thumb down the other. This links the canoeist directly to the blade of the paddle, making it easier to master the tricky co-ordination of this stroke. The top hand rests, palm up, on the head, ensuring a vertical shaft throughout the execution of the stroke. Once the change from one direction to another has been mastered, the paddler may resume the normal paddling grasp.

Figure 5:10a *Drawing the blade towards the stern.*

Figure 5:10b *Bringing the blade towards the bow with the opposite feather.*

Coaching Points

In the sculling draw it is important that fluency of movement is achieved, particularly while the blade angle is being changed. The more fluid the stroke, the more even will be the movement imparted to the craft. The stroke must be mastered slowly at first. Speed comes with familiarity.

Check to ensure that the loom is vertical throughout, and that the blade is fully immersed. Concentrate on ensuring that the paddler performs a symmetrical stroke, resulting in the boat moving directly towards the paddle and at right angles to the CLR. The paddler should also be coached into deliberately making the bow or stern lead during this sideways movement. This is achieved by opening the blade slightly more towards one end of the boat or the other whilst performing the sculling movement, enabling the paddler to observe the effect upon the movement of his boat, which will help him make adjustments to the stroke.

Common Faults

1   Paddle not vertical.

2   Blade not fully immersed.

3   Top hand altered to underhand grip.

4   Stroke not performed symmetrically, resulting in a diagonal or circular movement.

5   Stroke not performed in line with CLR, with the same consequences.

6   Blade angle too obtuse, resulting in crabbing movement, and requiring more effort than necessary due to the increased resistance.

7   Blade angle too acute, resulting in the blade slicing ineffectively.

General Comment
It is useful to practise this stroke without employing the top arm. This is done by laying the shaft across the clavicle (collar bone!) and nestling it behind the nape of the neck. Grip it by putting the head back slightly. The bottom arm can now perform the sculling movement. This is a very useful skill to master as it is the only real way that propulsion can be achieved using only one arm. The other arm can then be usefully employed to hold on to a capsized canoe during a rescue.

As an interesting variation this stroke can be performed with pressure on the back, rather than on the drive face of the blade. This moves the boat away from the paddle. With the paddle held as for the commencement of the stroke, previously described, set the blade. angle for the opposite scull. Tippy!

SCULLING FOR SUPPORT

Rather like the previous skill this is as much an exercise as an everyday stroke. The canoeist obtains support from his paddle, whilst in an unstable position, by sculling it backwards and forwards on or near the surface. The development of this ability to a high level can contribute an enormous amount to a paddler's confidence, and it is commonly used as a support stroke by white water paddlers. In fact, when performed in the extreme, it is virtually an eskimo roll, and is a very useful progression and confidence builder for this skill. The deep scull is the best support stroke for regaining balance after a violent loss of stability, as occurs often in really fierce white water.

The sculling action is identical to the sculling draw, except that it is executed with the loom near the horizontal, as opposed to the vertical position. The paddler reaches out to the side of the boat, lying back to reduce the CofG to a minimum. The blade of the paddle is laid flat on the water with the drive face down, and is then tilted, so that the edge nearest the bow is lifted slightly. The blade is sculled across the surface towards the bow for about three feet. The blade is then swiftly tilted the other way and sculled back again.

Throughout the exercise, the shaft of the paddle should be as low as possible, giving the stroke a wide radius, and presenting the flattest surface possible to the water, thus providing maximum support. Once the basic sculling action has been mastered without too much weight being applied to it, the paddler should begin to apply pressure by leaning the boat towards the stroke and gradually capsizing. The stroke will need to be performed faster as more weight comes onto the paddle.

It is possible to capsize completely, still keeping the head clear of the water, and support the upper body on the stroke, or to simply lie back and scull in a near capsized position for a long period. To recover from this unstable (if you stop sculling!) position, the legs and hips must rotate the kayak about the longitudinal axis, while the paddler's head is kept as near the water as possible. This action is enhanced by a press downwards on the flat blade. The action is identical to the final stages of a roll. Even when not practising the stroke in extreme positions, the recovery to equilibrium should be a hips, body, then head, action. This provides the pupil with an excellent educational exercise for the eskimo roll hip flick.

Progressions
1   Hold the paddle by the tip with the other hand on the neck close to the blade. The long lever this provides gives a great deal of support. Gradually reduce the length of the lever.

2   Raft students up facing in opposite directions, while they take turns in supporting each other, allowing for experiment without the risk of a capsize. First port to port, then starboard to starboard.

111

3   In a pool, or shallow water, stand behind a person and tip one way, then the other, to put pressure on the stroke.

Coaching Points
As with the sculling draw, stroke fluency is important. The paddler should be encouraged to produce an efficient, smooth stroke, as opposed to a violent thrashing of the surface. This is a committing stroke which inevitably results in capsizes, so choose carefully the time that you practise it. It isn't ideal as a warm-up exercise for novices in March, for instance! Watch that the loom is kept low, it should be almost on the gunnel when the boat goes on its side. Ensure that the CofG is kept low by the canoeist lying well back.

This stroke tends to be mastered to a very high level of skill by paddlers with access to a swimming pool, as the warm water encourages complete commitment. It is most important that this, and indeed all strokes, are practised systematically and symmetrically – that is, with equal enthusiasm on both sides. Eventually the paddler should be able to turn completely upside down and then simply scull back up again, regardless of which side he capsizes on.

Common Faults

1   Sitting upright – CofG too high.

2   Loom not horizontal, resulting in short radius, and reduced surface area of blade presented to the water.

3   Leaning away from the water during the stroke, causing an opposite and equal reaction of the hips, rotating the kayak about the lateral axis towards the stroke. Capsizes will result once the paddler reaches the point of no return, as support in this position is very difficult.

4   Blade angle too obtuse during sculling action, resulting in little support from the skimming blade.

General Comment
As with the recovery stroke, the sculling for support action is easier on the controlling wrist side. This is because the blade needs only to be rotated through 90° on the feathered side, but 180° on the other. On the non-feathered side, the arms can become uncomfortably bunched up, due to the extra rotation required. Practice will get around this. It is often helpful to shift the position of the inside arm, so that it is on top of the hull when in an extreme position, rather than leave it cramped by the deck of the capsizing boat.

BOW RUDDER

This is used to turn the boat, and at the same time provide support. Technically it is one of the most difficult skills to perform correctly, but once mastered is a very satisfying and aesthetically pleasing stroke to execute. The bow rudder can be used in a variety of situations, from turning on flat water, to breaking in and out in the wildest rapids. It flows into and out of the forward paddling stroke very easily, and is therefore most useful as a combination stroke, when turning momentum and power need to be alternately applied.

Leaning slightly forward, the blade is inserted level with the paddlers knees, drive face towards the boat, but the leading edge turned out at an angle of about 30°. The loom is as vertical as possible, and the arms bent dynamically. The lower wrist should be bent almost to a right angle, while the upper arm should have the back of the wrist in front of the forehead. The stomach muscles are employed to speed up the turn, with the legs gripping the deck firmly, so the boat is driven round the paddle with the opposite knee.

Sculling Support sequence

Figure 5:11a (top left) *Pushing the blade forwards.*

Figure 5:11b (top right) *The blade moving towards the stern with reverse feather.*

Figure 5:11c (right) *Commitment of body weight to the paddle. Notice low centre of gravity. Recovery is occasioned by hip flick.*

Figure 5:12 *Bow rudder. The top arm is deliberately held too high in order to show angle of the blade.*

Progressions

The simplest way to get into the basic bow rudder position is to place the blade in the water, loom vertical, as if preparing to do a draw stroke. Slide the blade forward, keeping the shaft of the paddle upright, until the blade is level with the knees. The blade is then opened with the wrists bending forwards, to an angle of 30-45°. This gives the basic position of the stroke. To execute it when the boat is moving, in a technically correct fashion, is not quite so simple, but if practised on flat water at slow speeds it will soon develop. Gradually introduce the stroke in different situations until the paddler begins to feel the support which is provided by the water pressure against the vertical blade.

Coaching Points

The most important points to consider are the position of the arms and the blade angle being presented to the water. The top arm should be bent in front of the forehead, with the wrist in front of the brow. The top hand is therefore reaching across to the other side of the boat, but the shoulder joint is not locked. This allows for adjustment of the arm's position during the stroke. The top arm is often spectacularly, but uselessly, wrapped around the head of the paddler. In this position, the arm is locked and very weak. The lower arm should be strongly bent to almost 90° and held close to the body. This utilises the strongest arm muscles and ensures that the levers involved are short and very strong.

Common Faults

1   Top arm reaching across under the paddler's chin to opposite shoulder – very weak position.

114

2   Top arm too high above head, or wrapped behind neck. Very weak and inflexible.

3   Top arm not reaching across far enough – loom not vertical enough.

4   Lower arm straight, or slightly bent – stroke too far from paddler and therefore weak.

5   Blade angle too obtuse.

6   Blade angle too acute.

7   Paddler not leaning forwards into the stroke.

8   Canoeist allows the paddle to be pushed backwards by the pressure of water. It must be firmly planted and *resisted*.

General Comments

This stroke is probably one of the most difficult skills to execute, and consequently is generally performed poorly. Lack of firm coaching information has not helped this. The foundation of this stroke is the draw. If that has been mastered correctly, then the component parts of the bow rudder are all there. It is vital, therefore, that the arm positions are educated early on, when the draw and sculling draw strokes are being practised, to ensure that the ranges of movement later employed in the bow rudder are simply familiar ones applied in a slightly different fashion.

Reference is sometimes made to a high telemark, and some would seek to differentiate this from the bow rudder. Originally the high telemark was performed at the very back of the canoe, in exactly the same way as the low telemark. The boat was leaned over to alter the water-line shape, assisting turning, and, in the early days, to lift it off the keel. The only difference between the two telemark turns was that the high telemark used the drive face of the blade, instead of the back.

Later, the name was applied to a stroke which placed the blade at about 90° to the paddler, with the drive face at 90° to the keel line. The canoe was pivoted around this. The modern bow rudder was the next development, and has made the high telemark obsolete, although there will be occasions when it is applied in much the same way.

TILTING THE CANOE TO ASSIST TURNING

Wild Water Racing paddlers use tilting to steer their V-shaped hulls. Racing canoes, and even kayaks with rudders, will be held on to their sides to assist tight manoeuvres – watch the K4s on a 10,000 metre turn! By altering the water-line length and shape of the boat, a turn is induced. It is essentially a matter of using the hips to rotate the canoe onto its gunnel to assist steering. The body will remain in the upright, efficient paddling position. Most canoes, when tipped to the left will turn to the right and vice versa.

Apart from the instances quoted above, this is a very necessary skill to acquire in order to control a boat in a cross wind on lake or sea. It is also useful when steering on surf waves, or white water.

Progressions

With the students sitting stationary in their canoes, get them to hold the boat onto alternate sides, by forcing the boat onto its gunnel through use of the knees gripping the decks. The body needs to counter balance. When paddling gently forward, the boat should be again held onto its side, and the result noted.

Coaching Points

There may not be a consistent turn at first – the boat could go either way. This is not significant, as when used in earnest, the effect will be consistent for the boat. A means of

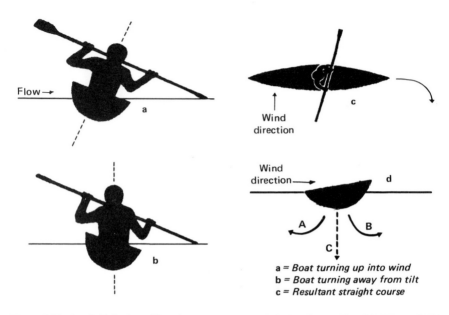

Flow →

Wind direction

Wind direction →

a = Boat turning up into wind
b = Boat turning away from tilt
c = Resultant straight course

Figure 5:13a (top left) *Body and boat leaning over as a unit for break out or break in.* **Figure 5:13b (bottom left)** *Boat tilted by use of hips only – body counter balancing.* **Figure 5:13c (top right)** *A moving kayak will turn up into the wind.* **Figure 5:13d (bottom right)** *The turn caused by tilting the canoe cancels out the turning affect of the wind.*

proving this is to find an open stretch of water where a moderate wind is blowing. Ask the paddler to move at good speed in a straight line for about 25 metres with the wind on the beam. The boat will tend to turn into the wind, and the canoeist will be correcting by tilting the canoe. Ask him or her to come back in the opposite direction, and the tilting bias will be the opposite way. Normally the kayak will be tilted towards the wind. The natural tendency of the boat to turn up into the wind will be counteracted by its turning away from the side towards which it is tilted. The result is that the kayak proceeds in a straight line. Steering in this way removes the need for sweep strokes, and other steering methods, which detract from the forward propulsion.

Tilting the kayak to aid steering is not the same as when leaning it to break in or break out of a fast current. Then, the body and boat will tend to come over as a unit. The body weight is committed to the paddle, and although the consequent tilting of the boat is assisting the sharp turn, different forces are involved. There is also the practical factor of ensuring that the hull is presented to the 'solid' water. For breaking out this will be the eddy which is stopping the boats velocity; breaking in, it will be the jet of water which the bow is entering and being swept away down stream on.

6 Reading Water

Compiled by the Editor

The skill of 'reading water' is fundamental to the successful negotiation of rapids. When canoeists use the term, they mean: the ability to identify from the wave shapes and patterns, and the appearance of the surface of the water, where the obstacles are located; where it is possible to shelter from the stream in an eddy, in order to rest, reconnoitre the next section, or see round a bend; where the real dangers exist; and where lies the route by which the rapid can most successfully be negotiated.

Why rapids exist

Rapids are produced where there is a marked gradient to the river and where obstructions occur, or where an irregular topography of the river bed confines the stream, so that a large amount of water is forced through a narrow gap. On the large rivers of the continents, the white water can be continuous for many miles. In Britain, however, it is normally a case of paddling varying distances between relatively short turbulent sections.

Types of wave

'Stoppers', 'standing waves' and 'haystacks' are the three distinct types of wave that need to be recognised. Each of these has different characteristics, but may change appearances in varying water levels. There is also an infinite variation of the situations and formations in which they may appear.

The stopper has been defined in the Safety chapter. It is recognised by the fact that the breaking foam is tumbling right the way down into the trough, or the hole behind the obstruction causing it. (See chapter 4.) A standing wave occurs also because of an obstruction, but the river bed beyond it does not allow a stopper to develop. The top may be breaking, but the foam will be tumbling at the crest and not roaring back down to the bottom, as with a stopper. The current is passing through a standing wave, and a canoe will normally be taken on through with it (figure 6:1a). Very large standing waves are capable of holding canoes at the top, however. The obstruction causing standing waves or stoppers can vary from an isolated rock, to a ledge right across the river. Haystacks, which are pyramid shaped waves, are created where currents converge (figure 6:1b). They normally mean a clear, bouncy passage through, although tell-tale signs such as a different pattern of breaking crests among them, could indicate the presence of a rock.

Other features

A 'riffle' is rarely mentioned in canoeing, being a very minor disturbance to the surface water, caused by shallowing.

'Fall' is used to indicate a specific change in level over a short distance, involving the canoeist in having to shoot the drop. It may be a few inches only, or a waterfall up to 30' –

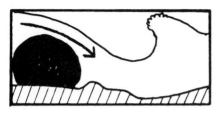

Figure 6:1a *A standing wave.*

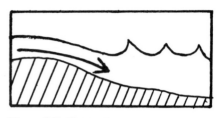

Figure 6:1b *Haystacks.*

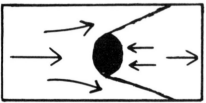

Figure 6:2 *The spiral currents caused by friction between the water and the river bank. There is a corkscrew effect from the surface down.*

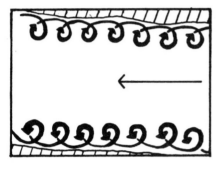

Figure 6:3a *The vee formed by the current diverging around the obstruction.*

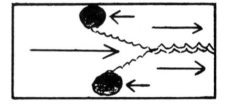

Figure 6:3b *The downstream vee formed between two obstructions, with the smooth tongue leading to haystacks where the currents converge.*

although these are for a very few experts only. Natural weirs occur on rivers, and come within this category.

The difference between an 'eddy' and a 'whirlpool' is that with the former, the vortex (centre) is rotating more slowly than the perimeter. With the whirlpool the opposite is the case. Very large whirlpools, in which the vortex does not change position, are to be avoided at all costs. Many fast rapids produce small whirlpools, and they occur in front of weirs. These normally move downstream and dissipate, and may cause a boat to dip under momentarily.

'Boils' can be seen on very large rapids, and beneath weirs when the river is in spate. This is an upsurge of water, which appears on the surface spilling outwards in the shape of a

Figure 6:4 (opposite) *Top picture: a canoeist's view downstream. Under the chain bridge on the Dee at Llangollen. There is an obvious break out behind the large rock on the right, but did you spot the break out on the left, or the number of canoes that could be accommodated – middle and lower pictures?*

119

mushroom. The demarcation line at the circumference of the area, can be quite difficult to negotiate, due to the instability caused by surface water sinking on both sides of the boat simultaneously.

When water piles up against a rock on the *upstream* face, a 'pressure area' or 'cushion' is created. The effect can be similar to a stopper, with a vertical eddy current of considerable holding power being generated under water, against the obstruction.

Where very powerful streams are involved, particularly in flood conditions, boulders are moved along the beds of rivers and finish up together, often at the end of the rapid. These are known as 'rock gardens', and may involve a portage when the river is low.

International system for grading rivers

There is an international system for grading wild water (table 1). The grading applies to normal summer conditions. If there has been a great deal of rain just prior to a trip, the chances are that the grading will be higher, or the difficulties encountered will be at the extreme of the category. Should the water be nearly at the top of the banks, therefore, and certainly if it is over them, great caution needs to be exercised. The grading given for the river should be well within the capability of all the paddlers involved. Inspection is always recommended for unknown rapids, or sections of rapids, and should be undertaken for familiar stretches in unfamiliar conditions.

On a simple rapid, the amount of steering necessary to link together sufficient paths through the obstructions, is minimal. The grading then increases according to the technical ability required to change course, the severity of the conditions in which manoeuvring has to be performed, and the likely consequences, due to the situation downriver, should a mistake be made – access to the bank, the size and location of eddies, whether or not the rapid finishes in a pool, or whether a further, perhaps more severe section follows.

In general, it is the river that is graded rather than individual rapids, or fall, although a particular isolated stretch of rough water could be above or below the general rating for the river.

Route finding

Negotiating rapids is more than just recognising the difference between one type of wave and another. It is essential to have a general knowledge of the behaviour of water.

In simple terms, where there are no obstructions, and an even depth of water, the current will be fastest in the middle of the river. Along the edges there will be an eddying effect. The friction caused by the banks, produces a continuous swirling, with water spinning and dropping as it reaches the edge of the mainstream again (figure 6:2). This phenomenon is the reason that it is often difficult to pull a swamped kayak right into the bank. When proceeding downstream, therefore, it is better to be near the middle of the river. In order to make headway against the current, a canoeist keeps to the edge. The bottom shelving steeply from the bank will indicate the passage of fast water, while a gently sloping bottom, means a comparatively slow current.

Any obstruction under water in a swiftly moving flow will cause a disturbance above and just beyond it. Look therefore for the small wave appearing on an otherwise smooth surface. There is a rock just under water upstream of it.

When approaching a section of rapid, the main route indicator is the downstream V. Wherever a rock is on or very near the surface in fast water the current will diverge (figure 6:3a). Where two diverging currents meet, the haystacks form, and it is the smooth tongue of water in between the apex of the vees, leading to the haystacks, which shows that all is clear (figure 6:3b).

Figure 6:5 *Making the breakout just to the left of centre in the previous picture. Notice the downstream vee to the right of the paddler who is facing upstream.*

Figure 6:6 *Using the face of a standing wave to ride across the stream.*

Table One   Wild Water – Grades of Difficulty

Grade I *Not Difficult*	Grade II *Moderately Difficult*	Grade III *Difficult*	Grade IV *Very Difficult*	Grade V *Extremely Difficult*	Grade VI *Limit of Practicability*
	passage free	route recognisable	route not always recognisable. Inspection mostly necessary	inspection essential	generally speaking impossible
regular stream	irregular stream	high, irregular waves	heavy continuous rapids	extreme rapids	possibly navigable at particular water levels
regular waves	irregular waves	larger rapids	heavy stoppers whirlpools and pressure areas	stoppers, whirlpools and pressure areas	high risk
small rapids	medium rapids small stoppers, eddies/whirlpools and pressure areas*	stoppers, eddies and whirlpools and pressure areas			
simple obstructions	simple obstructions in stream small drops	isolated boulders, drops and numerous obstructions in stream	boulders obstructing stream, big with undertow	narrow passages, steep gradients and drops with difficult access and landing	

* 'Pressure areas' refers to water piling up against a rock or other obstacle (sometimes called 'cushions' in this country).
N.B. Weirs are not classified as wild water and as such are not evaluated. They are (either) easily navigable or (very) dangerous.

Figure 6:7a (left) *A rock garden and sizeable fall on the river Ubaye, France. Photo: P. Knowles.*

Figure 6:7b (below) *Peter Midwood heading down the tongue of a vee in big water on the Orinoco.*

Figure 6:8 (top) *A stopper on the Serpent's Tail, river Dee at Llangollen.* **(below)** *Breaking out through the stopper.*

The fastest passage is usually just to one side of large waves, as it is slower to alternatively bounce over and cut through them. Unless canoeists are racing, however, they will generally choose the roughest route for the sheer exhilaration of the experience.

For kayaks, in minor rapids, the recommendation is to paddle hard in order to maintain steerage, and not be broadsided by the current. The opposite is the case for open canoes, however, where a great deal of reverse ferry gliding, or 'setting', is undertaken, to move the boat in one direction or the other across the river, in order to follow the route through. It is also necessary to hold back the speed to avoid being swamped. Kayakists in heavy rapids, also tend to let the water provide most of the power, and concentrate on aligning the boat in a similar way, to avoid the most serious hazards.

On bends, the fastest water sweeps around the outside, while eddy (reverse) currents are created on the inside. This can be clearly seen at low water. Large banks with gentle gradients are formed, created by the particles of matter dropped by the water when it slows down, as it rotates away from the fast moving flow, into the upstream eddy on the inside of the bend. In very high water conditions, whirlpools can be created there.

Figure 6:9 *A canoeist using the holding power of the stopper to attempt a loop, by riding upstream and down the face of the wave on the returning foam. When the bow meets the solid water proceeding downstream under the wave, the boat will be flipped end over end.*

125

Where a bend is very sharply angled there may be a danger of becoming pinned against the rock face or bank, and in heavy conditions, the spiral currents referred to earlier, may be sufficiently strong to take the canoe under.

The other great problem is to be taken by the current into overhanging, or, worst of all, fallen trees, which are common on bends, due to erosion undercutting the banks. The safe passage through is to keep well out and into the eddy, whenever such danger exists.

The importance of inspection

Inspection – getting out to take a look – not only enables hazards, perhaps invisible from above, to be identified, but presents an entirely different picture to that which it is possible to obtain from canoe height. Experience leads to the point, however, where a great deal of inspection can be carried out from a canoe. This is not something that can be learned from a book.

The behaviour of the element must be understood, and an ability developed to recognise the significant shapes of the waves, and the evidence on the surface of the water. It is then a matter of application, practice and hard experience. The more difficult manouevres should be deliberately tried. Paddling backwards in situations where the instinct is to go forwards. Break in and out, and sit in stoppers on the side you are least happy about. Work on these aspects in controlled situations, and eventually the ability will be gained that leads to mastery on mighty torrents.

Conclusion

Shooting rapids is probably, with surfing, the most exhilarating thrill obtainable in a canoe. The novice, who is able to control his boat, and change direction with reasonable competence, should be kept on grade I and II sections until he is able to handle them with confidence and commitment – breaking out on demand, and forward and reverse ferry gliding where required. If he is then introduced gradually to more demanding stretches, but where a mistake should not lead to disaster, the risk, for what is generally regarded as a hazardous activity, is minimal. Serious accidents occur almost exclusively to those who are allowed into situations beyond their competence, or to the expert who is deliberately pushing the limits of feasibility.

This does not mean that rapid river running should ever be regarded with anything less than respect. But treated with respect, the outcome is a lifetime of fun and excitement with minimal risk.

7 Moving Water Techniques

Jim Hargreaves

INTRODUCTION

Although there is much aesthetic pleasure to be derived from executing a technique perfectly on flat water, this in itself should never be the primary aim of learning the kayak handling skills. The canoe is a vehicle, and the basics necessary to propel, turn and manoeuvre it, are not the end of the sport of canoeing – they are the beginning. Moving water adds another dimension, and puts a new requirement on the paddler to apply his new found abilities.

There are a number of canoeists today who can perform every roll imaginable in a swimming pool, but come the day they experience a cold, unexpected capsize in murky water, the skill escapes them. Once a technique has been acquired well enough to be functional, it should be endorsed by the introduction of a factor which will draw the undivided attention of the paddler away from executing it. When the skill can be performed correctly whilst mentally attending to something else, it can truly be said that it has been completely mastered.

The diversion may be a game, a target, or a race, but there are few factors that will stimulate the pupil more than a first introduction to moving water. Although his canoeing career may develop no further than this tentative entry into a simple current, it may progress to the descent of some ferocious Himalayan torrent. Either way, coping with moving water will add an exciting and rewarding dimension to the acquisition of canoeing skills.

BREAKING OUT

Breaking out is the art of leaving a fast moving current and entering an eddy. It is a very important skill, as it is often the only way a paddler can stop for a rest, survey what is ahead, or break down a long piece of technical water into manageable sections. The sudden contrast between the speed of the current he is leaving, and the slack water he is entering, can catch the canoeist unawares, and cause a capsize. For this reason, a strong counter lean is necessary as an eddy is entered.

The paddler looks ahead downstream, and when a suitable break out is spotted, he starts to angle his boat across the current, and move towards the obstruction which is creating the eddy. As he draws level with the obstruction, his boat is ideally almost broad-side to the current. As soon as the upstream extremity of the eddy is reached, the bow is driven into the slack water. An upstream lean is quickly applied so that the hull is presented to the relatively stationary water of the eddy, with either a low brace or bow rudder being applied at the same time. The timing and judgement required to make accurate break outs takes

Figure 7:1 *Break out sequence using a low brace turn.*

Figure 7:2 *Break out sequence showing a forward sweep into the eddy followed by a power stroke converting into a bow rudder.*

much practise, and eventually the most minute eddies can become sanctuaries. The secret of breaking out accurately lies in the ability to spot the eddy from a reasonable distance ahead, thus allowing plenty of time to get to the correct position in the river, and drive for the slack water. The commonest fault in beginners is the lack of a forceful, determined approach to make the break out at all costs. Also the boat is often not driven deep enough into the eddy, so that the paddler is turned by the slack water, only to be plucked out again by the current, and carried downstream backwards. Almost as much skill is attached to *preparing* for the breakout, as actually executing it.

The bow must be swept into the slack, then driven in further with a power stroke, followed by a turning support stroke as the final entry is made. Students should be coached to a high level of accuracy in this skill as it provides an important safety factor when travelling on rivers. Allied to this is the art of using areas of slack water to help with turns. This basically means placing enough of the end of the canoe into slack water, so that the boat is turned, but then carries on downstream. This is useful when a paddler has been swung around inadvertantly in mid-stream.

BREAKING IN

Re-entering moving water in order to proceed downstream from an eddy, is known as breaking in. It is probably the main single cause of capsizes in beginners, followed closely by breaking out! From facing upstream in an eddy, the paddler must enter the current, turn with it, and proceed downstream. The reason capsizes are so frequent when practising this, is due to the contrast in speed between the boat entering the current, and the current itself. The fast water suddenly hits the side of the boat, pressure builds up on the gunnel, and the canoeist can be tipped in. Because of this, the paddler must first learn to lean away from the current he is entering, so that the hull is presented to the fast moving water.

The technique is best practised in easy situations initially, but the water must have

Figure 7:3 *Break in using a low brace turn.*

Figure 7:4 *Break in using a bow rudder.*

sufficient speed to define eddies clearly. The boat should be set an angle of about 45° to the current, if the eddy is large enough to allow for this, while it is accelerated towards it. As the bow enters the fast water, a strong lean down stream onto a low brace is executed. If the eddy is not large enough to allow for acceleration, strong paddle strokes must be used in order to enter the flow fully, otherwise the current will simply spin the boat around on the spot, and leave it perched on that unstable junction between the fast and slack water. The faster the current, the more speed must be used for the entry, and the harder must the lean be downstream. Only capsizing will convince the novice that he is not leaning sufficiently. After practise, the amount of lean required for a particular situation will come as second nature, as does the angle a motor cyclist needs to take a bend.

The strong and positive entry into the current should see the first third of the boat being thrust into the flow, before the turning stroke is executed. Once the turn has been mastered

131

using a low brace, a bow rudder should be tried. This is the stroke which eventually will invariably be used for this manoeuvre. Some advocate introducing breaking in and out using the bow rudder straight away. Because the flat, reassuring surface of the paddle blade is not there for support, however, many beginners find this skill unstable initially, and prefer the low brace.

Progressions

Breaking in and out should be practised on both sides. The key to success is repetitive training in a variety of currents. The co-ordination required to paddle into the current, and then perform a turning stroke, can be difficult to master. The one, two, three method may help. In this progression, the paddler executes three forward strokes followed by his turning stroke, be it a low brace, or a bow rudder. The first stroke is on the upstream side, thus providing a rhythm to get the timing right. One, two, three, turn!

Exercises are numerous, ranging from 'dancing' down the eddy line, consecutively breaking in and out of an easy current, to assisted turns – where the bow is introduced just sufficiently to turn the boat around on the spot. Then the stern is introduced to the current in the same way, to turn the boat back again. There should be no end to variations and methods tried to gently introduce this technique, but at the end of the day the paddler must go for it, and attack the current.

THE FERRY GLIDE

This technique enables a canoeist to cross a current without being carried downstream. It is most useful for checking downstream progress in order to make an inspection of what lies ahead, or for avoiding obstacles which have unexpectedly appeared. As its name suggests, the principle is similar to that of the old ferries that carried passengers across fast moving stretches of water. They were attached by a loop to a wire stretched across the river, and the steersman had only to move the rudder to angle the boat across the flow, for the opposing forces to cause the vessel to be moved across the stream.

The canoe is angled across the current and paddled in the opposite direction to the flow of the water. This will arrest movement downstream, and, providing the angle has been set correctly, the boat, caught between the opposing forces of the current moving downstream and the paddler paddling against it, will be moved in a sideways direction across the river. It is by gaining ground on a ferry glide across the current whilst facing upstream, that a paddler can work his way back up a simple rapid.

Slow, uniformly moving pieces of water should be used for practise until the basic idea is established. Thereafter, progress can be made onto faster, more difficult crossings. It is better to set the angle too acutely initially, as it is easier to broaden it than it is to regain a narrow one. The skill lies in judging the angle needed, and being able to maintain it, at the same time balancing the power of the paddle strokes, to cross the current. Tilting the canoe should be used as part of this balancing process. The slower the water, the more obtuse the angle needed. It is sometimes useful deliberately to gain or lose ground when appropriate, by over or under emphasing the angle of the boat to the current.

It is, if anything, more important to master the reverse ferry glide. The ability to check forward speed and move accurately across the current, can be vital to safety in any moving water situation, or to the ability to navigate technically difficult rapids.

Figure 7:5 Ferry Glide (top) *The stern of the kayak has been angled towards the left hand bank.* **(centre)** *By backward paddling, the canoeist is holding his position against the current.* **(bottom)** *The resultant of the opposing forces has taken the canoe to the left hand bank.*

133

Figure 7:6 High Cross. *The boat is accelerated into the flow, and shot across by the opposing velocities. Notice the paddle held ready for support on the downstream side.*

Figure 7:7 *The high brace position demonstrated statically.*

THE HIGH CROSS

The high cross is the name given to the technique of crossing a fast piece of water, usually at the nearest possible point to its immediate source, without employing a continuous, normal paddling action. On very fast water, this usually entails riding the face of a stopper or standing wave. The canoe will surf across if the current has been entered at the best angle and speed.

A high cross is usually approached at an acute angle. The boat is driven hard into the current from the slack water, with a strong downstream lean being applied. The speed of the water, opposed by the speed of the boat, will send the canoe across the jet very quickly. The skill lies in not losing ground if at all possible. The student must be encouraged to attack the water positively, at the correct angle. It is better to have too narrow, rather than too broad an angle of entry.

THE HIGH BRACE

This technique is used in big waters as a hanging support stroke. It is applicable in big broken surf, large stoppers, or break outs in heavy water. Care should be exercised as dislocations are not infrequent, because of the weak position of the shoulder joint. The drive face of the paddle is presented flat to the water, and the paddler hangs under the loom as if hanging from a bar. The upsurge of water acting on the flat blade gives considerable support.

By angling the blade, with the drive face still downwards, but opened up towards the stern, a pull can be applied in order to move the boat forward along a stopper or broken surf wave. Reverse movement can be obtained by opening the drive face towards the bow, and pushing. At the end of each relatively short stroke the blade is flattened and sculled back to the starting position.

8 Inland Canoeing

Graham Lyon

An unfinished Moonraker, left in his school workshop, was the start of Graham Lyon's canoeing career in 1964, and led to his helping a local youth club to build lath and canvas, and later glassfibre canoes. Although failing his Proficiency test at the first attempt(!) Graham later became an Instructor, and founder member of Shrewsbury Canoe Club, leading journeys on many well known white water rivers. An interest in sea canoeing developed in 1970 and a week is still spent annually on a self-contained expedition.

From Local Coaching Organiser, he was elected Regional Coaching Organiser for West Midlands in 1976, appointed a National Coaching and Development Officer a year later, and is currently Chairman of the National Coaching Committee. Graham still enjoys wild water racing in both kayak and C2, marathon racing – including Devizes to Westminster – and has competed in slalom.

INTRODUCTION

I can think of no other sport with such a variety of different, exciting and challenging aspects, as canoeing. With so many disciplines, there must be something that appeals to almost everyone. There is a vast range of craft to try, techniques to master, competitions to strive in, equipment to experiment with, and waters to explore. The inland canoeist should never become bored, because the moment that he feels interest flagging, he can take up and introduce a new branch of the sport to the club or group that he is working with. A new challenge is always there.

TYPES OF CRAFT

Basically canoes fall into two categories — the Kayak, and the Canoe. Let us first look at the Canoe.

Canoes

The most popular is the open Canadian canoe. Popular, that is in world-wide terms, because the possibilities of this craft have not yet been fully realised in this country. It is an excellent load carrier, and therefore ideal for camping trips, which is why it is so much used by canoeists in other countries for journeys into remote areas. Also it is a safe, stable and comfortable vessel, which would suit a family picnicing trip. Most people are surprised how well it performs in wild water, when operating in that element for the first time.

Canoes are paddled with a single blade, either in a kneeling or sitting position, very often with two paddlers on opposite sides at the bow and stern. However, they can be easily handled by one person operating from a central position.

The crossing of estuaries or large lakes should only be attempted in favourable conditions. The canoe is difficult to handle in a wind, and is easily swamped by waves. Spray covers are expensive.

The traditional Canadian canoe has been developed in two ways. It has been decked in, fitted with fairly small cockpits, and changed its shape to meet the needs of the white water canoeist, and it has been altered by the racing canoeists to produce more speed, at the expense of stability.

White water canoeing falls into two categories: Slalom, and Wild Water Racing. The slalom canoe is designed for touring and manoeuvring on wild water, and modern designs have a very low profile, making them less suitable for touring. Kneeling on both knees takes some getting used to, and successful manoeuvring in rapids with the single bladed paddle calls for great skill.

The Slalom double canoe requires team work. It is reasonably stable, and a very satisfying craft to paddle, as the two canoeists learn to work together.

The wild water racing canoe, like the slalom canoe, comes in both single and double form. Designed for speed in rough water, they are buoyant craft and less stable than a slalom boat. The canoe can be steered by leaning it to one side, or by paddle strokes.

Sprint canoes are built for one, two or seven people. The canoeist kneels on one knee only. Instability is largely a matter of comparison, and the adult who has paddled a stable touring or slalom canoe or kayak for years, will find singles and doubles 'tender' at first. However, a youngster with some natural ability will find racing canoes less of a problem to balance.

It is impossible not to be excited the first time you see a C7 flashing past. Most paddlers are impressed also when they see a sprint C1 perform a tight turn, with its gunnel almost under water.

Figure 8:1 *A traditional Canadian canoe. This one is owned by Frank Luzmore founder of the Canadian Canoe Association of Great Britain. Notice the pole (for poling, or 'punting') and the rig for sailing the vessel.*

Figure 8:2 *Slalom Canadian single (C1).*

Figure 8:3 *Slalom Canadian double (C2).*

138

Figure 8:4 *Wild Water Racing Canadian single (C1).*

Figure 8:5 *Wild Water Racing Canadian double (C2).*

Figure 8:6 *International Racing Canadian single (C1).*

Figure 8:7 *International Racing Canadian double (C2).*

Figure 8:8 *Racing war canoe (C7).*

Kayaks (for inland waters)

Having looked briefly at eight types of canoe, we must now look at the Kayak, where the variety is even greater. I shall refer to the paddlers of kayaks as 'canoeists' because that is the term generally used, although it would be more correct to refer to them as kayakists. For ease of identification kayaks are split into four main categories: touring, racing, white water and swimming-pool kayaks. All have their origins in the Eskimo kayak which was a narrow craft with a covered-in deck. As with the canoe, the design has been adapted to fulfil specific sporting functions.

The touring kayak is intended for trips of either a few hours, or several days, down rivers, across lakes or estuaries. Although there are a number of designs on the market, all have features in common. They should be easy to paddle in a straight line, and optional extras often include a rudder. The kayak must be comfortable to sit in for several hours, be stable, and fairly buoyant, giving ample space to pack camping kit. Large cockpits are often favoured for ease of getting in and out, and the kayak comes in either double or single form. Average length for a single is 14'-17'.

For touring down wild water of the type not easily accessible in this country, the design is rather different. The kayak is shorter (13'-14'6"), more manoeuvrable, often has rounded ends, remains very buoyant, the cockpit is smaller, and the paddler is able to brace himself in tightly.

The modern racing kayak has emerged from the tourer, being longer and narrower, and therefore faster. Used for both sprint and marathon racing, an under stern rudder is generally favoured for the former, and an over-stern for the latter. There are singles, doubles and fours (sprint racing only).

The excitement of racing kayaks is their sheer speed, and once able to balance one in a relaxed manner a canoeist will find they can make an excellent day touring boat. Because they are so fast, quite long trips can be attempted, and this is an area that has yet to be fully exploited.

Although a number of marathon races include shooting rapids and weirs, there are craft more suited to these conditions. The modern wild water racing kayak has evolved, using some of the design features of the sprint kayak's hull, but producing a more buoyant boat, with the seating and cockpit designed to allow it to be rolled, and for the paddler to brace himself in.

Some of the earlier wild water racing kayaks also make excellent day touring kayaks, since they are reasonably stable, fast, and have good carrying capacity.

At the present time the slalom kayak is a low-volume (or low-profile) boat, since the rules permit the kayak to be dipped under the poles. They are comparatively stable craft, highly manoeuvrable and designed for easy handling in rough water conditions. Earlier types, which were more buoyant, have tended to become the 'general purpose' kayak used frequently to introduce people to canoeing.

Modern competition slalom kayaks, because of their low profile and consequent lack of buoyancy, are not very suitable for long journeys. There is concern also at their use for wild water touring, away from the competition site. In 'heavy' conditions there is insufficient buoyancy for safety, and incidents of their 'folding up' have been reported. Particularly where they are of lightweight construction, it is not recommended that they be used in situations where help on the water, and access to support on the land, is not immediately available.

Swimming pools are widely used for introducing people to canoeing, practising rolling, capsize drill, rescues and other safety and skill techniques. Pool time is valuable and the length of a kayak prohibitive in terms of the numbers that can be got into a pool at one time. This led to the development of a short rounded boat commonly called a BAT (Baths

140

Advanced Trainer). So popular has pool use become, that it is hardly surprising that a competitive form of canoeing known as Canoe Polo has evolved, using these small craft. A modified BAT, which is a little faster, has now been designed for this game.

The Instructor's Kayak

It goes without saying that an Instructor's boat and equipment should be a good example to those that he is instructing. Obviously it must be in good repair, and careful thought should be given to the function that it is going to perform. Here individual preferences and invention play a large part, but some basic guidelines can be given. The level of equipment will vary if one is taking a group on a long river trip or just teaching the basic skills.

The kayak should be so constructed that it is strong enough to take the extra strains imposed upon it during deep water rescues. Remember that the inexperienced beginner often gets a lot of water in his canoe after a capsize.

A deckline system is useful for a swimmer to grasp, rafting and rescue situations, and lowering the kayak down steep banks. There is not universal agreement as to whether deck lines should be fitted to all boats for inland expeditions, particularly on white water. Suffice it to say that the more easily 'grabbable' a boat is in an emergency, the more likely is it that the problem can be quickly sorted out. There is a danger of ropes snagging in trees and other objects. However, the fitting of lines provided that they are taut, cannot come loose, and can never foul the cockpit area, is still to be recommended.

Make sure that you have plenty of buoyancy and if in doubt carry out a test. Pack your kayak with all the gear that you would carry as an instructor on a day's trip, fill it with water and then swim with it. This should prove fairly easy, and the canoe should offer you some positive buoyancy. An air bag system proves to be very satisfactory in this respect.

It is important that the Instructor feels comfortable in his boat for long periods of time. Some thought should be given as to how the kit is to be secured, and a few small loops on the inside for tying things in can be useful.

A towline is necessary, since you may need to tow a tired beginner or a capsized canoe. There are all sorts of systems, but the essential points are that you should be able to attach quickly and easily to the other canoe, and release quickly in case of an emergency. A paddle park is also useful.

OTHER EQUIPMENT

Spray covers

A spraycover keeps water from entering the canoe, and helps to keep the lower half of the body warm by sealing it off from the elements. Essential for white water canoeing, it is also useful for flat water touring in poor weather conditions.

Personal flotation aid

A personal flotation aid, either a buoyancy aid or a lifejacket, is vital for all beginners and for white water canoeing. The various types and their functions are described in chapter 4. Senior paddlers often race in marathons without personal flotation aids, and they are never worn by seniors at regattas, where a high degree of safety cover in the form of powered rescue craft is available. Statistics over the last decade clearly show that the wearing of a lifejacket or buoyancy aid for normal canoeing activities, virtually eliminates a likelihood of drowning.

Figure 8:9 *Touring single kayak.*

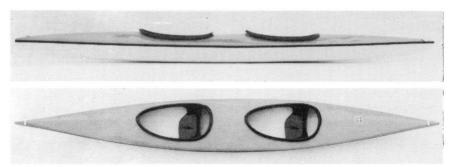

Figure 8:10 *Touring double kayak.*

Figure 8:11 *White water touring kayak.*

Figure 8:12 (top) *A modern international racing single kayak (K1)* **(centre)** *a more stable fast touring single kayak* **(bottom)** *Espada one-design single racing kayak (K1).*

142

Figure 8:13 *International racing double kayak (K2).*

Figure 8:14 *International racing four-man kayak (K4).*

Figure 8:15 *Wild Water Racing kayak (K1).*

Figure 8:16 *General purpose high-volume slalom kayak.*

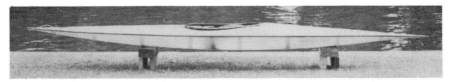
Figure 8:17 *Low-volume competition slalom kayak (K1).*

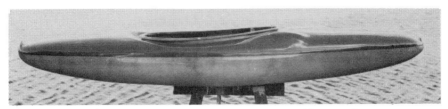
Figure 8:18 *Baths Advanced Trainer. This is one of the original BAT designs, 2 m in length. The maximum length (3 m) is now favoured.*

143

Safety helmets

Crash hats are compulsory in slaloms and wild water races. They are necessary for grade III water for touring, and advised at all levels of white water canoeing, where the emphasis is on practising technique. A person touring a grade I-II river, and merely shooting straight down the rapids, may prefer not to wear a hat. Rocks are hard, however, and heads are not.

Paddles

A curved slalom paddle can be used for most general types of canoeing although for touring on flat water only, spooned racing paddles may be preferred.

Clothing

In this country canoeing clothing can range from a pair of swimming trunks, through to a 6mm full wet suit with hood, such is the nature of our climate and the type of canoeing undertaken. Personal preference also plays a large part in the choice, as indeed does the level of the canoeists personal performance.

Canoeing requires the top half of the body to be as un-restricted as possible, but what is suitable clothing for a skilled canoeist on a particular day, may not be suitable for a novice. The expert will have arrived at the right clothing for his branch of the sport through experimentation and personal preference.

With fairly warm water, hot weather and dry clothes nearby, the canoeist could well wear just swimming trunks. One must guard however against the problem of sunburn, glare off the water and possible hyperthermia. As the sun goes down it may be necessary to put a jumper on to keep the paddler comfortably warm. Any further drop in temperature, or if there were any wind, then a waterproof anorak, or 'cag', would be the next line of defence.

The anorak is a fundamental piece of equipment. It needs to be wind and waterproof, and of single skin construction so that it does not absorb water, and dries quickly. If in doubt about the size, go for the larger one, since freedom of movement is all important for the paddling action, and you may wish to build up extra layers underneath in cold conditions. A close fitting, but comfortable, neck is required. This applies equally to the cuffs. Neoprene cuffs provide warmth round the wrist and the minimum of water is allowed to run up the arms.

As conditions become colder it will be necessary to put extra layers of clothing under the anorak. Although the spraycover helps to keep the legs warm, some covering on the legs will be necessary, and a pair of waterproof over-trousers are a useful addition. Remember to keep the head and back of the neck warm. Synthetic fibre-pile thermal clothing is good for canoeing, since it lasts well, remains warm when wet, and dries out quickly. However the material is not in itself windproof.

Wet-suits are popular with many canoeists for cold conditions, though less so with competitors as the paddling action may be restricted. They are particularly suitable for anybody learning white water skills or touring, in winter conditions, where swimming in cold water is likely. A wet-suit performs well under these circumstances in keeping you warm, provides extra personal buoyancy, and cushions the blows that may be received from rocks. In very cold conditions it is advisable to wear an anorak over a wet-suit, to minimise the chilling effect of the wind. Most canoeists find the full wet-suit with arms very tiring to paddle in and therefore the long-john is quite popular. You will probably need to wear a jumper and cag with the long-john, to keep your arms warm. Various combinations to suit individual preference are to be found, such as wet-suit vest or wet-suit trousers worn with other clothing on the upper body. 3mm neoprene is usually sufficient.

Tins, sharp stones and broken glass are all hazards to be found at the water's edge, on banks, and on tracks down to the water. Training shoes, or plastic sandals over wet suit boots are a sensible precaution.

In very cold conditions the head must be kept warm, and a woolly hat or wet-suit hood are suitable. Canoeists have been experimenting for years with keeping the hands warm. Some manage to paddle in gloves, but these tend to make it difficult to grasp the shaft of the paddle effectively. There are some good commercial solutions to the problem, including a 'glove' that attaches to the paddle. Some have found that rubber gloves, or wet-suit mittens with the palm cut out are effective.

It is very important that a person in charge of a group does not fall victim to cold conditions. In this position he may well find himself relatively inactive whilst watching others, and might have to enter the water to assist a canoeist in difficulty. Therefore, either wear clothing able to cope with this demand, or have dry clothing readily available.

PLANNING A JOURNEY

There are many factors which come into play when planning river trips, be they short one-day journeys, or camping expeditions, and it is not possible to produce an order of importance. The strength and ability of the group acts as the starting point. Consideration must be given to the time of year, the prevailing conditions of the water, and the weather, the equipment available, the presence or absence of a land support party, and the ability and experience of the instructor in charge. What are the aims and purpose of the trip? What do you really hope to achieve? Having taken these factors into account, the planning can start — where, when and for how long the journey will be.

Once a decision is made, carefully study the maps, sort out access arrangements, check out lunch stops or campsites, plan the distance to be covered each day, and of course look for suitable places to abort the trip should an emergency arise. It is desirable, but not essential, that the leader has canoed the route previously.

Background details

Whenever you are in charge of a group that is not known to you, it is advisable to get written permission from parents of any member of the party under 18 years. You should be satisfied beyond all reasonable doubt that all members of the group can swim. You are also responsible for their safety and well being and you should check through their kit, and pay particular attention to items of equipment that could affect the safety of the individual or group. If possible check canoeing equipment before the trip so that there is time to carry out any necessary repairs. A further check will be necessary just before getting on the water, and also test the fitting of lifejackets or buoyancy aids.

The next stage is to supply all members of the group with the information that they require: an equipment list, transport arrangements and times, what to expect en route. Depending on the nature of the journey this could require just a phone call, a duplicated sheet, or a full evening meeting. The less that you know about the group, the more thorough you need to be with the briefing. You may well wish to take a strange group on the water beforehand, to check on their canoeing ability and the capsize drill.

Transport

Transporting the canoes and paddlers to the start, and collecting them at the finish, needs to be well thought out. If a spouse, parent or friend, can be persuaded to act as 'support crew', this is the ideal. Various 'access' points en route can be planned in advance, and the group's progress monitored, besides help being at hand, should an emergency arise. The support driver can then ferry any other drivers back to the start at the end of the trip. This prevents delays at the commencement of the journey, when two cars have to be driven to the finish, and both drivers return in one, before canoeing can begin.

Organisation on the water
Before getting on the water, instructions should be given on what the system will be on the water and what signals will be involved. Here is a suggested series:

Stop and wait	Hand up
Move right or left	Hand moving in that direction
Go faster	Hands revolving around each other
Slow down	Hands moving down
Turn round	One hand – circular motion
Get on to the bank	Hand pointing
Your turn to come down	Hand beckoning
Well done	Thumb up
Lousy	Thumb down (if necessary!)

Courtesy to other river users is expected. Where there is traffic, it is usual to keep to the righthand side, but watch for anglers, and move out away from lines. In fast flowing streams, pass on the far side, or wait until the angler indicates that it is convenient to go through.

When approaching weirs or rapids, everyone should pull into the bank until the leader has inspected (if necessary), explained the route and made any necessary safety arrangements. Then organise the party through one at a time. For easy rapids, or 'safe' weirs known to the leader, it may simply be a matter of sending a competent helper down to demonstrate the route, and everyone following, ensuring that there is sufficient space between paddlers to allow for mistakes. For larger groups it is advisable to intersperse the group with other competent people, as the 'route' tends to become lost by novices following one another.

Once on the water the group leader must not only look to the safety of the group but to their enjoyment of the sport as well. Sheltered lunch stops, individual encouragement, pointing out things of interest, spotting potential hazards well in advance, and a cheerful presence, contribute to the safe enjoyable trip.

Stay alert, because there can be potential hazards on even the simplest of trips. Examples would be overhanging trees, rapids, weirs, shallows, mud banks, difficult access and egress points, fishermen and fishing lines, bridges, islands in the river, repair and maintenance work, reeds, other river weed, other river users, pollution, floating objects like logs and swans. In addition, the elements themselves cause problems, and not just rivers in spate, and cold weather, but strong gusty winds can cause havoc with a group. Tackling a rapid with the sun in the eyes is difficult.

Tail end Charlie

A golden rule is to appoint a 'tail end Charlie'. This person must be a competent canoeist for the situation, and never – but *never* – arrives at a point on the river with another member of the party out of sight behind him.

Equipment

Many a potentially dangerous situation has been rendered harmless because the leader of the trip has had the necessary emergency equipment to hand.

The risk of hypothermia (exposure) is always prevalent in Great Britain, even in mid-summer, and must be guarded against. The minimum requirement is to carry an exposure bag, and for colder conditions the addition of a sleeping bag is advised. A method of providing a hot drink is essential and some dry warm clothing. There are some very good single-skin survival units, which for a group that does a lot of expedition work in cold conditions, would be worthwhile. All can climb inside for lunch, or whilst waiting during the 'ferry' arrangements.

On the Continent whilst hypothermia must still be allowed for, there can also be a risk of dehydration and hyperthermia (heatstroke). It is advisable when planning a journey on the Continent in mid-summer, to take plenty of drink along. Often there is not easy access to shops once a journey is under-way.

In early summer particularly, Continental rivers are often composed of melted snow, with a consequent contrast between air and water temperature. This is difficult to allow for, and speed of rescue is vital.

A first aid kit, suitable for the time of year and the trip being undertaken is essential. Obviously the longer the trip, the more remote the area, the more comprehensive it needs to be. The most common complaints are: blisters, splinters, cuts, headaches, insect bites and sunburn in the summer. You may have to deal with a dislocation or a broken bone, however.

Another requirement is a repair kit, and wonders have been performed with adhesive plastic tape. The most difficult conditions in which to repair a canoe are when it is very cold, raining and with a gusty wind. Tape will not stick well to a cold wet boat so you will need some method of drying and warming the area to be taped. This can be done by pouring on methylated spirits and lighting it, with interesting results on occasions. A safer and more effective method of drying a damaged canoe is a small gas blowlamp, but you will need to carry matches which must be kept dry.

For a member of the party to break a paddle is not uncommon, so you will need a spare pair of split paddles in your boat. One pair to every four paddlers should be sufficient.

There are several good commercial throwlines available. However a small plastic bottle with some water in it, tied to a length of 6mm diameter floating rope will serve adequately. The weight of water in the bottle will help take the line out and also float on the water for the casualty to grab. A 100' line (8mm is even better) and float is an essential item.

An ordnance survey 1:25,000 map of the area is invaluable should an emergency arise, and help be needed quickly. A torch is a useful addition, particularly in the winter, together with a whistle.

All the kit in the world is only as good as the leader's ability to use it, and so practise is essential. Keep all emergency equipment packed and together when it is not in use, and in this way nothing is forgotten. Check for deterioration from time to time, and always take the opportunity to see what others have got, as canoeists are wonderfully inventive people. Encourage the attitude of self-sufficiency with all those who look like making canoeing a lasting hobby.

Other factors

No matter how well the basic preparation has been carried out, in the final analysis it is the conditions prevailing on the day that decide whether or not the plan is to be put into operation, curtailed, or cancelled.

On large lakes and reservoirs the existence of strong winds can create 'sea canoeing' hazards. In mountainous areas, the water temperature is often very low even in mid-summer. It would be advisable, if there is doubt about even a single member of the group, that canoeing was restricted to a shore onto which the wind was blowing. Provided the waves are not of a height to be dangerous, and this would be unlikely, and can be visually assessed, the worst that should then happen is a few capsized with everyone blown ashore.

When rivers are in 'spate', their character can change dramatically. The speed of the stream increases, canoeable weirs become places of danger, or for the expert only, and rapids increase their grading. Any obstruction in the water – trees, bridges and so forth – become sites where the unwary drown by being pinned against the obstacle, unable to move, and usually held just under water.

If, therefore, it is, or has been, raining hard, the river is muddy, swirling along and up to the top of the banks, great caution must be exercised.

An instructor's job is never finished —
Even after everyone is safely home the leader's job is not necessarily done. There may be letters of thanks to write where appropriate, and possibly arrangements to be made for the maintenance of equipment. If there have been any access problems you will need to contact the River Adviser.

RESCUES

The rescues described in chapter 10 are applicable to inland situations, although on a long rapid it will usually be necessary to tow a capsized paddler and his canoe at right angles to the current, into the nearest eddy, and empty the boat when ashore.

Insufficient attention is paid generally by canoeists touring on wild water to the necessity for packing a boat with buoyancy. It is a simple statement of fact that there is no situation in kayaking which is not rendered safer by having all available space taken up with buoyancy material. The less water that can enter a boat, the more quickly it can be emptied, the higher it floats, the more easily it is handled when swamped, and the less chance there is that it will become a 'write-off' through being pinned against an obstacle by the pressure of water.

A person who capsizes in a rapid should endeavour to grab hold of the paddle and upstream end of the canoe and swim with it, across the current, to the most suitable bank. Alternatively, slide the canoe across the downstream shoulder until the hands are on each side of the cockpit. Kick the legs strongly and lift the canoe as clear from the water as possible, at the same time pushing harder with the near hand, so that the boat flips over and lands the right way up. Then take hold of an end and shove the canoe into a suitable eddy, before swimming, with the paddle, to the side.

The carrying of a tow-line can also be a critical aid at times. It is particularly important that this is capable of quick attachment and immediate release, to avoid being taken into places where you have no wish to go. A tow-line should be carried in a manner that would not allow it to snag on an obstruction in fast moving water.

Stopper Rescues

'Stoppers' are created wherever water drops suddenly over an obstruction, be it a couple of inches over a rock, or hundreds of feet. There is a 'stopper' at the foot of every weir, and the forces creating them are described in chapter 4.

How to rescue someone held by a 'stopper' (known to water engineers as a 'hydraulic jump') is essential knowledge for the white water canoeist.

Many varied and devious ideas have been promulgated, and theories expounded. So much depends on the particular circumstances however: the size and severity of the 'stopper', the extent and strength of the reverse surface flow (known as 'back-tow'), whether there is a natural break in the stopper that will release objects, the depth of the water, and the nature of the river down-stream.

Figure 8:19 *'Digging' out of a stopper by use of a draw stroke.*

In a simple situation it may well be that the paddler can 'dig' his own way out by leaning well down-stream with a high draw, reaching the paddle deep into the flow, or work his way along to a natural 'break'. Where a 'stopper' is angled, this will inevitably be at a point down-stream. Natural stoppers on rivers are more likely to disgorge in this way than are stoppers on weirs. If the down-stream end of an angled stopper finishes against a wall, this could make it extremely dangerous.

If the paddler is unable to 'dig' his way out, and is not disgorged by a natural break, it may be that the leader or a more competent paddler, can 'barge' him out by dropping over the ledge and into the canoeist, broadside, from above. It is necessary to aim to finish up with your body just behind the body of the trapped person in order to avoid a clash of arms, heads and paddles. This should knock the trapped canoeist out and down-stream, leaving the more able performer to paddle or roll out. Even if the effort does not push the first canoeist out, the chances are that the two canoes together will come out more easily than one.

There is a risk in this manoeuvre of the rescuer's boat sliding under the victim's boat initially, and a buoyancy aid is therefore vital to protect the body. It would be foolish for the only competent paddler in a group to risk this move if there was a chance of his not being able to extract himself afterwards!

Another alternative has been mentioned. That is, for the canoeist stuck in a stopper to capsize, when the drag of the undertow on his body may pull him clear. Once out, he rolls up and continues down-stream.

If the above methods are not practical, but the tow-back does not make things impossible, a competent canoeist can approach from downstream, holding himself against the flow so as not to be taken right into the stopper, and present his bow to the victim. Once this is grasped the rescuer then back-paddles hard and pulls the trapped paddler free.

It may be that sufficient control is available to go in backwards and thus present the stern to the victim. This allows for far more power to be applied by the rescuer, who is now able to paddle forwards to release the trapped person. This process can be aided if necessary by

149

Figure 8:20 *Once the rescuer's bow has been grasped by the victim, other craft can raft across the towing canoe in the downstream flow, to assist with the pull.*

other canoeists 'rafting' broadside across the downstream end of the rescuer's boat. Provided the surface flow at that point is down-stream clear of the back-tow, the added drag will help to pull the victim free. Any number, almost, can be added in this way! But be careful of what is down river.

If tow-lines are carried (and they should be) a variation on this, and a possibility in a more serious situation with a lot of back-tow could be that the rescuer is attached to one or two other paddlers, who are then able to remain well in the down-stream flow, and ease the rescuer back onto the victim. Once he has grasped the rescuer's stern or bow, a great deal of effort can then be applied to pull him free.

It has often been said that when swimming in a stopper, the buoyancy aid should be removed, and the trapped person should dive, in order to be caught by the undertow and carried well down-stream, before coming up away from the surface back-tow. Those who have been involved in large, man-eating stoppers, will say, however, that it is impossible in that situation to know which way is up and which is down. Others would also be very dubious about removing a buoyancy aid in heavy water. If this is to be a serious consideration, however, a zipped buoyancy aid is vital.

Some of the rescue methods suggested for a canoeist could be tried, or the line and float used. In this instance, attach a buoyancy aid to the end, get as close as possible, and aim with an underhand throw just upstream of the victim. With the turbulence of the stopper it is often impossible for a swimmer to recognise when his hand touches the float.

The only advice that can be given to prepare people for this best-avoided eventuality is, if trapped in a large stopper, relax and attempt to work along the wave, breathing where possible.

Once a person is being carried downstream holding onto a line, be very careful to pay the line out gently so as not to hold them too hard against the current, when they will be forced under. Allow them to swing across the river downstream of you, until safely in an eddy.

When swimming free down a rapid, endeavour to travel feet first, using back strokes to control direction. A line thrown to a person being so carried, should be aimed just downstream of them.

Swimming in heavy water

In heavy conditions, such that it is not possible to swim with your boat to the bank, but with a rescuer at hand, it is often useful to hold on to your canoe for a while. Initially, it may help to pull you clear of stoppers. If you have hold of your boat, there is less chance of being hit on the head by it, and the canoe gives support while swimming. However, it is unlikely that a single paddler could tow you and your boat together to the bank in these conditions, but try and keep hold of your paddle, as this does not affect towing, and is difficult to find afterwards.

In big, technical water (grade VI, V and even IV) the boat, paddle and paddler are often separated by the water immediately. Survival is what matters. There is probably little anyone else on the water can do, and so the swimmer must be prepared to extract himself from the situation. Try to relax, and conserve energy. Do not struggle to keep your head above water all the time — allow the current to carry you under, but take big breaths when you surface. Keep your feet well up. Nasty accidents have occurred where swimmers have had their legs trapped between unseen boulders. Try and keep your head upstream and swim on your back. In this way, legs and backside (which should be protected by a wet-suit) take any knocks. If you do manage to get on to the back of a rescue boat, try to paddle with your hands, and keep your feet up, to make the task possible for the rescuer.

Practise makes a difference when it really matters — do not miss the opportunity therefore if you are at Augsburg at any time!

Avoiding obstacles

The worst hazard of all in moving water is to become entangled with a fallen tree. This is followed, in degree of calamity, with becoming wrapped around a single, narrow stanchion. In both of these cases, the safest remedy is to evacuate immediately. If, in spite of every effort to avoid the situation it has become obvious that a collision is inevitable, the following factors are critical.

Figure 8:21 *Fallen trees must be avoided at all costs. The above diagram was originally reproduced in* White Water Magazine.

If the obstruction is a rock or a horizontal tree, *throw* your bodyweight onto the obstacle, *at all costs keep your hull, and not the cockpit, presented to the flow.* If there is any danger of your not being able to maintain this position, immediately climb out onto the tree. Alternatively, work your way along, leaning hard onto the tree all the time, until able to pivot round the end and paddle free. For a rock, shunt your weight hard forwards or backwards (depending on the circumstances) and endeavour to 'wriggle' the boat free. If, however, you start to be overcome by the pressure, and feel the boat wrapping around, or you are being capsized upstream, and cannot contain the situation, evacuate immediately.

Should a collision with a single stanchion in heavy water be inevitable, it is best to be capsized upstream, so that the leg joints are stressed naturally, and control of them can be exercised. For a double obstruction — ie each end of the canoe held — the capsize must be downstream, otherwise the legs will be thrown up into the face as the canoe folds. Many boats are intended to break just ahead of the cockpit in these circumstances, thus freeing the occupants, but this is a factor that cannot be guaranteed.

To free a jammed canoe

There is such a variety of possible ways in which a boat could be trapped against an obstacle by pressure of water, that one or two basic principles only will be enumerated.

The cockpit needs to be turned downstream, thus, as the boat lifts clear, water will flow out, and the weight correspondingly decrease. There is no point in attempting to pull directly against the current. The boat should be lifted straight up, or dragged across the river, to clear the obstacle.

It may be better to attach ropes, which will allow the maximum of available effort to be applied from the bank, rather than a few people struggling to maintain balance on slippery rocks in fast flowing water. Look for the direction in which the boat is most likely to move, thus making use of the water's force, and pull in that direction. By attaching the line to a tree, and then pulling at right angles to that line from its centre, a considerable leverage advantage can be gained.

COACHING SESSIONS

Generally speaking, these are easier to organise than trips or expeditions, because they usually take place in one particular spot. If it is a fairly inexperienced group you will almost certainly have to teach from the water. Teaching a competent group might well be done from the bank, and you should organise a safety boat unless there are a number in the group capable of performing rescues. Whilst you should consider what emergency kit is available, it is seldom necessary to have such a comprehensive kit as required for a river trip. Neither is it usually necessary to carry it in your canoe.

Coaching an unknown group of young novices requires the greatest care. Firstly, decide what is to be done during the session. Decide what your aim is, and how it is to be achieved. Satisfy yourself as to the swimming ability of the group. Check the equipment, kayaks, fitting of buoyancy aids or lifejackets and give an initial briefing before getting on the water. Explain what they should do in the event of a capsize, define the limits within which they must canoe, and remember that the instructor should be first on, and last off the water. See chapter 12.

RIVER GRADING SYSTEM

A system of grading rivers has been devised so that canoeists have a common standard to go by when describing a river or section of water. The factors in identifying grading are shown in Table One in Chapter 6, page 122.

If one refers to a guide book e.g. *The BCU Guide to the Waterways of the British Isles* this will specify the grading given to different stretches of river or to major rapids. A person with a knowledge of the system will get a general indication as to the degree of difficulty he might encounter on a proposed expedition.

There are, however, reservations in considering the level of grading given in Guides:

1   Primarily it is a subjective system. One persons judgement will differ from another or may be affected by the observers canoeing ability.

2   Unfortunately, the *BCU Guide* is rather out of date. Changes in the river bed may have occurred due to either the passage of time, or man, building a weir, bridge or dam.

3   The performance of canoeists and boat designs have improved radically over the last twenty years. A rapid classified as grade IV then may now be considered an easy grade III.

4   The level or flow of water may drastically alter the grading of a river. A simple grade II rapid can become grade IV when the river is in spate. The change in water colour may make the route more difficult to discern. The increased speed of the river will give one less time to recover between one fall and the next. Flood conditions may also add temporary obstruction such as fallen trees blocking bridge arches.

ACCESS TO WATER

Access to water is the basic requirement for canoeing, but unlike the canoeist in Europe, in England and Wales we cannot paddle where and when we please.

The British Canoe Union is working for a fair share for canoeists. What can be achieved is greatly affected by the goodwill, or lack of it, between ourselves, riparian owners, and angling interests.

The law about trespass is different in Scotland and Northern Ireland, and it is important that canoeists from elsewhere obtain current information from the relevant National Association, as to the attitude that they should adopt.

Current legal position

Tidal waters.
Canoeists have the right to navigate waterways affected by the natural ebb and flow of the tides, although fees may be demanded where there are legally constituted harbour authorities, empowered through a byelaw to levy charges. There are a very few privately owned tidal stretches of river, where again payment may be asked, but where the right to navigate is firmly established. On Ordnance Survey maps, the tidal reaches of rivers are clearly indicated.

Navigations.
Canoeists have right of passage on rivers which are ancient navigations (eg Wye below Hay on Wye, Severn below Pool Quay). In many cases this right can only be exercised on

payment of tolls (eg Warwickshire Avon, Severn below Stourport, Thames, Surrey Wey). The right to navigate does not include the right to loiter, moor or land on private territory.

Canals.

Canoeists must obtain a canal licence (which will also cover them for British Waterways Board rivers).

Members can purchase licences at reduced rates through BCU.

NB *Negotiating locks.* The level of rivers is controlled by the installation of weirs. In order to bypass weirs, allowing boats to pass from one level to another, locks are necessary. It is usually quicker and safer to portage locks, and often the licence is cheaper. Should the lock be used, it is advisable to stay near the middle to avoid the turbulence as the water is let in or out. Be careful of other larger vessels which could crush a canoe.

Non-tidal Rivers

The riparian owner is usually the person who owns the adjoining bank. He owns the bed of the river to midstream, and the water whilst it is passing over it. Unless there is a public right of navigation, therefore, the passage of a boat over the river bed, without his permission, is equivalent to walking over his private land without permission. Unless the river bed has passed into the ownership of someone else, as does happen from time to time, he owns the right to take fish from his stretch, although these 'fishing rights' can also be sold or sub-let.

'Disturbance to fishing' can be a cause for legal proceedings in the civil courts and a case on the river Wharfe, which went to appeal, has set an unfortunate precedent in accepting that the passage of a canoe does disturb the right to fish even when no one is actually fishing. There is, as yet, no scientific evidence one way or the other. It is possible to establish a legal right of passage through long, uninterrupted use, but this is no mean task. In England and Wales the period is for 20 years, and in Scotland for 40.

It is usually necessary to cross private land in order to launch or disembark and permission, in this case, must be obtained from the landowner, unless there is a public right of way.

The position in practice

Current practice on private waters is to seek the permission of known objectors. When planning a river trip, members should contact the relevant BCU river adviser well in advance, sending a stamped, addressed envelope for the reply. The list of river advisers can be obtained (by members only) from the BCU headquarters. Information is also made available as it comes to hand, through the house journal *Canoe Focus*.

The river adviser will recommend if the trip should go ahead or not, and members must abide by what he or she says. An alternative time may be suggested, according to the fishing season, or the fact that angling is better early and late in the day, by the frequency of other canoeing parties on the river, or by water levels. Advisers will give details of any agreements in force, and of persons to whom prior application must be made for permissions. Advice may be given on access and egress points, and on the size and conduct of the party.

Should a bailiff, angler or other person, lodge an objection at any time, always try politely to talk him round in the first instance. If there is a possibility of making an agreement, it is essential to obtain the name, address and authority of the person concerned, the details of his permission/objection, and the boundaries of the stretch of river concerned. On a private river you will probably be in the wrong legally, and may be requested to make your way to a public highway. The police are not concerned usually unless there is a risk of a breach of the peace.

The river adviser then needs to be informed, as every report could be useful. Other matters, such as a tree that has fallen, or another unexpected hazard, should also be detailed.

Future Policy

The Union's approach may appear to be passive, but much hard work is being done at local and national level to secure a fair share for canoeists. Even more remains to be done, and the BCU is in consultation with such bodies as the Sports Council, the Water Authorities, the Country Landowners Association, the National Anglers' Council, the Water Space Amenities Commission, and the Central Council for Physical Recreation.

Evidence was submitted to a Select Committee of the House of Lords, and points worthy of mention from their report are:

(Para 35) *The legal question of rights of way over water must be settled.*

(Para 204) *Good management of facilities can extend their use. It can overcome the conflicts that sometimes arise between incompatible sports and it can produce far more co-operation than would come from a free-for-all. Sharing may take the form of zoning, dividing the use of water on a time basis, allocating a prime use, restriction on the number of users and so on.*

(Para 209) *Solutions are hardest to reach on certain privately owned waters where fishing has long assumed importance. If these solutions are to be reached the only feasible means will be by voluntary agreement, for coercion is out of the question.*

(Para 210) *In August 1972 ... it was the Government's intention to set out in legislation clear rights for the public in suitable craft and in a suitable manner to navigate all commercial and cruising waterways. In the particular case of private waterways to which the Wharfe appeal related, the law should also be such that equitable sharing arrangements between users can be negotiated.*

There is no sign yet that the Government will take up the Committee's Report as the basis for new legislation, but in the meantime we have the task of publicising the requirements of canoeists, so they are properly considered when the time comes. This may mean some payment and/or registration system, but the BCU adopts the principle that such arrangements would only be acceptable in return for a fair share of water space, and if the cost reflects the amenity enjoyed by the canoeists.

In the short term, Access agreements continue to be negotiated on the best arrangements obtainable. It is important that agreements are not entered into on a private piecemeal local basis. The BCU Access Committee should be involved, through the National or Regional Access Officer, so that the local negotiator can act in accordance with national policy. An arrangement that may look good in a limited local sense, could estabiish a dangerous precedent. Before conclusion, any agreement should be referred to the Regional Access Officer. The third-party insurance cover so very often required by the riparian owners is included as part of BCU membership.

Militant action is favoured by some individuals, but this is out of place. There are grounds for cautious optimism that canoeists will get a fairer share of water on a more clearly defined basis. A firm but reasonable approach has been adopted with a view to bringing this about as soon as possible. Success depends to a large extent upon the help and support that members and other canoeists give. We also need to win the sympathy of public opinion. Canoeists must make people aware that citizens do not enjoy a fair share of limited water resources in order to follow a healthy open air sport and recreation. The situation is developing all the time, which makes it necessary to keep up to date.

9 Sea Canoeing

Derek C. Hutchinson

Derek Hutchinson lives in South Shields and has been a school teacher since 1961. He attended South Shields Marine and Technical College, Durham Technical College and the Newcastle College of Art and Industrial Design. As a British Canoe Union Senior Coach he is now well established as an expert on Sea Kayaking.

His book Sea Canoeing, *published by A & C Black, now in it's 2nd edition, is sold all over the world and is accepted as an authoritative work on the subject. He contributed the Sea Canoeing chapter in* Canoeing Complete *published by Kaye Ward.*

He has led many advanced sea kayak expeditions. In 1975 he organised the first attempt to cross the North Sea in unescorted solo eskimo kayaks. It proved unsuccessful, but the following June, in kayaks of his own design, he and two others made the non-stop crossing in 31 hours. In 1978 he went to the Aleutian Islands where he organised and led a five man kayak expedition from Dutch Harbour on Unalaska Island, along one of the ancient Aleut baidarka routes, to the village of Nikolski, on Umnak Island.

In 1980 he designed the 'Ice Floe' sea kayak and this was the design used by the members of his expedition to explore the islands of Prince William Sound. During their 300 mile journey, the group paddled among the whales of the Sound, and filmed them. In all, Derek has designed five sea kayaks as well as a surf kayak and an open Canadian canoe. He travels extensively around the country, lecturing on his expeditions, advising on the general subject of sea canoeing and as a Senior Coach, training and assessing at the highest level.

INTRODUCTION

This is not meant to be a complete work on sea canoeing. That has been dealt with elsewhere, viz. *Sea Canoeing* 2nd Edition, by Derek C. Hutchinson, published by Adam & Charles Black, and *Sea Touring,* by J.J. Ramwell, published by the author. Nor is it meant to teach Seamanship, Navigation and Meteorology although all these subjects should be studied by anyone who intends to venture onto the sea in *any* boat of *any* size.

What I have aimed to do is to give some basic and necessary information and to point people in the right direction. I have tried to give some wider implications of the group leader's responsibilities as well as the obvious ones, an outline of the equipment needed, some of the basic techniques as applied to the coaching of sea canoeing and some aspects of group discipline and safety.

Some Responsibilities of the Leader /Coach

Because of the liaison that members of the sport have had with HM Coastguard and the good relations which have been built up with other rescue bodies, kayaking on the sea is held in much higher regard now than it used to be. However, there are still sections of the general public who regard the kayak as something of a toy, the seaworthiness of which they think lies somewhere below that of a small sailing dinghy. To help dispel any such notions, the group leader should set an example, having special regard to his equipment and general demeanour and having the foresight to realise what his wider responsibilities should be. He must think of himself not so much as a sportsman but rather as the master of a small vessel. This is not so absurd as it may first sound, when one considers what the experienced sea canoeist has to offer.

As a group leader, his main consideration is the safety and wellbeing of those who follow him. His concern for their safety should outweigh all other considerations. However, if it is possible for him to act without placing his group in any danger, then he must accept the fact that he also has responsibilities to others who share the open sea with him. It need not be only the users of small boats with whom he comes into contact. It could be water skiers, skin divers or the occupants of quite large boats. In some parts of the country, even rock climbers and those attempting to hang-glide may find themselves in the sea. The experienced sea canoeist who holds a coaching award is a highly trained operative who possesses the skill and facility to offer relief to many people in many different ways.

He carries distress flares and rockets which he can pass on to others or use on their behalf.

He can use his first aid kit to assist other small boat users and he might use his repair kit to assist with small engine repairs such as the sealing of a leaky fuel pipe.

He is trained in life saving and is proficient in at least one method of resuscitation and also carries the means of assisting those suffering from exposure. If necessary it would be possible for the canoeist to leave his kayak and board another larger craft.

He carries a compass, and in dense fog could act as a guide for less prudent water users.

He is able to navigate close inshore and among rocks, thus allowing him to offer relief to any cliff-fall victim.

He carries a tow-line. Any small vessel with engine failure could have its drift towards rocks, slowed or even halted by a strong paddler.

The lifejacket or buoyancy aid worn by the canoeist could be taken off and given to someone in greater need.

In the event of some small boat sinking, a kayak could be the means of supporting a large number of people if they were equally distributed around the gunwale.

Any one trapped in a large expanse of dangerous mud, could be assisted by a man using a kayak for support.

To sum up, the presence on the sea of a calm, experienced and well equipped man in a craft as seaworthy and as versatile as a custom built sea kayak, should be an asset and a comfort to all other water users. I have purposely excluded those specialist skills and rescues used by the Corps of Canoe Life Guards and have used as my subject the experienced sea canoeist who is also a Senior Instructor or Coach.

EQUIPMENT

Sea Kayaks

There are a number of very fine kayaks on the market in Britain today although there are also a number of kayaks of poor design. You might not be able to try them all but you can ask people who paddle particular kayaks what they think of them. I would also suggest choosing a boat that has been designed by a practising sea canoeist.

Two main types of sea kayak are now popular. The 'day boat' for coastal work and for the canoeist who does not want a boat which is too specialised. This type can be as short as 15 feet and have a slightly rockered hull. The other type is the specialised expedition boat. These are much longer, and have straighter keels, which give them more directional stability, and plenty of room to carry large amounts of expedition equipment. The cockpit of any sea boat should not be too large and it should have a good wide coaming upon which

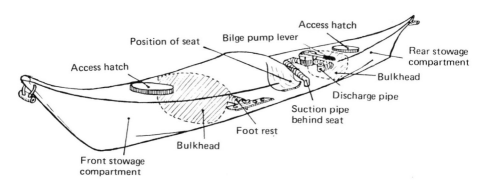

Figure 9:1 *The modern sea kayak shape, showing position of hatches, pump and bulkheads.*

the spray cover can make a watertight seal. The bow can either be straight, curved or clipper, depending on your fancy, but it should be powerful enough to cope with an oncoming sea. All kayaks should be fast enough to enable the paddler to get out of trouble quickly or to make headway against fast tidal streams and have enough buoyancy to float high out of the water even when turned on their side.

The greatest innovation in recent years has been the introduction of watertight hatches and bulkheads which makes the present day expedition kayak virtually unsinkable. Swamped boats were very difficult to empty at one time when fully loaded with equipment. Now little effort is needed, and rescues can be done quickly, as most expedition kayaks have small pumps fitted. These can be placed behind and to the side of the cockpit, and worked by a hand lever, or they can be situated inside the boat and operated by foot. Bulkhead compartments still need to contain positive buoyancy. Hatch covers must be tied in. An additional elastic over them gives double security.

Slalom kayaks fitted with a detachable skeg – a directional fin – can be quite adequate for sea work, but wild water racing kayaks are rather unstable.

Where non-specialist sea boats are used, careful thought must be given to making them sea-worthy. Opaque red and yellow is best for visibility. The buoyancy should fill all available space, apart from the cockpit. Deck lines should be fitted, which must be taut and not allowed to foul the cockpit area, besides toggles at each end. A paddle-park, consisting of either a length of shock-cord across the foredeck, or a length of line or thin shock-cord equipped to hook around the paddle, which is then left floating, is a necessity.

Some instructors, particularly when dealing with groups on their first outing on the sea, prefer to use more manoeuvrable and inherently stable boats. The 'general purpose' slalom kayak – not the modern low-volume type – lends itself to this when adapted as above.

Paddles

Like the kayaks the paddles are a personal choice. Paddles are available which are designed specifically for sea use. The blade is longer and narrower than the conventional type, but the surface area is the same. Spare paddles should always be carried at sea and should be of the type normally used by the canoeist. All paddles should be well maintained with paint or varnish if this is necessary.

Spray Covers

Make sure your group all have good serviceable spray covers with release straps or loops. Persuade them on serious journeys, to wear two, with the oldest one underneath. Some rescues, especially the 'T' Rescue can damage spray covers, so before starting the rescue take the top one off, then in the event of any ripping the cockpit can still be made watertight.

Emergency Gear

Each member of a sea canoeing group on expedition should carry in his boat at least a basic emergency kit, to cover both first aid and repairs to the kayak. These kits should be carried inside the boats in a position where they are easily accessible.

A basic repair kit should enable you to repair a split kayak, life jacket, spray cover or a buoyancy bag. As your experience increases so will the items in your kit.

The first aid kit should (at least), include assorted waterproof plasters, tweezers, scissors, pliers (for extracting fish hooks among other things), a few pieces of toilet paper and a little money for those *real* emergencies viz. Public Transport, Public Houses, Public Conveniences and Ice Cream.

The leader must carry a large polythene exposure bag and a sleeping bag, and his group members a change of clothing and some dry shoes in a watertight bag, a nourishing drink and something to stave off the pangs of hunger, and an exposure bag.

Bags and Containers

So long as equipment is kept dry, it can be carried in almost any kind of bag or container that can be repeatedly opened and closed without damage. Bags can be made from ex-army groundsheets but good waterproof bags can also be bought. The containers used for transporting chemicals are also useful but care must be taken in making them watertight. Any equipment which is carried inside watertight compartments should also be packed in bags just in case bulkheads and hatches leak.

All bags and containers should be made secure so that in the event of a capsize they cannot float away from the boat or entangle the paddler in long untidy securing lines.

Any equipment which is stowed inside a kayak must not only be secure, it must also stay dry. The salt water which seeps into worn, badly tied or poorly repaired waterproof bags and ruins clothing, food supplies, and sleeping bags and cameras, could be fatally dangerous to those people involved in extended sea trips. It could also cause an intolerable burden to fall on the rest of the party. In a situation where individuals carry items of a specialist nature common for the rest of the group, (some examples would be medical supplies, cameras and film, radio equipment and in some cases, fire arms and ammunition) any loss or damage from whatever cause could blunt the efficiency of any group and may even put them in grave danger. Members of the coaching scheme should be aware of the far reaching effects of wet equipment, and the inability of any candidate to keep dry the few items needed for a day trip, should be viewed as a serious fault.

Clothing

Canoeing on the sea is a dry sport – eventually, but during the early learning stages or during the training for the various awards, it can be a damp and often wet one.

Novices should wear high waisted wet suit trousers or Long Johns. 3-4 mm neoprene is sufficient, which should be lined for ease of getting on and off. It is possible to buy the materials and glue one's own suit together, or purchase ready-made.

Specially designed thermal jerseys or vests are excellent, but any warm, comfortable clothing would do so long as it is all covered by a waterproof anorak. An anorak for the sea canoeist, modelled on the eskimo hunting smock is made. The availability of chest-high

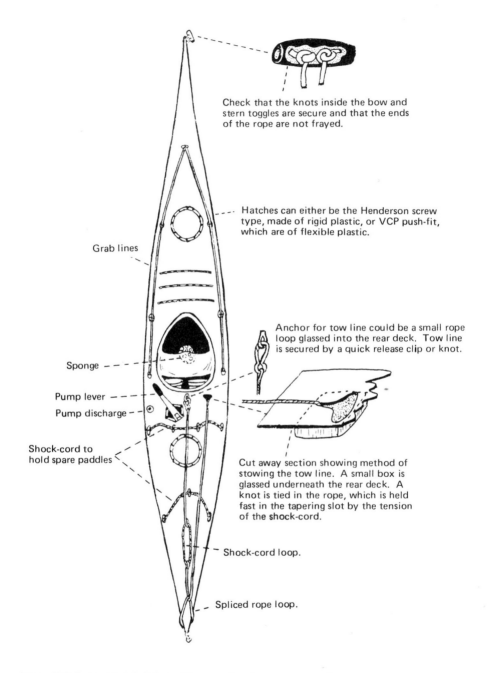

Check that the knots inside the bow and stern toggles are secure and that the ends of the rope are not frayed.

Hatches can either be the Henderson screw type, made of rigid plastic, or VCP push-fit, which are of flexible plastic.

Grab lines

Anchor for tow line could be a small rope loop glassed into the rear deck. Tow line is secured by a quick release clip or knot.

Sponge

Pump lever

Pump discharge

Shock-cord to hold spare paddles

Cut away section showing method of stowing the tow line. A small box is glassed underneath the rear deck. A knot is tied in the rope, which is held fast in the tapering slot by the tension of the shock-cord.

Shock-cord loop.

Spliced rope loop.

Figure 9:2 *A suggested deck layout for a sea kayak*

waterproof trousers can be an added comfort and safety factor, for wearing during meal breaks on journeys, and in cold conditions.

Full wet suit jackets can cause chafing and fatigue. If they are used, make very sure that there is plenty of room around the arm-pit, or better still make do without sleeves. A neoprene 'vest', covered by a thermal or other man-made fibre, or wool jersey is a good idea for winter paddling. The use of two medium-weight jerseys is recommended, rather than one thick one, allowing for better temperature control. This does not apply so much to thermal wear.

Feet should be protected from the cold and wet, but the footwear should be strong enough to enable you to wander happily on stones or over slippery surfaces when you land. Again, neoprene boots with oversize plimsolls or polythene sandals to protect them, are ideal.

Wear a hat, or at least carry one with you in case the weather turns cold. Brightly coloured crash helmets are useful for wearing when it is necessary to pull up anorak hoods. This maintains the paddler's vision, will not come off in an emergency, and aids detection.

Flares

Flares are part of a sea canoeist's normal paddling equipment. Carry them in a position where you can get at them in an emergency without removing your spray cover. Make two rockets and two hand flares the minimum if you are the leader, and encourage each member of your class to carry at least one distress signal.

Flares come in assorted types and sizes. To be recommended are those which fire high (approximately 1,000 feet) into the air and allow a starshell to float down slowly on a parachute. Hand flares are ideal to pinpoint your position once rescue is at hand.

Now available are flares which fire a cartridge about 100 feet in the air, but which do not require a fire-arms certificate. These are useful for pinpointing position, containing six to eight cartridges in a pack, although they are of dubious value in attracting attention in the first instance.

Smoke flares of a convenient size for a canoeist to carry do not give off enough smoke for high wind conditions.

White flares are *not* used for distress but to indicate your position, for example to prevent a collision in a busy shipping lane.

All flares carry an expiry date, so make a note of this inside any container you make to keep them in good condition. Paint these containers bright colours, and put your name and address inside.

In a case of emergency, do not hesitate to use flares. What people will say afterwards is no consideration as to whether or not you should send one off. If you think that any members of your group are, or are about to be in grave danger, send up a flare and don't wait until the last minute to summon help. It can take as much courage to send up a flare for outside help, as it can for some people to actually jump into the water and save somebody. Remember *the safety of the group is your first and main consideration*. The humiliation you may feel after having to call in the assistance of the gentleman from the RNLI or the criticisms of your 'friends', are just part of the burden of being a leader.

A good little exercise for a group, when they are out at sea, is to make the request 'Please hold a flare in your hand high in the air'. Then see who is last. They must not raft up of course while extricating them from the boats, or wherever else they may have hidden them.

Radios

A marine radio is an expensive piece of equipment, requiring a licence to operate, and with the price relative to its range and quality. Channel 6 is the 'ship to ship' frequency on which everyone chats, although strict RT (radio-telephone) procedure should be observed, and messages restricted to important items. Coastguard, port authorities, marine radio stations and others 'listen out' on channel 16, which is for calling and safety only. Other channels are used for organising rescue services.

The use of radio, or of emergency radio beacons, which broadcast, when activated, a constant distress signal on which rescuer's can 'home in', is a constantly developing field. Careful consideration and research is necessary before committing oneself to a purchase. The Advanced Sea Kayak Club is a good source of information on the subject.

TECHNIQUE

Of the basic paddle strokes used by all canoeists, some have particular application to sea canoeing, while others need a little modifying when used with long kayaks on the sea.

As far as technique is concerned, inshore 'rock dodging' can be classed with river slalom and surfing. In this chapter I am dealing only with deep sea techniques.

Forward Paddling

This is *the* basic stroke for any kind of sea canoeing and as you may have to do it for some considerable period of time, you may as well be comfortable while you do it. Most sea canoeists prefer some kind of soft firm back rest or support, thus emulating the Eskimos and making their seating position comfortable. Sea paddles are usually longer than those normally used inland so that the angle of the blade during the stroke can be much lower, giving a greater arc through the water and presenting a more acute angle with the upper blade, to any wind which might blow on the beam.

Unless the footrest is properly adjusted, efficient forward paddling is impossible. For the large exposed stretches of water involved in sea canoeing, the forward stroke should be strong, productive and economical. A weak forward paddling stroke is a sure sign of failure for a potential sea canoeist. Those who lead should be able to paddle long distances using only one paddle blade. Novices seldom carry spare blades at first and it is possible to have a number of breakages all at one time. Naturally, the leader will give up his own paddle if need be and use the broken one.

Reverse Paddling

It is often necessary for the leader of a group to fall back and check all is well with the stragglers at the rear. He or she should therefore be able to reverse paddle *fast* in rough conditions thus saving valuable time in an emergency. Groups should practise this in beam and following seas, in order to position quickly for rescues.

Paddle Brace

This is probably one of the most vital strokes in sea canoeing if one does not count the Forward Paddling stroke. The main use for the paddle brace of course is in surf. However, its application when paddling out at sea, in steep breaking beam waves is an important one, especially when paddling through a tidal race with white topped waves breaking continually upon one side. This would be a case for converting the basic paddle brace into what could be called a *mobile* paddle brace so that as you are paddling forwards and the wave is breaking onto you it is a simple matter to lean sufficiently into the wave to stop it knocking you over, angling the paddle blade, which is travelling rearwards, enough to support you but not enough to inhibit your forward stroke. When the paddle is at the end of the forward stroke near the stern of the kayak, the blade is no longer in a position to give support. The paddler could be vulnerable, so he must be ready to sweep the *back* of the same blade along the surface in the *low brace* position in case of any instability as the boat slips over and down the back of the passing wave.

Draw Stroke

This stroke is vital for the quick positioning of boats during deep water rescues. Insist that it is done well and with *determination* so that kayaks can be positioned *regardless of any chop on the surface of the sea*. Very often seconds count, especially with the Eskimo Rescue. It takes considerable strength to move a long kayak sideways against a beam wind. If, however, the stroke is helped by a high wind, it is all too easy for the boat to over-run the paddle blade and cause a capsize.

Turning the Kayak through 360 degrees

This is a very important manoeuvring stroke and not an easy one in a choppy sea with a strong wind blowing on the beam. The kayak is turned by *sweep strokes*; a reverse sweep stroke on one side and a forward sweep on the other. The paddle blade should be only just below the surface, the arm reaching out fully extended, the elbow only slightly bent. If the paddle blade is angled to give maximum support during the sweep, the kayak can be leaned *well* over, gaining an advantage from its width amidships, and thereby giving any long straight-keeled sea kayak a false rocker upon which to turn.

In beam seas created by high winds it is sometimes easier to perform three or four strong *reverse* sweep strokes (leaning the boat and allowing the wind to help blow you round) to start the boat moving. If this is timed carefully, approaching waves can be used to pivot the boat on.

Stern Rudder

The main application for this steering stroke is in surf or a following sea. The procedure for coping with the following sea should be explained to novices, so that capsizes and the resulting strain on your own nerves is kept to a minimum.

After a kayak has been overtaken by a wave it will be retarded in the trough. Forward paddling should then be eased off until the surge of the next wave is felt as the back of the kayak starts to lift. Full effort is used as the boat is pushed forward on the face of the wave. Once the boat is running, the stern rudder is applied to control the direction. If the waves are steep this can all be a little alarming to the inexperienced, so to combat any instability the back of the paddle blade can be trailed almost flat on the surface of the water behind the paddler.

Towing

Not only coaching members but any candidates for the BCU Advanced Sea Proficiency Test should also be able to tow their comrades to safety. Nobody enjoys towing, but one of your group could be exhausted or taken ill or injured. In such a case, getting them back to shore is of prime importance. Sometimes you may have to raft the patient up with someone else. This means you finish up towing two people back to land, an even less enjoyable task.

PLANNING A JOURNEY

With the aid of charts, tide tables, and tidal stream atlases, a journey can be planned a year ahead. It is the conditions which prevail on the day, that will determine whether it is to go ahead as planned, be revised, or cancelled altogether, however. The most accurate of weather forecasts is good for only up to six hours, and the immediate difference that increased wind strength, or the tide changing direction, can make, must be always foremost in one's mind.

The ability of the weakest member of the group is the factor which most governs the length of the trip, and the degree of commitment possible.

A knowledge of the coastline involved, and an understanding of the subjects which follow, is vital. Remember also that people have been known to become sea-sick in kayaks, to become affected by the sun's glare off the water, to become over-heated, or hypothermic, to lose their ability to balance following a capsize, or be taken ill. Never, therefore, undertake other than simple journeys with good escape routes, with unknown, untried or novice groups.

The average rate at which a small party of proficiency level candidates will travel is probably two knots plus the speed of the tidal stream. A strong head wind could drop this to one knot or less overall, and throw your estimated time of arrival (ETA) and subsequent estimated time of departure (ETD) into disarray. Your 'expedition base contact' therefore needs to be a person of sound judgment with an appreciation of the factors affecting sea journeys.

Preliminary information needs to be given, and permissions of parents sought, as advised under *Inland Canoeing* – Chapter 8. For sea journeys the ideal group should not contain more than 8-10 canoes, with a ratio of experienced paddlers to trainees as outlined in Appendix III.

Informing the Coastguard

HM Coastguard maintains a comprehensive lookout system right around the British Isles, although not every station is permanently manned. Responsible to the Government for the monitoring of all incidents off our coasts, requests for help from lifeboat or helicopter are made by them.

For any journey involving more than a local cruise along a sheltered coastline it is advisable to write out and give to the Coastguard concerned an expedition brief showing the names of the people involved, the types of boats, departure point and time, destination and estimated time of arrival, and the name and telephone number of the 'expedition base contact'. This must be a reliable person, who knows the details of your plan, has the names and addresses of all involved, and with whom you will communicate any change of plan. The 'base contact' **must alert the Coastguard** should you become seriously overdue. Contrary to popular belief, the Coastguard, who have many hundreds of passage reports from yachts and others to cope with, besides numerous other responsibilities, will not normally institute a search unless they are requested to do so. The 'expedition base contact' is therefore vital. Once the journey is over, the expedition leader, or the 'base contact' must inform the Coastguard, and should thank him for the surveillance and co-operation.

NAVIGATION

Navigation is a highly specialised subject and the more ambitious your sea canoeing the more you should know. The following aspects are particularly useful to the canoeist.

Charts

To plan any kind of adventurous sea trip you will need a chart, which is a map of the sea. Any chandlery will have a catalogue of Admiralty Charts covering the whole of the world's surface. There are three main groups: general charts on a small scale covering large areas, such as the English Channel, coastal charts of larger scale (1:75,000) and detailed charts of harbours and estuaries. Always quote the number as well as the title of the chart, when ordering.

There are also Stanford's Charts, which make more use of colour and include a tidal stream atlas of the area, which is a map on which arrows indicate the speed and direction of the tidal stream for each hour of the rise and fall of the tide.

A chart can be a little confusing at first glance because of all the tiny figures on the part of the map representing the sea, but these are only depth soundings. On older charts the soundings are given in fathoms and feet (one fathom equals six feet). Most charts now however are metric and have their soundings in metres and decimetres, eg 10_3 for 10.3 metres. All soundings on charts are taken from a point below which the tide is unlikely to fall, called the *chart datum*. This is the level of the *lowest astronomical tide*. Dry land is shaded a buff colour, but any area which is awash at high tide and *dries out* at low tide is coloured a nice seaweed green. These *drying heights* are also marked in metres and decimetres underlined, and show the height above the chart datum to which the area dries.

Obtain the little booklet entitled, *Symbols and Abbreviations – Chart 5011** you will find it invaluable.

Sudden differences in depths, drying heights and type of bottom – possibly indicating a long walk in deep mud at low tide – tidal races and overfalls, whirlpools, speed and direction of the tidal stream, types of shoreline, positions of buoys marking the navigation channels for large shipping, and conspicuous buildings is the information most relevant to a sea canoeist which is marked on a chart.

A long piece of thin fine chain can be used for laying on the chart to obtain distances. Its flexibility enables it to go in and out of small bays and around headlands. Only use a soft lead pencil, then any marks can be erased without leaving a deep impression.

Remember to measure distance by using the scale at the *side* of the chart, ideally in line with your position.

I find two set-squares easier to use than a parallel rule. Use good quality dividers with *fine* points – finger nail scratching on the edge of a torn off cigarette packet is not really setting a good example in equipment preparedness.

HMSO issue a series of *Pilot Books* for areas around the British Isles. They are filled with very detailed information, most of which is relevant to the sea canoeist and which is vital to the planning of trips in unfamiliar waters.

The Sea Touring Committee of the BCU maintains a panel of 'coastal advisers' who can give information on specific sections of coast. The obtaining of 'local knowledge' is a vital ingredient when planning a sea journey.

Ordnance Survey Maps

It is possible to plan coastal trips using only an OS map but you should have some local knowledge of the area and know the direction and speed of the tidal streams. OS maps should be used in conjunction with Admiralty Charts, and not alone. They are particularly useful in showing the position of telephone boxes, and pubs, etc!

---

* There is a complementary publication to Chart 5011 called *The Mariner's Handbook*.

Buoyage

The new system of buoyage is known as the IALA Buoyage System 'A'. Under the International Association of Lighthouse Authorities (IALA) system, due for completion around Britain at the end of 1981, there are five types of mark, which may be used in any combination:

Lateral Marks

These are either Red (port-hand) can-shaped buoys with a single red can as a top-mark (where fitted), and a red light of any rhythm (when fitted); or Green (starboard hand) conical or spar shaped, with a single green cone top-mark, pointed upwards (where fitted), and a green light of any rhythm (where fitted). These are generally still laid from seawards inwards in rivers and estuaries, marking well-defined channels. They follow a clock-wise direction around land masses when used in open water.

Basically, a canoeist should not cruise in a narrow channel marked by these buoys, and should, where necessary, cross such a channel at right angles.

Cardinal Marks

These are laid to indicate that the deepest water is on the *named* side of the mark, or which is the safe side to pass danger, eg a *North Cardinal Mark is passed to the north* (ie you must leave the mark *to the south* of you). A canoeist may well do the opposite, and so avoid being in an area which larger vessels are navigating.

North Cardinal Mark:

Topmark	–	2 black cones, one above the other, points upwards;
Colour	–	Black above yellow;
Shape	–	Pillar or spar;
Light (when fitted)	–	White, V.Qk.Fl.(b) or Qk.Fl.(c)

East Cardinal Mark:

Topmark	–	2 black cones, one above the other, base to base;
Colour	–	Black with a single broad horizontal yellow band;
Shape	–	Pillar or spar;
Light (when fitted)	–	White, V.Q.Fl.(3) every 5 sec. or Qk.Fl.(3) every 10 sec.

South Cardinal Mark:

Topmark	–	2 black cones, one above the other, points downward;
Colour	–	Yellow above black;
Shape	–	Pillar or spar;
Light (when fitted)	–	White, V.Qk.Fl.(6) + long flash(d) every 10 sec. or Qk.Fl.(6) + long flash(d) every 15 sec.

West Cardinal Mark:

Topmark	–	2 black cones, one above the other, point to point;
Colour	–	Yellow with a single broad horizontal black band;
Shape	–	Pillar or spar;
Light (when fitted)	–	White, V.Qk.Fl.(9) every 10 sec. or Qk.Fl.(9) every 15 sec.

Isolated Danger Marks

An isolated danger mark is a mark over an isolated danger which has navigable water all around it.

Topmark	–	2 black spheres, one above the other;
Colour	–	Black with one or more broad horizontal red bands;
Shape	–	Pillar or spar;
Light (when fitted)	–	White, Gp.Fl.(2).

Safe Water Marks:

Colour	–	Red and white vertical stripes;
Shape	–	Spherical, pillar with spherical topmark or spar;
Topmark (if any)	–	Single red sphere;
Light (when fitted)	–	White, Isophase, occulting or one long flash every 10 sec.

Safe water marks indicate that there is navigable water all round the mark; these include centre line marks and mid-channel marks. Such a mark may also be used as alternative to a cardinal or a lateral mark to indicate a landfall.

Special Marks:

Yellow. Not normally of interest to a canoeist unless used as a traffic separation mark where use of conventional channel marking may cause confusion, or, as is the case near where I live, where a yellow buoy marks the seaward extremity of an army firing range.

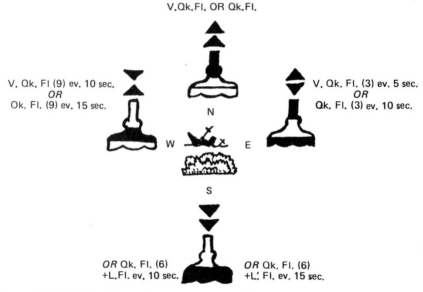

V.Qk.Fl. OR Qk.Fl.

V. Qk. Fl (9) ev. 10 sec.
OR
Ok. Fl. (9) ev. 15 sec.

V. Qk. Fl. (3) ev. 5 sec.
OR
Qk. Fl. (3) ev. 10 sec.

N

W   E

S

OR Qk. Fl. (6)
+L.Fl. ev. 10 sec.

OR Qk. Fl. (6)
+L. Fl. ev. 15 sec.

Figure 9:3 *Cardinal Marks. Lights when fitted are white*

In any case of doubt, it is of course possible to make for a buoy and wait there until a vessel has passed. One group, when 'threatened' by a 'Grey Funnel Line' ship (a RN Frigate) are reputed to have done just this, only to have the ship continue to bear down on them. Eventually they discovered that they had chosen her mooring buoy!

Beware of a fast tidal stream against a buoy – to be pinned against one could well be a drowning situation. This applies to any fixed object – eg moored boats – in fast moving water. Allow for the drift, and always aim to go behind the obstruction if there is any shadow of doubt. *Never attempt to race across in front of a large vessel.* 'Steam' has right of way in narrow channels, and quite apart from the personal danger involved, there is the risk to the ship should the pilot feel he has to try to take avoiding action. The chances of his being able to make a significant adjustment anyway, will often be nil.

As a ship turns, the stern sweeps round in a wide arc. Never therefore wait within the marked channel for a large vessel that is going to turn on a buoy opposite. It is extremely difficult to judge the path the stern will take.

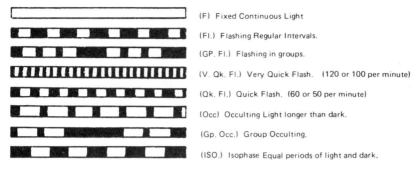

(F) Fixed Continuous Light

(Fl.) Flashing Regular Intervals.

(GP. Fl.) Flashing in groups.

(V. Qk. Fl.) Very Quick Flash. (120 or 100 per minute)

(Qk. Fl.) Quick Flash. (60 or 50 per minute)

(Occ) Occulting Light longer than dark.

(Gp. Occ.) Group Occulting.

(ISO.) Isophase Equal periods of light and dark.

Alt. — Alternating steady light changing colour.
Dir. — Directional light, a steady light.
Long flash — light not less than two seconds durations

Figure 9:4 *Recognising light patterns on buoys*

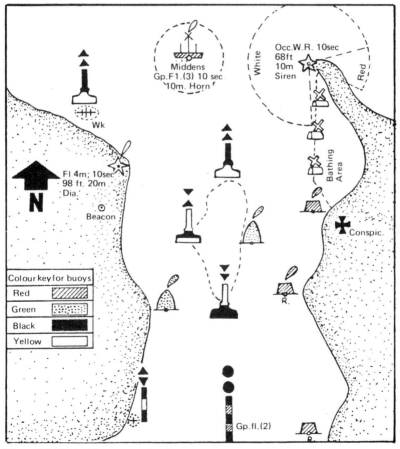

Figure 9:5 *Typical buoyage system in an estuary*

169

Compass

Always carry a compass even on short coastal trips. Summer fogs can materialise quickly and if you cannot see land or hear any fog signals you will need one. Be sure you have planned 'escape routes' and know in which compass direction to paddle at any stage of the journey, should fog set in. This applies equally to other contingencies, besides fog.

Even if the compass is not always carried on the deck, have a small emergency one hidden away somewhere. For long advanced trips, or where the compass may have to be stared at for long periods of time, and especially for night canoeing, the letters should be large, clear and luminous. When the compass is positioned on the deck you must ensure that it will not become damaged during rescues nor should it be influenced by metal objects nearby, either on or *under* the deck.

Remember there is a difference between 'true' and magnetic bearings, and always check with the chart as to the amount of 'variation' involved. ('Deviation' is concerned with metal, motors and similar affecting the performance of a magnetic compass when in position on a large boat, and is not applicable to canoeing, except to ensure that the compass is not so affected).

Transits

The time honoured method of navigation by transits has two great advantages; it is simple and exact. For these reasons the system is of more practical use to the coastal canoeist than any other. The principle is simply that of keeping two objects in line, one behind the other as you move towards them. If they appear to move apart from each other, then you are travelling or drifting in the direction which the marker farthest away is 'opening up' in relation to the near marker. *Example (Figure 9:6)* I am paddling towards the headland 'A', so I line up the marker flag on the water and the lighthouse on the headland. You can see by the direction of the waves that the wind is blowing from the right. I feel therefore that I should be blown sideways to the left. Things are not always what they appear however. In 'B' it is obvious that I am being swept to the right by the tide. It is the wind blown waves which make it appear that I should move to the left. Remember you move in the direction which the back marker opens up in relation to the nearer. If I *was* being swept to my left, the flag and the lighthouse would appear as they do in 'C'.

It is particularly important to understand transits in order to determine direction when paddling against a strong wind or current.

The intersection of straight lines drawn through two sets of transit markers will of course, pinpoint your position exactly. All groups should become transit conscious as soon as possible and relate transit marks on their charts with the objects they can see on land.

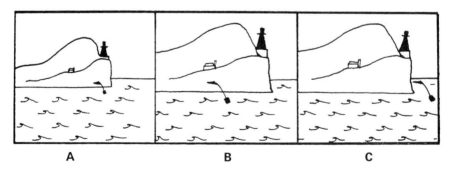

A   B   C

Figure 9:6 *Example of navigation by transits*

Tides and Tidal Streams

Tidal streams flow around the coasts of the British Isles in complicated but predictable patterns. Because these patterns are predictable, their direction and strength at different times can be published. The times and heights of high and low tide at any given port are contained in *Reeds Nautical Almanac* (local library ?) and the *Admiralty Tide Tables*. Local tide tables are usually available from newsagents, and times are often given daily in the local newspaper .

Tidal stream atlases, and charts, show the direction and strength of the tidal stream for any given hour of the range, while the *Admiralty Pilot* contains a great deal of information to aid navigation and warn of particular hazards for the area.

Tides are caused by the gravitational pull of the moon and, to a lesser extent, the sun. The moon and sun together exert their greatest pull when they are in conjunction (sun directly behind moon – new moon), or opposition (on opposite sides of the earth – full moon). The tidal range is greater at this period, and these tides are known as 'Spring Tides'. When the moon and sun are at right angles to each other (in quadrature) there is a lesser influence, and consequently a lesser tidal range, known as 'Neap tides'. Hence Spring and Neap tides occur every week alternately throughout the year.

On March 20 and September 22-23 annually the sun crosses the equator, and its declination is zero. The Spring tides occurring then are greater than normal, and care needs to be exercised when planning trips at this period, known as 'the equinox' – day and night are equal.

Because tidal streams are faster flowing during Springs, your passage will be easier and quicker with the tide and more difficult paddling against it. Any adverse conditions, for instance when a wind blows against the tide, or the stream rushes over shallows, will be worsened by Spring Tides.

On the open sea, a change in the direction of the Tidal Stream does not always coincide with the time of High Water (HW) and Low Water (LW) and you may find the tide running in the flood direction perhaps as much as two hours after the ebb has started, or vice versa.

The difference between HW and LW each day along the coast is 6 hrs 13 minutes and consequently the time of HW is approximately 50 minutes later each day.

When the direction of the tidal stream changes it is said to be 'slack water', although this may not last for very long. The 'twelfths' rule says that the level of water does not rise or fall at a constant rate throughout the six-hour period between LW and HW and vice-versa. The greatest rate of rise or fall (and hence the strongest tidal stream) occurs half-way through the tide in open water, but probably soon after the stream has commenced to run in the new direction in rivers and estuaries.

Twelfths Rule

Hour 1 of rise or fall – 1/12 of range	Hour 4 of rise or fall – 3/12 of range
Hour 2 of rise or fall – 2/12 of range	Hour 5 of rise or fall – 2/12 of range
Hour 3 of rise or fall – 3/12 of range	Hour 6 of rise or fall – 1/12 of range

Around the coasts of the British Isles the range of tides is from about 6' above chart datum for HW Neaps, and up to about 15' for Springs, with the largest range being the Bristol Channel area, where HW Springs can reach 45'. Spring tides are not only higher, they also go out lower.The bigger the range, the stronger the resultant tidal streams, which average ¼ knot–3 knots*. Off many headlands this can increase to 4-5 knots, and there are places around our coasts where the streams can reach 10 knots.

---

*One knot = one nautical mile (2020 yards) per hour.

Tidal Constant System of Tidal Prediction

As tidal streams are depicted simultaneously all round the British Isles, it is convenient to refer to a 'Standard Port'. This is usually Dover. To obtain the time of HW find the 'tidal constant' for the port you want, and either add or subtract it as directed from the time of HW Dover.

The time of HW at Dover is printed in many newspapers. Also that for London Bridge. Tables of Tidal Constants are printed in my book *Sea Canoeing*, on the maps in the *AA Handbook*, in *Reed's Nautical Almanack* and *Admiralty Tide Tables*. (When using a chart always check on which Port the tidal information is based).

Currents

These are also water movements within the sea but their origins are thermal rather than lunar and they have only a small influence on the sea canoeists around the British Isles. This is not the case in other parts of the world however.

Hazards Caused by Tidal Streams

Overfalls
Fast tidal streams passing over quickly shallowing underwater ridges cause tumbling, breaking waves. Their severity depends upon the depth of the water, the area covered by the shallows, the speed and direction of the tidal stream, the existence of any swell and the direction of the wind. Winds blowing against *any* tidal stream can create difficult conditions and when it blows against large extensive overfalls these could prove fatal.

Tide Races
This is the accelerated water flow caused by a tidal stream setting off a headland or similar, or through the restricted space between islands. Large standing breaking waves are common with the severity dependent upon the factors listed above.

Rips
A Rip could be likened to a river of water within the sea itself, moving at a different speed or in a different direction to the water adjacent to it. Rips often occur on surf beaches. A combination of tidal race, overfalls, and rips can often cause swirls, or whirlpools, represented on the chart as little whirlpools. When you paddle through them, they often appear as dangerous upsurges of water.

Training for the Advanced sea kayak award must of necessity take place in some of the dangerous conditions just described, and the leader of a group training in conditions such as these must be aware of his tremendous responsibilities. His role goes far beyond that of a Coach as defined in most other sports. His attitude must be like the Alpine Guide, who is prepared to give of himself physically, mentally and spiritually to bring them back alive.

Types of wave

The dangers of dumping waves are described in the chapter on surfing. Large waves breaking directly onto a steeply shelving beach are particularly dangerous, and can, in certain conditions, drag a person under, throw him back over, and keep repeating the process rather like a 'stopper' on a river, leading to a drowning.

Where waves hit a cliff and rebound, or sweep up a slope and reflect back out to sea, the ensuing turbulence as waves travelling in opposite directions coincide and collide, is known as 'clapotis'. This can be a lot of fun, or deadly dangerous, depending upon the circumstances.

THE WEATHFR

The wind, and the seas caused by the wind, are the greatest problem that you will encounter so make the wind and weather your particular study. Perhaps the best advice on forecasting weather based on personal observation is to be found in *Reeds Nautical Almanac*, but even then you will be lucky to have accurate predictions more than six hours ahead.

Weather forecasts are best obtained from the local weather centre, the number of which can be found in the telephone dialling code book. These are available pre-recorded or ask for a 'sailing forecast'. The radio and television forecasts are useful, and Coastguard stations, RAF and Civil aerodromes can also provide information. These latter three are able to give you an accurate report on current wind strength and direction. You may find it a help to carry a small transistor radio on any prolonged trip, to be sure of getting an up-to-date forecast even away from telephones.

To make the relaying of weather forecasts easier, the British Isles is divided into a number of specific sea areas. It is important that you know the names of these sea areas and their approximate location, especially those which are nearest to that part of the coast that you use most. The names and location of the weather stations are also important.

Remember that the shipping forecast is given for a large area of sea, and indicates the worst conditions likely in that whole area.

Beaufort Wind Scale

Wind speeds are categorised according to this scale. It ranges from 'O', which is 'sea like a mirror' to '12' which is a hurricane. The scale gives the Beaufort number, the speed range of the wind in knots, the descriptive term of the wind, the condition of the sea, and the probable height of the waves in metres. The wind direction indicates the compass quarter from which the wind is expected (eg a Westerly wind blows *from* the West). The scale is shown in Table One overleaf.

When winds are expected to gust to Force 8 (Gale force – 34-40 Knots) gale warnings are issued on the radio. Gale 'imminent' means within six hours; 'soon', between six and 12 hours; and 'later', over 12 hours. Gale cones are hoisted on Coastguard Stations, some harbour offices and fishery protection vessels, when a gale is expected within 12 hours. These are quite large, three feet high, painted black, and indicate the segment from which the wind will approach – if the point is upwards, the gale should come *from* the North, and if the point is down, the gale is expected *from* the South (of the East/West line).

The greatest single hazard when canoeing on the sea is the 'off-shore wind'. Even in moderate conditions beware of the effect on a novice group, who can suddenly find themselves in conditions they cannot handle. Remember, the further out you drift, the bigger the waves become.

Fetch

The height of any waves which are caused by the wind, is governed by the speed of the wind, and the 'fetch'. This is the distance across open water which the wind blows without hinderance. Therefore, if you are paddling a little way offshore, the 'fetch' may be only a few hundred feet if the wind is coming from that direction, and even though it may be gale force, the waves will be comparatively small. This, incidentally, is known as a 'weather shore'.

If the wind is blowing onto shore, this is known as 'lee shore' and the 'fetch' could be many hundreds of miles. For sailing vessels, and any large ship, a 'lee shore' is to be

173

avoided, and in heavy weather vessels will head well out to sea to avoid being blown there and wrecked, should anything go wrong. Provided there is not an impossible landing involved, a 'lee shore' is desirable for the canoeist, as in the event of an incident, the group is carried towards the beach, and not the open sea.

Table One: The Beaufort Scale

Beaufort Number	General description	Sea	Canoeists' Criterion
0	Calm	Sea like mirror	Suitable for initial training from 'safe' beaches
1 1–3 knots	Light air	Ripples appear	
2 4–6 knots	Light breeze	Tiny waves. No breaking crests.	
3 7–10 knots	Gentle breeze	Small waves. Crests begin to form.	Life gets interesting for all. Good for practicing capsize drill. Getting tough for beginners.
4 11–16 knots	Moderate breeze	Medium waves building up. Some white horses.	About the limit for the proficiency test standard canoeist if on journey.
5 17–21 knots	Fresh breeze	Decidedly lumpy sea many white horses	Anybody over proficiency standard enjoys this. Usually creates very good surf.
6 22–27 knots	Strong breeze	Large waves everywhere. Continually white horses.	Short journeys by advanced canoeists alright, but you are reaching the border line.
7 28–33 knots	Near Gale	Sea piles up and spindrift off tops of waves	Surf tends to be big. Experts are beginning to swear.
8 34–40 knots	Gale	The difference from a landsman's view of these is difficult to	Surf gets to be very big, and you spend your time hanging on to
9 41–47 knots	Strong Gale	say except that the sea looks lumpy,	your tent
10 48–55 knots	Storm	high breaking waves and spindrift following wind path.	Surf enormous, and you get blown away with your tent.

Fog

All advanced sea canoeists should be able to navigate in fog, but the training places great demands and responsibilities on the coach in charge. Before you vanish off into the murk with your trusting group, you must be completely familiar with the area you intend to use, indeed you should know it almost blindfolded. All the fog signals should be memorised by you, so that if necessary you can find your way without the use of a compass, before you even think about taking a group out into fog.

It is important that you know the names of the different audible fog signals and that you are able to differentiate between them. It is not much good if you don't know whether the wailing you can hear through the fog is a Typhon or a Diaphone, especially if the chart tells you that the two signals are ten miles apart!

When training advanced groups in fog, and the shore is invisible, have some well qualified helpers with you. Every member of the group should carry a compass and a whistle or a hand-held fog horn. In case of emergency, each should have a compass bearing that will get them back to shore again. It is best if the leader carried a loud audible signal which his group can 'home in' on.

Do not practice fog navigation in shipping channels. If you wish to keep shipping well clear of you and your group in an emergency, sound a 'D' in morse ie one long blast followed by two short ones and repeat this three times then a two minute pause and keep repeating. This signal will keep shipping clear of you *if they are small enough to manoeuvre* but please note, it is not a distress signal.

Audible Fog Signals
Diaphone – (Dia) This is a powerful low pitch sound finishing with a deep grunt.

Siren – There are various types of siren having different strengths and pitches.

Reed – This gives a feeble rather high pitched note.

Typhon – A strong medium pitched note that sounds like a ship's fog signal.

Horn – Some wail, some give off sounds of different pitches combined together, others give a long steady tone while some seem to waver up and down. These sounds are very distinctive and once heard are easily remembered.

Whistle – (Whis.) These are often worked by the swaying of the buoy. They can be shrill and clear, but if the swell is erratic the whistle will start and finish with a wheezing gasp.

Bells – Bells go ping, *Gongs* go bong – some even go clonk but you will be surprised just how far their sounds can carry.

ON THE WATER

Group Discipline
There should be no doubt in the group's mind as to who is the leader. The ratio of leaders to students should not be less than one to eight. The leader should appoint someone to go to the front of the group and lead. If the conditions ahead are questionable or the route uncertain, the leader should be at the front. Under normal conditions, the leader will act like a sheep dog, moving round the group offering advice and encouragement should anyone need it. Train your group to be aware of each other, show them how to turn their bodies around by trailing the back of the paddle blade on the water for support and looking right round on that side.

Members should not paddle too far from each other. In rough seas and big swells individuals can be hidden in the troughs. *The rougher the sea – the closer they be.* Some audible or visual signals should be agreed upon before the trip starts.

Leaders should be careful during 'rock dodging' exercises close in shore not to let the members of their groups get behind rocks or into caves where they can be out of sight for more than a few minutes.

Do not take untried novices into situations where they have to cope with steep following seas a long way off shore until they have done simple forward running exercises close in shore.

Coping with 'incidents'

When any incident occurs, such as a capsize, everyone should turn and face the oncoming waves, holding their position close to the 'action', but not knocking into one another or impeding those involved in sorting out the problem. There will be a constant tendency for someone to start paddling off, and the rest will follow. It is vital therefore that the leader ensures that this does not happen, and it is better that he or she is not personally committed to the rescue, repair, tow, or whatever it may be. There could be times when speed will be of the essence, however, and it is then that the leader must keep constant watch on the rest of the group, whilst dealing with the matter in hand.

'Rafting up' the rest of the party in this situation is not a desirable practice. The 'raft' will drift more quickly than an individual canoeist, and particularly away from someone who is in the water holding onto a boat. It will be extremely difficult in waves for the raft to be maintained, and when it comes to splitting up to re-commence, there will be considerable danger of capsizes.

Should a situation ever have got so out of control that help is needed, and individually paddlers are in danger of capsize, then rafting in pairs, facing one another, would be a way of containing matters until help arrived.

It would be better, however, if the likely result was that everyone would be blown further out to sea, for a course to be chosen which kept the group paddling into the waves, but which angled the boats slightly inshore of the wind. Thus, by 'ferry gliding' on the wind, the canoeists are pointing into the waves and are least likely to capsize. Eventually the party should make its way close enough inshore for the situation to be recovered.

The different effects of wind and tidal stream should be noted. With wind against tide, canoes being paddled or floating empty high on the surface will be more affected by the wind, unless the tidal stream is very strong, and the wind very light. A person in the water, or a waterlogged canoe, will invariably be taken in the direction of the tidal stream almost regardless of the strength of the wind. Where the wind is blowing across the direction of the tidal stream, then a waterlogged boat or person in the water, will be carried mainly in the direction of the tide, but will also be moved by the wind and wave action.

ON THE BEACH

As the kayaks of your group lie strewn about the beach ready for the signal to be off, certain thoughts should be racing through your mind rather like a pilots pre-flight check. I would suggest your thoughts are on the following lines.

1   Am I going far enough to merit notifying the coastguard?

2   Have all the novices had their Life Jacket fastenings checked?

3   Who looks like being the weakest?

4   Does anyone have any special disabilities? eg deafness, diabetes etc.

5   Am I taking them too far?

6   How many people have I got?

7   Have I taken into account any changes in tide direction?

8   Do I have enough help for what I intend to do with the group?

9   Are all the kayaks in good repair? – no loose toggles, footrests.

10 Are all the spray covers servicable?

11 Who is carrying flares?

12 Is everyone dressed adequately?

13 Are the boats full of buoyancy? Will what they have stay in?

14 Is the kit on their decks fastened on tight?

15 Did I get the Weather Forecast?

16 Have I got *all my own equipment?* eg compass, sponge, money, repair, first aid kit and car keys – did I lock the car?

Decision time

During your ponderings, you may consider that one of the group could eventually put you all at risk. This might be due to the distance involved, the condition of the sea and weather, the state of his equipment or his known physical or psychological condition. In a case such as this, he must be left behind. Be particularly careful where someone has been recommended to you by somebody else. Do not let feeling sorry for him or the persuasion of others deter you from a decision which you know is right and which has the best interests of the group at heart.

Launching

When launching (Figure 9:7) involve the group in a study of the sequence and pattern of the oncoming waves, so that they will become familiar with the driest and most efficient way of getting out through surf. Impress upon your group the importance of keeping dry during extended expeditions which involve camping.

Figure 9:7 *Different methods of launching from a beach*

If the surf is dumping the leader must leave the beach last of all. Launch your class one at a time. Hold each one steady at the waters edge so the wave will not sweep them sideways.

As soon as there is a lull in the oncoming sets of waves, push them off and out to sea. An out flowing 'rip' will help considerably to get them clear of the beach.

Landing

If you approach a beach where the surf is much larger than your group are used to, or if the surf is dumping dangerously, stop well outside the surf line and explain to everyone, what you intend to do, and what you intend they should do to get ashore safely.

Instruct the group to paddle in one at a time, then if there is a capsize you will only have one casualty to worry about. As they paddle into the shore they must keep turning round and watching for any large waves which might approach them unexpectedly from behind. As soon as a wave does reach them, and if it is steep, the student should stop paddling or even back paddle if the wave is very large. Once they have allowed the wave to pass under them, they must paddle fast again until the next wave catches up to them. As the paddlers reach shallow water where the waves are breaking, they must pause and wait for a lull in the big wave sets and then paddle in on the backs of the smaller waves. Appoint someone to take charge of the group and keep an eye on things while you go ashore first and land. The individuals can then be guided in *one at a time* with the help of some prearranged signals to indicate say: 'Take care wave behind', 'Slow down', 'Paddle fast' and so on. Once a boat reaches the beach grab the toggle quickly and pull the man to safety.

10 Rescue Techniques

Derek C. Hutchinson

INTRODUCTION

Capsizing is part of canoeing, at least during the early learning stages. The best remedy for a capsize is undoubtedly the Eskimo roll. It matters little, however, which method you use so long as you arrive on the surface, still sitting in your kayak at the end of it all.

Not everyone can Eskimo roll and some boats are almost impossible to roll due to excessive beam or poor deck design. There is always the possibility of failure, and so over the years various methods have been developed of putting people back into their canoes from the water. The water does not have to be very deep to merit this type of emergency procedure, in spite of the term 'Deep Water Rescues'. The water, in fact, need only be as deep as the tallest member of your group.

Since I began sea canoeing I have seen many methods of rescue tried with varying degrees of success. This ranged from group rescues, with as many as six people working out a complicated sequence, involving an ingenious system of levers and pulleys, brought about by the careful positioning of canoes and paddles before hand, to solo rescues – with a purple-faced man desperately trying to tread water, while at the same time blowing down a large 'U' tube which vanished up inside his inverted cockpit. This was an effort to expel the water and raise the kayak. Both methods had only limited support.

The methods of rescue and re-entry which follow should be practised in the calm waters of swimming pools or sheltered bays. It can be dangerous to practise in very cold or rough conditions without suitable clothing. Remember always that it is vital for the capsized canoeist to grab hold, and maintain a grasp of the canoe, immediately upon surfacing. This should be drilled into paddlers from the very first capsize practice, and particularly emphasised when initial training is taking place in a swimming pool, where the canoe does not immediately drift away as it does in most open air situations.

Beginners should also be trained to retain the paddle where possible, and to swim with the boat to the paddle, if it has been dropped.

All equipment should be securely stowed whether it is inside the boat or on the deck. After your rescue practice is finished, the surface of the sea should not be littered with floating debris such as flare containers, broken vacuum flasks, the contents of first aid and repair kits, sandwiches, or pieces of bloodstained polythene foam.

It is dangerous to perform any deep water rescue in surf. It is far safer to tow both paddler and kayak out of the danger area, whether it is amongst breaking waves or against rocks. Rough water practice may be made safer by wearing crash helmets.

Learning to Eskimo roll successfully is a sign of success. Once learned, having to roll is a sign of failure.

'HI' RESCUE ALSO KNOWN AS THE IPSWICH (Figure 10:1)

The rescue raft with paddles across forms the letter 'H', and when all three boats are in line, this becomes an 'I'.

1   A and B position their boats quickly, collect C's paddle, and then raft up facing him. C guides *the bow* of his upturned kayak between the two rescuing craft. A and B now lift the bow of C's kayak up and over the paddles which are positioned as shown, as quickly as possible, to allow the minimum amount of water to enter.

Make sure the cockpit is clear of the water before you start to pull the kayak over the paddles.

2   The upturned kayak now rests and pivots on the paddles. A and B hold the boat steady. If you are careful, you should not damage the paddle looms as you lift the boat

Figure 10:1a *'HI' rescue, the initial lift*

Figure 10:1b *'HI' rescue, rocking the boat over the paddles*

over. As C see-saws his end of the kayak up and down, the water drains out. As soon as the boat is empty, the two rescuers turn it over into its upright position and slide it forward off the paddles, to be in a position for C to re-enter by one of the methods described in Figure 10:6.

With practice, this rescue should be completed in under a minute. At no time must the man in the water let go of one of the rescuer's boats, as the wind will blow the two rescuers and the upturned boat away faster than it is possible to swim after them.

Some prefer that the rescuers come together facing in opposite directions, so that should the boat have to be emptied stern first, one of the rescuers is the best way round to assist with the re-entry.

In the event of the capsized boat being very heavily waterlogged, C can move to the other side of the paddles, either going around the outside of B's boat, holding on all the time, or coming between, and ducking under. He can then wrap one arm around a rescuer's boat, and with the other push *up* on his to take the weight. This will allow A and B to continue threading it along until the cockpit is over the paddles. C is then well placed to apply maximum leverage by pulling down to commence the see-saw.

It should never be necessary to 'swim'. The person in the water should always pull the boats around him. In essence, he stays still and manoeuvres the raft, or his own boat, as necessary. This is not what usually happens, where people naturally tend to pull themselves around the boats. There is a different action involved, which needs to be identified, thought about, and learned.

THE 'X' RESCUE (Figures 10:2a, 10:2b)

It is important that all leaders and instructors are able to empty a kayak without assistance. Two canoeists paddling together should also be able to rescue each other if the need arises. Both these requirements are met by the 'X' Rescue, so called because when one boat is pulled across the other, the raft forms the letter 'X'.

1   B lifts the kayak as quickly as he can so as to allow as little water as possible into the cockpit of the capsized kayak. Using his fore deck as a pivot B pulls the kayak across his boat until the cockpit rests near his own cockpit.

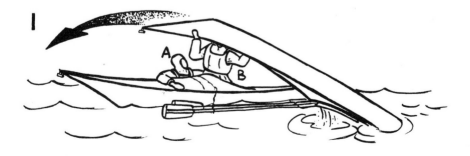

Figure 10:2a *The 'X' rescue, the initial lift*

Figure 10:2b *The 'X' rescue, emptying the kayak*

2   B see-saws the kayak by leaning his own boat from side to side. He is assisted by A in the water who helps to control the emptying movement by holding the bow. Once the boat is empty it is turned the right way up and A re-enters by the method illustrated in Figure 10:6.

It is easy for B to damage his spray cover as he tries to drag the partially waterlogged kayak across his own cockpit. It is as well to wear two spray covers, the oldest underneath, so that the top one can be removed before the rescue starts.

It is important that B looks after *both* pairs of paddles, this is when the paddle park is useful. If there is too much water in the capsized boat, its excessive weight will crack one or both of the decks during the see-sawing operation. It would be prudent to remove the worst of the water by The Curl (Figure 10:4) before attempting the 'X' rescue.

It is possible for two boats to empty a third in what would become a Rafted 'X' Rescue. In case of difficulty also, A can assist by placing both feet against B's hull, and straightening his body to pull the capsized boat across. He needs to push up as he does so, rather than pull down, which puts too great a strain on the foredecks.

CLEOPATRA'S NEEDLE (Figure 10:3)

Not a pretty sight – and hardly a situation a careful leader should get himself into if he has checked the buoyancy of all the kayaks in his group before setting off. It is possible, however, that on your travels you may come across some lone canoeist whose boat is floating like this, either because of no buoyancy at all, or because what little it has is badly distributed.

It will be your responsibility to instruct the man in the water what to do.

1   First the boat must be manoeuvred to the surface. This can be done by hooking the foot under the cockpit, or diving down and grabbing the coaming by hand and then lifting. Once the boat is level with the surface emptying can begin.

2   A supports the cockpit coaming on his shoulder. As he slowly lifts, he watches the water draining out. While A does this, C holds the kayak LEVEL. As soon as most of the water is out, the boat is flipped over so it is floating in the upright position. Any further water can be emptied out by the 'HI' method.

This method of emptying a swamped canoe can be very difficult, especially for people of limited strength and experience. After a great deal of experimenting I found a method which seemed to work every time and did not require an enormous amount of energy from the person is the water. This method I called 'The Curl'.

182

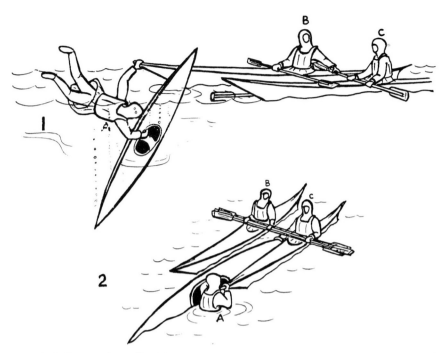

Figure 10:3 *Cleopatra's needle rescue*

THE CURL (Figures 10:4a, 10:4b)

1 The swamped boat lies alongside the boat of man B, its deck completely awash. A pulls himself over B's foredeck, as near as he can to B's cockpit without getting in the way of B's paddle, and then hooks his hands under the cockpit coaming of the swamped boat, his palms uppermost.

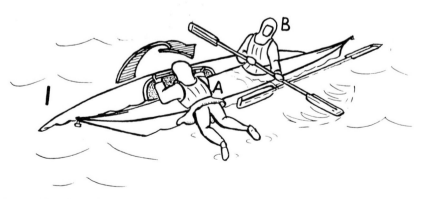

Figure 10:4a *Emptying a swamped canoe using the Curl*

183

Figure 10:4b *The rescuer assisting by leaning his canoe to empty the water*

2 A rests his elbows on B's deck, pulling the swamped kayak towards him and tilts the cockpit so that the water starts to drain out. Once his elbows are jammed against the deck by the weight of his kayak, B can then increase the draining angle by leaning over and sculling for support. Apart from making sure that the draining kayak is held firmly and perfectly level, no further effort is required on the part of A.

This method of rescue does not require exceptional strength, and as long as A can get his kayak on its side and *hold it level*, the water will drain out as B controls the angle of the lean.

The 'TX' rescue can also be used for a swamped boat. Here, the cockpit is turned towards the rescuer, who paddles his bow into it, thus forming the letter 'T'. The swimmer reaches under his own boat with both arms and joins his hands on the rescuer's bow, gradually levering up with his shoulders until the capsized boat is across the rescuer's. From there it is pushed along the deck, until the 'X' rescue described earlier can be completed.

ALL-IN RESCUE (Figure 10:5)

Weather conditions which are going to capsize all three members of a canoeing group at the same time, are bound to be bad. The remedy is tireing and the participants will have their anxious moments, even if they are only practising this in a swimming pool – especially if all the boats have had their buoyancy removed just to make things difficult.

1. C holds onto his kayak and looks after the paddles. If he wished he could hold the paddles between his legs, leaving his arms free. He must on no account become separated from the main rescue. A and B hold onto the upturned cockpit coaming facing in opposite directions. B lifts the *bow* of the kayak as high and as quickly as he can so that the cockpit clears the water. As B does this he will automatically pull down on his right hand. Any tilting of the pivot boat is counteracted by A, who holds onto the other side of the coaming. The less buoyancy the pivot boat has, the more important it is for both men to hold it perfectly level and still, otherwise the air inside will escape and the boat will fill up and sink.

2. B passes the kayak over the pivot boat to A, who continues taking it across until its cockpit rests on the upturned hull.

3. A and B see-saw the kayak until it is empty. Once this is done, it is turned onto its right

184

side and placed alongside the pivot canoe. B who wants to get in first, positions himself next to his cockpit.

4   The re-entry can be tricky in a rough sea. B passes his paddle across *the middle* of the pivot canoe. To gain entry, B will place his right hand at the rear of his cockpit and in the centre, whilst he holds the paddle and the front of the cockpit with his left hand. He enters the cockpit by kicking out with his feet, and pushing down with his weight upon his arms. To counteract any unsteadiness caused by B's re-entry, A pulls downwards on his end of the paddle loom.

As soon as B is secure in his boat, A's kayak can be emptied by a 'TX' Rescue, and C is finally put back in his kayak by the 'HI' method.

The order of leaving the water is important, and the leader will have to make some decisions before the rescue commences. The most scantily dressed should hardly be the last out of the water, but if the weakest is put into his boat first, he might not be able to undertake the 'TX' Rescue which follows next.

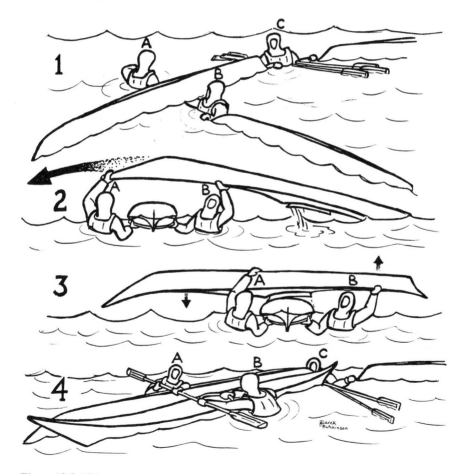

Figure 10:5 *All-in rescue*

OTHER METHODS

A number of other methods of emptying a capsized canoe exist, but those described are the most universally acclaimed and used. The most popular formerly was the 'H' method, whereby two canoeists positioned themselves on each end of the upturned boat, at right angles, forming a large letter 'H'. The capsized boat was then turned onto its side, kept level, and a gradual, even lift applied from each end. The problem with this method was that it is necessary to keep at right angles, and this involves a constant adjustment, the action of wind and waves tending to move the boats around. It also requires an equal effort to be applied at each end, otherwise one person ends up with all the weight, and an impossible task.

Other experiments, with paddles locked across shoulders, and the rescuers lifting the upturned boat (which is lying between them) with the opposite hands, and so forth, have been tried, but have not been generally adopted.

Self-rescue techniques, such as strapping the lifejacket to the paddle-blade, re-entering the inverted canoe, and rolling up with the benefit of the extra buoyancy on the paddle, are also advocated by some. These are not to be deprecated if they work for a given individual, but there is sufficient doubt about the wisdom of removing a life jacket in serious circumstances, and insufficient support generally for such innovations, for this book to give them approval.

Rescue methods particularly applicable to inland situations, eg rescues from 'stoppers' are included in Chapter 8 'Inland Canoeing'.

METHODS OF RE-ENTRY

Face up from the stern (Figure 10:6a)

This is probably the most widely used method of re-entry. The paddles are made secure and both A and C have a firm hold on the centre kayak with both hands. If they wished for an even firmer grip they could hold that side of the coaming farthest away thereby crossing their arms. B does not have to use a great deal of energy to get back into his boat, but he may feel slightly undignified.

It is important that the 'victim' lies back in the water, letting the lifejacket take his body weight, and puts his legs in first. The arms must reach right across the rescuer's boat and his own, and his push down applied to the outside of the boats, in order to keep them together. Occasionally, a less well co-ordinated person will have extreme difficulty in finally bringing his or her body weight in. It is then necessary that the rescuer C lies firmly across the victim's canoe, with near arm wrapped around, far hand gripping the centre of the coaming at the front, body-weight on the empty boat, and knees pulling strongly to keep his own boat close. If the paddles are across in front of the rescuer the person re-entering can put one leg into his boat, hook the other over the paddle shafts, and thereby gain some added leverage by pulling down with that leg.

Face down from the stern (Figure 10:6b)

Some people prefer to get in like this but in rough seas many people finish up like this anyway, even though they may start differently. This method can be uncomfortable if the rear deck is carrying spare paddles, flares and perhaps a fishing-line, especially as you start hitching forwards towards the cockpit. It is as well to remember where you put the fish hooks.

Over the side re-entry (Figure 10:6c)

I settled on this method some years ago as a good method of re-entry involving only two people. A has one arm under the paddle loom and is gripping the coaming with both hands. This will keep the raft stable, and as B exerts his weight down onto the paddle it will increase the stability. If B needed assistance, A could quite easily take his left hand off the cockpit coaming and grasp the others life-jacket without any loss of stability.

Figure 10:6a *Re-entry face up from the stern*

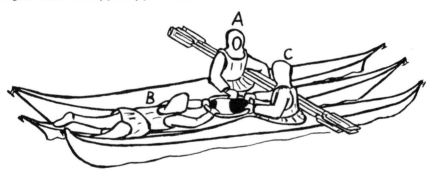

Figure 10:6b *Re-entry face down from the stern*

Figure 10:6c *Re-entry over the side of the canoe*

ESKIMO RESCUES (Figure 10:7)

This type of rescue requires a patient who has water confidence and faith in those around him, and a rescuer who can position his canoe quickly and carefully.

The Side Rescue

1　This is the most useful method. The capsized man bangs on his upturned hull with both hands to attract attention of those nearest to him and then moves his hands to and fro in an arc. This will save unnecessary manoeuvring on the part of the rescuer.

2　Once alongside, the rescuer puts the patient's nearest upright hand onto the paddle loom which is placed across the two boats. If the rescuer does not locate the hand on the loom, the distraught victim may try to pull himself up to the surface on the side farthest away, with disastrous results.

3　As the patient hip-flicks, and then pulls his body to the surface, he must change his hand grip position when he reaches the half up stage.

4　It will be seen that it is possible to give assistance by presenting the bow of the rescuing kayak to the patient, but this can be dangerous. If the rescuer approaches too fast, and there is a collision, an arm can be crushed or a skull cracked. It would be safer for the rescuer to execute a quick turn and come in from the side. During training, the rescuer must paddle forward as the patient, holding his bow, pushes himself up, otherwise the rescuing craft tends to be pushed away by the patient, who will then fall back into the water.

R & R RESCUE (Figure 10:8)

(Re-entry and Roll H & H – Hutchinson's horror!)

The golden rule is "less than three there should never be'. The reason is that in case of accident or illness, one person can stay with the casualty whilst the third can go and seek help. If a tow is needed, support is usually essential, and a unit of three competent canoeists is as safe as it is possible to be in small boats on the sea. With the advent of single-handed rescue techniques, however, many canoeists have happily operated in pairs, and with the development of bulkheaded boats and efficient pumping, more and more people are seeking adventure by going out to sea alone. I wrote elsewhere* 'To condemn the adventurous is pointless; it is more important to develop rescue techniques which enable them to pursue their own particular road to Valhalla with at least some margin of safety'. If a man is a competent eskimo roller it is going to be a rough sea or some unfortunate circumstance which forces him out of his boat and into the water. Any subsequent re-entry balancing act which requires a man to sit on top of his deck and start hitching about in that same rough sea is out of the question. It was for this reason that I introduced the R & R Rescue into print. It takes nerve and needs practice for it to be successful – but then doesn't everything?

1　The canoeist faces the stern of his boat holding the cockpit coaming with both hands. He holds the paddle ready on the side on which he intends to roll up. In the illustration he is preparing to 'wind up' on his left hand side. He then takes a deep breath, throws his head back and then swings his legs and feet upwards and into the cockpit.

---

*Sea Canoeing, Second Edition by Derek Hutchinson published by A. and C. Black, Ltd.

Figure 10:7 *Eskimo rescues 1, 2, and 3, demonstrating the side rescue and 4, showing the presentation of the bow*

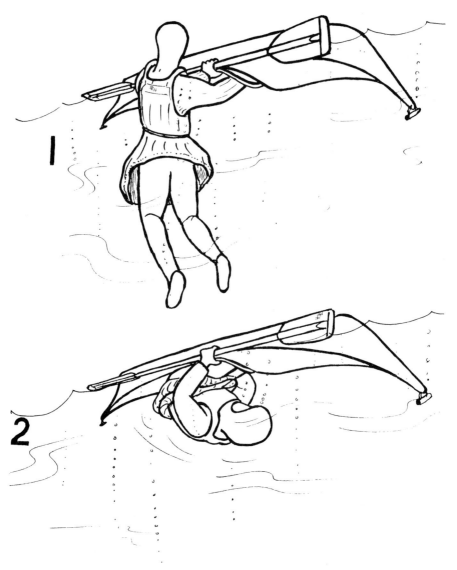

Figure 10:8 *Self rescue – R and R (Re-entry and roll)*

2   Once back in the cockpit, the man can now roll up. With practice even the spray cover can be put back on upside down, but it is hardly necessary, as the amount of water taken into the kayak is not a great deal if it is fitted with bulkheads. A small pump takes care of the rest.

Once upright, the canoeist should put on his spray cover immediately, to stop any breaking seas filling the boat further. If the kayak feels unstable due to the water inside, it is possible to scull for support, resting the extended paddle over one shoulder, while pumping out with the other hand. A foot operated pump has been designed and this can be fitted instead of, or as well as, the hand operated type.

REPAIRS AT SEA (Figure 10:9)

Undertake any of the rescues mentioned previously in anything but calm water and you'll find it all too easy to damage a kayak. As the boats swing about, cracks across the head will not be a rarity. Most serious damage to boats seems to occur when the group is running before a following sea. Kayaks in the hands of novices tend to run out of control and harpoon each other. Until a few years ago it was recommended that the occupant of a damaged kayak *got out of his boat and took to the water* while his boat was being repaired. This seemed a little silly to me, so I encouraged all my students to keep dry during the time it took to do the repair, by sitting astride the rescuer's boat.

If the patient is nervous it would be better to choose the rear deck to sit astride. He could use both hands to hold onto the rescuers life jacket, or he could scull for support on one side with the extended paddle. Unfortunately, in this position the patient is unable to assist with the repair. Sitting on the fore-deck however, the patient can hold the kayak or help with the repair. He can also hold the paddles against the side of the boat with his leg, in the absence of a paddle park.

It is in the best interests of the leader if all the members of his group carry their repair kits in a position which is easily accessible. Then the person doing the repair can use the kit from the damaged boat, which when it is across the other boat acts as an outrigger and stabilizes the whole operation.

Figure 10:9 *Repairing a damaged kayak at sea*

191

RESCUES TO NON-CANOEISTS

The sea canoeist, with his speed and skill through surf, offers a fast method of rescuing anyone who is in difficulties. They might not be canoeists, and their physical condition may vary from normal fatigue to complete unconsciousness.

It is a prerequisite of the coaching awards that candidates have a specified life-saving qualification. The BCU Lifesaving Test incorporates certain specialised rescues which are also used by the Corps of Canoe Life Guards.

Stern Carry (Figure 10:10)

If the patient is co-operative and not completely paralysed with fear, carry him on the rear deck. It is probably about the best way to carry anyone as the bow does not dig in, nor is the paddler retarded by the man in the water. The patient however must keep his body low onto the deck, so that the balance of the boat is not affected. It is possible to carry in through surf, but it takes practice, and a patient who is determined to hang on tight.

If the person being rescued is fairly small, it might be better to carry them in pillion style. In this way, the child will feel more secure and if their body is close to you, as well as having their arms wrapped around, there is less chance of them becoming dislodged. You will also find the kayak easier to control this way (Figure 10:10b).

Bow Carry (Figure 10:11)

This method is ideal for someone who is tired and nervous, because in their position on the bow you can watch and encourage them as you paddle them in to shore. If you must come in through surf, it would be better to approach the shore backwards. It could be distressing for the patient to have the rescue canoe loop on top of him.

Always ensure that the bow of the canoe is over the swimmer's shoulder, so that his teeth are not likely to act as shock-absorbers.

If the surf is large and you think there may be a chance that your exhausted patient will be washed off the boat, stay outside the surf line, send up a distress rocket and wait until help arrives.

Panicking swimmers should be approached with caution. If they make a wild grab and clutch your kayak in a way which may cause you to capsize, use your paddle and push their hands off the deck swiftly and firmly with the blade. Talk to the patient and calm him down, then direct him as to what is best to do. In your enthusiasm to escape his clutches do not break his fingers or beat him about the head.

Raft assisted resuscitation (Figure 10:12)

Using kayaks rafted together, expired air resuscitation (EAR) can be carried out successfully on the water. Probably the best way to go about this, is for the rescuer in the boat nearest to the patient to turn round so that he is facing in towards the raft. The canoeist in the boat farthest away from the unconscious person then reaches across his partner's boat, grasps the patient's wrists and with a concentrated heave, pulls him over and across the raft. The patient is then turned over and resuscitation can begin.

It is possible for the two man raft to be towed to shore by a third canoeist, but it is far more prudent to send up a distress rocket the moment the unconscious person is sighted. Thus professional help can be on the way whilst resuscitation is in progress. Remember that anyone who has been unconscious *for any reason* should be examined by a doctor as soon as possible.

Figure 10:10a *Rescuing a swimmer using the stern carry*

Figure 10:10b *The Pillion carry*

Figure 10:11 *The bow carry rescue method*

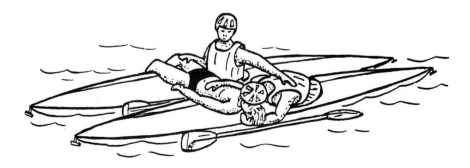

Figure 10:12 *EAR being carried out across the decks of the canoes*

Resuscitation in the water – Kayak support (Figure 10:13)

To do this you must first jump out of your boat, but be careful not to capsize it, and don't forget to put your paddle in the paddle park. Hold onto the front of your kayak by its lifting toggle. Using this as a support, bend the patient's head well back over your arm (keep your hand off his throat) and start EAR. This is not easy, and you will find it awkward and exhausting work.

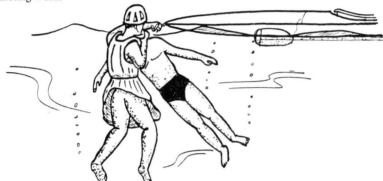

Figure 10:13 *EAR being carried out in the water using the bow of the canoe for support*

DEPENDENT FACTORS

The success of the rescues illustrated depend very much on a number of factors:
1 The age and physical condition of the participants
2 Their level of competence and their general morale
3 The type of personal buoyancy and the clothing they are wearing
4 The distance between group members at the time of the capsize
5 The skill level of the group and the speed they can manoeuvre
6 The condition of the sea and the strength of the wind
7 The distance from shore and the proximity of rocks
8 The temperature of the water
9 The weight of the equipment inside the upturned boat
10 The amount of equipment carried on the deck and how secure it is
11 The time of day
12 The prevalence of shipping
13 The amount of buoyancy inside the kayaks
14 The personal qualities and experience of the leader.

Capsizes can be infectious, causing others to follow suit, and your attention may be split between calamities. If a rescue lacks supervision, it is possible that the sense of urgency may be lost, which is so important in getting people out of cold water as quickly as possible. You many often find it necessary to use a combination of rescue techniques to solve a difficult capsize situation.

The key to success is plenty of practice against the clock in controlled choppy conditions, even if it means doing it artificially in a swimming pool. Any practice is better than no practice at all.

11 Canoe Rolling

Compiled by the Editor with Canadian Rolling contributed by Martyn Hedges

Brin Hughes, Local Coaching Organiser for North West London, a commercial photographer, took the photographs for figures 11:1 to 11:8.

The section on 'Learning to roll without the aid of a swimming pool' is based on the recommendations developed and proved by Captain Barry Lillywhite, S/Sgt Bob Hawkes and the staff of the Joint Services Mountain Training Centre at Kingussie.

Martyn Hedges is currently British and European Canadian singles Slalom Champion. Because of his outstanding ability he was awarded the first sports scholarship at the University of Bath and is one of a small band of sportsmen to have gained a Sports Aid Foundation Elite Grant.

INTRODUCTION

There is nothing particularly mysterious or difficult about the art of eskimo rolling. It is simply a matter of turning the canoe or kayak upright by rotating at the hips. At the same time the body weight is pushed up by using the support obtained when the paddle blade is pressed sharply on the water. Man is not at his happiest when suspended upside down in an unnatural element, however, and the action necessary to sweep the blade on the surface in that situation is difficult to translate. This can lead to unnecessary confusion.

It must be emphasised that there is no single best, or right, way of learning to roll. Many instructors achieve equal success with a variety of teaching methods. What is universally accepted, however, is that in order to eskimo roll consistently in all conditions a canoeist must be able to rotate the boat upright by a method known as 'hip flick'. Attention paid to this element of the skill, and its performance in a smooth, reliable manner is vital. The better that the hip flick is performed, the more efficient and more consistent will be all subsequent rolling.

At what stage should a canoeist learn to roll? The answer for some, could be 'never'. The skill would be largely irrelevant to a person who was going to do nothing but flat water or marathon racing, or merely tour placid rivers in large-cockpit boats. For a canoeist aiming to tackle white water, surf or sea touring, however, the ability to roll is important, and many would argue that it should be regarded as a basic skill. Certainly, the total safety of an individual or group is, to a large extent, affected by whether or not a person can roll in serious conditions. It is the refinement of rolling techniques that has made possible the successful negotiation of the more advanced situations tackled by modern canoeists.

Concern has been expressed that if paddlers learn to roll too soon, there can be a tendency to 'give in' and roll, when in fact all was not lost, and a capsize could still have been prevented by the use of good recovery strokes. There are grounds for this reservation, and it should always be remembered that it is safer not to be upside down. Used properly though, the ability to roll at an early stage leads to the quicker learning of more efficient support strokes, together with most of the other controlling skills.

The same principle is involved when considering the use of a swimming pool, and aids such as face masks, nose clips and goggles. All these things are a means to an end only. After their initial exploitation to assist learning, emphasis must be laid on acclimatising to the real situation. This applies also to buoyancy aids and lifejackets. Where they have not been used in a swimming pool initially practice should occur with them in the pool, before the paddler reinforces his newly acquired skill in the great outdoors.

Background

The Eskimos have been rolling their kayaks for many centuries. It was only in 1927 however, that Edi Pawlata, an Austrian, became the first European to perform a roll, having studied the writings of Nansen and Jophansen.

In 1930 Gino Watkins, an Englishman who had gone to the Arctic to survey for a possible air route, learned rolling directly from the Eskimos and undertook kayak hunting expeditions in order to survive. Regretfully he died on one of the expeditions.

A study of the BCU film loops, or the memories of those who learned to roll prior to about 1965, will serve to show that the art of returning to the upright position following a capsize, was largely a matter of levering the body out of the water by dint of a prodigious sculling sweep, the boat being recovered by hip rotation as an after-thought. The Eskimo kayaks then available were popular for learning in, together with the latest slalom boats.

Interestingly enough, a missionary writing in 1765* describes ten methods by which an Eskimo righted his craft – the variation being by use of his full paddle, half a paddle, harpoon, until finally he would resort to hands only – although this, the writer observed, did not always work! A significant observation in the account is that once the paddle was positioned, the kayakist then applied 'a flick of the hips' to recover. It was the re-discovery of 'hip flick' in about 1965 that revolutionised the learning of rolling, and this, together with evolution of boat design, has led to its much greater incidence of successful application.

THE KAYAK ROLL

Equipment (see also pages 224-227).

Any kayak with a beam of 24" or less can be rolled quite easily, provided the paddler is able to hold himself in. A firm grip of the deck needs to be maintained with the knees, and a footrest is an advantage. The better the spraydeck, the less time will be wasted in emptying. Beginners should make sure that they are happy with removing it in an emergency. Maximum buoyancy in the boat is also an advantage, but beware polystyrene blocks which can crumble and pollute the pool. Paddles should not be metal-tipped, to avoid possible damage to baths. Any type will do, but ideally the paddler should be used to the pair chosen.

Face masks or nose clips and/or goggles can be useful in enabling the learner to obtain a clear vision of the paddle on the surface, and in preventing water entering the sinuses. Learn to breath out through the nose when under water, by practising in a quiet corner – exhale very slowly. This also prevents water penetrating the sinuses.

Hip Flick

It is assumed that the canoeist is happy in the boat, and is able to capsize, stay under and release the spray deck before coming to the the surface, holding on to the canoe, moving the canoe along untill he can grasp the end, swimming with the canoe and emptying it. See

---

Birch Bark and Skin Canoes of North America – Smithsonian Institute.

Establishing the hip flick

Figure 11:1a *The canoeist should grasp the paddle with knuckles uppermost. Note the under-hand hold by the instructor.*

Figure 11:1b *The half-way stage – concentration on hip flick only.*

Figure 11:1c *The kayak is now nearly upright with the paddlers head still in the water. Ideally, both hands should be on the rail, knuckles uppermost.*

chapter five – Basic skills. Initially, mobility of the hips can be learned by sitting upright in the kayak and wobbling it from side to side – the body remaining upright, and the knees in firm contact with the deck. Another useful drill which can also be practiced at any time when canoeing, is to place one paddle blade on a firm surface – another boat, or the bank or shore – and hang your body weight from it. Again, turn the canoe over as far as you can and recover it. The body should remain still.

Eskimo rescues are excellent practice for establishing hip flick technique. Hold onto the bow of another canoe, rest your body on your arms, without putting your head under water initially, take the boat over as far as it will go, and then recover it. Your body should not have moved. Gradually try further and further over until finally you are upside down, still holding onto your partner's bow. Hip flick up, concentrating on the boat rotating upright first, and your body following. The head should come out of the water last.

Most people have a 'preferred' side, which may or may not be related to their right or left-handedness, or their controlling wrist. Quicker results will be obtained if you commence to learn by coming up on your most comfortable side.

Where a swimming pool is available, use the rail at the side. Place both hands on the rail, knuckles uppermost, and practice hip flicks as before. Remember, the body should remain still and the boat be moved independently by the action of your hips, gradually allowing yourself lower into the water, until you are able to recover smoothly and consistently when upside down (Figures 11:1a, b and c). Never practice these techniques unless a helper, able to pull you upright, is at hand.

When an instructor is holding a paddle shaft he can assess the effectiveness of the hip flick by the amount the canoeist is pulling down on it. This should be minimal.

Some prefer to continue with hip flick practice, using a life-jacket or buoyancy aid, and then a swimming float with which the learner is coming up successfully, before proceeding. Provided the hip flick is effective as described, however, success is usually obtainable by proceeding to the next stage.

The half-roll

Not everyone will agree that this stage is necessary or desirable. Instant success can usually be guaranteed, however, which increases the confidence. It introduces the paddle, and indicates that provided the blade 'bites' the water, sufficient purchase is available to enable hip flick to be applied, and the body weight finally supported out of the water.

Move the hands along the shaft until the hand on the non-rolling side touches the blade. If desired, this hand can hold the very end of the blade, thus extending the lever, although there may be a tendency for a hand so placed to slip off.

The instructor takes the tip of the blade and the paddler capsizes, allowing his arms to the surface as he does so (Figure 11:2a). What follows is really a recovery stroke performed when upside down. Pull down on the paddle and *hip flick the canoe upright*. A roll performed in this way, with the paddle at right angles and pulled straight down, is known as a 'put across' roll (Figures 11:2b and c).

Whilst it is a good idea for the instructor to support the blade tip, to ensure that the paddle stays on the surface until required, he should, after the first couple of tries, be able to take his hand away before the canoeist 'strikes' – the paddler is thus rolling. All that follows is merely variation and improvement.

The Main Rolling Methods

Pawlata Roll
Some instructors will prefer to move directly to the 'screw' roll, but the advantage of the Pawlata is that the extended lever (Figure 11:3a) allows for maximum support.

The put across half-roll

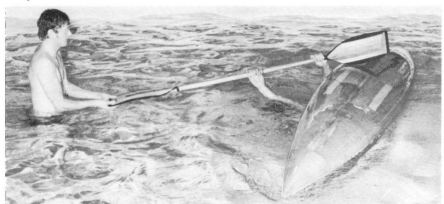

Figure 11:2a *First, allow the arms to surface.*

Figure 11:2b *At the half way stage the head is still under water.*

Figure 11:2c *Notice the mobility at the waist. The canoeist is now leaning well back.*

Figure 11:3a (above) *The Pawlata 'wind-up' – starting position.*

Figure 11:3b (right) *Before the capsize the instructor checks the angle of the blade on the deck.*

Figure 11:3c (below) *After the capsize the instructor sets the blade and the canoeist should 'feel' the water in this position.*

Figure 11:3d(top) *The instructor guides the sweep of the paddle.*

Figure 11:3e (centre) *The roll is completed with the canoeist applying hip flick, and lying back.*

Figure 11:4 (left) *It is often advantageous to practice the Pawlata sweep with the instructor supporting the canoeist.*

Notice the 'wind-up' (pronounced 'wined-up' – there's nothing to be afraid of!) with the rear hand wrapped around the end of the paddle blade, and the top edge biting into the forearm. The leading hand needs to be placed on the shaft naturally, and then the wrist rolled out, so that the edge of the forward blade nearest the water is tilted down towards it. This will in fact be the leading edge when upside down and ready to roll. The paddle will be swept round on the surface and so the leading edge tilted upwards will prevent the blade from 'diving'. The action is really a scull sweep from the bow.

Instruction needs to be given on the arm action, and the movement practised before capsizing to roll. The following is recommended: 'Imagine the paddle is a pitch fork, and that you have a load of hay on the end which you are going to pitch up and over your opposite shoulder into a loft above you. Let your head follow the path of the hay'. Let the student practice this, concentrating on feeling that the paddle is a pitchfork with a load of hay on it.

Initially the instructor should hold the blade (Figure 11:3b) and bring it to the surface after the capsize (Figure 11:3c). It is a good idea for the instructor to tap the blade on the surface a couple of times, having told the paddler that he is going to, and encourage the canoeist to 'feel' the blade there. Then he can bang the bottom of the canoe with one hand, at which signal the paddler sweeps the paddle around, guided by the instructor. He hip flicks upright when the blade is at about 45° from him (Figures 11:3d and e).

Notice in Figure 11:3d that the beginning of the sweep has brought the canoeist's body nearer the surface – it is not possible to hip flick from a completely upside down position, which is why a lifejacket or buoyancy aid *should* be an advantage. This however happens naturally, and should not normally be stressed. In figure 11:3e the paddler has rolled by hip flicking the boat upright when the blade was at the greatest point of leverage – nearly at right angles to the body. There is a similarity here, with the 'put across' roll. In fact, most canoeists nowadays roll by pulling down on the paddle – the various wind-ups and sweeps are merely a means of getting the blade to the point at which maximum leverage is obtained before pulling down.

Practice should now enable the canoeist gradually to do away with the instructor's help until he is completing a full Pawlata roll unaided.

Should difficulty be experienced with the sweep of the paddle, concentrate on the top of the near blade digging into the forearm, and the cocking of the forward wrist. It might be helpful for the instructor to support the paddler as shown (Figure 11:4) in which position he is able to practice the sweep, being gradually lowered into the water until successfully completing a half-roll.

If this does not lead to success in a reasonably short time, go back to basic hip flick routines. Older people will almost invariably have greater difficulty than youngsters, due to decreased mobility around the middle, and a tendency to want to work things out in their minds, rather than just doing what they are told!

When the paddle reaches a point about 45° behind the canoeist, a reverse sweep, or scull, must be applied if needed.

Once the canoeist is attempting to roll unaided the instructor should take up the position shown in Figure 11:5, in order to be able to pull him upright in the case of a failure.

Screw Roll

Rarely nowadays will a competent roller move his hands along the paddle in order to come up. The 'Screw Pawlata' roll is merely the routine described above, performed with the hands maintaining their normal hold on the paddle (Figure 11:6a and b). Ensure that the controlling wrist is used to set the angle of the blade. The same practice as above should lead to success. An extended lever can be obtained by positioning the hands as shown in Figure 11:2a.

Figure 11:5 *The instructor can rescue the upturned canoeist by reaching over the hull of the boat, grasping the canoeists arms or the gunnel, and right the canoe using his own body as a counter weight. He stands on the opposite side to the paddle.*

Steyr Roll

There are those who believe that rolling should be learned from a lying back position. Certainly, the centre of gravity is lowered by this, and properly performed, the Steyr roll is the simplest of all. The paddle is merely swept forward and you sit upright. However, rather like the 'put across', the simplest in theory often proves most difficult in practice. It is possible, in both surf and heavy water, to be knocked backwards, and it may be an advantage to be able to roll without having to bring the paddle to the bow of the canoe first. Many white water paddlers are opposed to any leaning back, however, due to the danger from submerged rocks. They advocate that all rolling should be accomplished with the head and shoulders tucked forwards.

To wind up for the Steyr, first adopt the Pawlata position. Then sit upright, bringing the paddle perpendicular. As you do so, push the insides of the wrists outwards. Continue backwards until you are lying along the stern deck, with the drive face of the blade uppermost (Figure 11:7). The roll is performed by capsizing towards the paddle, bringing the blade to the surface, and sweeping it forwards, pushing yourself up as you do so. Some merely use the sweep to move the blade to right angles, when the normal pull-down and roll up with hip flick is applied.

You may care to practice 'dry' by sitting on the floor with legs out in front of you. Wind up as for the Pawlata with the forward blade and drive face uppermost then into the Steyr as described, so that you are lying on your back. Roll over, the paddle coming underneath you, ensuring that the wrists follow round as they would do, with the drive face ending up face downwards on the floor. You are now lying on your belly. You will then see just how little effort is needed on the paddle blade to roll yourself over and sit upright. In the swimming pool, help can be given by an instructor in similar ways to those previously described.

Figure 11:6a *The start, or wind-up position for the screw roll. Note the hands are in the normal paddling position with the controlling wrist setting the angle of the blade.*

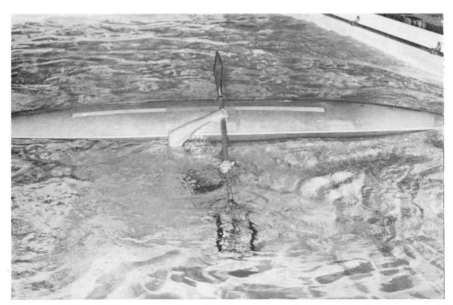

Figure 11:6b *The half-way stage – the paddle has swept round, the canoeists body has neared the surface and he is about to 'strike' and hip flick up.*

Screw Steyr Roll
As above, but with the hands in their normal position on the paddle.

Hand rolling (Figure 11:8)
Once a person is rolling easily and consistently with a Screw roll it is posible to move on to hand rolling, but it is probably worthwhile mastering all the rolls described above and below, first.

As has been stressed, the fundamental constituent of rolling is the hip flick, and the more effective this becomes, the less leverage will be required from the paddle. To consolidate this movement therefore, a series of practices should be carried out as before, but moving on to the use of a lifejacket or buoyancy aid for support. Place the float just behind the line of the hips and well out to the side. Hold with fingers on top, and thumbs underneath, and strike down with the hands in order to hip flick upright. When this can be done consistently, using a single swimming float, try recovering by striking down on the blade of a paddle left floating alongside. Once this is working, it should be possible to hand roll.

You may find that in order to recover using the floating paddle, the top arm needs to be flung across the canoe, and this will almost certainly be the case when using the hands only. Start with both hands close together, lying well back. Capsize, wait until the boat is settled, with hands near the surface. Strike down and hip flick upright (Figure 11:8c). Notice how the head comes out of the water last, and is close to the back of the canoe, keeping the centre of gravity low.

Storm Roll
A study of films from Greenland shows that the Angmassalik Eskimo at least does not usually use the Pawlata. The starting position is more or less the same, except that the forward blade is above the water, is about 30° from the side of the kayak, and has 'inward wind-up' – that is to say that the edge of the blade nearest the canoe is the higher, instead of the outer edge as in 'Pawlata'. Leaning well forward, the paddler pulls violently down. As he comes up he pitches so violently forward that the working blade comes out of the water behind him. The arc described by this blade is vertically downwards instead of horizontally outwards.

This can be performed with the normal, instead of the extended hand positions on the paddle, and most canoeists with good hip flick technique will come up well before the paddle has completed the full arc described.

Figure 11:7 *The wind-up or starting position for the Steyr roll.*

Hand rolling sequence

Figure 11:8a *The canoeists lays well back with hands close together.*

Figure 11:8b *Capsize and wait for the boat to settle.*

Figure 11:8c *Strike down and apply hip flick to right the canoe.*

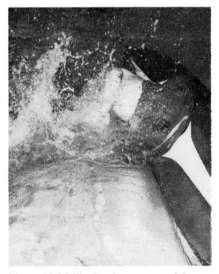

Figure 11:8d *The head comes out of the water last close to the back of the canoe.*

206

Perpendicular Paddle Roll
This is really a draw stroke performed when upside down. Often a capsize will occur when a high brace or draw is being applied. It is a matter, therefore, of keeping the paddle upright, but reaching out underwater with the lower arm and pulling sharply inwards – as for a high draw stroke – hip flicking upright as you do so.

Stunt Rolls

Clock roll
Hold the paddle as for the Pawlata roll, but with contrary (Steyr) wind-up. As you capsize, push the blade outwards and fall backwards into the Steyr position. Roll up on the Steyr, and bring the paddle forward into the starting position. Repeat as often as you like. To onlookers it appears that the paddle makes a big, sweeping circle like a hand of a clock. To get the 'hand' to move the right way, it is better to execute this roll left-handedly.

Rotary Roll
Capsize, holding the tip of one blade so that it is horizontal with the bottom when your body is pointing straight down. With your arms above your head (below you!) merely wind the paddle round and round, changing your grip as necessary. The far blade must remain perpendicular throughout, and thus the canoe spins round on the surface. When you've had enough, roll up.

Top Hat Roll
Probably still a favourite at demonstrations, the idea is to roll without getting your hat – preferably a 'topper' – wet. If you are holding your paddle on the left, take your hat in the right hand as you capsize and keep this arm above the water. When upside down reach across and give the hat to the left hand – which is holding the blade of the paddle – then bring the right arm under the canoe, grasp the paddle, and roll up.

Conclusion

The techniques described are not the only ways of bringing a Kayak upright, and as with all advanced skills, a paddler would not necessarily use only one movement to achieve recovery. Hopefully what has been written will help all to obtain early and continued success. Purists may argue that the skills outlined are not the original techniques involved under those headings, and they are right. They are, it is believed an accurate account of their application today. What matters, however, is whether or not a person can right him or herself following an accidental capsize – not the name of the method by which it was accomplished.

Various exercises are known, and others can be invented, to improve technique, to train for the real thing, and to maintain interest. Some ideas are outlined in the next chapter. Remember always that rolling is not an end in itself, neither is canoeing in a swimming pool. Properly learned and then re-learned in cold, moving water, the ability to roll effectively can safely open up experiences that would not otherwise be feasible. Consistent rolling on both sides must be the aim if the skill is to be relied on as a major safety factor.

LEARNING TO ROLL WITHOUT THE AID OF A SWIMMING POOL

Provided a person is confident under water, having performed capsize drills, eskimo bow or stern and paddle rescues, and has begun to control the canoe with the knees – using hip flick for recovery strokes and so forth – it is possible to obtain a fairly high success rate in the following manner.

Figure 11:9a *Working from his canoe the instructor holds the blade in position during the capsize.*

Figure 11:9b *The blade is smacked on the surface of the water.*

The instructor sets the student up in the Pawlata position described earlier. He then tells the student to imagine that the paddle is a pitch-fork and that he has to pitch a load of hay up over his right shoulder (right-handed paddler wound up with the paddle on the left). Let the student practice this, *concentrating on feeling that the paddle is a pitch-fork with a load of hay on it,* the head to follow the paddle around.

Directions should then be given along these lines: 'I am going to hold your paddle blade and guide it while you capsize. When you are upside down I will lift the blade up and slap it down onto the surface twice. I want you to feel the blade striking the surface. Then you must pitch that forkful of hay over your head – concentrate on following the paddle blade with your head and eyes. Your head must leave the water last – and you will come up.'

As the student capsizes, the instructor holds the blade by winding his arm under the canoe (Figure 11:9a). Then carry out the procedure of smacking the blade on the surface (Figure 11:9b). As the student commences to roll, *push his canoe away strongly with your paddle* (Figure 11:9c). This takes the paddle out to the side and around in an arc, keeping the blade on the surface. The student should roll. It may be necessary to call 'hip flick' as the head appears.

Progress can then be made by making the student do all the initial work in feeling for the surface and so forth, until finally he is rolling unaided. If success it not obtained in a reasonable time it may be necessary to return to hip flick practice and the other techniques described earlier. It is unnecessary for a student to come out of his boat as the instructor can immediately position himself for an eskimo rescue should an attempt fail.

Figure 11:9c *As the roll commences the instructor uses his paddle to push the canoeists boat away.*

THE CANADIAN ROLL

Introduction

For anyone learning to paddle Canadian canoes in rough water the need to be able to roll becomes important very quickly. The use of a single blade, coupled with the high centre of gravity of the boats can lead to frequent capsizes. While the single blade simplifies the mechanics of the stroke, the high centre of gravity and wide beam couple together to make this roll a challenging prospect.

Fittings

Whatever fittings the canoe possesses, whether aluminium, or webbing straps, they must enable the paddler to grip himself tightly in the canoe when capsized. They must be positioned in such a way that exit from the canoe in an emergency is a quick and easy task, not requiring any unbuckling of straps by hand. It is essential that before paddling a Canadian canoe for the first time, capsize drills be performed. The dangers connected with overtight, badly positioned fittings are very real. Never cross your legs beneath the seat in a Canadian canoe.

Terminology

Throughout the article, the expression 'top hand' refers to the hand holding the handle of the paddle. 'Lower hand' means the hand nearest to the blade. 'Drive face' indicates the side of the paddle blade which is pulled against the water *when paddling forward.* The 'back' of the blade is the opposite face.

Drills

Initial drills that can be practiced by the paddler to acquaint himself with the roll are as follows:

1   Capsize practice to overcome the fear of being trapped and ensure a quick release from the boat.

2   Swimming in the canoe to the bank after a capsize – after capsize, lean back in the canoe and slightly to one side, swim with hands (breaststroke or dog paddle) and the head will break surface. In this position it is possible to swim along whilst breathing satisfactorily. Practice both sides and swapping over.

The Canadian screw roll sequence

Figure 11:10a *Shaft parallel with boat. Blade out in front. Top hand slightly to rear of hip. Lean forward. Rotate wrists outwards. Capsize towards paddle.*

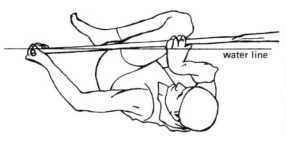

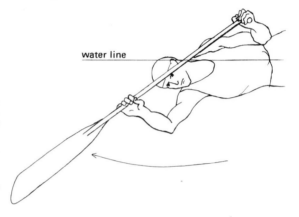

Figure 11:10b *Give canoe time to steady. Paddle and both wrists to surface. Control blade angle with top hand – too much 'bite' and canoe will turn; too little, the blade will slice.*

Figure 11:10c *Keep body just below surface. Top hand fairly still, close to gunwale and following as it begins to lift. Blade, lower hand and torso sweep out in wide flat arc. Keep face and chest down towards bottom of pool. Use hip-flick to thrust hull upright.*

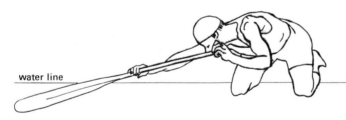

Figure 11:10d *Keep body weight as low as possible. Reverse sweep (see 11:10e) if necessary to complete recovery.*

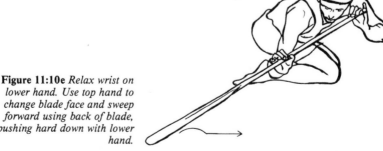

Figure 11:10e *Relax wrist on lower hand. Use top hand to change blade face and sweep forward using back of blade, pushing hard down with lower hand.*

3   Righting the canoe by use of the bank or a partner. Capsize onto partner's arm or side of pool and use arm strength in conjunction with hip flick to right the canoe. The hip flick is the most important part of the Canadian roll and practice is essential.

The two main rolls practiced today have their origins in the kayak Screw and Steyr rolls. A third – the cross-bow – is advanced, and peculiar to the Canadian.

Rolling Methods

Screw Roll
Hold the blade in the normal manner. Place the shaft parallel to the side of the boat on the side you wish to roll with the blade stretching out in front of you. The top hand should be positioned slightly to the rear of the hip. Lean forward and ensure that the wrists are bent, so that the outward edge of the blade turns towards the surface of the water (Figure 11:10a).

Capsize towards the paddle and allow boat to turn over fully. Leaning forward, thrust the blade towards the surface, ensuring that the top hand is clear of the deck, or in a comfortable position. Keep both wrists bent, so that the outboard edge of the blade is slightly turned towards the surface. (Figure 11:10b).

Keeping the lower arm straight, sweep in an arc from the bow, pulling firmly down. The action should be swift, and a sharp hip flick introduced when the paddle passes through 45°. Keep the body low until the boat is almost fully righted. This is of great importance, due to the amount of body which is out of the boat (Figures 11:10c and d).

If difficulty is encountered in this procedure the following addition should be made. As the blade has passed the centre of the boat, say about 130° during the initial sweep, drop both wrists to reverse the blade and push down hard while moving forwards (Figure 11:10e). Whilst pushing down, the hip flick should come into operation. Keep the body low as outlined before. This addition allows more strength to be used to ensure success. However, in competition, the first method is preferred, due to speed and superior finishing position.

Steyr Roll
Many Canadian paddlers prefer this method, as it offers stronger leverage, which aids success.

Hold the paddle as normal, lean back, and bring the blade upwards and over the head into the Steyr position but rotate the wrists as for a screw roll – the drive face should be flat against the canoe, so that the back of the blade is presented to the surface when you are upside down. Capsize towards the paddle and allow the boat to turn over fully. Ensure that the outward edge of the blade is uppermost on the surface by moving the lower hand towards the surface and thrusting the wrist upwards (Figures 11:11a and b).

Begin the sweep by arcing the paddle from the stern with a straight arm, pushing down using the back of the blade. Maximum downward thrust and hip flick should begin when the blade passes through 45° (Figure 11:11c). As the boat rises, ensure that the body position is kept low, as this will assist in the success of the roll (Figure 11:11d).

In contrast with the Screw roll, where the thrust for the roll comes from a downward *pulling* action using the drive face, the Steyr relies on the more powerful *pushing* action using the back of the blade.

Cross-bow Roll (Figure 11:12)
This is an advanced roll which enables C1 paddlers to roll on their wrong side without changing hands, and C2 paddlers to roll without one partner changing sides. It is awkward to execute, with the additional disadvantage of a very unstable finishing position.

The Canadian Steyr roll sequence

Figure 11:11a *Take paddle up and over head. Shaft parallel with arm on non-paddling side. Lie well back. Capsize towards that side. Keep blade close to gunwale and steady while canoe settles. Top arm relaxed. Lower forearm across face. Knuckles of blade hand near ear. Torso roughly in line with stern deck so that back of head, both hands and paddle are just under surface when capsized, with face and chest turned towards bottom of pool for as long as possible.*

Figure 11:11b *Relax grip on lower hand. Use top hand to set blade angle. Leading edge slightly raised. Strong pushing action required as blade is swept forwards. Top hand fairly still, close to gunwale and following as it lifts. Push blade hand away, and follow with body. Keep face and chest turned towards bottom of pool. Use hip-flick to thrust hull upright.*

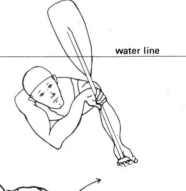
water line

water line

Figure 11:11c *Boat should be upright before paddle is at 90° to keel line. Keep chest and face turned towards bottom of pool as much as possible.*

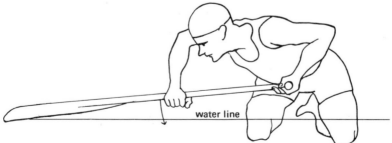
water line

Figure 11:11d *Keep body weight low. Top hand acts as a pivot and controls blade angle. Don't get it higher than necessary or support will be lost.*

213

The cross-bow roll sequence

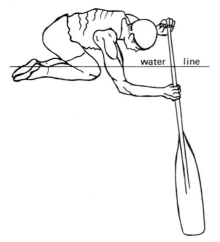

Figure 11:12a *Bring body weight close to deck. Top hand across. Forearm near head. Blade hand under water. Paddle as vertical as possible. Capsize maintaining this position.*

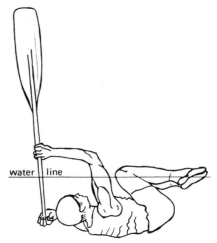

Figure 11:12b *Blade and some shaft in air. Keep paddle vertical.*

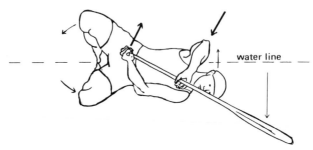

Figure 11:12c *Push out with lower (blade) hand. Pull top hand in across body. After blade has smacked surface keep pushing down hard with blade hand and pull inwards across thighs with top hand. Apply hip-flick.*

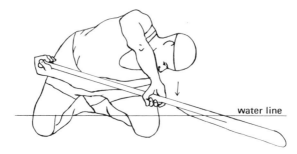

Figure 11:12d *Push down with blade hand. Keep body low until stability is achieved.*

214

Hold the paddle as normal, but feather it so that the drive face is towards the canoe, parallel to the gunwale. Place it in a vertical position, blade in the water on the paddling side beside the body, top hand shoulder height. The bottom hand should be in the water. Capsize either side (practice will be required in capsizing both ways) holding the paddle firmly in the starting position until the boat has turned over fully. In this position the blade will be in the air pointing vertically upwards. Now the hand nearest the blade pushes out, as the other hand pulls inwards towards the body. When the blade meets the water, resistance is felt. Push violently down with the hand nearest the blade. The other hand will continue moving towards the body. At the same time, hip flick.

As the boat is righted, the body must be kept low until stability is reached. This is the most difficult stage of the roll as it is so unstable.

Rolling the C2

C2 paddling is all about co-ordination between two individuals, and this is never illustrated better than during a roll. The methods used are based on the C1 rolls, Screw, Steyr or Cross-bow. If one paddler does not use the Cross-bow, then the partner must change hands to roll.

When capsized and ready, both paddlers must act together. The one who will take the longest to get into position must signal. Two or three regular hits on the boat with the paddle is the signal to start – the pair rolling up on what would be the third, or fourth 'hit'. This works reasonably well initially, but the following faster sequence should be encouraged. As before, the slowest paddler into position should initiate the roll. In this case, however, the 'signal' is the beginning of the roll itself. When the other partner feels this initial pressure causing the boat to begin to roll up, he joins in to produce the maximum force. This is a subtle advanced method dependent on a good sense of 'feel' for the boat, which works very neatly between paddlers who are well co-ordinated. With one partner using the Cross-bow roll, the return to the surface can be remarkably fast. Practice in a C1 is invaluable for achieving good results in a C2.

Canoeist shooting Richmond Falls. Photo: Bill Sampson.

12 Teaching Techniques and Use of a Swimming Pool

Compiled by the Editor

INTRODUCTION

Canoeing is fun. It can also be challenging, exciting and adventurous, and for some, that is what makes it fun! This does not hold true for everyone however, and so an instructor needs to be sensitive to the varying aptitudes and requirements of his students. Some will want to hurl themselves into every situation of apparent danger. Others, who might have been put off for ever if 'thrown into the deep end' too soon, will, through careful coaxing, eventually find fulfillment in adventurous canoeing. Many will never want to commit themselves to heavy rapids or surf, but may well achieve a lifetime of enjoyment in pursuing the path of the paddle in racing, or touring in kayaks or Canadians.

The instructor will inevitably gather about him a keen band who will follow his personal enthusiasm. He should, however, be prepared to allow for all interests to develop. Where this is not possible, and it would be in that person's best interests, an individual canoeist should be introduced to another group or club which caters for his potential.

A leader must be careful to ensure that he does not become a 'one man band' ending up as child-minder to myriad youngsters, whose total ongoing demands he cannot possibly satisfy, and whose immediate needs are met only at the expense of his personal canoeing time. This leads nowhere in the long term. The aim, therefore, should be to recruit and train other adult helpers, and to establish a club – even when it has to be a wholly junior club – where parental involvement is insisted upon at least in helping with transport and general supervision on a rota system. Club management functions – particularly for fund raising and similar activities – are another area where parental help can lift many unnecessary burdens from the instructor. The booklet on club formation, structure and management, available from the BCU, should be consulted in this respect.

There will be areas where this cannot be the norm, and here specialist advice should be sought, and investigation made of resources available through plans to combat inner city or urban deprivation. The National Association for Outdoor Education may well be able to give guidance in these circumstances.

'Example is better than precept' is a maxim which still holds true. Whilst the instructor, or other experienced paddler, will often be working in situations where buoyancy aids, for them, are superfluous, the novice will seek to emulate. He wants to be like them, and the only possible imitation he can achieve in the early stages is in style of dress, and approach. Your good example could therefore save a life.

The principles and ideas outlined are related to a general introduction to the sport in all purpose kayaks. It is assumed that the advice on safety equipment and procedures detailed elsewhere will be applied throughout the following.

PRINCIPLES OF GOOD INSTRUCTION

The success or otherwise of any session will be directly related to the care taken over the planning of the content, and the preparation of the equipment and the group. *The instructor needs to have an overall aim for each session,* ensure that the site chosen is suitable for that aim, and see that any aids needed are set up well in advance of the pupils' arrival. He also needs to have various ideas 'up his sleeve' so that the session is kept alive should interest wane at any stage. When students appear, their gear should have been checked and ready.

Practical lessons, lectures, club evenings, day trips, courses, all need planning in advance and must be relevant to the needs of the group, and the conditions suitable to their ability.

Try to ensure that there are sufficient canoes to go round – singles are normal when kayaks are used nowadays – or consider carefully how to achieve equal time sharing, and ways of keeping the non-paddlers gainfully occupied. Where first sessions are involved, it is best to prepare a handout listing the clothing and equipment necessary, remembering that those concerned are unlikely to possess wet-suits or thermal gear, and similar. Insist on light footwear – it is always better than having to perform first-aid!

Much of the art of instruction develops with experience, and there is no single method of approach, or sequence of teaching, that is universally applied. There are, however sound basic principles which will help an instructor in the early stages, and which hold true however well his personal style of tuition may develop. An instructor needs to be:

1 *Firm but understanding.* It is vital for safety, in most situations, that individuals respond immediately to the instructor's requests. These should not be beyond the ability of the student to comply with, nor order him to do something that makes him afraid.

2 *Aware of the environment.* The prevailing conditions should be used. It is no use proceeding with a lesson plan that requires a calm, controlled situation, in a howling gale. Always talk from upwind, and ensure the sun is not shining into the students' eyes as you demonstrate your best Colorado hook! Set bounds if necessary when students first go afloat.

Figure 12:1 *Canoeing is fun – for all ages!*

218

3   *Enthusiastic.* If you are not really interested in what you are doing, neither will the group be. Remember always that what may be tame, old hat, and boring to you, could be the biggest challenge that your student has ever faced!

4   *Responsible.* When individuals or groups are under tuition, the situation chosen must always be intrinsically safe, although it may well appear to the novices to be very exciting indeed. There is never an excuse for anyone to be led into real danger merely because the instructor, or his helpers, want a personal challenge.

INSTRUCTION TECHNIQUES

A high work rate is important for enjoyable and successful sessions. Remember the truism:
   The majority of what you *hear,* you forget
   Some of what you *see,* you retain
   What you *do,* sticks.
   When first imparting skills to others, it is a good idea to follow a teaching pattern. One in common use is known as EDICT:
   Explanation
   Demonstration
   Imitation
   Correction
   Testing

1   *Explanation.* Tell your group what they are going to learn and how the skill is performed – but remember KISS: keep it simple, stupid! Refer to the vital ingredients only. Use simple language – avoid jargon. Break the skill down into easy stages. Your students will want to *try* first, and *learn* later.

2   *Demonstration.* This should be competent, correct, and convey the vital points. The class needs to see how easy it really is, not how flashy it can be made to appear.

3   *Imitation.* Let them try.

4   *Correction.* Help the paddlers to get it right. The instructor must be able to identify and overcome the root cause of any problem. This is often the most difficult part of teaching canoeing, for it is not sufficient to know that something is wrong. All the elements of the skill must be fully understood – study carefully the relevant chapters. Patience and encouragement are necessary to obtain success.

5   *Testing.* Set exercises or goals which require application of the skill, and suggest routines for future practice.

Group control

The most effective form of group control – essential to the safe enjoyment of the activity – is achieved through well structured *activity.* Even in fairly placid water situations, groups can easily become dispersed if individuals lose interest and drift off, while in circumstances which are not ideally sheltered from wind or current, care must be exercised to contain matters. This may mean taking less people afloat than planned, or using an assistant. The person in charge must always remain observant, ensuring that all his group are accounted for and are working within the bounds set.

Practical sessions

The Star Tests provide a natural learning progression, although the teaching of skills should not be over-done. Basic techniques are a means to an end, and where possible, for every new ability learned, a situation should be devised for its natural application. Look also towards logical progressions, and the setting up of exercises that require the skills learned to be applied in a naturally flowing sequence. Figure of eight courses around buoys, slalom gate wiggle tests, and similar, are simple examples which provide for this.

Another factor, when working on the improvement of skills, is to relate an exercise to a 'goal' by the use of a stop-watch, or very precise requirement. For example, having learned stern rudder, it could be used to hold a straight course through a narrow gap, gradually increasing the speed at which the obstacle is approached, and decreasing the distance from it at which the stern rudder is applied.

An awareness of the whole body should be incorporated into your teaching methods. Rather than saying 'keep your bow pointed towards that tree', try 'keep your feet pointed towards that tree'. Or have your group paddle with eyes closed, concentrating on feeling the blade in the water, and exerting an even pull on both sides. Sometimes the desired result can be best obtained by finding a way of removing from the student any anxiety about failure to achieve the standard being set. Little work has been done within canoeing on these lines, and the application of 'inner game' theories to the sport opens up a new and fascinating field of discovery.

When steering, or practising the various skills, give thought yourself to the part that your lower body is playing, and pass on to your students the tips that will enable them to master the techniques more quickly and fully. Again, virtually nothing has been written on the part the lower body plays in turning and steering the kayak, although the importance of controlling lateral stability with the hips has been well documented.

Initially, one to two hour sessions are usually long enough, while sleeping muscle tissue is being organised. Ensure everyone knows the boundaries and what to do in the event of a capsize. Where small cockpit kayaks or canoes are involved, the instructor, or a competent helper, should always go afloat first.

There is little point in spending a great deal of time on land drill, but some indication of holding and feathering the paddle, forward and reverse control, and the sweeping action, can be useful. With less able groups, or where a mass of youngsters are merely 'having a go' in a canoe, it may be useful for paddles to be unfeathered, but this is not advocated for normal situations.

When beginners first go afloat they have two main problems, both of stability – lateral and directional. It is useful to prepare them psychologically for this, although care must be taken to ensure that they are 'prepared' for it – not 'put off' altogether!

Progress will vary according to the individual, the group, and the conditions. Where possible, it is best to achieve a balanced group – one person well below the general standard can spoil the activity for everyone. Success will also be related to the staff-student ratio – six to eight per instructor is ideal, 10-12 is manageable, but beyond that meaningful activity is difficult to organise.

What follows are simple examples of games and exercises that can be devised to build up confidence, reinforce a skill, or restore a 'flagging' session.

Steering and stopping exercises
Sweeping to correct or turn, and paddling backwards to avoid collisions, are obvious early priorities. A course around two buoys, canoes or other obstacles, can be established. Paddlers must use *forward* sweep strokes only to turn. Forfeits such as having to stand up in the canoe, or receiving a paddle-full of water from the instructor, can be devised if

backward strokes are used. Such penalties would probably be inappropriate to an adult group – teaching methods must always be related to the type of student involved. By changing to a figure-of-eight course around the buoys, an element of speed and stopping control can be brought in, whereby canoeists have to take avoiding action when passing each other. Ensure the course is long enough for the number involved.

A soft ball, or sponge, carried by the Instructor can be used for 'King'. Set bounds. Collisions, or breaking bounds, bring a forfeit. The ball or sponge must hit the body. The game starts with the instructor hitting someone, and finishes when only one paddler is left not caught. Variations, where the students have to remove a twig or similar from the instructor's toggle, can also be played. Making a race out of any technique learned, such as draw stroke, sculling draw, paddling backwards, is always a useful aid.

Rafting

Rafting-up is probably the most satisfactory way of keeping a group together in order to chat or demonstrate to them. Ensure, however, that there is no danger of a large raft drifting onto moored boats, or a bridge arch, or becoming a hazard to other traffic. It could take several minutes for a party of inexperienced canoeists to disentangle themselves in an emergency.

All kinds of fun, which increases confidence and enjoyment, can be had from a raft, which should not become a captive platform to which the instructor talks endlessly. Simply by making every other person hold firmly to the cockpit coaming of the canoe on each side of him, with the alternative people standing up, is a basic exercise. The paddlers from each end can be made to change boats, with one running along the foredecks, and the other the stern-decks. Rafts of three, with the outsiders paddling, and the middle man keeping the trio together can enjoy a race – use extended paddles so that the canoeist in the centre does not lose his head! Try 'chariot' races, where two canoeists raft together with one person sat between the canoes on a paddle which is placed across just behind the two cockpits, keeping the raft together with a foot in each boat. The partner stands, again with a foot in each boat, and operates the other paddle. Races can include swapping positions at a half-way point (Figure 12:2).

Simple 'changing places' events teach balance. The canoeists sit in pairs facing the same way. One sits across onto the partner's stern deck and supports, whilst the partner moves over into his canoe, and then supports while the first paddler sits down. Emphasise that balance is maintained by pushing down equally on both hands, or by holding directly in the centre of each canoe.

Hip flick exercises

Use the bank, or another canoe, to teach committal of the body weight to the paddle. Place the blade on a solid object and hang on the paddle, rotating the canoe over and back again with hip flick. Ensure the canoeist hangs under the shaft, and does not allow the arms to become extended – a little practise only is usually required. This is a good precursor to learning the recovery stroke.

Mobility exercises

'Cross deck paddling' gets the learner pivoting about the waist (Figure 12:3). Turn head 90° then shoulders, in order to be able to paddle the boat sideways by operating the paddle as 'normal'. A slight counter-balancing lean away from the paddle is necessary. This can be varied with a 'turning' race, using the same paddling position as before, but drawing in with the blade nearest the bow, and pushing out with the blade nearest the stern to turn 360°, and then vice-versa. By the time this has been performed on both sides, the canoeist is becoming quite versatile! Although not used in modern kayaking, the cross-bow rudder, or Colorado hook, is fun, and a useful mobility exercise. (See cross bow cut, p245).

General confidence building fun and games

Where white water canoeing is the eventual aim, and rolling is an end in view, occasional 'wet' sessions are necessary. Often a simple water fight can be the start of a period that will be remembered for a long time, and lead to the overcoming of any fear of capsize. Beware of making such activity the norm however. Racing whilst sitting on the stern deck, with feet in the boat, or kneeling up in the cockpit paddling on one side only, or standing up races, are all events that can lead to people enjoying falling out.

Follow the leader, doing exactly as he does, where he does it, can cover the whole repertoire of skills. Joining the stern toggles together, by slipping one through the other, or taking a carabiner or short piece of line afloat with you for the purpose, for tug of war between two canoeists, can restore interest and involvement, and improve paddling power (Figure 12:4). Crocodile races, with two or three canoes clipped together at the toggles, is also easily organised, and involves the participants in developing and applying controlling skills.

Forward paddling on one side only, for intermediate groups can include the requirement to keep the paddle in the water all the time. An 'Indian' recovery – feathering the blade forward through the water – is necessary. This can also be made into a race. Turning a canoe by using a bow draw, slicing the paddle through to the stern – 'Indian' or feathered recovery as above – then pushing out at the stern, and slicing the paddle forwards for another bow draw until the boat has turned 360°, involves considerable feel for the action of the blade in the water, and for balancing skills. Again, make a race of it.

Lessons and lectures

There will usually be a need to give both lessons and lectures. Properly presented, a short talk and classroom illustration of canoeing techniques can aid understanding and so speed up the learning process. The following should always be considered:

1   The venue should be moderately warm, well ventilated and well lit – brighter at the instructor's end. Everyone needs to be comfortably seated, and have somewhere to write. The blackboard, or other visual aids must be visible to all. Avoid distraction.

2   The lesson plan should be sketched out in note form to ensure you fulfil your aim and to guide you through your introduction, main subject matter and conclusion, and remind you of the vital points that you need to make. Consult, but avoid reading from, your notes. A suitable anecdote, or similar, to illustrate your message, can be usefully pin-pointed.

3   Audio or visual aids can include the use of blackboard, slides, tape recordings, overhead projector, prepared drawings, flannelgraph, and so forth. It is not possible for a listener to concentrate on talking alone for more than 20 minutes. For young people, the period is much less. 'Question and answer' is a means of breaking a monologue. Where lengthy notes are required write them on a blackboard, overhead projector, or large sheets of paper in advance, and reveal them gradually. Handouts, summarising the session should be circulated at the end, not at the outset.

4   Avoid distracting habits – jingling coins in the pocket, or throwing chalk up and down as you talk, are favourites – and endeavour to alter the pitch and volume of your voice. Try and look around your audience. Admit when you are wrong – never attempt to bluff your way through if asked a question to which you do not know the answer.

Figure 12:2 *The 'chariot' race adds interest and develops confidence.*

Figure 12:3 *Cross deck paddling is a useful mobility exercise.*

Figure 12:4 *A tug of war between two canoeists can add interest and develop paddling power.*

Conclusion

All that has been written is merely a basic outline to help develop the art of good instruction, together with a few ideas for having fun and increasing confidence and skill. Imagination and innovation are the vital tools which can be gained through experience approached with an open mind. The instructor should not always paddle and teach at the same level, but seek the company of better canoeists in order to improve his personal standards. Working with others, observing their teaching techniques, and gaining experience of different water and types of canoeing will develop a knowledge and love of the sport, which will in turn communicate itself to others.

THE USE OF A SWIMMING POOL

Swimming pool time is as valuable for training purposes to the canoeist, as it is to the skin diver. Properly used, it provides a controlled situation where skills and water confidence, vital to the paddler's safety, can be most efficiently developed.

Care must be taken to ensure that all equipment used in swimming pools is suitable and clean. Always arrange for facilities to be available for washing out boats prior to putting them on the water. Those who use swimming baths have a moral obligation to every other canoeist to see that their conduct, and the care they take, ensures a good relationship with the pool management. A booklet entitled *The Canoe and the Swimming Pool* is available to help in situations where superintendents may be reluctant to allow time to canoeing groups.

Metal tipped paddles are best avoided – or the ends must be well protected. Pointed kayaks or canoes should have the bow and stern padded. Old rubber balls with a hole dug out, can be taped on. Hold the ball on the canoe by taping lengthwise along the canoe – about nine inches and around the ball: two lengths crossing the ball at right angles. Then bind round and round the taped canoe and the ball. If canoes with polystyrene buoyancy blocks have to be used, take along a biology net, or similar, in order to skim the surface of the pool for crumbs of polystyrene at the end of the session. Ideally, a fleet of boats for pool use should be maintained and kept on site. BATs are specially designed for this purpose.

The size of classes should be monitored so that the number of boats in the pool at any one time is manageable. When rolling is being taught, two to three persons can share, the others acting as 'instructors' to the person in the canoe, under the supervision of the coach in charge. Where a series of weekly sessions is run as a course, careful thought must be given to an ongoing programme of activity. Classes must not lose their purpose, or there could be degeneration into rowdy or meaningless activity.

As has been stressed, a swimming pool is an artificial environment, and most skills learned there will have to be re-learned in the open air. Overdone, a breed can develop which does not canoe outside a pool, and this is undesirable for a natural sport like canoeing. When transferring groups to the real situation, be careful to work them up gradually, and do not assume that because a person is handrolling in a swimming pool, he will be able to tackle difficult conditions of river or sea – or even paddle in a straight line to start with!

The swimming pool is of paramount importance as a *training* aid. Work done there must supplement, not replace, practise under natural conditions.

Practical work

A depth of as little as 3′6″ is adequate for learning capsize drills or the eskimo roll. It is vital at all times that the person in charge is in a position where he can see all that goes on – this is necessary for coaching as well as for safety. Never let swimming be permitted in the area where canoes are operating. A whistle, and a stop watch, are worthwhile accessories. Where instructors are having to stand by in the water for any length of time, wet suits are advised.

There is a case for developing confidence under water prior to sitting a person in a canoe. Let the students perform hand-stands in the water, progressing to forward rolls, and then somersaults, forwards and backwards – a nose-clip will help. Try the routines with eyes shut, moving on to swimming ten strokes under water comfortably with eyes shut. Roll and cavort, the body forgetting its usual vertical orientation. Get the students to count the tiles on the pool bottom, or lie back and blow bubbles, watching the pearly globs wobble to the surface. Let people paddle themselves around the pool without a canoe.

Then put the boat in, upside down. Let the candidate put his head up into the cockpit and breathe, then swim under water away from the canoe, back to it, and again breathe from the cockpit, keeping under water and using the cockpit as a base. Move on to somersaulting into an upside down sitting position in the boat and somersault out again. Finally, fit spraydecks and proceed, if necessary, with the normal capsize routine. Never try to find out who can hang upside down in a canoe the longest.

When performing the eskimo roll, it is essential that the head leaves the water last. Some instructors feel, therefore, that learning to swim the canoe whilst still in the cockpit should be left until after rolling has been learned, in case it induces a tendency to bring the head up first. It is hard work, mechanically, however, to keep the head above the surface when swimming a canoe or kayak in this way. The technique should be to take a breath, and then drop the head back in the water, easing air out of the mouth as the boat is swum. When air is needed, the head bobs up – a breath is taken – and back down again. The ability to swim the canoe to the edge and roll up without getting out is a great confidence booster, and, properly taught, should assist, rather than detract from rolling skills.

A game which develops an ability to hold firmly with the thighs, and is a great source of fun, is for two people to take hold of a canoe, capsize it, and endeavour to shake the occupant out into the water. The game is over when the canoeist falls out or gives in by slapping the hull – the helpers must then immediately roll him upright (Figure 12:5).

Figure 12:5 *A rocking exercise to train the paddler to stay in an inverted canoe.*

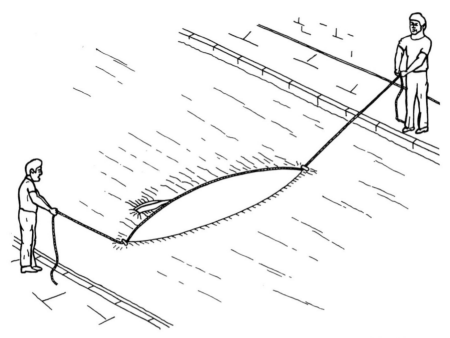

Figure 12:6 *A rope is tied to the canoe whereby the pullers capsize the canoeist, and drag him along when upside down to develop rolling ability.*

The rolling programme

A programme of sessions should be worked out emphasising certain skills to be mastered each week, with competitions or sequences involving that skill designed to enliven the programme. The whole repertoire of basic and rolling techniques can be utilised for this purpose, together with rescue drills – not forgetting the 'all in' rescue.

Once consistent rolling on both sides is achieved, and probably during the learning process, it will be necessary to introduce games and activities to consolidate achievement, and again, to bring variety to sessions.

Various practices can be organised to create a more realistic situation in which the eskimo roll must be applied. Tieing a rope to each end of a canoe, with a helper on each side dragging the canoe along, is a useful exercise. Be careful that the 'pullers' do not become over-enthusiastic, as a rope breaking can cause accidents. A continuous length of line which runs from one side of the pool to the other, passing through each end loop of the canoe en route, can overcome this problem (Figure 12:6).

Students can line up at one end of the pool and create waves by kicking up and down. The canoeist should practise throwing his paddle away, swimming to it, and then rolling up. The paddler should capsize, release the spray deck, come to the surface, then go back under and get back into the canoe with a reverse somersault, replace the spray deck, and roll up. Two canoeists can capsize and swim to each other (no paddles). One flicks up by holding on to the other canoe, and then the other eskimo rescues on him.

226

Team relays can be arranged, with a race to a first position, where the boat must be turned 360°, then race on to a second position where a roll is required, then race on to the change-over position (well away from the pool side). A rope across the pool, to which the canoe has to be paddled, capsized, and swum under before rolling up, can also provide interest.

General fun and games

Polo practise is worthwhile at all stages, or an enjoyable game can be obtained by using hands only – no paddles. This is particularly useful with small pools, or before candidates are very proficient. In this case, capsizing opponents should not be permitted. Figure 12:8 shows a training programme for canoe polo – more benifits will be obtained if your session is well structured.

Various obstacle courses can be organised using rubber rings or plastic containers with weights attached. A slalom gate, or gates, can usually be strung across a pool. The wiggle or wriggle sequence can be used – with a stop watch timing the event. Make competitors use identical boats. Although dipping techniques can be taught, it is better for the wiggle gate test to concentrate on turning skills, by hanging the poles in the water, so that canoes cannot be ducked under them (Figure 12:7).

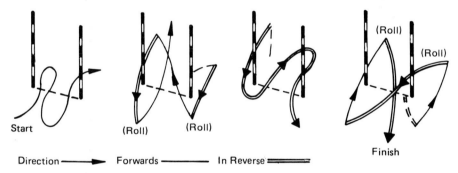

Figure 12:7 *The wiggle test, as performed without the rolls becomes the wriggle test when the rolls are included.*

Synchronised canoeing programmes can be devised, and a demonstration programme arranged, which works to music, or to timing, without the requirement for continued called instructions. The possibilities here are endless. Various demonstrations of technique, with boats turning together using the same number and rhythm of strokes, patterns being formed, crossing over in figure of eight routes, rolling in unison, and in sequence, and so forth.

Try obstacle relay races – boat in the water, enter from the water, hand-paddle to middle, the boat must pass under a rope and the canoeist over it, hand paddle to far side, unassisted swap over in the water.

Fastest roller contests are also easily set up, with one person timing and another counting, to see who can achieve the greatest number of rolls in 30 seconds, or 60 seconds.

Conclusion

With prior thought given to an overall plan, and a purpose worked out for each session, swimming pool training can provide tremendous enjoyment and fulfilment, as well as enabling the groundwork for the essential skills of the canoeist's trade to be mastered.

Canoe Polo Training Programme

PASSING   (1) In Three's, moving freely around the pool passing.

(2) Three + players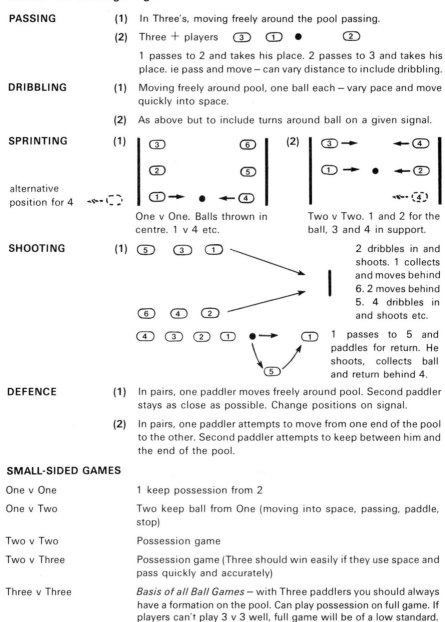

1 passes to 2 and takes his place. 2 passes to 3 and takes his place. ie pass and move – can vary distance to include dribbling.

DRIBBLING (1) Moving freely around pool, one ball each – vary pace and move quickly into space.

(2) As above but to include turns around ball on a given signal.

SPRINTING (1)

alternative
position for 4

One v One. Balls thrown in centre. 1 v 4 etc.

(2) Two v Two. 1 and 2 for the ball, 3 and 4 in support.

SHOOTING   (1)

2 dribbles in and shoots. 1 collects and moves behind 6. 2 moves behind 5. 4 dribbles in and shoots etc.

1 passes to 5 and paddles for return. He shoots, collects ball and return behind 4.

DEFENCE   (1) In pairs, one paddler moves freely around pool. Second paddler stays as close as possible. Change positions on signal.

(2) In pairs, one paddler attempts to move from one end of the pool to the other. Second paddler attempts to keep between him and the end of the pool.

SMALL-SIDED GAMES

One v One   1 keep possession from 2

One v Two   Two keep ball from One (moving into space, passing, paddle, stop)

Two v Two   Possession game

Two v Three   Possession game (Three should win easily if they use space and pass quickly and accurately)

Three v Three *Basis of all Ball Games* – with Three paddlers you should always have a formation on the pool. Can play possession on full game. If players can't play 3 v 3 well, full game will be of a low standard.

Figure 12:8 *A training programme for canoe polo showing a variety of manoeuvres and set plays which can be practised in the pool.*

228

SET PLAYS

 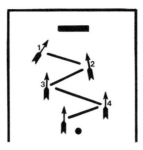 

1 Free Throw 1 and 2 move first, then 3 and 4.

2 Under Goal 1 has ball – passes to 3, who is shielded by 1 and 2. 3 shoots.

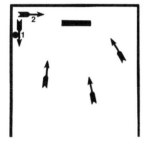 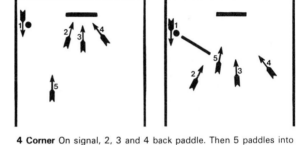

3 Corner 2 has ball, 1 comes in, in reverse, to take corner. 1 passes to 2 who shoots. Other paddlers keep away from goal area.

4 Corner On signal, 2, 3 and 4 back paddle. Then 5 paddles into space, receives ball and shoots.

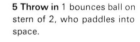

5 Throw in 1 bounces ball on stern of 2, who paddles into space.

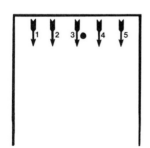 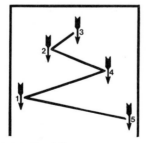 

6 Goal throw 1 and 5 move away, then 2 and 4.

7 Goal throw 1 or 2 pass to 3 or 4

229

An Open Canadian Touring Double shooting a fall on the New French Broad River, USA.
Photo: Pete Midwood.

230

13 Canadian Canoeing

An introduction to the art and lore of the Canadian Canoe compiled by the Editor.

INTRODUCTION

Canoeing is a much neglected pastime in Great Britain, when compared with kayaking. This has boomed and is invariably the activity that is taught in the hundreds of centres, schools, scout units and clubs where 'canoeing' is a main, or subsidiary pastime.

A trend is discernable, however, in that more and more centres and clubs are now involving 'open canoe' work, while some commercial concerns, which use canoes on camping cruise holidays, and some specialist canoe suppliers, have recently established themselves. Many of the British manufacturers have, in fact, been making canoes by the hundred over the years, but these have largely been exported to the Continent.

There is a difficulty in dealing with canoeing in this manual, in that in spite of the comparatively small following at home, in total it is a far more complex sport than is kayaking.

The repertoire and application of skills is more diverse. All the kayak techniques described earlier are in fact borrowed from canoeing – the recovery stroke being the only one that was invented by kayakists and is now used in canoes. There is a different application of the strokes for solo or doubles technique. Trim has to be adjusted by the paddlers themselves deciding on the most advantageous position for a particular circumstance. Poling is a separate art, and is reckoned to be canoeing's fastest way to ascend a stream by human power. The craft lends itself to being sailed, as well as allowing for the successful attachment and use of outboard motors. It can also be rowed. All these outlets should be explored by those who would truly call themselves 'canoeists'.

We would need to go back many centuries to discover the beginnings of the paddling skills that Milo Duffek successfully translated to kayaks in the early 1950s, and the canoe that has been adopted. This originated in North America, which includes, most importantly for our purposes, Canada. The 'dugout' was followed by the 'birch bark' canoe, which comprised a timber frame covered with the bark of birch, or other suitable tree. Early explorers, missionaries and traders, obtained these craft from the Indians, and used them as a major means of transport. Often the canoes were large, crewed by many paddlers. Some early settlers who were trappers, hunters and traders, became the 'voyageurs' of the 17th and 18th centuries, obtaining their living by transporting goods and passengers in native-built canoes hundreds of miles across the network of waterways that comprise much of Canada. Their journeys, and ability to cover vast distances, living off a hostile land and 'portaging' heavy loads from one river or lake to another, are legendary.

It was not until about 1870 that a modern canoe building trade became established by Whites, and all-timber, and then lath and canvas construction methods developed. These were followed eventually by boats made of aluminium, glass-fibre, and now ABS and other substances even more resilient. Currently there are over 600 designs of open canoe available in America, serving a canoeing population estimated at around 2.5 million. Over 100,000 craft are sold annually.

Besides sailing their canoes, poling was a skill developed by the voyageurs, and largely lost with the advent of down-river recreational canoeing. In recent times there has been a resurgence of interest, with contests in poling canoes up rapids being staged. Many will be surprised to learn that in England there are canoe poling races held at boating club regattas on the Thames today.

Five different designs of 'shoe' or 'spike' exist for poles, which themselves are made of wood, aluminium or fibre-glass. It is not necessary to be able to reach the bottom, however, as poles can be used as paddles, and another repertoire and application of skills is then involved. On long down-river trips, a period of poling can bring relief by allowing for a changed position, and utilising different muscles.

In the light of this brief summary, it will be appreciated that the treatise is necessarily superficial, and that the adaptation that has been made for 'British' purposes of the open canoe skills, which developed in a wilderness context, less than comprehensive. It is beyond the scope of this chapter altogether to develop further the areas of poling, sailing and powered canoeing. Those interested are urged to study the American Red Cross manual, *Canoeing,* available from BCU Supplies.

The basic skills applicable to the competent handling of Canadian canoes have been set out in logical progressions as an aid to learning. A competent demonstration of all these arts makes for a proficient canoeist, able to take charge of his craft on an extended journey. A system of canoe handling tests and tests of touring proficiency are administered by the BCU.

Camping is dealt with in chapter 15. The open canoe, which is a substantial load carrier, allowing greater ease of packing and unpacking, and keeping its occupants much drier than a kayak, is purpose-built for this activity.

The system that follows has been based on the Canadian Recreational Canoe Association's Standard Tests of Achievement in Canoeing, and the very fine Path of the Paddle Film *Solo Basic,* now in the BCU film library, together with advice from George Steed.

CHOICE OF BOAT

For mainly solo work, a length of 15'-16' is ideal, and 16'-17' for solo or doubles. If doubles use is paramount then 16'-18' should be considered, with the longer length (or even greater) being applicable if the carrying of large loads, or extra paddlers on long cruises, is to be the norm.

With the bewildering array of designs available, only general guidelines can be given. The boat should be light enough to be lifted comfortably by an adult crew; have modest tumblehome – an excess makes the boat difficult to empty; be slightly rockered (if manoeuvrability is important); have no keel strip if manoeuvrability on white water is the biggest factor; or a shoe keel (very flat, single strake, wider than it is deep) if a compromise is required; for touring in a straight line, a conventional keel, or keel supplemented by bilge keels, is recommended; wide, flat-bottomed boats are stable, but more cumbersome for solo paddling; narrow bows and stern however will cause the canoe to 'knife' into waves and so ship water; the fullness of the bottom needs therefore to be carried well fore and aft, for general purpose boats; the sheerline should not have excessive rise at bow and stern, nor an excessive dip in the middle.

For canoes up to 17' in length there should be three thwarts (or seats) and the centre thwart can be 14" off-set from the centre of the canoe. The distance between the middle

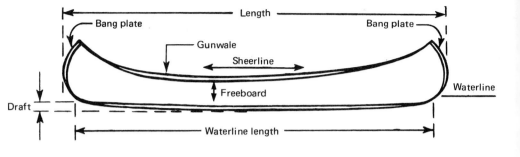

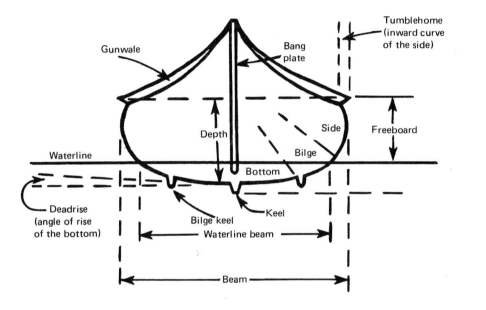

Figure 13:1 *The parts of a canoe.*

thwart so positioned and the beginning of the deck at the far end, divided by two, is the distance that the bow and stern thwarts should be located from the centre thwart. In this way, the stern thwart is nearer its end of the canoe, than is the bow thwart, and the best combination of paddling positions is allowed for.

For lakes and placid river canoeing a painter (up to 15′ of 6 mm line – preferably floatable) should be located at each end. These are always kept loosely coiled in the bottom, clear of the paddlers. They are not recommended for white water because of the danger of snagging. Buoyancy (minimum 12½ kg each end) for white water should fill most of the free space. Closed cell foam pads glued to the floor for kneeling on, complete the fittings, except that where rapid rivers are to be run, a system of quick-release thigh straps should be incorporated.

CHOICE OF PADDLE

Correct length is the most important factor, and it should be such that the handle is level with the forehead when the blade is just buried in the water, with the paddler kneeling on the bottom of the canoe, his posterior resting on the thwart. A rough gauge is to stand, holding the paddle with the blade on the ground. The top of the handle should be at eye-level. For racing, or slalom, this may well vary. The blade itself should not be too long, and it is best to avoid the very wide blades used by white water canoeists, in the early stages. Choice of grip is a matter of personal preference, although the T-grip is the more positive.

BASIC SKILLS – level 1

Paddling position

To commence the paddler should kneel on the bottom of the canoe, with the knees spaced comfortably apart, resting on the pads, his posterior supported on the thwart. It is better, for learning, that the beginner first adopts the bow position in a double, with a competent paddler in the stern. Once a 'J stroke' is performed successfully, however, there is no reason, provided the wind is not blowing too strongly, why the beginner cannot learn solo. Obviously, the opportunities that Canadians give for twice as many people to be afloat in half the number of boats, to have plenty of fun, and yet still be fully occupied, will be exploited by most.

Launching and embarking

Remember always to lift the bulk of any object using the muscles of the legs, rather than the back. Squat, rather than bend over to pick up a heavy weight. Any efficient method of carrying the canoe is acceptable, including above the head, with the thwart resting on the shoulders, a hip or shoulder carry, one person each end, or each side as appropriate.

The canoe can be placed on the water, either by a straight lift down, or feeding it in end first, and bringing it parallel to the bank once afloat. Where two crew are concerned, the bow-man normally enters first. Facing the bow, the outer foot is placed on the keel-line and both hands grasp the gunnels, with the paddle held across so that the blade is on, or towards, the shore. The other foot is then brought across and the paddling position adopted.

'Forward' or 'power' stroke (Figure 13:2)

The choice of paddling side will depend on the individual's preference, remembering that generally strokes are performed on one side only. A recreational canoeist should, however, aim to be ambidextrous, able to control the boat from all four stations. A double is paddled with bow and stern man working on opposite sides, the stern man being responsible for the general steering.

A method of determining the position for the hands on the paddle is to place the grip well up into the arm-pit and hold with the bottom hand where the fingers lie when the arm is stretched along the shaft.

Place the paddle blade in the water with the blade at 90° to the keel line, by extending the lower arm and reaching forward with the body, but not producing an exaggerated lean. The top arm guides, in order to keep the paddle upright, and an equal distance from the keel line, throughout the stroke. The trunk should be rotated about the spine, and it unwinds, with the body coming back to the upright position, as the lower arm pulls the blade through

Figure 13:2 (top left) *The paddling position. Commencement of the power stroke.*

Figure 13:3 (top right) *The 'J' stroke.*

Figure 13:4 (left) *Draw stroke.*

the water. Remember that in theory the blade should remain still, by gripping the water, and the boat is levered past it.

When the bottom hand is level with the hips, the blade is lifted cleanly sideways out of the water, and taken forwards to recommence the stroke by the top arm dropping, and the top wrist feathering the blade with the thumb pushing forwards. The blade should be feathered with the top edge high in case of catching a wave.

Backwater stroke

In order to stop a canoe, or go backwards, a backwater stroke is applied. This uses the non-drive face of the blade – the 'drive' face being the side of the blade that is pulled against the water in a forward power stroke. Commence where the power stroke finishes, by leaning slightly back, inserting the paddle blade, and pushing away with the bottom arm, again using the powerful abdominal muscles. Recovery is the reverse of the forward stroke recovery process.

'J' stroke

A solo paddler, or the stern man in a double, will have to control the direction of the canoe by using 'J' strokes and sweep strokes as necessary.

If the boat is turning away from the steering side, as will inevitably be the case with solo paddling – for then power is being applied to one side only – a steering element needs to be introduced to the power stroke, to bring the canoe back on course. (Figure 13:3)

When the paddle blade reaches level with the canoeist's hips, instead of lifting it from the water, the blade is turned through 45° while still fully immersed, the stroke continued, and the blade gradually taken away from the side of the boat. In the early stages the gunwale may well be used for leverage.

To turn the blade through 45°, the wrists are rotated so that the wrist of the top arm is turned with the thumb pushing *forwards* – the drive face of the blade turns out away from the side of the canoe. As will be seen, this forms the shape of the letter 'J' when performed on the left side, and it is the tail of the 'J' – the blade gripping the water and pushing sideways – that gives the correcting moment.

Goon stroke

The 'goon' stroke is the method of steering a canoe most likely to be adopted by those left to their own devices. It is performed in exactly the same way as the 'J' stroke, except that the paddle is rotated so that the drive-face of the blade is turned towards the canoe during the steerage part. It is less efficient than the 'J' stroke, because of the 'drag' that is caused by the angle of the blade, but it allows for more support.

Draw stroke (Figure 13:4)

This is used to move the canoe sideways or to turn it. At this level, the concentration should be on a simple, functional draw-stroke. Kneeling in the normal paddling position, first turn the head through 90°, then turn the shoulders – rotating at the waist – and reach the paddle well out, with the forearm of the lower arm at 90° to the shaft. The drive face of the blade is towards the canoe. Pull the blade in, keeping the paddle upright, until about 6" from the side of the canoe, when it is lifted out, and the action repeated.

When some measure of competence and confidence is achieved, the blade should be kept in the water after each stroke, and rotated through 90° by the wrists bending out. The paddle is then returned to the commencement of the stroke without the blade being lifted from the water. A canoe can be turned in a circle by a doubles pair each performing a draw stroke on his or her paddling side. The blade needs to be deep.

236

Forward sweep stroke

To turn a canoe away from the paddling side, or correct its course if it is turning *towards* the paddling side, a forward sweep stroke is used. Remember that a canoe rotates around its centre of gravity. When operated solo, it will rotate around the paddler, and for doubles, in an arc that passes through the shoulders of the bow and stern man. The maximum effort should be applied along this circle in order to achieve the most efficient turning.

Reach well forward, with the top arm low. The bottom hand can be brought up nearer the grip to allow the paddle blade to be inserted further forward, and achieve a wider sweep. The paddle shaft will be at about 45° and body rotation used to achieve power.

For solo paddling, the blade is inserted near the bow and continues in a wide arc, the blade just covered, until reaching the stern. The top arm will push across to drive the blade into the stern, once it reaches the stern quarter. For doubles, the blades's arc is 90° only. The bow-man reaches almost directly ahead, and rotates until the blade is at right angles to his body. The stern-man commences the stroke from right angles to his body, and finishes with the blade well astern.

Recovery is as for the forward power stroke, with the blade feathered and kept close to the water, except that the top hand will remain close to the paddler's waist.

Reverse sweep stroke

Sweep strokes can be applied in reverse, by doing the opposite of that which is described above for the forward sweep stroke. The non-drive face of the blade is used.

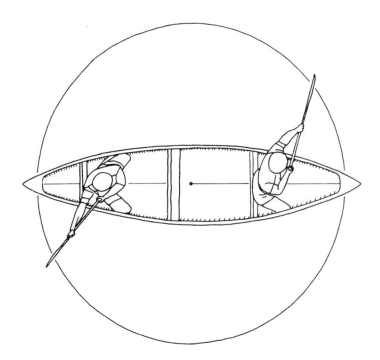

Figure 13:5 *A canoe rotates around its axis. Force is only effective when it is applied on this arc.*

237

Figure 13:6 *Practising the recovery stroke 'dry'.*

Stern rudder

See entry on stern-ruddering under kayak skills chapter five. The paddle is trailed using the 'goon stroke' angle – driving face towards the canoe.

Recovery stroke (low brace) (Figure 13:6)

The non-drive face of the blade is presented to the surface, with the paddle held as near horizontal as possible. Lean the canoe towards the paddle, and recover with a sharp push down onto the blade. The skill can be effectively practised 'dry' as shown, and in doubles, tried one at a time!

Coming alongside

The canoe is turned into the current, or wind, depending on the circumstances, and the upstream (or up-wind) paddler disembarks first. The paddle can be used as a brace by holding it across both gunwales and resting the blade on the bank. Stand, but remain in crouched position, and place the near foot on to the bank, maintaining balance by holding both gunwales. Then bring the far foot ashore. Once ashore, the boat is positioned and held to enable the other paddler to disembark.

The canoe can be lifted out sideways on, with the crew's toes protruding over the bank to prevent damage, or one end lifted ashore first, allowing the water to support most of the weight.

Capsize, swim ashore and empty the canoe

A swamped canoe should be swum to the shore – for test purposes 10 metres is sufficient – by holding on with one hand and swimming using the other arm and legs. Rest as often as necessary. Where two paddlers are involved hold onto opposite sides.

When emptying, remember that there is no point at all in lifting water. When two people are present, the simplest method is to stand at each end of a canoe that is swamped, turn it the right way up under water, and merely lift with a continuous rolling action, until it is upside down above the water, empty. Then turn it the right way up and place it back on the water.

For situations where access is more difficult, there are several possible methods, including the gradual lifting of one end. This will expel water over the other. Gradually bring the end ashore, until two people can turn the canoe over, and then lift it out.

A way to empty a canoe solo from a bank is to grasp the far gunwale near midships as the swamped canoe lies alongside, and gently roll the canoe towards the bank. Then, standing up, lift the canoe just enough to let the end of the bow and the stern overlap the edge. Resume rolling the canoe until it is out of the water and up on the bank.

Rescuing a swimmer

A swimmer can be brought aboard by the crew sitting low in the boat, and balancing by holding both gunwales, while instructing the swimmer to grasp the far gunwale, or a thwart beyond the mid-way point, get his feet near the surface, and keep them there with a strong kick. Pull the canoe under the body by continuing a vigorous kick and exerting pressure on the far arm. When a point of balance is reached, roll backwards and sit in the canoe.

Balance

Learn to stand solo, with feet shoulder width apart, and separated fore and aft, with the body facing diagonally forwards and the knees slightly bent. Keep the tip of the paddle blade in the water.

BASIC SKILLS – level II

Paddler positions and trim

Alternative stances should be learned and adopted to relieve the stress on the knees. In the early stages, only short periods of kneeling on two knees should be tried. The one-knee cruising position can be adopted, with the bulk of the weight on the thwart. Kneel on the knee that is on the paddling side, and brace the forward foot in some way. Alternatively, it is possible to kneel in a full upright position on both knees, away from the thwart. The thwarts may be used as seats when there is no rough water to be negotiated. The high-kneeling position is the most dynamic, and is the one used for flat-water racing – see chapter 14.

A comfortable flat-water cruising position for solo paddling, is to kneel off-set on the paddling side of the canoe, with the knees closer together than before, and with the paddler located ahead of the stern thwart. When this stance is adopted, the canoe will be tilted to the paddler's side, and the bow will be high.

Where two or more paddlers are involved, the canoe should sit evenly on the water, and in particular the bow should not be lower in the water than the stern.

Pitch stroke

This is an alternative to the 'J' stroke, having a more delicate application for situations where minimal correction only is required. When the blade is half-way through the power stroke, the angle is gradually altered to about 45° and the stroke continued so that the blade remains at a constant distance from the keel-line throughout. The drive face is rotated outwards, as for the 'J' stroke, but the blade is clipped smartly out of the water towards the stern.

Bow cut

The skill described here is the ancestor of the modern kayak bow rudder, which used to be applied with the blade near the front of the boat. The blade is taken forward and out from the side of the canoe by the lower arm. It is turned, with the wrists pushing in – top thumb pointing back towards you – so that the drive face of the blade is towards the canoe, but the leading edge and tip is angled out away from the boat. The shaft should be at about 45° with the top hand just above the shoulder. Both wrists will need to be pushed well forward to achieve the correct angle on the paddle.

For the stroke to be effective, the canoe must be making good speed. A solo paddler or bow-man then places the rudder firmly in, and holds the paddle in position, resisting it solidly. The bow will be drawn towards the bow rudder, and the turn can be assisted by the stern man sweeping or drawing. The position of the top hand as described is important, as if it is held in front of the face there is a danger of injury should the blade strike an obstruction (Figure 13:7).

Reverse 'J' stroke

In order to maintain a straight course when paddling backwards, the direction of the canoe will need to be controlled by a reverse sweep, or a reverse 'J' stroke, depending on which way it is veering.

The paddle is taken through the water as for a simple backwater stroke, and the blade rotated through 90° with the non-drive face turning away from the canoe – the top thumb will be pointing backwards. The effort is applied as for the 'J' stroke.

Sculling draw

Turn the head, then the shoulders. The drive-face of the blade is turned towards the canoe and the paddle remains the same distance from the keel-line throughout the stroke. With an upright paddle, inserted ahead of you towards the bow, the blade is set to 45° from the keel-line – the drive face towards you – and moved from fore to aft. At the end of the stroke, the blade is turned so that the drive face remains towards you, but the opposite edge is now leading and is pointing out 45° from the keel-line. Move the paddle from aft to fore, when the angle is again reversed, synchronising exactly with the change of direction, and the action continued.

This will draw the boat sideways through the water. The relative position of the bow or stern can be corrected by adjusting the angle of the blade, or extending the length or strength of the pull.

Pry or pushaway (Figure 13:8).

To move the boat sideways away from the paddling side, a pushaway or a pry stroke may be used.

For the Pushaway, the paddle is placed upright in the water, near the canoe, with the body turned as for the drawstroke. The bottom arm pushes out, using the non-drive face of the blade. Start with the lower elbow close to the hip, and wrist and forearm lined up behind the heel of the hand. The recovery is made by flattening the blade through 90° and returning to the starting position.

The Pry does the same job, but the gunwale of the canoe is used for leverage. Slice the paddle in behind the paddling position and lever the non-drive face of the blade out, by pulling on the paddle shaft, using the gunwale as a fulcrum. A pry can be combined with a power or sweep stroke, and is best applied towards the end of the effective part of the stroke. It should not be used on the down-stream side in shallow water, as it may capsize the canoe if it catches a rock or hits the bottom.

240

Figure 13:7 (top left) *Bow cut – used to turn the canoe towards the paddling side.*

Figure 13:8 (top right) *The pry. The gunwale is used for leverage.*

Figure 13:9 (left) *Compound back stroke. Starting position.*

Inside pivot turn

This is a modified sweep for solo paddling. Reach out as far aft as possible on the paddling side, and by using the non-drive face of the blade begin an extra-wide reverse sweep stroke. When the mid point of the sweep is reached, turn the paddle over so that the power face of the blade completes the arc. Do not change your paddle grip.

Recovery stroke (low)

The canoeist should, by now, be able to take the canoe over and recover effectively with the gunwale on the water line.

Draw strokes on the move

The draw stroke learned at level I should now be used to ease the canoe to one side whilst it is travelling forwards. For doubles, the partner uses a pry.

Cross-bow draw

The draw stroke can be applied, with the canoe stationary, on the opposite side, without changing the paddle grip, by dint of efficient trunk rotation.

Changing positions

The paddler(s) should demonstrate an ability to shift to various positions in the canoe, by holding on to both gunwales and keeping the body weight low, whilst moving.

Balance

Balance is demonstrated by holding onto both gunwales, near the centre, moving the feet up on to the gunwales, and then standing upright. Conditions should be calm!

Jump out and climb in unaided

With help near at hand, the canoeist should be able to jump out, retaining contact with the canoe, and re-enter by employing the method explained for collecting a swimmer.

Capsize and paddle a swamped boat ashore

Place both hands in the bottom, and raise the legs to the surface behind you. By kicking and pressing down gently with the hands, half drag and half swim your way over the near gunwale until your chin reaches the far gunwale. Keeping your body in the water, roll over on the back of your neck, spreading your arms along the gunwale and resting your legs in an extended position over the opposite gunwale, producing an outrigger type of balance. Gently sit down into the bottom and slowly pivot around to a position where both legs are under the midship thwart, with your thighs (just above the knees) pressing firmly up against the thwart near each gunwale. The arms and legs may be extended sideways, and sculling may be done as necessary to maintain stability. Then hand paddle, or paddle the canoe ashore.

BASIC SKILLS – level III

Trimming the canoe to cope with varying wind conditions

Remembering that the canoe pivots around the position of the paddlers, it is necessary to alter the trim according to wind and water conditions. For a doubles pair, it will be necessary in waves to move close together in the middle, lightening the bow and stern, thus allowing the canoe to ride up and not ship water. In this instance, the canoe should be turned around so that the bow-man kneels ahead of the centre thwart, and the stern-man the stern thwart.

When paddling into a wind solo, it is necessary to move forward, in order to keep the bow in the water, and allow the stern to pivot down-wind. For a following wind, the weight should be shifted back. A beam wind is best counteracted by paddling on the opposite side to the wind, and trimming the canoe so that the bow is blown down-wind sufficiently to counteract the paddling effort. In this way, the wind is providing the steerage, and no 'J' stroking should be necessary. If you have to paddle on the windward side, then move forward so that the stern is light. Canoeists should be able to maintain directional control in force three winds at this level.

The Canadian stroke

Also called 'the knifing J' this provides another variation on the forward steering cycle. The paddle is pulled through the water using the normal 'J' stroke, but instead of lifting the blade out of the water at the end, it is carried forwards and out from the side while still under water. The drive face should be upwards with the leading edge slightly high. Pull up on the paddle as it is knifed forwards.

'C' stroke

In order to maintain steerage in certain conditions, particularly of wind, it is sometimes necessary to commence the power stroke with a draw. The paddle is inserted forwards and out from the canoe, and drawn in, so that the movement blends into the normal power stroke. End with a 'J', or Canadian recovery.

Compound back stroke (Figure 13:9)

For efficient paddling in reverse, the compound back stroke is used. To commence, the paddler turns his head, looking back over his shoulder, then turns the shoulders and rotates the trunk for maximum effect. The drive face is used until the paddle is level with the body, when it is reversed, and the non-drive face of the blade pushed forwards, as for a normal back-water stroke, finishing with a reverse 'J' if necessary.

Sculling over the stern

The paddler should be able to reverse his canoe, with diagonal displacement, by applying a sculling draw at the stern, utilising the initial position described for the compound back stroke.

Box stroke

The stroke commences with a bow-draw as described for the 'C' stroke, but at the end of the power stroke the blade is turned through 90° and a push-away applied, using the non-drive face of the blade. Recovery is through the water, keeping the blade set at that angle, in order to go straight back into the bow draw.

Outside pivot turn (Figure 13:10)

Using the drive face of the blade throughout, the turn commences with a cross bow draw, with the paddle being carried smoothly across the bow and continuing in a sweep as previously described. Recovery as for the power stroke, but the paddle has to be taken back across the bow and twisted so as to initiate the cross-bow draw as near abeam of the paddling position as possible.

Pry on the move

With the canoe under-way, slice the paddle into the water alongside your paddling position, the blade slightly in under the canoe. Using the gunwale as a fulcrum, lever the blade outwards, using the non-drive face.

The pry can be used to move the canoe sideways, to initiate a turn, or to lever one end of the boat across the stream. Canoeists should be able to move sideways, or turn, using a pry.

Recovery stroke (high brace)

The technique is the same as for low-brace, but the drive face of the blade is presented to the water, with the paddler 'hanging' – wrists under the paddle shaft.

Reverse sculling

As the name implies, this is the sculling draw used in the opposite way, and moves the boat away from the paddle instead of towards it. The drive face of the blade, set at an angle of 45° from the centre line, remains towards the canoe throughout, but the non-drive face does the work. Commencing forward of your position, with an upright paddle, the drive-face of the blade is towards the bow, and the paddle is drawn through the water towards the stern, being kept an equal distance from the centre-line throughout, so that the non-drive

Figure 13:10 *Outside pivot turn. This is also the starting position for the cross-bow cut or cross-bow draw. The 'drive' face of the blade is used.*

face is working against the water. Then continue the stroke, synchronizing the change of angle and direction.

Hanging draw

The north-American term for this skill is 'Stationary draw', in that the paddle is kept stationary, but the movement of the boat and/or the water cause a diagonal displacement of the canoe.

With the canoe moving at reasonable speed, the paddle is placed upright in the water, well out from the side, with the drive face parallel, towards the canoe. Turn the leading edge about 30° outwards, and firmly resist the paddle. The canoe should be drawn sideways across the water. Partner prys.

Cross bow cut

This enables the solo paddler or bow-man to safely turn the canoe away from his paddling side. The paddle is lifted across to the opposite side without altering the hand positions, and by employing good trunk rotation (see Figure 13:10). The drive face of the blade needs to be towards the canoe, but the top edge further away than the lower edge. The paddle shaft is at about 45°. Forward sweeps or draw strokes from the stern man assist the turn, which is occasioned by the paddler holding the position as the bow draws round.

Canoe over canoe rescue (Figure 13:11)

Direct the capsized canoeist(s) to hold on to the end(s) of your canoe while latching onto the capsized canoe with your paddle. If the capsized canoe is upside down, roll it slowly towards you, and place any loose gear in the bottom of your boat. Move your canoe to one end of the capsized boat, maintaining a hold at all times. Grasp the end and lift it slowly onto your canoe – no more than two to three feet. Roll the canoe bottom-up and draw it across your gunwales until it is resting empty in a balanced position. Then roll it upright, and slide it back onto the water. Hold both canoes tightly together while the victims climb back in one at a time.

Figure 13:11 *Canoe over canoe rescue*

Balance (solo demonstration)

'Gunwale bobbing' is a means of propelling the canoe without paddling! Stand near the stern deck, with one foot on each gunwale. Sink the stern by bending the knees, and kicking the legs downwards. The canoe will shoot forwards and as the stern rises again allow the legs to bend and repeat the driving downwards action. You should be able to travel 25 metres without falling off. Alternatively a 'gunwale walk' on all fours, jumping over a thwart, or a headstand is acceptable!

PROFICIENCY

The Canoe is the simplest yet most efficient vehicle designed by man for travelling under his own power on nature's highway – unspoiled rivers and lakes. The repertoire of skills so far described, are those necessary for a person to master before tackling open lake crossings, or venturing on rapid rivers. In order to be competent in these situations, an ability to use the skills in order to achieve a technique for coping with certain situations, and a knowledge of other factors, is necessary.

Switching

There is no reason why the paddle should not be changed to the alternate side, provided it is done for a specific reason, and not merely because the paddler cannot control the canoe in normal circumstances any other way. The technique is known as 'switching', and is advocated by some marathon canoeists in particular. An efficient method of transferring the paddle, is to bring the top hand down and hold the shaft just under the lower hand, which then slides up to the grip while the paddle is being moved over to the opposite side.

Break-out and break-in

The stern-man must control the direction of the canoe so that the bow will slice into the eddy behind a rock. The bow paddler uses a bow, or cross-bow draw in the eddy, to hold the bow and pull it into the slack water, allowing the stern to sweep around. The stern man will be bracing, and both paddlers will allow the canoe to be leaned upstream so that the hull is presented to the eddy.

An alternative method is to reverse ferry glide across the stream, ensuring that the stern of the canoe can be slipped into the eddy immediately behind the rock.

To break out of the slack water and into the fast current, to continue down-stream, the canoe is driven into the fast water, aiming for a crest or down-stream face of a wave when possible. The lean must be down-stream onto a low brace.

The ferry glide

As for a kayak, the ferry glide is an essential part of river running. It is more used with Canadians however, particularly the reverse glide, in order to 'set' the canoe across the stream. Unlike a kayak, the canoe is slowed down on moderate rapids, which allows for a good measure of control. A crew must be able to take the boat across a flow, maintaining the angle of the canoe to the current, in order to move in a straight line across the river relative to the banks.

When running down a rapid, the stern man still supplies the main steering, but the bow-man takes avoiding action as necessary. He will draw or pry to avoid a rock, and the stern man merely matches this action to keep the canoe running straight. In order to control the general direction in the rapid the stern man shouts commands such as 'OK – do nothing;

Figure 13:12 *Gunwale-bobbing – a balancing exercise.*

Figure 13:13 *Running heavy white water. Notice the large buoyancy bags and block. Photo: Ottowa River Kayak and Canoe School.*

247

'forward' – paddle on; 'back' – reverse paddle; 'left' – do what is necessary in the circumstances to move the boat to the left; 'right' – opposite of 'left'.

To initiate a reverse ferry glide, the stern man first shouts 'back', and both paddlers check the speed. At the right moment, the stern paddler, using a draw or a pry, swings the stern in the direction in which he wants the canoe to move. The stern will be pointing towards the bank toward which the canoe is moving, and the bow will be pointing towards the far bank, at an angle, in general terms of around 30°. Both paddlers work to maintain this situation.

Lining and tracking

Lining is the art of letting a canoe down a section of rapid that is too difficult to run. Tracking, is the art of towing the canoe up against the current. The upstream line in both cases must be attached to the forefoot of the canoe, and a second line to the down-stream thwart. One or two paddlers, by keeping the upstream end of the canoe further out from the bank than the downstream end, in both cases, can control the direction and descent.

Capistrano flip

Once a canoe is capsized and swamped, it can be rescued in the following way by two swimmers, by first getting as much air as possible trapped under the inverted hull.

1   Turn the canoe upside down over yourselves.

2   Trap air under the hull.

3   Lift one gunwale slightly to break the suction.

4   Give a strong kick up and push on the gunwales.

5   At the top of the thrust, push harder with one arm than the other, thus causing the canoe to be flipped over in mid-air, landing alongside you. Properly done, the flip will land the canoe almost empty, and ready for re-boarding.

Portaging

The paddles (there should always be a spare) can be used as a 'yoke' for carrying the canoe on the back, by tieing them length-wise between the middle and bow thwarts.

14 A Club Based on Flat Water

David Train

David Train commenced paddling as a family man, originally with the Viking Club at Bedford. He has, in recent years, made an impact on the marathon and sprint racing scene nationally. Architect of the Open Racing Scheme, in 1973 David moved to Fladbury, a small village situated on the placid river Avon in Worcestershire. There he established a club which, in five short years, became a major force in the marathon and sprint racing world, largely because of the interest of parents, as well as its youngsters. It is now a club of over 200 members of all levels of ability, from parents who started in their forties, to top class Olympic squad paddlers.

David has given a great deal of thought to the system which is necessary for the success of a club based on flat water, and here expounds his views, which can best be described as 'The Fladbury Philosophy'.

INTRODUCTION

Formal canoeing instruction in this country has evolved around the premise that everyone eventually wants to paddle on rough water. In consequence, small cockpit, manoeuvrable boats are used, where a great deal of attention has to be given to capsize and rescue techniques, rolling, struggling to keep in a straight line, and generally getting very wet.

This chapter is therefore about being *on* the water, not *in* it. It is about travelling, and not going round in circles, looping or rolling. It is about using the many miles of flat water rivers and canals which predominate in this country, using kayaks and canoes which are suitable for this type of canoeing. It is about running a club based on travelling on placid water in suitable craft.

More importantly, the teaching methods which have been developed mean that it is possible to teach *anyone* to canoe. People of all ages have been provided with an activity based on flat water, which they can develop, each to his own full potential.

The philosophy is simple. It is canoeing for fun; canoeing for the family; canoeing for fitness. It really is *canoeing for all*. Any canoeist, particularly at the instructor level, with the motivation and following a few key points, could create a major club within three years, by following the progressions in this chapter.

To create successful top paddlers we must concentrate on technique at a very early stage, so if you are teaching youngsters, please read both the Canoe and Kayak paddling forward skills sections carefully.

TEACHING KAYAKING

It is possible, with proper progression, to teach any person, whatever the age, to paddle. Whether this is done in a kayak or canoe, the boats used should meet these criteria:

1   Craft should have 'open cockpits' – ie the knees are not trapped under the deck. This relieves the fear of being stuck in the event of a capsize.

2   All boats should have little rocker, so they are easy to paddle in a straight line.

3   The kayaks recommended are illustrated in Figure 14:1:
     a) A 15' long, by 24" beam very stable touring kayak.
     b) A 17' long, by 22" beam fast touring kayak with a rudder.
     c) The Espada. A stable racing K1 for adults.
     d) The latest design of K1.

The method of teaching can be very simple. In the first session the following points should be covered.

1   A brief session on safety
     a) Wearing of a buoyancy aid.
     b) Danger of weirs.
     c) No wellington boots – they are dangerous.
     d) What to do in the event of a capsize.
     e) Importance of dressing according to conditions.

2   How to use the paddle.

3   How to paddle forwards, stop, reverse.

4   How to get into the kayak.

5   Stress that everything must be done gently at first.

6   Steering the kayak with paddle or rudder.

Once afloat it is important that the pupil is carefully *watched*. Whatever the age, there are some people who have natural balance and are relaxed, and others who are tense and will sit stiffly. Some take a few sessions to get used to feathering the paddle, others pick it up quickly. The coach must watch and decide when to change to the second level – the fast touring K1 with a rudder. For some this could be within a few minutes, with others a few sessions. Eventually, even the most apprehensive will progress to the fast tourer.

For many adults the fast tourer will be as far as they wish to proceed. It is a beautiful kayak for touring, and it can be used at a reasonable level for racing in marathon and sprint. For those who wish to become more skilled, the progression is then to the Espada, and the racing K1. Speed is a function of the person *and* the boat. It is no good having a theoretically fast boat, if the person cannot stay upright in it! Using the four types of kayak,

Figure 14:1 *Foreground: 15' × 24" stable touring kayak; 17' × 22" fast touring kayak; Espada; modern K1 (furthest from camera).*

250

people ranging from under three, to over 75 years old, have been successfully taught. The level they reach, and the type of kayak they will use, depends on each individual. All will start with the first kayak. Some adults will conquer the Espada and the latest design K1. Under–nines often paddle the most unstable K1 within a few hours of starting.

After a very few sessions, and with only the knowledge outlined, paddlers are ready to take part in the Club Fun Race activities. The progress with some can be quicker, and youngsters have been taught to canoe, and within a week have raced in open competition.

TEACHING CANOEING

Until recently, canoe racing has had little support in this country, and consequently there are few craft in which to learn. As with kayaks, it is important to have a progression of boats, to develop gradually the skills and balance necessary to paddle the racing C1. The basic boats and teaching philosophy are as follows:

1   The Open Canadian. This is used primarily to get people used to handling a single blade. Often youngsters will learn by merely 'playing around' at the end of a session.

2   The C7. This is a stable racing canoe in which the less experienced can paddle with competent canoeists whose style they can copy. It is easy to build and transport, and a mould is available.

3   The touring kayak. Due to the shortage of Canadians, it is often necessary to improvise using a kayak to learn single bladed paddling.

4   The racing Canadian

The method of teaching canoe is the same as for kayak: Safety. Then basic instruction in the use of the paddle. Most of the progression in C1 can be made step by step in the touring kayak. The method, as follows, is shown in figures 14:2a–14:2e.

1   Sit in a kayak with a short single bladed paddle, getting used to paddling on one side. The rudder may be used at first, but the paddler will soon experiment with steering with the paddle. At this stage teach the steering stroke.

2   Kneel in the kayak on both knees, sitting back on the heels. This is very much the same balance as for sitting.

3   Gradually kneel upright as confidence develops.

4   From the position of kneeling upright on two knees, transfer all the weight on to one knee. The paddler is now in the racing position, for in racing there should be *no weight on the forward leg*.

5   Finally move the forward leg into position.

6   Having got to this position, the paddler should be able to progress to the racing C1, with a low knee block.

Teaching Racing C1 to Youngsters

Questions are asked about one-sided development in people taking up C1. Many sports are one–sided, such as tennis, squash, golf and so forth. Do not train paddlers too hard when they are young, and all should do other activities such as running, swimming and weight training when old enough. So, for kayak and canoe, if you train people, then give them a balanced programme.

Progression sequence for teaching canoeing

Figure 14:2a *Use kayak with short single blade. Paddler sitting. Note straight lower arm. Allow for play and experiment.*

Figure 14:2d *The final position in the touring kayak. Allow paddler to gradually develop thigh muscles with short play sessions. Gradually increase distance paddled.*

Figure 14:2b *Change position so that paddler is sitting on his heels, using a cushion for the knees.*

Figure 14:2e *Move to racing C1 using a low block or cushion. Go back to touring kayak for distance work.*

Figure 14:2c *Youngsters will naturally move to this position. After practice get paddler to concentrate on kneeling with weight on one knee (same knee as paddling side) while remaining in this position.*

Figure 14:2f *The final stage: a high kneeling block in the racing C1. Pictured Steven Wickens.*

Figure 14:3a *Body rotates as paddle goes forward. Straight lower arm throughout pull. The head visible under the top arm which is coming in towards body. Kneeling leg should be forward or at 90° – never back. There is no weight on the forward leg. Pictured Stephen Train.*

Figure 14:3b *Clean entry of blade. Good body rotation. Relaxed upper arm. Remember power is provided by back muscles with lower arm pulling. Do not push with top arm.*

Special Injuries

Most sports have specific problems if there is over-indulgence at an early stage. With kayaks there are wrist problems, with canoes, it is the knee that could suffer damage. If sufficient time is given to adapt, then the risk is removed. When starting beginners off do not keep them at it too long before a rest. Make sure they have an adequate kneeling block – a cushion will do at first. Do not let paddlers kneel in the boat without some support.

Teaching Canoe Paddling Techniques

As has been stated, the teaching of correct technique to youngsters is vital. The basic principles are:

1   Imagine you are kneeling in your canoe and in front of one side of you are a series of stakes coming up from the river bed, and they are at intervals of a few feet, just above river level.

2   Reach for the first stake with the pulling arm, by leaning forward and rotating the body around the spine.

3   Get hold and pull back by lifting the body and rotating back. The canoe will move past the stake. *Your pulling arm is straight.*

4   When the hand reaches a point just in front of the hips leave go and reach for the next one.

The paddle is simply a convenient way of carrying the stake, in which the essential principles are:

1   The boat moves past the stake (paddle).

2   The power is provided by the back muscles which, through the lower arm, *pull.*

3   The top arm guides only – *it does not push.*

4   The blade should go into the water without power, as though into a slot – *no splash.* The power is applied afterwards.

Length of Paddle
For paddling from a high kneeling position, the handle needs to be at eyebrow height. Consequently, youngsters will be changing paddles quite frequently as they grow.

Steering the Racing C1
Teach the above points as soon as you can, but it is obviously difficult for the paddler to learn them before he is able to control the canoe. Steering is the most difficult part of the single bladed paddle technique:

1   Assuming the canoeist is paddling on the right hand side, to steer to the left is simple – just use a sweep stroke.

2   To steer to the right or keep the boat straight, it is more complicated. To the experienced paddler, steering becomes part of the normal forward stroke. For the beginner, these are the essential points:

When the bottom hand is at a point just in front of the hips, the blade is kept deep and turned through 90° by the top hand (thumb forwards as for 'J' stroke – see chapter 10). The top arm has moved inwards and dropped in a continuous smooth movement, and the blade grips the water for steerage as it is lifted clear by the action of the top arm as described, together with the bottom arm pulling the paddle away from the side of the boat.

Steering the C1 Figure 14:4a (left) *At half-way stage paddle is turning by action of upper arm. Note straight lower arm throughout stroke. Top arm moves forwards and down.* **Figure 14:4b (right)** *Paddle blade has turned through 90°. To the experienced paddler steering is an integral part of the stroke. Beginners need to push the paddle away from the canoe with the blade kept deep in the water to start with.*

COMPETITION AND CLUB ACTIVITY

Whilst some adult members will like to go out for a gentle paddle, there are few who do not at some time take part in racing. Here again, the gradual step method works, commencing at the club level with the weekly Club Handicap Race. Then the now Open Racing Scheme, run by the BCU Marathon Committee, provides a natural progression up to whichever level people wish to progress. There is also Sprint Racing, where the system is being reviewed to allow for a natural introductory sequence, although it will have less appeal to the older adult joining the sport.

Canoeing, unlike some other sports, has a weak club structure – generally, that is, there are a few notable exceptions. A great number of popular and successful activities such as golf, sailing, squash, tennis, cricket and football, revolve around a club base, where people meet and take part in their sport. Why then is canoeing different? Many reasons are suggested, but proof exists that a successful club can be established *with only a couple of miles of flat water available to it.*

With the increasing costs of petrol, and the shortage in this country of white water sites, the only real expansion possible must be on the hundreds of miles of placid water that is mainly available, particularly in England.

The Club Handicap Race

This is the event which binds the club together – the weekly Club Handicap Race. This one activity alone can be the basis of a successful club. The principles are:

1 That each paddler has a standard time for the course based on previous performance.

2 That the race is run with the slowest off first and the fastest last. If the handicapping is correct, then all will cross the finishing line together!

This type of race gives something to everyone in the club. All can improve. The beginner competes with the top paddler. The fastest canoeist always has another boat to try and overtake. A safety factor is built in, because competent paddlers are always coming up behind, able to sort out a problem, should one occur.

How it is done.

1   Hold your Club Handicap Race every week. Club members will then know that if they turn up there will be an activity. It is vital that it is run even if most of the club are away at a national competition.

2   Plan a course suitable to your river or canal. You may wish to have more than one distance – eg 2 miles, 3.5 miles, 4.5 miles. Out and back is easiest to organise.

3   Set standard times. To initiate the system, take a rough guess at what each paddler might do and work on that.

4   Recruit a starter, finishers, someone to work out the results, and someone to provide a cup of coffee at the end. In cold weather a safety boat may be desirable to pick up any stragglers.

5   Having calculated the standard times from the previous race, list the competitor's names, starting with the slowest and ending with the fastest.

6   The start time for each paddler is calculated by subtracting their standard time from the slowest competitor.

eg. slowest was 55 minutes = start time 00.00 minutes

next was 47 minutes = start time 08.00 minutes

next was 44.15 minutes = start time 10.45 minutes.

7   Each paddler is started at the appropriate time, and at the end of the race his finish time is recorded, then his actual time worked out.

8   If his actual time is faster than his standard (previous) time his standard time will be reduced, giving him a greater handicap.

After the race, a chart showing start times, finish time, position, and the new standard on which future handicaps will be based, should be displayed in the clubhouse. This is shown in Table One and can be paramount in providing continuing interest and motivation.

The Open Racing Scheme certificates can be used, so that all competitors have a chance of a good prize with a benefit to the club. Details from the BCU. The scheme allows for competition within the club for division 8 and 9 events. If there are enough of these paddlers in a Club Handicap Race, it is permissible to promote on a time basis.

Table One – Weekly Handicap Race

Name	Boat	Std. Time.	Start Time	Finish Time	Position	New Time Calculated
Fred	C1	55	00	53.30	2	53.30
Jack	Touring K1	44	11	54.00	3	43.00
Susan	K1	40	15	55.00	7	40.00
Bill	C1	36	19	54.45	6	35.45
Roger/Phil	C2	35	20	53.00	1	33.00
Stephen	K1	34	31	54.30	5	33.30
Andy	K1	32	23	54.15	4	31.45

Marathon Racing in the Open Racing Scheme.

It was stressed that the Club Handicap Race should be the regular activity of the club. Racing within the club however will lead to national competition. The Open Racing

Figure 14:5a (left) *The Weekly Club Handicap Race. The first competitor is under starter's orders. The handicap system should mean that the paddlers arrive at the finish together.*

Figure 14:5b (centre) *General fun and games, splashing about and the opportunity to try different craft, should all be encouraged.*

Figure 14:5c (bottom) *The Fladbury C7 crew which represented Britain, in action. The boat is popular and lends itself to both training beginners, and providing opportunity for fun and enjoyment.*

Scheme provides a very natural extension of the Club Handicap Race. It is canoeing that all can join in, and the gradual progressive structure allows people of all abilities to develop to their natural potential. The competition for the premier team prize in marathon racing – the Hasler Trophy – has rules which make it possible for small and large clubs throughout the country to have a chance of winning.

Do not be put off by the word 'marathon'. The lower divisions cover only 3 or 4 miles. On the other hand, if you are the sort of person who wants to race longer distances, there are a number of marathons and time trials available. The toughest of these is the annual Devizes to Westminster race which is 125 miles with 72 portages.

Sprint Racing.

Another outside activity for a club based on flat water to progress to, is Sprint Racing. A small club arriving at the National Watersports Centre at Holme Pierrepont, Nottingham, surrounded by international paddlers and officials, may well find it daunting at first. Don't be put off by this, but persevere. There are many friends there willing to give advice, and you will soon be part of the scene.

Sprint Racing is a great sport, and the next few years will see a real growth, with developments at regional and club level. Racing started a hundred years ago, and yet in 1981 there are less than 1,000 registered racing paddlers. It is a sad reflection on this oldest established canoeing competition. I hope you will help to change it.

Training for Competition

If the flat water canoe club is to gravitate towards competition, then supplementary activities are important – particularly in the winter. Whilst not within the scope of this book, such activities that may be considered are:

1   Weight training for muscular strength.

2   Circuit training for muscular endurance.

3   Flexibility exercises.

4   Running, football, basket ball and similar team games for cardio-vascular efficiency.

'Fun' or 'Rag' Regattas

Not everyone in a flat water canoe aspires to be a national champion. The provision of 'fun' activities, where all can participate, is important to a balanced programme. Mini sprints over, say, 100 metres can prove interesting, whilst K2 races – fathers with sons – can provide a diversion that involves the family. Standing-up races in K1s will give the smallest junior a chance to shine, or a tug-of-war between two K2s, or land-based teams on opposite sides of the river, can be hilarious. To the imaginative mind, the combinations are endless.

Whilst a barbeque, disco, or cheese and wine party can be the perfect end to an enjoyable day's canoeing, remember that it is the sport that the club is all about. Never let the social side, which, used properly, can complement the canoeing, become the main function of the club.

Conclusion

At the beginning I said that any instructor, using a few simple principles and methods, could create a major club within a short time. Now is your chance, and your challenge. Start to use your flat water, teach your paddlers, form your club, and enjoy a great sport – one which has as much appeal to participants as any other I can think of.

15 Canoe Camping

Ric Halsall

Ric Halsall has been a keen canoeist for 14 years, and a member of the Coaching Scheme for 12. He is currently Deputy Head at Buckden House Outdoor Centre and is BCU Regional Coaching Organiser for Yorkshire and Humberside.

One popular definition of camping, held particularly by mountaineers, claims that 'camping is the ability to live as comfortably as possible under any weather conditions in remote areas with the minimum of equipment needed to ensure adequate shelter, feeding and expedition activity.' It would not take a lot of imagination to put those words into the mouth of a canoeist, for the sentiment of 'getting away from it all' is common to many disciplines. The advantages of being able to continue an activity until the very end of the day are far more numerous than those of mere additional miles paddled.

To a person who enjoys canoeing canoe camping appears to be a logical next step. Whether the expedition be of a night or a month's duration, the same basic principles hold good; preparation, both mental and physical, are of paramount importance to ensure a successful venture. An attitude of 'that's good enough' will probably result in forgotten or badly packed equipment, whilst even the most straightforward trip along the local canal will benefit from the attention paid to details. Route planning can be as simple as trying to ensure that most portages are downhill sessions and that there are adequate access points along the route for vehicles, either as support crew or to pick up the canoes at the end of the journey. Is there to be a non-canoeing driver attending the party or have vehicles already been positioned at the end? Is a 'there and back', or a round trip, envisaged, or a straight A to B? All these questions (and of course many others) can quite easily convince folk that camping from a canoe will turn out to be hard work. This need not be the case and with practise the opposite point of view becomes the norm.

Unlike the walker and the cyclist the canoeist has no problems in storing his equipment; in effect the canoe becomes a large waterproof rucsac which is paddled rather than carried. Weight therefore is not the prime concern of the canoe camper, as the way in which the equipment is packed into the canoe is far more important than the weight of the individual items. It is essential that the place of each item is known so that it can easily be found even in the dark. It is equally essential that the items first required at the campsite are stowed in the most accessible places. There is no point in decorating a field with food, spare clothes and sleeping bags in a frantic search for a well hidden tent. A policy therefore of first in, last out, must be adopted, whilst maintaining the trim of the craft. Time should be spent in looking at items of camping equipment in an attempt to choose the type most suited to the needs of the individual. Talk to others who have carried out similar ventures, successfully or otherwise – much can be learned from other people's mistakes.

When purchasing equipment it is always best to visit a light-weight camping specialist, as rarely will the local sports shop, or family camping centre, have the range or know-how to advise you properly.

TENTS

A cheap tent may be adequate under ideal summer conditions, but in strong wind and driving rain will offer little in the way of comfort and protection. A buffeting wind and persistent rain, a double act encountered at most times of the year, can wreak havoc with unsuitable equipment. A fly-sheet that is a separate covering over the top of the main tent, will cut down on the chances of the rain spraying through the inner walls, whilst the layer of still air trapped between these two skins will act as insulation and maintain a higher temperature within the tent. This space can be used for storing wet clothing, stoves, cooking utensils and any other items not required inside the tent.

Ideally the tent should be of simple construction, weather proof and designed to be stable in adverse conditions. It should be easy to erect, have a sewn in groundsheet, and sufficient

Figure 15:1 *". . . Ensure that most portages are downhill".*

260

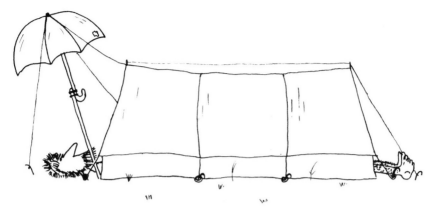

Figure 15:2 "... *the selection of the right size tent can be important*"

space to cook at the entrance if necessary. It is always worth studying the way in which the manufacturer has folded the tent as it left his factory. If the tent is repacked in the same manner on subsequent occasions, the bulk can be effectively reduced. Alternatively, if the available space dictates, the poles, pegs and tent can all be packed individually, thus creating a set of much smaller units.

After every trip the equipment will need cleaning and careful checking. Pegs need washing and straightening if necessary, missing items replaced, and the tent cleaned inside and out. Wet tents, whether cotton or nylon, will suffer if they are not opened out and dried as soon after the trip as possible, and the guy lines will be to hand if they are properly tied up at this stage.

SLEEPING BAGS

As the quality of sleeping bag is reflected in the quality of sleep achieved, it is well worth spending as much as you can afford. The majority of heat is usually lost towards the ground and to counteract this adequate insulation is essential. The construction of the sleeping bag should be such that at no place is there a cold spot caused by the sewing of the inner and outer skins together. A system of baffles or walls will contain the filling and prevent the heat from escaping. If a zip is included make sure that it has a flap either in front or behind it for the same reason.

The bag can be filled with either down or man made fibre, both of which have excellent heat-retaining properties, but bear in mind that down will lose these properties when wet. Because the warmth of a sleeping bag is achieved not in any 'electric blanket' manner, but through layers of trapped still air, it always pays to shake the bag prior to getting in to allow the fibres to separate and collect more air. The use of a sheet liner will not only make for a cleaner bag, but will provide yet another layer of trapped air.

No matter how good a sleeping bag is, the filling will become compressed underneath the camper, and when that happens much of the insulating layer of air will be lost. This cannot be helped but in an effort to reduce the amount of heat lost thought should be given to providing alternative methods of insulation. Spare dry clothes, layers of newspapers, or foam pads all have proved to be effective. Whilst these suggestions will offer some degree of warmth they will not offer much in the way of comfort. For the camper who wishes softness as well as warmth, an air bed comes into its own, providing enough energy is left at the end of a day's paddle to inflate it. It must be remembered though that the air bed initially will be quite cold as there is a vast amount of air drawing away valuable warmth. A closed cell foam pad will warm up almost immediately, will roll or fold into an acceptable size, and most important for a canoeist, will not absorb water.

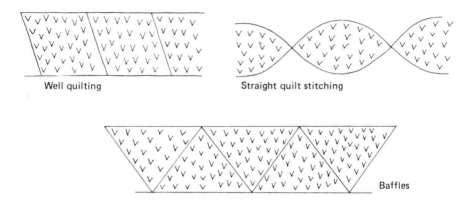

Well quilting   Straight quilt stitching

Baffles

Figure 15:3 *Methods of sleeping bag construction*

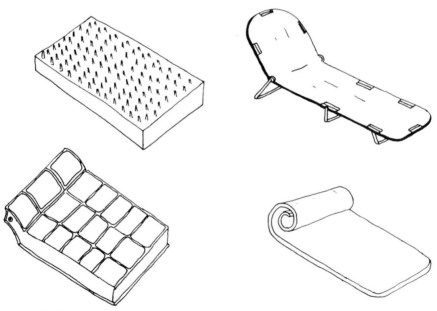

Figure 15:4 *Foam pads, camp beds, air beds and closed cell foam are all methods of improving your comfort*

STOVES

In most places in this country the building of open fires is actively discouraged. As a result the camper has to take his own cooking fire. At first sight the choice seems overwhelming as there are numerous alternatives on the market. Basic principles are more important than details at this stage, so the stove should be straight forward in operation easy to maintain and cheap to run. It must also be capable of working easily in wet cold conditions as this is the time that hot food is most required. The type of fuel needed is one of the easiest ways of classifying stoves, as the availability of spare fuel is an important consideration when making the initial choice.

Gas stoves have the advantage of being clean, relatively cheap to buy and almost impossible to use incorrectly; on the other hand the spare containers tend to be rather bulky, towards the end of the cylinder the gas pressure drops off, making boiling a long and labourious job, and the gas has difficulty vapourising in low temperatures. It must also be pointed out that a number of young people have been involved in accidents whilst changing cylinders, so always ensure that there are no naked lights in the vicinity during this operation.

Pressure stoves, burning either petrol or paraffin, have been with us in various shapes and sizes for many years and will always have a strong band of devotees. The main advantages of the paraffin burning stove are its efficiency, economy, dependability and perhaps most particularly, the availability of paraffin almost anywhere. It is often claimed that the taste of paraffin pervades even the best wrapped food, and that the priming procedure is unnecessarily complicated in that a different type of fuel (ie methylated spirits) needs to be carried. Many people now use solid fuel priming blocks, which although more expensive, avoid the risk of spillage whilst in transit. Petrol stoves have many of the same advantages but represent a considerably greater safety risk. Stoves burning methylated spirits are expensive to run and the fuel may be difficult to obtain; in fact in some parts of the world it may possibly be illegal. Set against this however is the fact that the stove contains no moving parts, hence reducing the maintainance costs to almost nil and producing a nearly child-proof unit. Whatever type is eventually chosen regular care and attention will prolong its life. Stoves should be handled with great respect as a tent fire can be horrifyingly final. It will not take many seconds to burn down a tent, and all the equipment manufactured in man made fibre will melt, perhaps even splashing on to the unfortunate occupant. Always remember that any cooking will not only use up oxygen but will also produce carbon monoxide, a deadly vapour not easily detected. Adequate ventilation must be ensured at all times and only in extreme cases should cooking be undertaken within the tent. Stoves should be stored under the fly-sheet at night, giving extra sleeping space and removing any danger of poisonous fumes. The propane gas used in the canisters is heavier than air and with a faulty switch could produce disastrous results.

Most stoves will require some sheltering from the wind otherwise the heat generated will be dispersed and wasted. The metal wrap around type used on pressure stoves will only help at the pre-heating stage, and a wind-shield of canvas on light metal supports will protect the stove from the wind once it is alight.

POTS AND PANS

A set of cooking pans must also be bought, preferably a set of aluminium ones which will nest inside each other. The lids should be capable of doubling as frying pans or plates and a secure handle is essential. (Detachable handles have an annoying habit of becoming detached at the wrong time!)

Washing-up can be done in a canvas or polythene bowl carried for the purpose, but most people find that a large pan will do just as well. Carry a small supply of liquid detergent and a nylon pan scrubber, and think about heating washing up water at the same time as making the end of meal drink. The washing of dishes should always be done in a bowl or a pan and never in the river. Greasy particles will foul a campsite long after the passage of a canoe camper. The only sign that the place has been in use should be the flattened area where the tents have been. All the rubbish will have been taken home. No matter how well we think tins have been hidden and buried, animals will find a way of uncovering them.

FOOD

The days of being able to live off the land with a bow and arrow, or hunting spear   ..g gone, and the canoe camper of today has to take the majority of his food with him. Unfortunately the choice of types of food is almost as overwhelming as the choice of tent. It would appear unreasonable to consider carrying fresh vegetables and real meat, as the problems of transporting and cooking this are, on the whole, greater than the satisfaction gained from eating it. Low bulk, easily prepared food is the order of the day. Long cooking times require additional fuel to be carried, which in turn poses storage problems, so food which can rapidly be brought to an eatable state is much favoured. Although this may be a dehydrated powder it need not be unpalatable. Time and effort spent in the early stages of the meal preparation will ensure a satisfying result.

Dehydrated or freeze-dried meals will taste more appetising if a selection of spices are carried, which can be added as appropriate. Beef extract cubes are worthwhile, as they can be used to make a hot drink, as well as adding them to any meat dish. Curry powder, however, does tend to rival fibreglass resin in its ability to flavour everything packed close to it, so care must be taken to ensure that all members of the expedition like curry! If the dehydrated meal is put into a pan to soak, whilst the tent is being erected, the length of cooking time, and therefore fuel consumed, can be reduced. Horrific tales are frequently exchanged of instant potato being added to cups of tea, so it is imperative that powders are clearly identifiable. Practise preparing camp food in the controlled environment of the kitchen before venturing outside – at least attention can then be concentrated on the food, rather than the conspiring elements. Make sure that the capacity of the various cooking containers are known, so that accurate measurements can be made – potato soup has graced the grass of many a camp site! A useful tip is always to add the hot water to the powder, as this allows for a more controlled mixture. Experiment with as many different brands and combinations as possible.

Dehydrated food must always be re-constituted and cooked thoroughly, or abdominal disorders – which could be severe — may result.

With the wide selection of easily prepared instant meals now available, a varied and interesting menu should be easily achieved, but in amongst all this food should be a small package which, it is hoped, will never be used. An emergeny pack need not take up much space, but should contain items which will, if called upon, rapidly convert into energy: eg sugar concentrate bars. Wrap these tightly so that they are definitely separated from the rest of the food, and yet are easily recognisable. A selection of commercially produced emergency kits are available on the market, but health food and confectionery shops will yield the necessary ingredients. It is also worth making sure that this pack does not contain favourite sweets, otherwise emergencies tend to crop up at regular intervals! A 'treat bag' can be packed elsewhere to improve flagging morale.

CAMP WEAR

In addition to normal canoeing clothing some ideas of camp wear must be considered. The wide range of fibre pile and thermal clothing currently available on the market widens the choice almost infinitely, but the criteria of warmth to weight/bulk should offer some guide lines. Items not being worn should only take up a minimum amount of space in the boat and should certainly weigh as little as possible. Woollen hats, scarves and gloves all deserve a place in the kit, as does a pair of dry socks to put on last thing at night.

Commercial plastic containers.   Homemade waterproof bags.

Figure 15:5 *Adequate waterproof protection is essential to keep clothing and equipment dry*

LIGHTING

Some form of lighting will be required, both in the tent and around the campsite. This can vary from a heavy duty rubber torch, through a lamp with a head band thus keeping both hands free, to a candle. If candles are used, which certainly warm up the tent, make sure that the risk of fire has been ruled out as much as is possible, breaking candles in half, using the night type of stubby candle, and standing it in a metal container are all sensible suggestions for safeguarding property. Matches and box need protecting against dampness and it is always worth taking well packed spares. A cigarette lighter is less likely to be affected by wet hands and damp tents.

PACKING THE CANOE

Having eventually amassed all the necessary equipment some method of storing and protecting from dampness must be sought. In the event of a capsize it is imperative that the contents are dry and that they stay with the canoe, so all the containers must be secured within the craft. Watertight bags can be bought or made simply at home, but in either case the bags can be made to fit not only the contents but also the available space in the canoe. The simplest type of container is a sausage shaped waterproof bag with the top folded over and fastened with a clip, rubber band or string. More robust plastic containers with screw tops have been used successfully in recent years, although the amount of equipment that can be carried in each bottle is limited. Obviously the size, shape and number of containers will be controlled by each individual canoe, so that all available space is utilised effectively.

Heavy-duty polythene bags will provide the necessary water-proofing, but are susceptible to snagging on splinters of fibreglass. They need always therefore to be protected. An old canvas kit-bag, or a sausage-shaped cover made of calico will suffice.

An open Canadian canoe, designed originally as a load carrier, will present fewer problems in terms of packing equipment than will a slalom boat. One or two large bags, or barrells, are common. Self-sealing polythene equipment bags, with protective covers complete with dog-clips and straps for attaching to thwarts, are obtainable. It certainly pays to take the time to test the effectiveness of watertight containers prior to the expedition, as the sight of a waterlogged sleeping bag reduces morale to rock bottom.

The length of the trip will affect not only the amount of equipment to be carried but as a result will increase the weight of the canoe. In turn this increased weight will affect the handling of the craft and many basic skills may have to be relearned. When loading equipment, including crew, remember to avoid any tendency to overweight the bow – the canoe should float level or very slightly stern down. If this loading is carried out with the canoe in the water, then less strain will be put upon both craft and canoeist at a later stage, and also the trim can be checked as the kit is stowed.

CHOICE OF A CAMPSITE

The choice and preparation of a campsite is equally as important as the selection of equipment; imagine the site in bad weather and make arrangements to protect yourself - sooner or later it will arrive.

The spot chosen should be above the level of possible flooding as mountain rivers can rise several feet over-night, from rain falling many miles away. Spend time searching for signs of previous high water and use that as a guide. Beware of cattle coming to the water's edge to drink. Not only do they break the bank into muddy slopes but they are very inquisitive of strange beings in their field.

In strong winds make sure the back of the tent points into the wind and is well clear of mature trees. If there is no wind apparent at the time of pitching check for evidence of the prevailing wind (ie bent trees, distorted shrubs).

Fresh water should always be carried, as rarely in Britain nowadays is river or stream water fit to drink. Never drink from stagnant or slow moving water - the freshest is found where the current is strongest. Purifying tablets are available from chemists for emergencies, and a 'pump' which purifies water is also on the market.

River banks are usually privately owned and therefore permission to camp must be sought. It is a good idea consequently to start looking for a campsite about three hours before the proposed end of the day, unless sites have been previously arranged.

Figure 15:6 *". . . will present fewer problems in packing equipment"*

Figure 15:7 *". . . less strain will be put upon both craft and canoeist"*

Figure 15:8 "*. . . imagine the site in bad weather. . . search for signs of previous flooding*"

Despite all the lists of equipment and the demoralising tales told by not so fortunate associates, the thought of leaving the trappings of civilization for a short period of time, is attractive to many people. Age proves to be no barrier nor really does canoeing ability - the standard of the trip is suited to those taking part. Routes and equipment will be chosen in the light of experience, items once considered essential will be discarded in favour of those things found to be of more use. Be ruthless in the amount of equipment taken - only take again what has been used. Develop the ability to pack up and leave at a moment's notice. Enjoy the experience for what it is, for it is only by going that you will have tales to tell others.

For more serious expeditioning, much can be learned from reports of previous exercises, and copies of these, or information on where they can be obtained, is available through the BCU.

16 Surfing

John Hermes

Jean Pierre Hermes learned to canoe in 1969 on a course in Cornwall, where he still lives. He became secretary of the steering committee which brought about a BCU Canoe Surfing section in 1975, and has been annually elected Chairman ever since. Using mainly slalom boats and skis, John has held most British titles, except for the Cornish, the first non-national championships, which he inaugurated!

An Honorary Surf Coach of the BCU, he holds the Bronze Medallion of the Surf Life Saving Association of Great Britain. John has surfed extensively the South Wales, Devon and Cornwall Coast, the West Coast of France, and the Severn Bore.

INTRODUCTION

Given the right weather conditions, surf can be found almost everywhere around the coast of Britain, and a surfable wave has been recorded on less likely waters, from flooded streets, and storm swept inland waterways, to the phenomenal 'Severn Bore'. For the instructor and his group however, the recognised surfing beaches, particularly those of the South West peninsular and South Wales, provide the warmest and most consistent areas for surfing. Details of all the British surf beaches are shown on a map available from BCU.

Although many factors may determine the formation of a surfing wave, the essential ingredients are a long, gently sloping (preferably sandy) beach with swell or wave action. This ideally requires the beach facing out to several hundred miles of uninterrupted water, enabling a far-off storm or wind to create a sizeable swell.

Having satisfied these basic conditions, the beach must be considered in more detail, as some seemingly good surf can be fraught with dangers. The canoeist must be familiar with all the problems likely to be encountered. Should there be any doubt about any aspect of the safety, or the ability of any of the party to handle the known dangers – look for another beach!

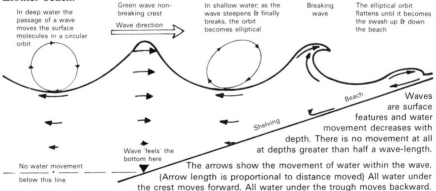

Figure 16:1 *Wave Profiles*

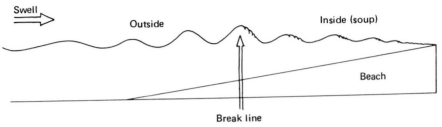

Figure 16:2 *Waves on a typical surf beach*

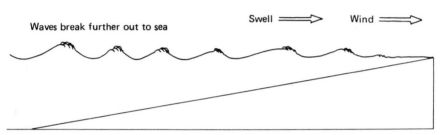

Figure 16:3 *Waves caused by an on-shore wind tend to be flatter and are often closer together*

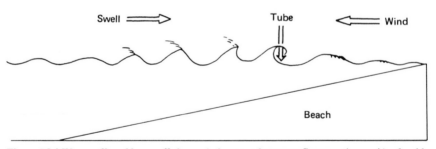

Figure 16:4 *Waves affected by an off-shore wind are much steeper. Spray, or 'spume' is often blown back from wave.*

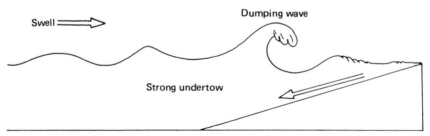

Figure 16:5 *Waves breaking on a steeply shelving beach. The swell outside the dumping wave remains flat.*

270

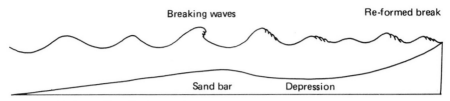

Figure 16:6 *Waves affected by bar or depression on beach.*

THE CRAFT

There are three different types of craft available to the surf canoeist and each has its own advantages and disadvantages.

Slalom Kayaks

The modern GRP slalom kayak of almost any design, provided its construction is not too light-weight, can be surfed. The choice of design can be left to the individual canoeist, as each has points for and against. Whatever the design chosen, the kayak should be fitted with the features listed in the section on safety. Low-volume boats, with very pointed ends can be extremely hazardous to other surfers and have been banned for use in competition.

The main advantages of a slalom kayak in surf are:

1   Of all surfing craft the slalom kayak can be paddled out through breaking waves most easily.

2   They are usually readily available.

3   They are easy to paddle into the correct position to catch a wave.

4   A slalom kayak can start its runs on a wave further out to sea than any other craft, giving a longer overall ride.

The main disadvantages are:

1   The length makes it more difficult to manoeuvre on the wave;

2   The tendency to broach (turn sideways) makes it difficult to control, and once broached, the kayak carves a 4m danger zone through the surf as it is swept towards the beach.

3   The canoeist needs to be reasonably competent before tackling surf in a slalom kayak.

Surf Kayaks

A kayak specially designed for surf, overcomes some of the disadvantages of the slalom kayak, but also loses some of the advantages. As with the slalom kayak, the manufacture of surf kayaks has led to many different designs and again, choice is a matter of personal preference.

The GRP surf kayak is manufactured in the same way as a slalom kayak and should always include the additional strengthening required for surf. An extra feature found on the surf kayak is the skeg, or fin, fitted to the hull just behind the seat. It is advisable for the skeg to be fitted, not directly to the hull, but by means of a 'skeg box' which allows the position to

271

Figure 16:7 *A surf kayak*

be moved, and different sizes to be fitted (to suit differing surf conditions). This also allows the fin to be knocked out, rather than risk damage to the hull.

The advantages of the surf kayak are:

1   Its greater ease of mobility
2   Higher planing speed
3   Ability to ride in front of a broken wave (ie not to broach)

Surf Skis

The newest breed of canoe craft, the ski, is more of a surf board which is paddled, than a canoe, in appearance, though techniques used in paddling the ski are wholly canoeing techniques. The ski originated in two separate sports, and these origins have gradually welded together. The first to be used by canoeists were based on surf kayak hulls, with a closed ski deck added. They were constructed in much the same way as the surf and slalom boats. The second form of surf ski originated in the surf-boarding world. Here the ski is found in two forms – the long (6 metre +) racing ski, and the short lightweight, wave-riding ski. The former are used only in surf races (a feature of Surf Lifesaving Association

Figure 16:8 *A surf ski, or 'wave' ski. There are also rescue skis and racing skis.*

272

Championships) whilst the latter closely resemble the canoeist's ski concept in construction. These are often made in the same way as a surfboard, with a strengthened foam blank covered with GRP. The advantages of this form of construction are:

1 The overall strength/weight ratio.

2 The very lightweight craft produced.

3 The infinite variety of designs possible by shaping the foam blank.

There are disadvantages:

1 The difficulty in making a satisfactory repair.

2 The possibility of damage allowing water to penetrate the construction.

As with the other craft, a great variety of designs exist within the basic outline. There are also several different devices for keeping the paddler on his craft. These vary from lap straps, outside thigh grips and thigh belts, to a central 'tree' which is gripped by the thighs.

The advantages of the ski, are those of the surf kayak, with the addition:

1 If separated from his ski, the paddler has no difficulty in regaining the craft (provided a 'leash' is used).

2 A ski can be used to some effect by paddlers with very little canoeing experience.

Skegs

An important feature of both surf kayaks and surf skis, is the skeg, or fin, mounted on the hull. Because both types of craft have a reduced length, particularly behind the paddler (the stern) the craft has a tendency to slip sideways when travelling on a diagonal run, or to turn very quickly. The skeg is designed to stop these traits by creating sideways drag, without slowing significantly the craft's forward motion. The basic skeg design is shown in figure 16:9.

The skeg shape and length can be varied according to the surfer's needs. For waves up to about 4 feet, most surfers use a small skeg, about 3″ deep.

Problems can arise, however, when a surf kayak or ski is used on steep waves, and for radical manoeuvres. The diagram shows a ski in position, being surfed on the 'rail' (edge or gunwale) of the craft. (Figure 16:10).

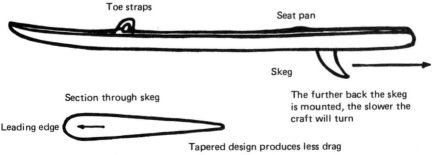

Figure 16:9 *Basic skeg design*

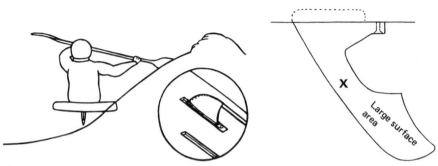

Figure 16:10a (above) *The skeg has lifted clear of the water and is having no effect. Although this may be an extreme case, it is obvious that on steep waves, the amount of skeg out of the water will vary. This can be overcome by using a longer skeg, with most of the side surface area deep in the water.* **Figure 16:10b (right)** *This has the obvious weakness of the area marked x being liable to break when very fast turns are performed. This weakness can also cause 'fin flutter' – vibrations in the skeg, which can produce increased forward drag.*

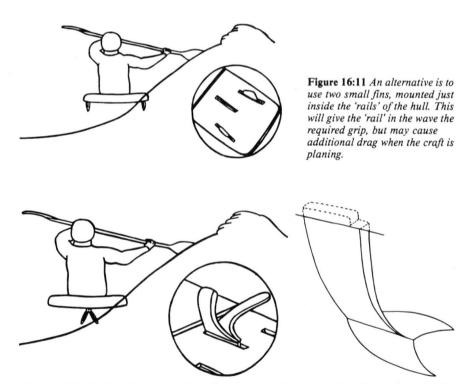

Figure 16:11 *An alternative is to use two small fins, mounted just inside the 'rails' of the hull. This will give the 'rail' in the wave the required grip, but may cause additional drag when the craft is planing.*

Figure 16:12a (left) *A design, popular with surf board riders, is the 'butterfly skeg', a twin skeg design mounted in the central position.* **Figure 16:12b (right)** *The T skeg, also enables the fin to 'reach sideways'.*

Enthusiastic surf kayak and ski riders follow closely the design development within the surfboard world, and many innovative designs come from board manufacturers. It must be said though, that many skeg designs have as many drawbacks as they have advantages, and often are a matter of fashion, rather than real advantage. As a general rule, the simpler the better. Surf kayak and ski paddlers, once they have mastered the basic technique of their craft, should, however, experiment, and may well find that 2 or 3 different types are needed for different conditions.

The use of skegs on slalom kayaks has not yet been fully explored. The slalom canoe, with its long stern, and softer rails (gunwales) tends to side-slip. On very steep waves, a slalom canoeist on a diagonal run can lose control of the stern to such an extent, that the craft turns back up the wave and over the top. A fin mounted on the rear of a slalom canoe, however, makes turning extremely difficult, because the increased length between skeg and paddler creates far greater leverage.

Although no really satisfactory fin design has been found for slalom kayaks, a final thought should be given to the 'retractable skeg'. The idea of having one which can be lowered when required has been tried with limited success on surf kayaks. This type, if robust enough, would appear to be ideally suited to the slalom kayak.

Canoeists should not forget that the 'ultimate' skeg is the paddle. When a craft is planing, the paddle can be used to achieve the same affect as a skeg, and many of our top surfers rely entirely on their paddles, and shifting their body weight.

SAFETY

As with any aspect of canoe sport, the instructor's first duty must be to the safety of all members of his group. Provided a comprehensive series of checks are made before and during each session, the likelihood of serious accidents will be reduced. Safety checks can be divided into five categories:

1   Conditions.

2   Boats.

3   Personal equipment.

4   Back-up safety.

5   Organisation.

Conditions

Before starting any session, local weather forecasts, together with their likely effect on the proposed beach, should be considered. Obvious hazards such as rising wind speeds, or very low temperatures, should be avoided. Attention should also be paid to the direction of the wind and the possibility of moderate off-shore winds, for, whilst providing excellent conditions for the more experienced surfer, they may create havoc with a party of beginners. With capsizes likely, you may end up with boats, paddles and bodies being blown out to sea. Unlike open water canoeing, the effects of wind strength are difficult to generalise, as the position of land shelter, headlands and so forth, may have a considerable bearing on the surfing area. The influence of the wind may also vary with the state of the tide. However, off-shore winds greater than force 2-3 should be avoided with beginners in surf.

The state of the tide will also determine conditions. For example, low tide often produces a 'dumping' wave, with the likelihood of greater exposure to the wind. High tide may leave very little beach (especially if there is a sea wall) together with the possibility of

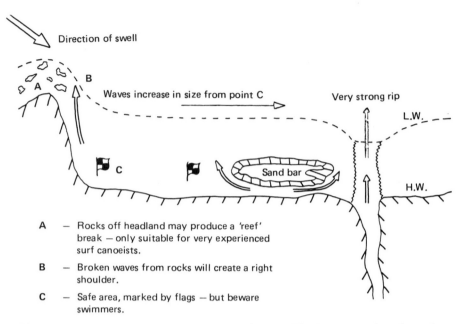

Direction of swell

B Waves increase in size from point C

Very strong rip

L.W.

H.W.

C Sand bar

A — Rocks off headland may produce a 'reef' break — only suitable for very experienced surf canoeists.

B — Broken waves from rocks will create a right shoulder.

C — Safe area, marked by flags — but beware swimmers.

Figure 16:13 *A typical surf beach. The arrows indicate possible rip currents where the surf may appear smaller and safer. The reverse is true. Avoid areas where the waves are flatter*

reflected waves from sea walls or cliffs. Rising or falling tides can produce very dangerous swimming conditions (rips, undertows) and at certain states, swimming may be prohibited altogether. Tidal stream charts do not give enough detail for these currents to be recognised and local information must be obtained from lifeguards, surf lifesaving clubs, or other surfers.

Surfers should be familiar with the various structures on the beach which are likely to create danger zones, as outlined in figure 16:13, but always be advised by the professional lifeguards patrol. Also take note of any signs posted.

When sharing the beach with others (especially swimmers) canoe surfers need to take special care. Observe the beach safety zones. Do not canoe in swimming areas marked by red and yellow flags. Surfing zones are indicated by black and white chequered flags. Red flags show danger areas, and are often flown at low tide, or when there is no lifeguard patrol.

It is necessary to assess the height of the surf before committing a group. Beginners and intermediate surfers will often become too nervous to turn around in large waves, and may continue out through the break-line in a lull between heavy breaks. A 'rule of thumb' system is to commence by standing right at the water's edge and look at the horizon. If peaks break the horizon, it is BIG. If not, kneel and again look at the horizon. If occasional peaks break it, then probably the larger waves are around three to four foot, and the surf useable *inside* by novices. Less than this, the surf is probably ideal, but beware of conditions changing and waves building up higher, particularly as the tide rises.

Boats

For beginners using slalom or surf kayaks a good plan is to have two pupils per craft, with one surfing, and one on the beach, or standing in the water, to assist. One instructor to four craft (eight pupils) is then a good working ratio. For beginners, who are unlikely to canoe past the break-line, it is not necessary to have anyone patrolling outside the break, although when possible it does reduce the concern for instructors within the break, or on the beach.

All equipment should be carefully checked before the group go on the water. Slalom and surf kayaks should have:

1   Strong construction.

2   Block buoyancy fore and aft to prevent collapse of deck, and solid buoyancy right up to the footrest to prevent paddler from shooting down inside the boat in the event of a 'pearl dive'. All other available space should be filled with buoyancy.

3   Fail-safe footrest in full working order.

4   Toggles, not end loops, at each end.

5   Uncluttered deck.

6   Smooth cockpit edges. Most minor cuts and grazes are caused by poorly finished craft.

Surf skis should be equipped with a leash, attached to an off-centre point at the bow. The leash may be attached to the paddler's ankle, or the centre of the paddle shaft, by a velcro'd strap.

Personal Equipment

Each canoeist should have:

1   Suitable warm clothing (wet suits are ideal). Beginners should in any case wear something on their legs and feet to avoid cuts during the inevitable capsizes.

2   A correctly fitted buoyancy aid which covers most of the trunk region. This provides protection against knocks as well as providing buoyancy.

3   A tightly fitting helmet.

4   A strong pair of paddles – at all levels of surfing, this is essential. The construction of the paddle used is often determined by price, but better to pay a little more for a strong pair, than break a plywood blade in the first session. Most surf canoeists use wooden slalom paddles, and modern trends tend to favour a very short length (under 200cm) for fast paddle strokes with rapid accelleration and 'take off'. A short leash from wrist to paddle is sometimes used by surfers to avoid the loss of the paddle in large waves.

5   An efficient spray deck. These must be tight fitting to prevent water entering the boat. Consequently decks must have a good release strap or toggle. Nylon spray decks tend to come off or be stoved in heavy water, and so neoprene covers which leave a flat deck are more suitable. Otherwise, the wearing of two nylon spraydecks can be effective.

6   Nose clips can be used by those paddlers who prefer not to get water in their synuses.

Back-up safety

Instructors or group leaders must be familiar with:

1   Rescue services available.

2   Use of reel and line (if available).

3   Position of nearest telephone.

4   A system of signals, clearly understood by all members of the group.

The leader must also have confidence in his or her own ability to perform a rescue on any member of the group who might be swept outside the break line. If in doubt – don't go out. Those who intend to be involved with surfing on a frequent basis should consider taking some form of surf lifesaving award, as swimming is often the only suitable form of rescue for surf. The Surf Life Saving Association Bronze Medallion is an acceptable standard. You should be familiar with the international surf lifesaving signals (see Appendix V) and the use of a reel and line.

Canoe to canoe rescues should not be attempted where there is the possibility of breaking waves. Instead, rely on the canoeist swimming his craft ashore. It is vital that he remains to seaward of his boat – otherwise the overtaking waves will throw the canoe onto him.

Toggles are essential, for hands or fingers in loops can be tourniqued by a canoe rotating on the front of a breaking wave.

Should it become necessary, a simple rescue can be effected by the capsized canoeist lying full-length on the stern-deck of a rescuer, with his arms around the paddlers waist, and legs wrapped around the hull. Quite large surf can be safely negotiated in this way. This does require confidence on the part of the victim however. If in doubt, a bow-carry may be more appropriate (see Chapter 10).

Organisation

The 'buddy' system has been advocated, whereby one person paddles, and a second is available to help with emptying and launching, the canoeists taking turns to ride the surf.

Make the group paddle out at either end of the marked zone, so that the area is not full of two-way traffic, with consequent danger and spoiled rides. If the beach is not marked, indicate a 'paddling out' area. There may be a friendly rip which can be used to aid this chore, but be very sure of its strength and length before allowing novices to use it.

The person on the wave has priority, and a canoeist should not 'drop in' on the side the paddler on the wave will first manoeuvre towards. It is particularly important not to impede board riders in this way, as the surfer may well have waited the best part of a day for this particular spot on this particular wave, only to be barged off it by a canoeist, who can in fact paddle in and out at will and ride virtually anything. Beginners must be particularly careful not to ride in close together on a wave, for if one loses control, or releases his 'rudder', the canoe will immediately charge along and back up the wave, possibly at around 30 mph, with potentially disastrous results for anyone in the way. The risk of collision is a serious one. If a paddler is unable to control direction, and there is anyone or anything in his path, he must immediately capsize. The drag of his body in the water will stop him.

TEACHING PROGRESSION – KAYAKS

Surf canoeing for beginners can be tackled in two distinct ways.

1   The introduction of reasonably proficient paddlers (2 Star or above) to using their craft in surf.

2   The introduction of complete beginners to surf using the Surf Ski.

With the former the paddler will almost always use a slalom kayak and the learning sequence is:

1   Getting into the kayak and onto the water.

2   Paddling through broken waves or 'soup'.

3   Paddle brace for support.

4   Sideways run in the braced position ('bongo-slide').

5   Running forward on soup, then turn and brace into a sideways run.

6   Riding green waves.

Taking each point in turn the instructor should maintain close contact with pupils and demonstrate each technique when possible. Looking at each of these techniques in detail, some of the likely problems may be as follows:

Launching

On most surfing beaches the 'seal' launch is the most effective as it allows the paddler to adjust and check all his equipment before tackling the water. The problems of entering a kayak in shallow surf include: being swamped by a slightly larger wave before the spray deck is properly adjusted, having paddler washed up the beach whilst putting the spraydeck on, or being turned parallel to the surf – and a probable capsize! With the 'two pupils to one craft' system, the 'buddy' can help his partner and avoid these situations. Points to remember when making the 'seal' launch.

1   The craft should be at right angles to the waves – not all are parallel to the beach.

2   The craft should be as close to the water as possible – certainly in the area which is being reached by the last run of larger swells.

3   When the paddler is ready to start, the canoe should be lifted by placing both hands, or one hand and the paddle, on the beach, and sliding forward by shunting his weight. This process is repeated until the craft is afloat.

4   Seal launches should not be attempted if the craft is fitted with a skeg.

5   Beginners should always be made aware of the areas safe for launching. *Do not* launch near a strong rip current, near rocks, near swimmers or a swimming area.

Paddling out

Initially the technique for paddling through broken waves is to keep the craft at right angles to them, and paddle forward, continuing the paddling strokes as the wave passes the craft. With larger waves and more experience, presenting the hull to the leading edge of the breaker (see ski section) is more effective. With a slalom kayak, much of the force of the wave can be avoided by leaning right back on the rear deck as the kayak passes through the broken crest, thus presenting less surface area to the wave.

The paddle brace

A static paddle brace with the craft parallel to the broken wave. As the waves reach the craft the paddler leans into the wave, with the paddle resting on or behind the crest. The first few times, this technique can be helped by the 'buddy' standing in the water on the seaward side of the boat and supporting the paddle. This leads to the:

Figure 16:14a *Incorrect. Body bent this way causes inshore rail (gunwale) to be forced down.*

Figure 16:14b *Correct. Body bent this way lifts inshore rail and forces seaward rail down.*

'Bongo' slide, or broached run

If the broken wave is big enough it will carry the craft towards the shore. Provided the paddler remains in the 'braced' position and continues to lean into the wave, he should not capsize. The commonest fault amongst beginners is to not lean hard enough towards the wave and the wave rolls the boat over towards the shore. Another common fault is not bending correctly at the hips as shown in Figure 16:14.

Wave riding

Once the 'feel' is achieved, and successful rides are being obtained on both sides, the next stage can be proceeded with. Paddling out a little further, or even 'outside' if the surf is less than two feet, turn quickly between waves, and learn how to paddle hard to get the canoe moving in order to be picked up by the following swell. The canoeist must be ready to lean hard onto the wave, once the broach starts, and not be tripped over the 'downhill' gunnel.

A common mistake with beginners is for them to keep paddling, and end up ahead of the wave, looking rather like a windmill. Once the surge is felt, as the boat is accelerated by the wave, the paddling forward should stop, and the 'stern rudder' applied (see chapter 6).

Initially, it is a good idea to let paddlers endeavour to keep the boat straight for short distances, and then release the rudder and so turn back off the wave, to try again. Although the eventual aim must be to maintain a straight course, with the rudder applied on one side of the canoe only, initially it will be necessary to change sides frequently, or be ready to lean hard into the wave once a broach is inevitable.

When success is being achieved consistently, a 'diagonal run' should be introduced. Once the boat is moving on the wave, the paddler should turn away from the break, and apply a stern rudder on the 'downhill' side of the wave, preventing the broach. In this way, it is possible to move along the wave considerably faster, and for longer distances, than with a straight ride. Control is aided by tilting the kayak onto its 'uphill' gunnel (i.e. leaning away from the stern rudder). This causes the bow to want to turn downhill, and so aids steering. As the wave starts to break on the boat, the paddler must be ready to bring his paddle across and throw himself onto it, bracing on the top of the wave.

From this point on, it is a matter of building a repertoire of skills, paying careful attention to the shape and pattern of waves, looking for the wave that is going to break evenly along its length, and applying those skills to maintaining the maximum length and variety of ride possible in the circumstances.

TEACHING PROGRESSION – SKIS

The surf ski provides instructors with a new medium to pass on their skills. Because of its unique design amongst canoe craft, the ski provides an opportunity to teach surfing first and foremost, with canoeing skills playing a secondary role. The following suggestions therefore apply only to instructors who are starting with non-canoeing beginners, and whose aim is to teach *surfing* with a ski, rather than 'canoeing'.

This programme is based on the assumption that the instructor has made the necessary preparation with regards to safety and that the pupils are paired in the 'buddy system', each pair having a fully equipped, but basic design ski (those with lap straps, trees, thigh grips are not suitable). The programme can be divided into sections, each leading in natural progression to the next:

1   Familiarity with the craft.

2   Development of balance and weight shift.

3   Using the wave for forward propulsion.

4   Paddle techniques.

Initially the instructor is not concerned with paddle technique, and during stages one, two and part of three paddles are not required. It is now best to look at each item separately.

Familiarisation

To familiarise pupils with the craft they are using, calm water can be used. The aim is to enable the beginner to master simple techniques, such as turning the craft upright from a

Figure 16:15 *A diagonal run. The rudder is applied on the shoreward side, and the kayak is tilted towards the wave. Photo: Peter T. Young.*

Toe strap

Figure 16:16 *Using a shoulder carry. Depending on the style of ski, carrying can be either across the back holding the toe straps as illustrated, or using a specially designed handle which is moulded into the craft or attached to each end of it and looped over the shoulder.*

swimming position, mounting the craft from deep water and getting feet into toe straps quickly, once mounted. Another very basic, but nevertheless important feature, is carrying the craft on land. The instructor may have his own personal preference for dealing with each of these but certainly with younger pupils teaching by using 'games' requiring the various skills, often works well. For example: swimming to an upturned craft, turning it from the water, mounting, attaching a leash to an arm or ankle, capsizing and swimming back towing the craft to a finish line, might form a 'race', or game after each skill has been practised individually. For games like this it is better for the craft not to have a skeg fitted.

Depending on the style of ski, carrying can be either across the back holding the toe strap or using a specially designed handle, either moulded into the craft or attached to each end. The ski is carried using the shoulders, as demonstrated in Figure 16:16.

Developing balance

The next stage is to become thoroughly familiar with balance. Again, through games: sitting or kneeling hand paddle races; standing; standing on one foot; and so forth. Up to this point the beginner will not have used a paddle or a skeg. The desire to use the paddle increases, and as the art of good ski surfing lies in the control of body weight, and balance, the next move is to the surf.

Forward propulsion

Here the 'buddy' system is essential. Initially small surf (waist deep) can be used. With one partner sitting on the ski, the other tows it out to a suitably sized wave and turns the craft to face inshore. A gentle push, just as the wave reaches the stern, will set the ski in motion. By lying back, the rider can keep the craft surfing just in front of the wave. With toes in the straps, and hands gripping the 'rails' at the stern, the rider can control and correct any deviation from a 'straight' run. Should pupils have difficulty mastering the leaning control, the ski can be used like a belly board (provided it has a fairly smooth deck). The emphasis at this stage must be on keeping the rider's weight at the rear of the craft – too far forward and the ski will 'pearl dive'. The rider must, however, be prepared to adjust his position to keep the ski on the wave. If there is continued difficulty in controlling forward direction, a skeg should be inserted into the skeg box.

Once the rider has controlled a forward run on soup, he can then try to 'steer' the ski using his hands. At all times the appropriate safety precautions should be observed by both pupils and instructor. The use of an ankle leash will save a considerable amount of time.

Using the paddle

The ski surfer can now be introduced to his paddle. Although the feathered paddle is used almost exclusively amongst 'canoeists' when surfing, the unfeathered paddle is used by many ski paddlers who have graduated from the surfboard riding ranks. Unfeathered blades are certainly easier for the beginner to use, but whichever form is chosen, the surfer should now be encouraged to use the paddle to steer and correct his craft, and to propel the ski, and turn to catch a wave. Beginners at this level will tend to make the same sort of mistakes as canoeists in conventional craft – e.g. paddling too soon to catch the wave. Errors should be corrected if and when they occur.

Paddling out through broken waves on a ski tends to be more difficult than for kayaks. There is a tendency to 'backward loop' on steep or powerful waves. This can be overcome

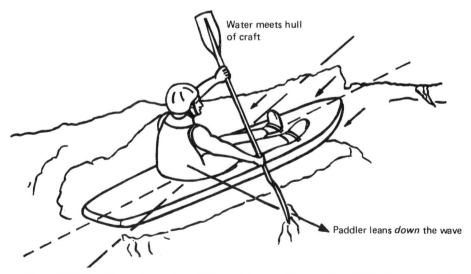

Water meets hull of craft

Paddler leans *down* the wave

Figure 16:17 *Paddling out through surf. The craft is steered between 5° and 10° off course, and the canoeist leans away from the wave to present the hull to the breaking wave.*

by either increased speed, or moving the weight forward as the ski meets the wave. A useful technique when paddling through broken water is to meet the wave at a very slight angle from the 'right angle', and lean down wave, thus preventing the hull of the craft to the oncoming breaker (Figure 16:17). This causes the water to lift the hull, as a larger surface area is presented to the wave. The conventional 'paddle forward and punch through the wave' often causes the bow to dig into the face. The crest then breaks along the deck, and hits the paddler. It is the force of the water against the paddler's body that stops the forward motion, and often causes him to be 'caught' by the wave and carried inshore.

Having mastered the basic techniques of paddling out and catching the wave, the ski rider should progress to green (unbroken) waves, where the shifting of body weight becomes even more important. When riding a green wave the paddler should experiment with moving as far along the seat pan (i.e. with fixed feet, moving his bottom as close to his heels as possible) as he can. This will increase speed on a diagonal run, and when combined with a rapid backward movement and lean to one side, will turn the ski. Tyros should also be encouraged to try running without a skeg, as this develops delicacy of touch. Finally, ski paddlers should experiment with the various devices produced: skeg designs, gripping devices such as 'trees' and lap straps, to find which suits them best.

SURFING TERMINOLOGY

Blown Out – When the wind destroys the shape of the waves.

Bongo-slide – This picturesque name is given by some canoeists to the sideways push from a large breaking wave, when a kayak is broached and taken down the face of the wave by the force of the tumbling crest.

Bottom Turn – A turn performed after accelerating to the bottom of the wave, with the kayak or ski climbing back up to continue riding near the 'break'.

Break Line – Sometimes called 'surf-line', this is the area in which the waves are first breaking. Between this area and the shore is called 'inside', and beyond it, where the 'green waves' first build, is called 'outside'.

Broach – When a boat is swung sideways onto a wave, it is said to have been 'broached'. As a boat runs down a wave, three forces are accelerating it: gravity, because it is on a hill; water, because the molecules of water in the wave are acting on the hull (figure 16:1); wind, if it is following. These forces are mainly accelerating the stern, however. The bow is tending to dig in ahead of the wave, and is being slowed by friction with the water, and by the action of water molecules moving back against the bow and returning into the wave. These opposing forces cause the stern to want to overtake the bow. Consequently, the boat 'broaches', or, in extreme situations, 'loops'.

Catherine Wheel – Surf Kayaks and skis can be induced to spin in a 360° circle on the face of a wave. Performed as a 'trick', to gain points in competition the manoeuvre must be part of a programme aimed at keeping the craft in the best position on the wave.

Climbing & Dropping – By body lean, and with a minimum of paddle steering, the canoe can be made to climb the face of the wave and then drop down it again in a series of graceful curves.

Closed Out – When a wave drops instantaneously along its length, making it unrideable, or when the height and weight of the surf on a beach make conditions very dangerous.

Cut Back – The paddler moves away from the break and turns towards it again.

284

Drop In – To take off on a wave when there is a surfer between you and the shoulder, spoiling the other person's ride.

Dumper – When a section of a wave breaks, instead of the break running evenly along the length of the wave, it is said to be 'dumping'. The term is more generally used to indicate when these sections are dropping particularly hard; or when there is a heavy shore-break; or when the breaking crest is throwing ahead of the wave, creating a hollow (or 'tube' – Figure 16:4).

Figure of Eight – A cut-back with two turns up the green wave.

Green Wave – A well-formed wave before it breaks.

Humper – A very large, green wave.

Line-up – Surfers waiting to catch a wave.

Locked in – Usually used to indicate when a surfer is in the best position for riding, especially in a 'tube'. Also known as 'in the slot'.

Loop – A manoeuvre performed in kayaks (but not surf kayaks). The wave is ridden normally until it is about to break. The kayak is then kept straight and slowed to stay well up the face of the wave. As the wave breaks, the kayak is backed up and kept on an even keel by a couple of short, sharp back strokes. The breaking crest will then throw the stern over the bow, and when all has settled down, the paddler rolls up.

Outside – The area beyond the 'break line'. Sometimes shouted as a warning that larger waves are approaching, which could break further out.

Pearl Dive – When a boat shoots down a wave, submerges ahead of it, and hits the bottom, it is said to have 'pearl dived'. This can be damaging to boat and paddler. The footrest can break, and if the bow is not packed with polystyrene or similar, the canoeist may end up jammed down inside the boat. In controlled conditions, experts can use the bottom to contrive a loop call a 'pole vault', or to quite deliberately stand the canoe on its nose.

Pirouette – Kayaks (but not surf kayaks) are ridden as for a loop. When in the perpendicular position, the paddler places a bow-rudder in the wave, and flicks the hips to face the kayak out to sea. This is known as a 'dry loop' as he then lands the right way up, instead of having to roll. Those with very flexible hips should be able to spin a complete 540°. If the moment of pirouetting is left until the kayak is past the perpendicular position (i.e. stern ahead of bow) it is possible to land on the breaking wave, be carried in, and repeat the whole manoeuvre in reverse. This should not be attempted in large waves breaking in shallow water, however, because of the danger of the stern hitting the bottom and causing a spinal injury.

Pop-out – Kayaks (but not surf kayaks) are ridden as for a 'loop'. Instead of using final back-strokes, however, the boat is allowed to drive down the face of the wave and under water. As the wave breaks it 'swallows' the boat, and the buoyancy causes the kayak to shoot out the back of the wave, often becoming completely airborne. Also known as a 'sky rocket'.

Re-entry – Following a cut-back the surfer uses the 'break' to accelerate back onto the shoulder.

Reverse Rides – It is extremely dangerous to ride surf backwards, as even for experts, the degree of control available is suspect. Reverse loops, should the kayak hit the bottom hard, could result in serious back injury.

Right Run – Surfing to your right.

285

Rip – When surf is piling ashore on a beach, the water level can increase relative to the rest of the sea. Water – which must find its own level – therefore has to return quickly to restore the balance. This often results in a fast 'river' of water streaming back out to sea, often at the edges of a bay. This stream can move from one to four knots and can be used by experts for a speedy passage through the surf. A swimmer caught in a rip should swim at right angles to it (parallel to the beach) until clear of its influence – which is usually only a matter of yards – and then return to shore using the surf.

Set – A group or 'box' of waves.

Shoulder – Ideally a wave breaks evenly from one end to the other. The art of surfing is that of keeping one-self positioned right in the 'pocket' just ahead of the breaking part of the wave. A 'left shoulder' is a wave breaking from right to left as viewed from the sea, looking towards the beach. A 'right shoulder' is the opposite.

Soup – The white foam tumbling down breaking waves inside the break-line is known as the 'soup'.

Stall – Slowing down, in order to regain the shoulder.

Swell – Waves created by a far-off wind or storm. These tend to traverse the ocean in patterns called 'boxes', the pattern moving at about 70 mph.

Tube – A hollow created by the crest of a wave throwing forward as it breaks. Boards, skis and surf kayaks can ride inside this hollow – to many, the 'ultimate experience'. Tubes are not common in Great Britain.

Wave – Wave height is measured from 'crest' (top) to 'trough' (bottom), and this height is invariably exaggerated. Wave-length is the distance between crests. A molecule of water in a wave rotates as indicated in Figure 16:1. When the depth of water is only one and a half times the height of the wave, the friction slows down the bottom of the wave, and the crest overtakes the bottom. Thus, the wave 'breaks' and the water itself then moves and tumbles ashore.

17 Forms of Canoeing Competition

Compiled by the Editor

INTRODUCTION

Standards in all sports have been rising consistently for many years. This has lead to specialisation, and craft and techniques have developed in all the disciplines of canoeing which, in the main, are suitable for one purpose only. It is still possible for a performer of high calibre to enjoy good competition and good canoeing in many different ways, but it is less likely now that an individual will rise to the very top in more than one type of event. There is no reason, however, why a canoeist cannot compete at an enjoyable level across the board. Many do, and pursue touring, expeditioning and other recreational pursuits as well. Most of the major white water river expeditions, for instance, have been undertaken by leading slalom and wild water racing paddlers.

During the past decade greater emphasis has been laid on the importance of training and coaching in order to achieve success. With the continual increase in knowledge about how to attain maximum physical fitness, develop the specific muscles to cope with the power requirement, and the science of psychological preparation to motivate the athlete, it is essential that coaches take the necessary steps to keep themselves informed and up to date.

This chapter does not attempt to provide that specific training or coaching information for competitive canoeists, but reference is made in the Bibliography to the sources from which help can be obtained at the present time. A manual is in preparation which will eventually cover these aspects in detail.

In general terms, a canoeist needs to develop the cardio-vascular system, in order to supply the oxygen required to break down the muscle glycogen which enables them to function. Running, circuit training and swimming are generally reckoned to be the best forms of exercise to achieve this. Cycling is also useful. Interval training, both in the canoe, and running, is good, because the recovery period immediately following the flat-out burst of effort where high heart beat rates are achieved, has a significant affect. Interval Training should not however be used with young paddlers (under 16 as a rough guide).

Power training must be specific. There is no point in developing strength in muscles that are not required, nor in ways in which a muscle is not used for canoeing purposes. Various apparatus has been designed to accurately imitate the paddling action, enabling the canoeist to develop his ability to pull with trunk rotation and the lower arm. Heavy weights should not be used by young people until after puberty, due to the adverse effect this has on bone growth.

Local muscular endurance is improved by circuit training exercises with weights but again, the routines chosen must be relevant to the use to which the muscles will be put in propelling the canoe. There will be differences between slalomists and racing paddlers in this respect. In all training routines involving the use of weights expert advice should be sought before starting. Mobility exercises help to keep muscles supple and extend the range of movement. They should be part of the canoeists training programme and can be incorporated in a 'warm-up'. Some coaches feel that diet is important but generally speaking properly balanced meals will provide adequate nutritional intake. Women and girls may require iron supplements which should be prescribed by a doctor.

Research has shown that excessive fitness training applied to young people before puberty does not significantly improve performance. Some may enjoy a certain involvement with suitable programmes. There is no point, however, in pursuing this to any great extent, and the use of heavy weights must be discouraged.

Training in the boat is the most relevant of all, but a proportional balance must be maintained in order to provide variety, and to improve most efficiently those components which together allow maximum performance to be achieved. For juniors, the greatest emphasis should be on developing technique, allied to maintaining interest, having fun, and increasing the ability to cover distances at a steady rate.

MARATHON RACING

The term 'marathon racing' should not deter anyone from entering a local event, whatever their age, or type of kayak or canoe owned. Most people enjoy touring, and marathon racing enables a canoeist to proceed uninterrupted at his own best pace, on different and varying waterways.

Racing for fun

A recent revision of the marathon racing scheme has led to the development of a divisional system, in which all types of craft and all ages of people of either sex can compete on equal terms. Known as the Open Racing Scheme, events can be held on any type of water, at club, local, regional and national level, and cater for any number of participans from a minimum of five. The lower divisions 8 and 9 – race over a *maximum* of only four miles. Full details of how to stage club or local races are available free from the BCU. A network of regional advisors exists to help with enquiries.

Promotion, which from the lower divisions can take place at local level, is organised on a percentage basis, and all competitors receive a certificate which also entitles them to an entry in a national draw, which takes place several times each year. Once a paddler begins to move up the divisions he will normally compete at regional, and then national level events, but the system enables everyone, in any type of kayak or canoe, to find his level and enjoy continued good competition.

Serious marathon paddlers usually gravitate eventually to international racing K1s or K2s, C1s or C2s and compete over distances which vary between 10 and 80 miles. At the time of writing consideration is being given to the adoption of a standard Canadian for international marathon racing, but this may well remain as an open event.

The Racing Yearbook published annually, gives full details of rules and events, with advice to organisers, and shows the ranking lists of paddlers for Divisions 1-7, based on promotion achieved throughout the previous season.

Figure 17:1a (above) *Preparing for the start of the classic Gudena Marathon, Denmark.*
Figure 17:1b (below) *The field spreads out. Photos: Vakd Vedel*

Boat designs

Any type of canoe or kayak may be used but only within the ICF regulations for length, breadth and weight, as shown:

	Maximum length	Minimum beam
Single kayak	520cm (17')	51 cm (20")
Double kayak	650 cm (21'4")	55 cm (21½")
Single canoe	520 cm (17')	75 cm (29½")
Double canoe	650 cm (21'4")	75 cm (29½")

Boats over 460 cm in length must not have concave sections. Propulsion shall be by paddle only, the paddle being supported solely by the hands. In essence, the class rules above mean that most canoes or kayaks can race. Obviously, those that conform most closely to the limits are likely to be the most successful in the right hands. When used for marathon, racing kayaks will usually be fitted with an over-stern rudder, which lifts if it meets an obstruction.

There are different classes of event dependent upon the standard of course and organisation involved, and particular races are nominated to count for various perpetual awards such as the Hasler Trophy, for which the rules are designed to enable any club with an interest in marathon racing to compete on equal terms.

Marathon Racing Rules

Boats must be rendered sufficiently buoyant to stay afloat and support the crew in rough water when capsized, and adequate spray decks must be worn on open water. Competitors must be competent to swim in the waters on which the race is held, and life jackets or buoyancy aids (minimum inherent buoyancy 6 kg) must be worn by all those under 16, and by others at the organiser's discretion.

Competitors may not wash hang on powered craft during a race, nor change boats. They may receive food and drink, but no other assistance, unless permitted by the organiser (eg a disabled person whose boat is carried for them at a portage). Paddles may be changed in the event of a breakage. A code is used to identify the type of water, and the number of portages involved:

'A' denotes sea, tidal estuary, lake or other open water

'B' denotes fresh water rivers and canals

'P' denotes portages.

A numeral following the symbol shows the length in miles or the number of portages: eg A5B6P7 indicates a race of 5 miles on open water, six of closed water, and seven portages.

Tactics and Portaging

Apart from developing the physical ability to paddle at top speed for the duration of the course, serious competitors pay a great deal of attention to race tactics. The whole concept of marathon is that it should be held on natural waterways, and involve taking whatever steps are necessary to navigate the canoe to the finish. It may be necessary to cross large lakes, or estuaries, shoot weirs, or portage the canoe around obstacles or potentially dangerous situations.

Attention has to be paid to the vagaries of tide and current, reading the water to spot rocks and shallows, and practising techniques to ensure a swift transition at portages. Especially important is the development of 'wash-hanging' skills. By sitting close to another canoe, dependent upon the speed of travel this is usually with your bow about a third of the way back from his – it is possible to obtain a considerable 'lift' from your

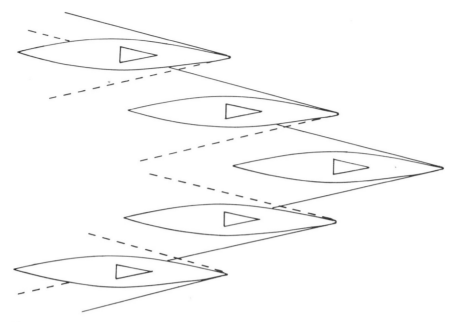

Figure 17:2 *Wash hanging*

Figure 17:3 *Portaging – not time for resting!*

291

opponent's wake. Thus you are conserving energy for the time when you sprint, and hopefully leave him behind. He meanwhile, will try to cause you to drop back off the wash, which is invariably extremely difficult to regain.

Most marathons commence with a mass start, and the ability to gain the first portage ahead of the field, can be critical. Many paddlers fix foot-rest pumps to enable the boat to be kept dry, and attention needs to be paid to ensure that spray decks keep the water out, but can be quickly removed and fitted when portaging.

National and International competition

A National Championships is held in which all age groups are catered for. The ICF awarded marathon racing international recognition in 1980, and whilst it still does not have world championships status, a number of major events between nations now take place, including a European grand prix series. Some races in other parts of the world – notably Australia, South Africa, the USA and Canada involve hundreds of miles of lake and river, maybe crossing mountains, and are occasionally up to a month's duration. The longest race in Great Britain is the annual Devizes to Westminster canoe race, traditionally held at Easter, which is of 126 miles duration and requires 72 portages. Seniors race non-stop, while Juniors have three compulsory overnight stops.

Conclusion

Marathon racing has the greatest potential for expansion of all the competitive forms of canoeing. It is now within the scope of any and every local group, club, or individual to stage a low-key event, with a minimum requirement for facilities and organisation. The emphasis is on fun and enjoyment for all the family, but feeding into the national system.

CANOE POLO

A game for teams of five players, who endeavour to pass a ball to each other, avoiding the opposition, until scoring by striking it against their opponents' goal.

This description does not begin to reveal the excitement and enjoyment that is engendered in having to control a small, unstable craft, propel it at maximum velocity, spin, and balance it, while hurling the ball, with opponents permitted to capsize the paddler by pushing him off balance when he is in possession. Neither does it convey the fierceness with which games are contended at all levels.

Canoe Polo can be played on any area of water that enables a pitch of regulation size to be laid out, and goals – consisting of boards 1 metre square with the lower edge 2 metres from the water – erected. For British games, the goals currently should be between 20 and 50 metres apart, but with fast development occurring at home and abroad, rules have occasionally to be reviewed. An attempt is being made to reconcile the British and continental games, to allow for growth in international play.

At present the differences are considerable, particularly with regard to the German tradition, where Polo has been played for many years. Well supported national leagues exist there, and matches used to attract great numbers of spectators. Teams consist of six, as opposed to our five players. Their boats are a one-design scaled down kayak, whereas in Britain the BAT, between 2 and 3 metres in length, and between 50 and 60 cms beam, is used. The pitch can be football size, using water polo goals, laid out on a lake, while swimming pools are the normal site for matches at home. The ball can be propelled by striking it with the paddle, whereas in Britain the paddle may be used to stop, deflect, or

Figure 17:4 *Goal! A game in progress at Crystal Palace*

flick, but not to strike it. A football 'kick-off' is used, as opposed to our teams lining up at each end, with the members of each team being permitted to race for the ball, which is thrown in to commence, or re-commence the game.

Safety

Crash helmets are compulsory, together with full-length buoyancy aids to protect the trunk and lumbar region. Although dangerous use of the paddle is penalised, polo is a close contact game and a wire visor worn to protect the face is a sensible precaution. Paddle blades must not be metal tipped and a minimum thickness at the edge is stipulated. Neither deliberate ramming nor obstruction is permitted.

Contests

Many friendly inter-club games are played, besides local and regional leagues operating. Nationally an 'A' and a 'B' league are organised, and may well be extended. There is an annual national knockout tournament with initial games played at regional level, leading to the finals for youth and senior teams, currently held at the Canoe Exhibition at Crystal Palace in February each year. A training programme for Polo is detailed in Chapter 12.

RACING

Previously know as Paddle Racing, and commonly called Sprint, this branch of the sport is a competition for canoes and kayaks over a course as flat and as still as can be obtained of distances up to and including 10,000 metres. Competitions may be organised for any craft, but the normal classes of boat are K1, K2, K4, C1, C2 and C7, which is raced internationally by juniors only. The distances are 500 metres, 1,000 metres, and 10,000 metres. Nationally juniors race 3,000 or 6,000 metres as a distance event, and ladies 6,000 metres.

World championships for seniors are held evey year except Olympic year, when canoe racing forms part of the Olympic games. For juniors, a junior world championships is held every two years. Olympic canoe and kayak racing involves 500 and 1,000 metres for men and 500 metres for women. Figure 17:6 shows the usual international and Olympic racing events, while figure 17:5 identifies the classes of boat and shows their dimensions. C7 events are competed for by juniors only.

For national championships and international purposes, no turns are permitted for distances of 1,000 metres or less, and the start and finish must be at right angles to the

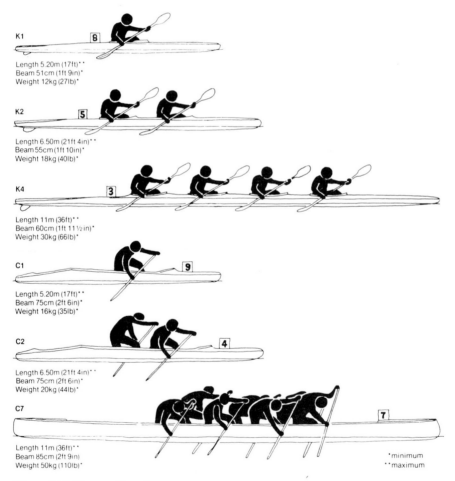

K1   8
Length 5.20m (17ft)**
Beam 51cm (1ft 9in)*
Weight 12kg (27lb)*

K2   5
Length 6.50m (21ft 4in)**
Beam 55cm (1ft 10in)*
Weight 18kg (40lb)*

K4   3
Length 11m (36ft)**
Beam 60cm (1ft 11½in)*
Weight 30kg (66lb)*

C1   9
Length 5.20m (17ft)**
Beam 75cm (2ft 6in)*
Weight 16kg (35lb)*

C2   4
Length 6.50m (21ft 4in)**
Beam 75cm (2ft 6in)*
Weight 20kg (44lb)*

C7   7
Length 11m (36ft)**
Beam 85cm (2ft 9in)
Weight 50kg (110lb)*

*minimum
**maximum

Figure 17:5 *Classes of boat for sprint racing*

	World Championship Events			Olympic Events	
	500m	1,000m	10,000m	500m	1,000m
Men					
	K1	K1	K1	K1	K1
	K2	K2	K2	K2	K2
	K4	K4	K4		K4
	C1	C1	C1	C1	C1
	C2	C2	C2	C2	C2
	C7				
Women	500m			500m	
	K1			K1	
	K2			K2	
	K4			K4	

Figure 17:6 *World championships and Olympic sprint racing distances*

course. Where possible there must be at least five metres between boats, which should be able to race in clearly marked lanes. Wash hanging is not permitted for races up to 1,000 metres, nor during the last 1,000 metres of longer distance events.

The premier site in Britain for Racing, is at the National Water Sports Centre at Holme Pierrepont, Nottingham. This purpose-built course accommodates nine buoyed lanes for canoeing and is equipped with modern timing and control equipment, including a photo-finish facility. Local regattas can be held on any river or open area of water which permits a 500 metre straight course, and is ideally a minimum of 1.5 metres deep. Full guidance on how to set about staging a regatta is available from the BCU, and whilst there is every reason for the event to be run as well as possible, an approved chief official, when appointed, will be able to advise on the essentials.

Racing registration scheme

When entering a ranking regatta for the first time, paddlers register with the BCU Racing Committee on production of a BCU membership card. A team leader must be identified who is responsible for making all entries, and attending the briefing, known as the 'team leaders meeting'. A well-run regatta is an extremely busy affair, with races starting and finishing every few minutes throughout the weekend. As many events may be entered as the competitor wishes, and the greatest headache for organisers is to schedule the classes and distances to ensure that a competitor has a reasonable chance of being able to do so. The annual calendar of events is published in the Racing Yearbook together with all other necessary information – rules, advice to organisers, names and addresses of officials and coaches, team leaders handbook, and so forth.

Equipment

Until recently, in spite of the advent of fibreglass, wood veneer boats were favoured by most for racing, and with notable exceptions still are at international level.

Sandwich construction methods, whereby a lightweight plastic foam honeycomb aluminium or paper core, is trapped between two layers of fibreglass have, however, enabled rigidity combined with lightness to be achieved. Competition among manufacturers of boats and other equipment connected with racing is intense, as, more than any other branch of the sport, with all else being equal, the faster boat will win the day.

Rudders are normally under-stern, for maximum effectiveness, and in any case are not included in the maximum length restrictions. Spooned assymetric paddles are mainly used, which enter more evenly, present a balanced face when pulled, and allow maximum 'grip' of the water. Lifejackets or buoyancy aids are usually unnecessary, except for the very junior classes, as racing is closely supervised by umpire and safety launches.

Skills and tactics

A 'closed skill' is one where an identical movement is repeated consistently in order to achieve the given end, whereas an 'open skill' requires a fluidity of reaction to constantly changing circumstances. Flat water racing is therefore towards the 'closed skill' end of the spectrum so far as canoeing is concerned, and great attention must be paid to the development of a strong, efficient and consistent forward paddling technique, that does not break down when the canoeist is under pressure.

Apart from the distance events, where positioning and behaviour on the turns can be vital, tactics largely consist of paddling at the limit of one's aerobic capacity, until timing a burst to leave the opposition behind at the finish.

Getting started

The marathon Open Racing Scheme is probably the best introduction to sprint racing. A K1 or C1 needs to be mastered to the point where it can be comfortably balanced, and so

Figure 17:7 *Start of the K2 10,000 metre event at Holme Pierrepont*

296

successfully raced for the duration of the course. The Racing Encouragement Tests are a means to this end, and the advice given in chapter 14 is pertinent.

Changes have taken place in the organisation of domestic sprint racing at club level, with the policy being to cope with the present expansion and encourage an even greater participation. More competition will be available which will be easily accessible to all at the lower levels.

The New Divisional system for Sprint Racing

The racing divisional system for sprint is different from marathon. There are separate races for men, ladies, seniors, juniors, canoe and kayak. The number of divisions at present for each class is shown below. These are being increased as more people take part in the sport. For senior competitors, the starting point is the Senior 'D' division. Promotion depends on performance. Juniors (under 18) start in their age divisions. They are promoted by age or by performance.

Class	Divisions
Kayak Men	4 Divisions: A, B, C, D
Kayak Ladies	2 Divisions: A, Novice
Kayak Junior	4 Divisions: Under 18, Under 17, Under 15, Under 13
Kayak Junior Girls	4 Divisions: Under 18, Under 17, Under 15, Under 13
Canoe	2 Divisions: A, Novice

Seniors race over 500m, 1,000m, and 10,000m. Ladies race over 500m and 6,000m. Junior paddlers race over different distances depending on division – the bottom division distances are 500m and 3,000m. The under 18's race over 500m, 1,000m and 6,000m.

The 10,000 Metre Award

10,000 metres is a standard racing distance, competed over annually in the world championships, and is the longest distance raced under sprint racing conditions. To be able to paddle 10,000 metres in a racing kayak or canoe without stopping is an indication of a fair degree of competence and paddling fitness. A paddler who can do so would feel that he

Figure 17:8 *K1s wash hanging on the 10,000 metre turn*

or she could enter a regatta or race without being likely to disgrace him or herself. Members of the BCU coaching scheme may assess this test of competence in any racing K1, and may obtain badges and certificates from the Award secretary.

It is suggested that the test should be made something of an occasion, the culmination of a winter's training, perhaps, with spectators, and an interesting course exactly the right length, with notices every 1,000 metres and so on. The assessor must use his experience to ensure safe practice and the proper sort of safety regulations for the 10,000 metre course he is laying out.

The Espada Award Scheme

The world's foremost kayak designer, Jorgen Samson of Denmark, designed the Espada in 1961. It was built in cold moulded veneer, and the design enjoyed success until being superseded. In 1970 the BCU obtained the right to produce the boat, launching it as a one-design class to encourage young people into racing craft. Moulds exist, for amateur building, and the boat is still widely used. In recent times however, moulds have become available for more modern racing K1s to be built. The Espada in comparison, is less suitable for smaller paddlers. As a consequence of this development, together with the changes which have occurred to the structure of marathon racing, and the marketing of a touring K1 more stable for older or bigger people to learn in, the Espada as a one-design class has been phased out. This does not mean that the boat itself cannot be raced – it is still an adequate K1 for the beginner, or young canoeist. Youth paddlers entering the sport would be well advised, however, to obtain a more modern racing kayak. Although the Espada Award Scheme is still available, apart from the 10,000 metre award, it is now moribund.

SAILING

The International Ten Square Metre Sailing Canoe is today the fastest single-handed sailing dinghy. It evolved from sailing races between touring canoes which took place well over 100 years ago. These led to canoes being designed specifically for sailing competition, developing into the establishment of an international class in 1933.

The excitement and enjoyment of sailing an International Canoe comes from meeting the challenge of learning to sail a high performance, thoroughbred racing craft, and then through practise and experience finally mastering this modern, efficient and beautiful boat.

Skills and tactics

The deck layout, fittings, rig and sails are allowed to develop within rules which ensure fairness in competition, whilst encouraging experiment. An ability to rig and tune the boat for maximum performance needs to be brought to the same high standard as does the skill to sail it at its fastest, without mistakes, in all conditions of wind and sea. These factors need then to be allied to a sound knowledge and use of the rules, and an ability to read and respond to the conditions in order to win races.

High level fitness training is not a major factor in canoe sailing, and helmsmen and helmswomen compete on equal terms. The practical limitations are a minimum body weight of about 50 kgs, allied to reasonable agility.

Figure 17:9 *Righting an international 10 square metre sailing canoe*

National and International competition

Competition ranges from club to frequent international level. An annual national championships is staged, while world championships have traditionally been held tri-annually.

Further Information

A newcomer can take a standard boat and learn to sail it well, leaving the finer points until later. The Secretary of the sailing section will supply details of old and new boats for sale, and plans for self-building, or how to fit out a glass shell. Advice is also available on how to tune boats, where canoes are sailed, and where your nearest canoe sailor can be located.

Training is largely a matter of individual responsibility, but newcomers are welcomed and helped by other sailors. There is a national training programme which provides help and advice, and which consists of at least two practical weekends each year aimed specifically at helping individuals to improve their performance.

SLALOM

Introduction

The object of a slalom is to test the canoeist's control of his boat in agitated water. This is achieved by hanging a series of 'gates', consisting of pairs of poles between 1.2m (4') and 3.5m (11'6") apart, over a course up to a maximum of 800 metres in length. Between 18 and 30 gates are arranged in such a way that the canoeist has to use every skill of manoeuvrability that he possesses, allied to an understanding of the behaviour of water, to enable him to negotiate between the poles in a set sequence, without touching them with body, boat or paddle. Red and white bands (left hand side) and green and white bands (right hand side) indicate which way the gate has to be tackled, together with an identity board which shows the number of the gate, and whether it requires a forward or reverse presentation.

Every feature of the rapid is used, and the gates may be set downstream or upstream. At least four have to be paddled through backwards (reverse gates). Slaloms are held on weir pools, as well as rapids, although the less constant behaviour patterns of weir water has led to restrictions on their use for top level events.

Two timed runs are allowed. Touching poles, missing, or facing in the wrong direction on the way through gates, attracts penalties, which are awarded as varying numbers of seconds – 5, 10 or 50. These are added to the time taken to complete the course. The better of the two runs is counted when determining the result to give the competitor's final score. Outside assistance is not permitted, but a team member may perform an eskimo rescue on another. Crossing the finishing line upside down disqualifies.

Competition is for single kayaks (K1) men and women separately, or for single or double canoes (C1, C2). A divisional system operates. Newcomers first enter Novice events, where the site used is often little more than a swiftly moving stream, and gradually work their way up through immediate or seasonal promotion, dependent upon results achieved, to the premier division, where the water involved is often very 'agitated' indeed – grade III-V.

An event known as Grand Prix is sometimes added to a competition. Here the emphasis is on speed over the course, which is indicated by the gates, but without penalties being awarded for touching poles.

Boat dimensions and classes

	Minimum length	Minimum beam
K1	400 cm (13')	60 cm (24")
C1	400 cm (13')	70 cm (27½")
C2	457 cm (15')	80 cm (31½")

Competitors in the lower divisions and novice events, who have not reached their 13th birthday, may use scaled down 'junior' kayaks which do not conform to the above standards.

Around 1975 is was discovered that by reducing the volume of kayaks and canoes at the bow and stern, the ends could be 'dipped' or ducked under the poles. This shortens the distance around the course, and led to a new range of skills being developed to take advantage of the phenomenon. Although still a necessary art to learn – it is sometimes quicker to turn by dipping and spinning for instance – the establishment within the rules of a standard height for the ends of the poles from the water, has reduced the necessity for deep dipping, or for extremes of design.

Classes include individual and team events for K1, C1 and C2. Teams consist of three kayaks or canoes negotiating the course together, the time being counted from when the first member starts, to the last finishing. A 'team gate' is featured, and this must be cleared by all three competitors within 15 seconds, or an additional penalty is awarded.

Safety

Crash helmets and buoyancy aids or lifejackets (minimum inherent buoyancy 6 kg) are compulsory for slalom competition, together with requirements for end loops (6 mm line sufficiently large and accessible to enable the whole hand to be easily inserted) or toggles, and adequate buoyancy. Competitors must be prepared to rescue another competitor if he is in difficulty on the course during their run, and to stay near the finish until the following competitor is through in order to render assistance if necessary.

300

Figure 17:10 *Nicky Wain of Great Britain clearing reverse gate 11 on the Afon Tryweryn – World Championships 1981. Photo: S Brighton*

International Competition

World Championships are held every other year – in odd numbered years – and in 1972 Canoe Slalom appeared in the Munich Olympics. Continued efforts to have it included again have so far been unsuccessful, due mainly to the fact that suitable water usually occurs only in remote areas, while the costs of creating a purpose built course, such as that provided at Augsburg, grows increasingly prohibitive. Regular International events take place annually, with a Europa Cup series occurring in alternate, non world championships, years.

Preparation, tactics and further information

Technical ability on the water, and in negotiating gates, both vital components for success, are nullified if the competitor does not use his organised practise and his free time, to study and memorise the course. Before entering the first gate it is vital to know the course sequence, exactly where the boat must be placed for each gate, and which strokes will be applied to position it there. Various systems are used to break out and paddle through gates, and there are many ways to tackle a given pattern. Advice on techniques, and on all aspects of preparation for slalom including fitness, is given in the *Slalom Handbook*.

A yearbook is also published, and sent free to all 'ranked' paddlers – ie all except Novice division. This contains the rules for competition, entry fees, the annual calendar of events, constitution of the committee, names of officers, advice to organisers, and a complete list of ranked paddlers.

A Slalom Organisers Handbook is also available which gives full information on how to set about finding a site and organising a slalom, including practical hints on course design and erection, right through to the facilities required, timing and control equipment available, and the recruiting of judges, officials and helpers. A free leaflet *Starting in Slalom* is available from BCU Headquarters, containing details of the current year's entry fees and requirements.

SURFING

A system of judging the technical and artistic ability of a canoeist when riding a surf wave has gradually developed. The rules once favoured 'tricks' whereby loops, pirouettes and pop-outs were scored heavily. With the development of surf kayaks and skis, however, the emphasis has changed to allow maximum points to be awarded for the application of skills and techniques which maintain the paddler in the most advantageous position on the wave. Riding close to where the greatest power is generated by the breaking wave, using the energy to the best advantage, and for the maximum length of time, is what counts.

Contests and championships are held in areas where the most reliable surf is formed. In order to cope with increasing entries, a system of qualification through performance at lower level events has been inaugurated before acceptance at the national championships. There are now two main classes. Surf kayaks and skis compete together, while slalom boats perform in the other class.

A series of heats, depending upon the number and seeding of the competitors, is decided upon. Each heat of up to six paddlers are given a short time period – usually 20 minutes – in which to perform, while judges count the number of rides, the type of waves chosen, and analyse and score the techniques used during that period. The best five waves per competitor only are counted.

Figure 17:11 *Chris Weaver's surf kayak takes a bottom turn on a big day in Brittany, 1982. Photo: Vyv Cox.*

Safety

Crash helmets and buoyancy aids or lifejackets (minimum inherent buoyancy 6 kg) are compulsory, and different colour bibs are worn to identify competitors. Boats must be strongly built, with maximum buoyancy, and equipped with end toggles. Leashes or seat belts are compulsory for skis.

International Competition

At present canoe surfing is practiced mainly in Britain (all four nations and Jersey fielding teams) the USA, South Africa and Australia. Some French canoeists surf also. It is only here, however that to date the governing body has adopted the sport, and whilst friendly international events have been encouraged and promoted, a great deal of work has still to be achieved before representations can be made to the International Canoe Federation for recognition for offficial international status.

WILD WATER RACING

A wild water race is one that covers a minimum distance of 3 kilometres, with grade III water during its course. A race run on a lesser grade of water under the auspices of the Wild Water Racing Committee is known as a Down River Race. There must be a continuous route along the course without the canoe or kayak touching the river bed, and there must be continuous navigation – no portages are permitted.

The art of wild water racing is mainly two-fold. One factor is the ability to propel the canoe at maximum speed throughout the duration of the course. The other is the skill of reading water, in order to gain the greatest advantage. That is, to determine from the current patterns and wave shapes on the surface, where the fastest route through the rapids exists.

A competitor must endeavour to use positive, forward propelling strokes, resorting to back-paddling only if absolutely necessary. Steering his craft by tilting, or forward sweep strokes and tilting, are vital skills for the racer to develop.

A wild water race is held on a time trial basis, with competitors departing at set intervals, which must be a minimum of 30 seconds, from a standing start. An overtaking competitor must be given way to if he shouts 'water' – the word 'free' is used in international events. Outside assistance is not permitted, and while a competitor may roll, crossing the finishing line upside down, disqualifies.

Boats

Boats to conform to certain specifications:

	Maximum length	Minimum beam
K1	450 cm (14'9")	60 cm (24")
C1	430 cm (14")	70 cm (27½")
C2	500 cm (16'5")	80 cm (31½")

A minimum weight restriction is currently under consideration. Craft have become increasingly light, and are built to the limits of the standard, producing a vessel that is considerably less stable than its forebears. There is no restriction with regard to concave sections for wild water racing boats, and so the minimum beam requirement is often met by a pair of integral 'wings' flaring out behind the cockpit.

Classes

Classes include single kayaks (K1) for men and women separately, single canoes (C1) and double canoes (C2) for men and mixed couples. There are also various youth age groups and a veterans class. Competitors are separated into divisions according to results, with a promotion and relegation system.

Safety

Boats must be rendered unsinkable, and possess a handle which permits easy insertion of the hand at each end. Where rope is used it must be at least 6 mm in diameter. Buoyancy aids or lifejackets are compulsory (minimum inherent buoyancy 6 kg). A competitor must stay near the finish until the next paddler is safely home, and is required to assist another competitor who may be in danger during the race, or risk disqualification for life. Juniors should be accompanied by a responsible adult, who is able to interpret the advice given by the organisers concerning conditions on the course, and advise the junior competitors in his charge accordingly.

International events

Wild water racing is linked with slalom internationally, and world championships are held in alternate, odd-numbered years. There is an annual programme of international events and a Europa cup series. In the latter the Slalom and Wild Water Racing events' results are combined to decide the top nation.

Further information

The season in Britain runs from October through to June, and a yearbook is published, which is sent free to all ranked paddlers. This is available from the BCU and shows the rules, committee structure and officers names and addresses, the full calendar of events,

Figure 17:12a (above) *A competitor in the men's K1 event.* **Figure 17:12b (below)** *Graham Goldsmith, Great Britain, competing in the C1 event on the Afon Tryweryn, World Championships 1981. Photo: Keith Williams, Sports Photography.*

and advice to organisers. The *Wild Water Racing Handbook* gives training methods and schedules, and offers advice on race tactics.

Spector Scheme

A 'one-design' wild water racing kayak, known as the Spector was produced with moulds available for hire, to encourage more canoeists, particularly juniors, into wild water racing, with a competition scheme, similar to the 'Espada' scheme for Racing and Marathon, being built up around it. This has, unfortunately not developed so well as had been hoped, and has now been discontinued.

HOT DOGGING

Hot dogging has not caught on in Great Britain as yet, but has good potential as a less formal type of canoeing competition. The site needed must provide a large, friendly stopper, and competitors merely perform various tricks of balance and canoemanship on its face. Loops, pirouettes, pop-outs and similar are the order of the day, but the art is developing fast in America, where a contest was won by a Canadian paddler who threw his paddle away and juggled with three oranges, while balancing his boat with his hips.

Playing in stoppers and standing waves in this way has been a canoeing pastime for many years. Perhaps the future will see a more formal approach – and, heaven forbid – a BCU committee to organise and promote it.

GLOSSARY OF TERMS

When competitors and coaches are talking a number of expressions are used which may be confusing to the more casual canoeist. An attempt has been made to identify the more common terms and types of exercise involved. Some definitions are related to extremely complex physiological functions, but are stated as simply as possible.

Aerobic activity The muscles are fuelled by an intricate system of chemical reactions which require an adequate supply of oxygen. When the demand from the muscles is within the capacity of the heart and lungs to supply the necessary amount, the athlete is performing 'aerobically'.

Anaerobic activity If there is insufficient oxygen available through the cardio-vascular system to meet the requirement of the muscles for the demands being made upon them, maximum power is still possible for a limited period, anaerobically – literally 'without oxygen'. A chemical known as lactic acid is produced, however, and whilst this re-converts, it also becomes a 'waste product' and a build-up diminishes performance.

All canoeing competitions (including 500 metre races) are basically aerobic events, with the competitor relying on using the body's anaerobic capacity (approximately 45 seconds) to enable him to perform beyond his natural limit at a carefully timed stage. It will be seen from this, that the development of the cardio-vascular system is vital to improved performance.

Fartlek Literally, 'as you feel'. A system of training devised in Scandinavia, where bursts are followed by periods of more gentle exercise, as the mood dictates.

Fast-twitch and slow-twitch muscle fibre. Muscles are comprised of two types of fibre in proportions which are determined genetically. In general terms, a sprint racer, slalomist and surfer would ideally have greater proportions of fast-twitch fibre to slow-twitch, wild water racers a more even balance, and for endurance events paddlers the slow-twitch fibres should be in the majority. There have been some notable exceptions to this rule, however, and while biopsies are performed to determine the balance, many are opposed to such experiments in an area in which little can be done to change matters, although fast-twitch fibres can, through training, be adapted to some extent to perform more like slow-twitch fibres.

Glycogen boosting (boosting reserve carbohydrates). This is a process of raising the carbohydrate (glycogen) reserves in the body to approximately twice the normal level. It is achieved by diet over a seven-day period leading up to an event. Extra energy is made available, enabling a higher performance to be achieved for special events which must be of at least two hours duration. If used more than twice a year the body is likely to acclimatise to the process and no benefit would be achieved. Psychological stress may be increased, because at a certain stage in the process, while training is continuing, the athlete will feel physically depleted.

Interval Training Set periods of work with set periods of relatively short rest. The periods of rest might be a previously agreed time – for instance, 30 seconds – or could be based on the length of time it takes the pulse to drop below 120 beats per minute (generally accepted as recovery). Interval training should not be performed with very young paddlers (approximately under 16 years).

Isokinetic These exercises require a special apparatus, such as a multi-gym, where the force increases as the speed of muscle contraction increases.

Isometric exercises. When a muscle is tensioned without being shortened, the activity concerned is known as an isometric exercise – it does not produce movement – eg pushing against a wall.

Isotonic exercises. If a muscle is allowed to shorten during tension an isotonic exercise is involved – eg where a weight is lifted through a range of movement by the body.

Kinaesthetic A word that means 'awareness of muscle action'.

Multi-gym A device which incorporates a range of types of exercise, with easily adjusted loads, in a single compact unit.

Peaking This refers to the stage at which all facets of training come together to produce either one, or perhaps a period, of outstanding performances, generally confined within a three-week time span. Minor peaks should occur in training as major events are approached. However, the athlete must appear at the major event(s) of the year paddling fit, cardio-vascular fit, not overtired, and mentally prepared to achieve.

THE AMATEUR RULE AND OTHER INFORMATION

Amateur status

An amateur canoeist is a sportsman who devotes himself to the sport for pleasure and for his own moral and physical well-being without deriving therefrom, directly or indirectly, any material gain. He is not permitted:

1   to engage as a professional in any sport, or to receive

2   compensation for loss of earnings;

3   to participate in competitions in which money prizes are given;

4   to use championships titles for the purpose of financial or

5   material gain which does not represent payment for actual work done – for instance, payment for the use of championship titles in the publicity of commercial firms. (He may, however, receive travelling and subsistence payment corresponding to his actual outlay during a competition, and for a limited period of training, and he may receive clothing and equipment as required for practising the sport – but only through his national federation). A full-time teacher who is employed as a general instructor of canoeing should not find his amateur status affected. Because of the complexity of the 'amateur status' situation, an explanatory leaflet has been prepared which is available from BCU headquarters, and an 'eligibility committee' has been established to make recommendations in specific cases.

Sponsorship

From the above it will be seen that for an individual to receive direct payment to help him with his training or competition, from whatever source, is an infringement of the rule. This does not debar members from receiving bursaries or other forms of assistance, however – it merely means that these must be declared to, and organised through, the governing body.

Advertising

For events run under ICF rules, only the normal trademark of the manufacturers, which must conform to limitations of lettering size are permitted. It would not be allowable for an individual to compete in a boat carrying any other form of advertising, except by arrangement with the specialist committee concerned.

Sports Aid Foundation

A firm known as Sports Aid Foundation Ltd., dedicated to the raising of funds to assist competitors of high potential with their legitimate training costs, operates on a national and regional basis. Canoeists who qualify for national teams are automatically considered for national grants. Those who are just below the standard set, may be considered for regional Sports Aid Foundation grant.

A number of local authorities and other bodies exist to help local sportsmen of high potential. Application should be made to your local or regional sports council for information.

18 Canoeing for Disabled People

Ron Moore

Ron Moore is currently Headmaster of a school for mentally handicapped children, having worked in special education for the past 15 years. He has had a good deal of experience in teaching canoeing to physically handicapped groups also, working mainly in the local community.

Now Regional Coaching Organiser for Devon and Cornwall, Ron joined the coaching scheme in 1967, having commenced his paddling career in 1953, using a folding double.

POLICY OF THE BRITISH CANOE UNION

The British Canoe Union wholeheartedly supports the promotion of canoeing for the disabled and encourages members of its several disciplines and particularly of the coaching scheme to contribute to this aim.

No group of people suffering from a particular disability should be barred from canoeing. The decision regarding the suitability of canoeing should in every case be a personal one.

Disabled canoeists are encouraged to take BCU tests. The Union's policy is to avoid a separate system for handicapped canoeists. Where a specific disability precludes a candidate from completing a particular part of a test, the award may be given with a suitable endorsement setting out the parts not completed.

Normality should be the aim and, if possible, disabled canoeists should be encouraged to join existing clubs and use standard canoeing gear. However, the formation of special groups and the development of specially adopted gear is positively supported whenever this is necessary.

WHY INTERVENE?

Why ask people whose lives are already burdened with some problem to take up a demanding and dangerous activity? The answer is three-fold.

First, canoeing can be specifically therapeutic for certain physical disorders such as hemiplegia. Second, the disabled are more likely to have suffered some loss in the quality of life, and a place in a special canoeing group can begin to redress that loss.

Third, all the reasons why the able-bodied like canoeing apply to the disabled too. It's healthy, it's fun, it's beautiful.

However, intervention will usually be necessary in the form of positive encouragement to overcome the fear or reluctance felt by parents, medical authorities, the disabled themselves, and sometimes the helpers as well!

MEDICAL ADVICE

Before looking for clients the leader must first seek medical advice. Everyone should be free to decide whether the pleasure derived from an activity is worth the risks involved and an objective medical report will be an important factor in making this decision. It is unfair to ask a doctor to sign a form indicating that a disabled person is fit for canoeing, especially if he is not familiar with the standards of care and protective equipment which may be available. Ideally, a medically qualified person will be closely associated with the club or group and will be someone with the insight to distinguish between temporary problems caused by lack of exercise and real disabilities which will be more long-lasting or permanent. The medical report will alert the leader to some of the problems he might encounter, some of which are described here:-

Several clinical conditions including cerebral palsy, spina bifida, multiple sclerosis, muscular dystrophy, polio, and similar, may result in sensory loss to various parts of the body. Consequently injury to the lower limbs when entering or leaving the canoe may go unnoticed, pressure sores may develop from imperfect seats or cockpits, and impaired circulation may result in the development of chilblains or skin ulcers. The wearing of protective clothing will reduce all of these risks.

Most disorders are exaggerated by fatigue. Thus the spastic client may become more rigid and the atoxic less co-ordinated, but for some the avoidance of fatigue is even more necessary. This includes those with muscular dystrophy, multiple sclerosis and, of course, heart complaints.

Epilepsy should not necessarily prevent someone from considering canoeing. The frequency and severity of attacks, the degree of control achieved by drug therapy and the closeness and skill of the instructors available must all be considered before a decision is made. It should also be borne in mind that those who have suffered any kind of brain damage may be more susceptible to sudden loss of consciousness when taking part in strenuous water sports and provision must be made for this when training assistant instructors.

Hardware such as calipers or artificial limbs may suffer from contact with salt water and may be an impediment in the canoe. On the other hand they provide a degree of independence when the user goes ashore, so it may be decided to take certain aids in the boat when going on an expedition.

Asthmatics are often hard to recognise as disabled and the leader should beware of over confidence. Inhalers must be easily available and are usually best kept in the instructor's boat.

The deaf and the blind will need a high degree of individual tuition, and if diabetic students are taken it is essential to discuss briefly with them their dietary requirements in case of emergency.

This list is by no means exhaustive but serves merely to illustrate the kind of preliminary information which the medical report should provide.

Finally, care should be taken to recognise multiple disabilities where the most obvious condition might hide a more serious complaint. In one case, for instance, a student who was totally deaf was accepted in a disabled group and attended for several weeks before it was discovered that he was also diabetic.

At the outset it was stated that medical advice must be sought. At the end of this chapter is a suggested enquiry form. It is very important that this form be used for each individual disabled person whom you are going to take canoeing. If the medical advisor for that person says something on the form which you do not understand, get a clear explanation so that you know exactly how you must react to any misadventure. This is most important.

OTHER CONSIDERATIONS

Insurance

There are two kinds of insurance to consider. The first is *Public Liability* otherwise called *Third Party*, which protects you and your students from claims for damages from anyone or anything damaged by you or your canoeists. Individual members of the BCU are insured for claims of this kind as are members of groups which are in the charge of members of the BCU Coaching Scheme. It would be unwise to start unless all members of the group were covered.

You should also consider *Personal Accident* which recompenses the insured himself for any injury he suffers in the course of the specified activity. This is often left for the person or his parents to take out for themselves. Here, all individual members of the BCU are so covered. Others should be informed of the situation.

Swimming

The definition of swimming usually implies moving measurable distances through water. The minimum requirement for the safety of a canoeist in an organised group is to be able to float with confidence after capsizing and coming safely out of the canoe. Severely physically handicapped people sometimes find it difficult to achieve the normal requirement to swim 50 metres but this should not prevent them from taking part provided that the extra supervison needed to preserve a reasonable standard of safety is available.

Assistant Staff

It is unhelpful to specify staff/student ratios as these will depend on the degree of handicap and the standard of skill achieved by the students. In extreme cases it may be necessary to have three or four instructors to one disabled canoeist in order to guarantee a deep water rescue but generally one to one is the most demanding ratio that will be necessary.

Assistant instructors need not all be members of the coaching scheme but they must be proficient canoeists and they will need a period of special training before taking on their new responsibilities. Young people can often provide most of the help required but a minimum number of qualified instructors may be needed for insurance purposes.

Assistant Instructor Training

Assistant instructors must acquire two different kinds of skill in order to help the disabled. They must be expert in rafting, supporting, towing, deep-water rescues, including swimmer to canoe for an unconscious patient and resuscitation.

Equally important are the more subtle teaching skills which allow the disabled student to enjoy the adventure and independence which comes from canoeing, and at the same time to feel secure and closely cared for. There are times when a student will need help or he may be so frightened that he will not come again. There are other times when he should be left to struggle alone to overcome his fear. Only the experience of the leader will tell him which course to take, but it is easy to be too ambitious on the water and not sufficiently demanding on dry land. For instance a student looking worried when the wake of a passing boat rocks his canoe might well be supported by his instructor. On the other hand, a student who has difficulty in walking should be allowed to do his fair share of carrying when the gear is put away at the end of the session. (Figure 18:1).

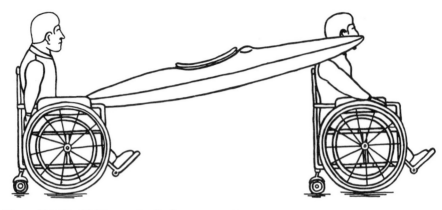

Figure 18:1 *Disabled innovation in the carrying of a canoe*

FORMING A GROUP

Finding disabled people is not always easy. A canoe club may find that mere willingness to accept disabled members results in a very poor response and until you have developed a reputation for child care you may find local schools, clubs and centres reluctant to send their children to you. Adults may be found, through rehabilitation centres, sheltered workshops, social workers, the Spastics Society and many similar organisations which support those suffering from other disabilities. The first principle should be to start in a small way and a group of three or four students with a similar number of assistant instructors would be appropriate. Numbers might well grow later but leaders should beware of over confidence following early success and as the variety and degree of handicap increases with your local reputation it is wise to gain experience slowly and resist the temptation to expand too soon.

Preliminary Meeting

Before starting canoeing there should be a preliminary meeting of students, parents and assistant instructors, where the group leader can explain his requirements and describe the programme. A paper can be distributed giving the leader's address and telephone number, so that he can be informed if a student or instructor is unable to attend a session. The need for reliability and serious commitment should be made clear to both sides. Students can be advised what clothes to wear, and at this stage particular attention should be paid to those with sensory loss in the lower limbs. Loose fitting wet-suit trousers are helpful in these cases. Life jackets and helmets can be tried on and adjusted ready for the first practical session, and parents and care staff can be told of the part they can play. It is good policy to encourage their active participation at least on the pool side in helping to change students, to handle gear, and in some cases to help with supervision. A parent who learns to perform a swimmer to canoe rescue from the pool side can be an invaluable assistant.

A course of instruction

The course should start with a swimming session in a heated pool in Winter or early Spring. Life Jackets should be worn and it may be found that some students are unable to swim with them in a conventional way. It may be necessary for some to have their life jackets partly inflated (this is always helpful to boost the confidence of a timid student, or to provide an extra margin of safety at any time).

From the start, an instructor should beware of moving too fast. After observing the student's swimming ability, canoes may be put in the water and games like 'under and over' and 'sitting on the deck' should be played. This enables students to get wet without the trauma of capsizing while sitting in a canoe. Next, everyone may be taught how to enter the cockpit from the side of the pool. Capsizes can be avoided by having instructors stand in the water at the side of the boat and supporting it firmly. (Figure 18:2). It may be necessary to invent unconventional ways of entry for some students, but the aim of independence should be borne in mind and any help which is necessary in the earliest stages should be withdrawn as soon as possible.

Those with impaired use of one arm may find that entry is easier if the strongest arm takes the weight on the side of the swimming pool.

Those without use of the legs can usually develop a completely independent technique by sitting first on the rear deck and lifting the legs in one at a time.

Instructors should stay in the water and hold onto the canoe while balance, hand-paddling and basic strokes are learned. Later, as confidence is gained, they may supervise their student from the side of the pool, but in some cases this could take several sessions to achieve.

A conventional teaching programme follows, bearing in mind the need to accept slow progress. About ten sessions of an hour's duration would be appropriate for teaching basic

Figure 18:2 *Capsizes can be prevented by standing in the water to support the canoe*

313

strokes, some games, and helpful group skills like rafting up and how to be rescued. Capsize drills should not be taught in the early sessions, but should be left until confidence and enthusiasm have developed.

Having learned basic skills in a warm pool, the transition to cold water outdoors brings fewer dangers, but the leader should be aware of the greater challenge. Some students may at first be intimidated, and will need close support again for a time. The problems presented by poor circulation are greater, and protective clothing should be checked to ensure that all students are warmly dressed.

The outdoor programme will probably involve greater distances, but the weaker members of the group need not be left behind. They can be helped to new and interesting areas of water with a tow from an instructor, or in a double canoe.

Towing is best done from the bow with the instructor paddling backwards, so that he can watch his student and avoid capsizing him if his boat yaws and is pulled sideways. If the distance to be towed is too great for this, one instructor may tow conventionally while another escorts the student.

Students who have great difficulty in steering may be helped by using a detachable skeg, and it may be necessary for the most seriously handicapped to have two instructors, one nudging the canoe on either side.

It is wise before starting an outdoor programme to read again the medical reports for all students. Close association for several weeks with an enthusiastic group can create a feeling of over-confidence.

SPECIAL AIDS

The Canoe

Normality should be the aim and most students can cope well in a conventional canoe. A roomy, buoyant slalom canoe used commonly for group teaching is suitable. Students who find it difficult to get into this kind of canoe will find the larger cockpit of a touring canoe easier, while extreme difficulty caused by stiff legs can be overcome by using a double tourer (which also gives more lateral stability than a single-seater), or an open Canadian. Even more room and greater lateral stability comes from the VCP 'Caranoe' and the Hotelcraft 'Duette'. The Caranoe can be fitted with a velcro spraydeck and can be used for moderate sea trips and wild water at least to Grade 2.

Paddles

Blind students sometimes find unfeathered blades less confusing in the early stages. They should use ovalled looms with a taped-on mark where the hand grips the paddle to indicate the angle of the blade. (Figure 18.3).

Unfeathered blades, also help students with weak grip, who find the flexing of the wrist required with feathered blades too demanding.

A weak grip can also be helped by using a very thin loom, extra light paddles, and custom made hand grips taped onto the loom. Such paddles need not be expensive as there is no need for the strength required in normal blades. If there is still a problem in gripping the loom, the following may be tried.

1   *Mitts* with one side of velcro sewn to the mitt and the other side epoxy glued to the loom. Alternatively, the velcro can be sewn into a ring which slides along the loom, allowing rotation of the paddle to take place more easily. (Figure 18:4).

2   *Patent Neoprene mitts* which fix the hands to the loom, bearing in mind the extra risk involved and the need for individual supervision.

Amputees may find Canadian blades easier to handle. Thalidomide damaged students with rudimentary limbs may find an extra long unfeathered paddle can be tucked under the armpits and paddling strokes are performed entirely by movement of the trunk.

Backrests

Many serious problems associated with poor balance or paralysis of the lower limbs can be completely overcome by using a backrest. This can be a simple rectangle of marine ply, a plastic swim-float or a hinged model of tubular steel and canvas (supplied by Ottersports). (Figure 18:5).

Buoyancy

All students should try an inflated life jacket in controlled conditions as some handicaps, particularly the loss of one or more limbs, can result in strange attitudes in the water. If a life jacket does not have the desired result, for example, if the student floats face down, then

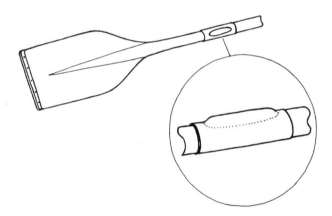

Figure 18:3 *Paddle with taped-on mark to indicate the angle of the blade*

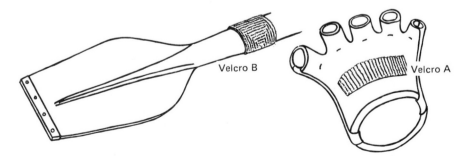

Figure 18:4 *Velcro mitts or paddle ring can help those with a weak grip to hold the paddle*

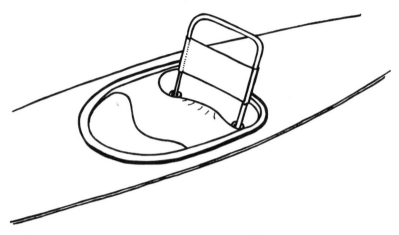

Figure 18:5 *A backrest may assist in overcoming many problems.*

other buoyancy aids must be tried. There should be no confusion over the issue of insurance here. No handicapped person should be deprived of the right to canoe because of an insurance requirement. If lifejackets are compulsory for trainees, but it is dangerous for a particular trainee to wear one, the problem should be resolved by consultation with the governing body and the insurance company. In some extreme cases, with the loss of all four limbs, even a buoyancy aid may float the student face down, and in this case a neoprene waistcoat will provide minimal flotation. However, an acceptable degree of safety might be achieved only by providing an individual instructor for such a student.

Protection from Cold and Abrasion

Paralysis of a limb is usually accompanied by poor circulation. In addition to this there is the danger of injuries going un-noticed because of the lack of pain and a subsequent risk of infection.

Protection can be provided in two ways. First, the cockpit should be free from cracks, and sharp edges can be covered with adhesive tape or neoprene. Second, the limbs at risk should be protected at least with trousers, socks and plimsolls, but ideally with full length neoprene trousers, fitted with long zips for easy dressing.

It may be necessary to make a special neoprene protector for a rudimentary limb. Protection from cold is otherwise done in conventional ways, using woollen hats and jerseys and windproof outer clothing.

Aids for the Visually Handicapped

Bells, bleepers and complex electronic devices have been tried and should not be condemned. However, the less dramatic ways have had most success, and the best aid seems to be a sighted canoeist paddling close by, giving occasional directions. The helper should ideally paddle behind the student, so that he can quickly detect any divergence from the proper course. He is also out of the way if the student over-corrects and swings sharply to one side.

A helper behind is also placed well to be heard clearly. Blind students above all, need directionally stable boats, and slalom boats are least suitable unless fitted with skegs.

Touring singles are much more desirable, and the simplest solution is to use doubles with a sighted companion.

The use of raised markings on the loom and the possible use of unfeathered blades has already been mentioned.

Blind students can often paddle for long periods without verbal directions, by using reflected sounds from large objects nearby. For instance, it may be possible to paddle unaided alongside a harbour wall or along a steeply banked river, and such opportunities for independent activity should be exploited by the leader, without neglecting his responsibility to preserve a proper degree of safety and discreet supervision.

Conclusion

The effort needed to provide an apparently simple piece of apparatus should not be under-rated, and it may happen that a suitable modification is painfully perfected over a number of weeks, only to find that the student drops out. Nevertheless, to give a disabled student a greater degree of mobility and independence is a challenging and fascinating technical problem.

Having considered briefly some of the practical problems and the means to overcome them, care should be taken to avoid bizarre modifications made for their own sake.

The student should, as far as possible, use conventional gear for reasons of economy and to achieve a high degree of normality.

CANOEING FOR THE MENTALLY HANDICAPPED

Wide range

The term 'mentally handicapped' covers a very wide range of ability. Those at the top of the range can learn in the same way as ordinary students, but will just take longer.

The less able will need special techniques, which are quite simple to adopt, and are described here.

Don't depend on words

Some students may not know 'right' from 'left', and instructors using these terms will merely confuse them. The term 'paddle forwards' may be meaningless, or may be associated with paddling at the sea-side. In this case it is better to demonstrate, and say 'Do this' or 'Do it like me'. With exceptionally slow learners, the instructor can physically place the blades in the right position and guide the student through the motion.

Free play

Failure to teach forward paddling at this stage should not discourage the instructor. A period of free play, leaving the handicapped students alone to enjoy the activity, will often result in their discovering the technique themselves.

Suitable equipment

Stable canoes, unfeathered blades, and skegs, make early success more likely.

Suitable environment

Elementary canoeing in a protected area will be sufficiently demanding to sustain the interest of mentally handicapped students for a long time. It is not always desirable to seek more demanding canoeing, as the degree of adult intervention in order to be safe, will be much higher. Better to provide a simple activity with a lot of independence.

Timid students

Some will be excessively timid, and will need individual care and encouragement in the early stages. An instructor in the water, holding the bow of the canoe, can keep the boat stable, and encourage the student face to face.

317

Ambitious students
Some will be unaware of objective dangers, and may not act in a normally expected way. For instance, they may paddle into the path of an oncoming boat, and be unable to respond to verbal instructions to come back. This can be simply overcome by providing sufficient assistants on the water.

Involving specialist staff
Mentally handicapped people will usually be accompanied by staff, or parents, and their co-operation will be invaluable. They may w. be taught canoeing alongside their students, and will certainly learn the basic skills as quickly. Even if they cannot be persuaded to join in, they can give valuable advice at the water's edge regarding the degree of each student's understanding, and the need for extra care or encouragement.

Small steps
The key to success in teaching the mentally handicapped is probably best crystallised in these two words. There is no need for super-human patience, kindness, skill, or virtue. Ordinary people with ordinary tempers can achieve success if they remember to teach in, and to be content with, small steps.

SUMMARY

Many disabled persons can gain great benefit from canoeing. Their introduction to the sport requires careful preparation with attention to medical advice, the enrolment of sufficient helpers, insurance, hiring a pool and not least, finding the disabled canoeist. Numbers of students will, of necessity, be small, and the effort demanded will be large. Nevertheless it is commended to members of the coaching scheme as a rewarding and worthwhile facet of their work.

A suggested form of medical summary is given below which should be adapted as appropriate. This should be completed by a medical advisor.

An initial paragraph, describing the nature of the course and stressing the fact that there will be expert instruction and supervision throughout, should accompany the form.

SECTION 1

a) Nature of disability ....
b) Any other relevant disability (e.g. epilepsy/diabetes) ....
   ....
c) If so, how well is it controlled? ....
   ....
d) What drugs are being used? ....
   ....
e) Any known allergies/skin conditions? ....
   ....
f) Are there likely to be any incontinence difficulties? ....
g) Has the applicant a particularly nervous temperament? ....
   ....
h) Does the applicant require a special diet? If so, please give details ....
   ....

SECTION 2

Please delete where appropriate:
a) The applicant is ambulant/partially ambulant/non ambulant
b) If non-ambulant is he/she able to propel his/her wheelchair?
c) Degree of strength in legs: Right: Good/Poor/nil   Left: Good/Poor/nil
d) Degree of control in legs: Right: Good/Poor/nil   Left: Good/Poor/nil
e) Degree of strength in arms: Right: Good/Poor/nil   Left: Good/Poor/nil
f) Degree of control in arms: Right: Good/Poor/nil   Left: Good/Poor/nil
g) Are the back muscles strong/weak? ....
h) Is the applicant likely to have spasms? ....
i) If so will the spasms be increased in cold water? ....
j) Degree of balance and postural sensibility ....
k) Has the applicant deficient sensation in any limb? If so, please state which limb(s)
l) Has the applicant good vision? If not, to what extent is it impaired ....
m) Has the applicant good hearing? If not, to what extent is it impaired ....

Figure 18:6 *A suggested form of medical summary*

Appendix I

British Canoe Union, BCU Coaching Scheme and British Schools Canoeing Association Structure and Policy

INTRODUCTION

The British Canoe Union is a limited company, recognised by the Sports Council and in membership of the Central Council of Physical Recreation, as the governing body of the sport of canoeing in the United Kingdom. It is affiliated to the International Canoe Federation (ICF) and represents the interests of canoeists at home and abroad.

The aims and objectives of the BCU are:

To encourage health, enjoyment, and care of the countryside through the use of canoes and kayaks in competitive and recreational activities.

To promote canoeing in all its forms.

To organise and assist in promoting and organising canoeing meets, regattas, championships, trials, training sessions, tours, rallies, demonstrations, festivals and other competitive and recreational events.

To select, train and administer competitors to represent the United Kingdom.

To give encouragement and support to canoeing expeditions.

To promote international co-operation and friendship by encouraging participation in canoeing activities between nations.

To arrange and provide the holding of courses of instruction and exposition in canoeing skills and techniques, the establishment and conduct of a system of tests and qualifications, and the promotion of safety.

To issue guidelines and make regulations for all forms of canoeing, as appropriate, and to encourage the observance by canoeists of a code of conduct.

To protect the interests of canoeists, and to work for improved facilities and for greater access to waters.

To support administrative or legislative measures which will improve facilities for canoeing and to act to prevent the introduction of such measures injurious to the sport.

To create and promote by publicity and education an informed and interested public opinion on the value and importance of canoeing in all its forms.

To provide and supply information and advice to members by means of books, periodicals and other methods.

To foster technical improvement and development of canoes and equipment.

To investigate and research rights of passage.

To arrange for insurance, travel facilities and the purchase of goods and equipment to be available to members.

To provide services as possible and appropriate for other organisations, clubs and persons interested in or associated with the sport and recreation of canoeing.

Separate Associations exist for Northern Ireland, Scotland and Wales which are recognised through an agreement with the Council of the BCU as the governing bodies of the sport within their respective countries. They have right of representation on the Council, the Management Committees, and the Specialist Committees of the BCU to ensure their interests are served when matters of a federal (United Kingdom) nature are discussed.

There are full reciprocal rights of membership between the Associations and the BCU.

Membership of the BCU

Membership of the Union is open to organisations within the United Kingdom, and to men, women and young people of any nationality who are interested in canoeing. There are three types of membership. No 'entrance fee' is charged.

1 *Individual membership,* which consists of:
   a) *Full Membership.* For adult members over the age of 19 years.
   b) *Youth Membership.* Those who have not reached their 19th birthday by 1 January may, if they wish, become Youth members. All the privileges of full membership apply except for voting rights and the right to sit on Specialist Committees.
   c) *Family Membership.* Provided that at least one member of a family joins as a Full member, spouse, and children under 16 *resident at the same address* may become Family members by paying a reduced annual subscription. Family members *have all the privileges of a Full member,* except voting rights and the right to sit on Specialist Committees. They do not receive individual copies of the magazine or any other general correspondence.
   d) *Introductory Membership.* For adults over the age of 19 years who do not wish to take part in the coaching scheme. Introductory membership, which includes the right to take part in competition, is available at a reduced fee.
   e) *Basic Membership.* For those who wish to support the Union in its endeavours to maintain and improve access and facilities for canoeing. Basic members pay a small annual fee, and may take advantage of the various discount schemes, but are not entitled to compete in national ranking competition, or be a member of the Coaching Scheme.
   f) *Cadet Membership.* Those who have not reached their 17th birthday may, if they wish, become Cadet members. All the privileges of full membership apply except for voting rights and the right to sit on Specialist Committees. Cadet membership is available for the first year only, and is not renewable except as a Youth member.

Benefits of individual membership
Individual members in categories a, b, c and e have the right to take part in competition, touring, and other events sponsored by the BCU. Adult full members take part in the management of its affairs, and all have the right to wear its badges and tie and fly its pennant. All members receive the regular house magazine free, together with annual calender of events and courses, and current happenings and events in their region. They are covered for third party insurance claims. Full, family and youth members also enjoy automatic boat damage insurance, personal accident and life assurance whilst engaged in canoeing activities. Low price extra canoe insurance is available together with British Waterways Board licences at reduced fees. Advice and information is available to members on all canoeing matters and events, including the services of the river and coastal advisory scheme.

2 *Affiliated members*

Affiliation is open to any canoeing club or body in the United Kingdom. Service Unit Canoe Clubs stationed overseas may also affiliate. There are two types of affiliation:

a) *Open Clubs.* Senior clubs are those whose membership is comprised of more than 15% adults. Such clubs, provided that at least ten of its members are full individual members of the BCU, have the right to nominate two of those members to each of certain Specialist Committees, and the further right to a vote and a voice at the annual general meeting of the BCU.

b) *Junior Clubs.* Where 85% or more of the members are under the age of 18 and still in full-time education, a club may join the British Schools Canoeing Association, with full rights of BCU membership apart from those stated in the previous paragraph. In addition, a named leader receives full individual membership rights as a privilege within the club fee.

An Affiliated body has the right to seek recognition of its canoeing events, to purchase certain goods and publications at preferential prices, to receive the Club Newsletters and BSCA Newsletters, and are protected by third party insurance.

Affiliated bodies agree to bind their members by the Rules and Regulations of the BCU whether or not they themselves are members.

3 *Associate members*

These are organisations with an interest in canoeing who wish to support the objects of the Union. Associateship is open to any *non-canoeing* body who wishes to have contact with the BCU – eg local education authorities. Associates have no voting rights, but may seek advice and will receive magazines and club news as they are published.

Insurance benefits

The insurance policy indemnifies the British Canoe Union and/or its officials, and/or members and/or affiliated clubs (insofar as concerns canoeing and social activities) against claims for legal liability (personal injury and property damage) to third parties. Indemnity against third party risks required by many local authorities before canoe surfing is permitted, is covered by this policy. All canoeing and related activities are included and there is member to member liability. It covers the use of swimming pools and other premises hired, except for the first £100 where the damage is not due to fire or explosion. Premises and equipment owned or rented by the club (but not property held in the custody or control of the insured) are covered for third party risks only. The policy also indemnifies members of the Coaching Scheme for legal liability arising out of, or caused by, wrongful advice.

The Structure of the British Canoe Union

The affairs of the BCU are managed by a Council who employ a Director, responsible for the general administration of the Union. As Chief Executive of the Secretariat, the Director is responsible for all its activities and directly or indirectly the management of all its staff. He is responsible to the Executive Committee of the Council for management of the Secretariat, and to the Council for achieving the objectives of the BCU and carrying out the policies laid down for him.

The Council consists of:

The President (elected annually at the AGM)

The Chairman (elected annually from within the Council)
The Treasurer (elected bi-annually at the AGM)
10 members (elected for two years at the AGM)
One nominee from each of the National Associations
One nominee from each of the Specialist Committees
One nominee from each of the English regions

Council has over-riding authority in all matters, but delegates its responsibility to the standing committees, formed from its own members, namely:

1 *The Executive Committee* – responsible for financial and administrative matters.

2 *The Sports Management Committee* – responsible for oversight of the affairs of the specialist sports committees.

3 *The Access, Coaching and Recreation Management Committee* – responsible for oversight of the affairs of the other specialist committees.

4 *The Committee for English Affairs* – responsible for oversight of the English regional committees, and for endorsing where necessary the selection of English teams.

Further delegation of Council's responsibility for the day to day conduct of its affairs is made to the specialist committees, who are authorised to act in all matters connected with their own branch of the sport, and to draft regulations for the proper management of their discipline.

These specialist committees are:

Access	Marathon Racing	Slalom
Canoe Polo	Racing	Surf
Coaching	Sailing	Touring
Corps of Canoe Lifeguards	Sea Touring	Wild Water Racing

The national associations, BCU regions and clubs nominate representatives to the specialist committees, though the qualifying criteria for membership varies between committees. All committee representatives must be full members of the Union.

If every organisation entitled to representation exercised its right to nominate members to every specialist committee, the size of each would be such that it would be quite unmanageable. In practice, organisations tend only to nominate members to those committees in whose activities they are particularly interested. Most, though not all, specialist committees, organise annual general meetings which elect a chairman and executive committee to administer their affairs.

Council has also delegated responsibility for the promotion of canoeing, and the improvement of facilities and access to Regional Committees. These have been established within geographical boundaries based on the Sports Council's regional boundaries for England. Members within the region elect a committee which is responsible to the Council. The constitutions of regions vary, but all are subject to ratification by Council. The regional chairmen form the 'Committee for English affairs' pending the introduction of a formal federal structure and a separate association for England. The aims of regional associations are:

1 To maintain and establish access rights and facilities for canoeing.

2 To provide a regional programme of activity.

3 To make the services of the Union more direct and meaningful to individual members.

4   To provide a link and encouragement to full membership of the Union to periphery groups and persons.

The Union maintains liaison with and is represented on, a variety of national, regional and local organisations, by voluntary officers, and by members of the headquarters secretariat. These include nominees to the Management Committees of the Holme Pierrepont Water Sports Centre, and the Plas y Brenin National Centre for Mountain Activities, Regional Councils for Sport and Recreation, the Central Council for Physical Recreation, and many other voluntary and statutory bodies.

COACHING SCHEME

Director of Coaching

A Director of Coaching is employed who is responsible for the proper administration of the whole of the Coaching Scheme. He is supported by National Coaches working within regions, and National Coaches with special responsibility for the training and qualifying of competition trainers and coaches. The Director of Coaching will, on invitation, visit local, regional and national association coaching panels throughout Britain.

Each region (as previously defined) is sub-divided, for Coaching Scheme purposes, into its county or other administrative area as convenient, each with its own Local Coaching Organiser (LCO). Every qualified member of the Coaching Scheme (including Trainee Instructors and Competition Trainers) is automatically a member of the local coaching panel. The LCO is informed of their name and address, and is kept up to date. He is therefore able to supply names of instructors who may help with training or testing local individuals, groups or clubs as the need arises.

The LCO will know of courses for rolling, introductory and advanced skills, tours, the clubs in the area, and so forth. He is the person to contact for such information – name and address from BCU Headquarters. Local Coaching Organisers usually circulate periodic newsletters to their panels to keep everyone in touch, and should call occasional meetings. It is advantageous for this workload to be spread by the appointment of District Organisers, willing to call members of the Coaching Scheme together on an even more local basis in order to promote the activity thoroughly, and to ensure that all the needs of the area are being met.

LCOs are elected by their local panels, every three years. Normally the LCOs elect the Regional Coaching Organiser (RCO) who is responsible for representing the view of the region to the National Coaching Committee and the BCU Regional Executive, and National Coaching Committee policy back to the region. Essentially he administers, supports and enthuses LCOs, who in turn should seek to involve and service every member of the scheme within their jurisdiction. The RCO is responsible for authorising all national courses within the region.

Tests of Personal Performance

A number of tests are available covering most aspects of canoeing. They break down into general introduction, touring, and specialist tests.

There are **Star tests** (grades 1 to 5) which follow a natural learning progression for kayaks or canoes, and provide certificates and badges as each 'milestone' in a paddler's development is achieved. At 4 or 5 star level these tests separate into wild water or surfing techniques.

Proficiency tests (at Intermediate and Advanced level for kayaks or canoes for inland waters or the sea separately). There is a requirement for expedition preparedness and ability, and the Proficiency Tests are essential pre-requisites for certain coaching awards.

Expedition awards at bronze, silver and gold standard are encouragement tests for expedition work, and are administered by the British Schools Canoeing Association.

Racing encouragement tests (grades I-IV), and the **10,000 metres Award,** are related to paddle racing. The Encouragement Tests introduce a paddler to international sprint racing kayaks. The 10,000 metre award shows competence in racing, and is administered by the BCU Racing Committee.

The **Canoe safety test** is administered by the Corps of Canoe Lifeguards. Its purpose is to introduce at an early stage in a canoeist's development, simple concepts of practical techniques for saving others from drowning. It is a pre-requisite for the Instructor Award.

BCU lifesaving test. This test is a pre-requisite for Senior Instructor assessment. It covers basic lifesaving technique, and use of the canoe as a life saving medium. The Corps of Canoe Lifeguard Award is an identical test. RLSS Bronze Medallion (General) is the minimum RLSS award recognised as an equivalent.

Coaching Awards

Entry to the general Coaching Scheme of the British Canoe Union is as follows:

1 Be 16 years of age

2 Obtain the relevant Proficiency Certificate*

3 Become an individual member of the BCU

4 Successfully complete an approved two-day Training course.

Apart from Trainee Instructor status, all the Awards are valid indefinitely subject to annual return of Coaching Registration Form and renewal of membership.

The general Awards and their scope are as follows:

Trainee instructor. Minimum age 16. A Trainee Instructor has successfully completed a two-day training course and should *assist* a qualified Instructor or Senior Instructor. Valid for 3 years (maximum).

Teacher/Leader Endorsement. Trainee Instructors who are Teachers or Youth Leaders may be 'endorsed' to be solely in charge of small groups in a stipulated sheltered area in summer conditions.

Instructor. Minimum age 18. For those introducing others to canoeing on placid (grade I) water only. Applicable anywhere throughout the year. Instructors may test for 1-Star.

Senior Instructor. Minimum age 18. Senior Instructor is the correct grade for a person to be in charge of canoeing activities for a club or school which includes expeditioning and/or white water (grade II) or open sea (including surfing). Senior Instructors may test for 1-3 Star, and Proficiencies (subject to Examiner grading).

Coach. Minimum age 21. The Coach Award is designed for experienced Senior Instructors of Advanced Proficiency ability. It is an indication of a wide all-round knowledge of the sport and coaching techniques, club management, and the staging of

---

* Proficiency Tests, Training courses, and Senior Instructor qualification are separated into Sea or Inland (Kayak or Canadian) syllabus'. Proficiency tests can be examined locally by arrangement with the nearest qualified Examiner. Applications to Local Coaching Organiser (address from BCU HQ). Leaflet T1 gives syllabus and entry details.

courses. Coach is the correct grade for a full-time person to be in charge of canoeing activities in a Centre.

Examiner Gradings
There are four grades of 'Examiner'. E1 – Proficiency Test; E2 – Senior Instructor Training, Instructor and Senior Instructor Assessment; E3 – Advanced Proficiency Testing; E4 – Coach Assessment.

Competition Coaching Awards:
There is direct entry at both **Trainer** and **Coach** levels.
   Competition Trainer. Minimum age 18. For those introducing others to the lower levels of competition.
   Competition Coach. Minimum age 18. For those involved in coaching competitors at Club level. Coaches may test for 1-Star, and 2-3 Star by arrangement with the Regional Coaching Organiser.
   Senior Competition Coach. For those coaching at regional/national squad level.
   NB. There are separate courses for Polo, Racing, Slalom, Surf and Wild Water Racing at all levels.
   Full details on any aspect of the structure outlined in this appendix, together with information on any and all other sides of the sport can be obtained from the BCU. A stamped, addressed envelope should accompany all enquiries.

THE BRITISH SCHOOLS CANOEING ASSOCIATION

The British Schools Canoeing Association was formed in 1970 to encourage, promote and help canoeing in schools. It is concerned with the development of canoeing within the curriculum, with the provision of information, and the staging of events for schools participation.
   The BCU recognised the part that canoeing in schools and education centres plays in the overall growth of the sport, and the importance of forging links so that young people who wish to, may more easily enter the main stream of the activity.
   In consequence, a special relationship has been brought about, through which, whilst maintaining the autonomy of the BSCA, the Association as a whole is able to take advantage of the servicing facilities of the full-time secretariat of the BCU. Teachers and leaders of youth canoeing groups receive the benefit of both BSCA and BCU club and individual information, by payment of a single fee.
   Membership of the BSCA is open to individual school and youth canoeing groups where 85% or more of the membership are under the age of 18 and still undergoing full time education.
   The formation of regional and county associations is encouraged, but these do not have direct representation on the Council of the BSCA.
   Member groups receive BSCA newsletters and information sheets as they are produced, and also BCU club newsletters, besides benefits of the third-party insurance scheme, discounts on goods and BWB licences, recourse to the river and coastal advisory service, and the general help and advice which is available. The leader is automatically a full individual member of the BCU through the club fee, is entitled to take part in BCU events, and to hold BCU coaching qualifications.

Appendix II

Canoeing Activities of other Organisations

CORPS OF CANOE LIFEGUARDS

Introduction

The main work of the Corps is carried out by members who patrol beaches wherever the general public is likely to get itself into difficulties. The main purpose of the Corps is still to train young people into a state of proficient canoe handling to be able to render assistance to anyone who may be in distress or difficulty in water. Since the risk is not inconsiderable, the training is rigorous and well worthwhile.

The aims of the Corps of Canoe Lifeguards

1   To set a high standard of canoemanship.

2   To come to the aid of anyone in difficulties or distress off any beach, or any river, lake or canal, and to this end to work in co-operation with any other rescue organisation or club working for the same purpose.

3   To be available to local authorities or the police, to assist in relief work during times of flood or similar emergencies.

4   To act as a guide or assistant to parties of canoeists who are on more adventurous expeditions, especially parties from schools, youth clubs or youth organisations, both at home and abroad.

5   To teach the skills of canoeing, especially to their fellow club members, and other young people from schools, youth clubs and youth organisations.

Canoe Lifeguard Training

This covers a very wide and varied programme, and is constantly reviewed in the light of experience, changing conditions, new equipment and improved techniques. Initiative and new ideas for training are always welcome. All lifeguards are trained in the following:

1   A high standard of canoeing ability.

2   Surf Life Saving Association and Royal Life Saving Society methods and awards.

3   First Aid.

4   Canoe Lifeguard methods of rescue using a combination of canoeing and lifesaving ability. Techniques vary from Unit to Unit, depending upon local conditions.

5   Methods of patrolling.

The Rescue Canoe

The idea of using a canoe for lifesaving is now well established. The skilled Canoe Lifeguard can operate in heavy seas, surf or weirs, and works in conjunction with the Coastguard, RNLI, Police and the Services.

There are times when a lifeguard has to leave his canoe to go to the aid of a patient and a canoe gets filled with water. Because the Rescue canoe has two buoyancy chambers the lifeguard is able to empty his waterlogged canoe single handed and re-enter. In addition it can be used as a stretcher, and even be paddled when it is upside down.

The Rescue Canoe, with red and yellow stripes, is available only to qualified users, but the Instructor Canoe is supplied in plain colours to any canoeist. Both versions are supplied with toggles, handles, towing point, paddle park, hatch and buoyancy. All authorised canoes are registered with the Corps and have a registration certificate glassed into the cockpit.

Awards and Appointments

The scheme is based upon five awards, each stage being levelled at a particular function within the Corps, and emphasis is placed on gradual progression of knowledge and skill. This should be gained by working with an operational unit. The five awards are:–

Canoe Safety Test
An award for all members, testing certain elementary skills. The holder cannot be regarded as a Lifeguard.

Assistant Lifeguard
The basic award for all members, giving the basic skills required to enable the holder to work with a Lifeguard or be able to carry out a simple rescue by him/her self if ever required. This is identical to the BCU Life Saving Test.

Lifeguard
This is the desirable award for all operational members, and essential for Patrol Captains. It should enable the holder to co-ordinate, on the scene, a rescue using several canoes, or various rescue craft, and be able to carry out more complex rescues by himself when required.

Senior Lifeguard
This is the desirable award for Patrol Captains and essential for Corps Training Officers or Duty Officers. The Senior Lifeguard should be able to organise and co-ordinate any rescue, using whatever equipment.

Chief Lifeguard
This award is made by the National Executive Committee to a holder of the Senior Lifeguard Award who has the necessary administrative experience.

In addition to the above awards, the National Executive Committee have the authority to appoint a person, who has sufficient insight into the work of the Corps, coupled with known administrative ability, to the position of *Honorary Chief Lifeguard.*

In recognition of the valuable public service rendered by Canoe Lifeguard Units, the BCU offers honorary membership of the Union – with full affiliation rights as follows: 'That any groups of persons using canoes in their duties as life saving organisations, wherever they may be in the United Kingdom and regardless of whatever organisation to whom they may be affiliated or with whom they may be working, may on application be accepted free of all charge as full member Units of the Corps of Canoe Lifeguards.'

Award for Valour
An Award for Valour has been instituted. The criteria for nomination is as follows: 'The Award shall be made in recognition of any canoeist whose gallantry and devotion in bringing assistance to others in an aquatic situation shall be considered to be of outstanding merit. For the purpose of this Award 'gallantry' and/or 'devotion' shall be seen as an act of quite exceptional quality and perseverance bearing in mind the severity of the climatic or aquatic conditions obtaining at the time. Neither the success or otherwise of the mission, nor the survival or loss of the rescuer or victim shall detract from the qualification. The Award may be made posthumously.'

DUKE OF EDINBURGH'S AWARD SCHEME

Canoeing is applicable to the following sections of the Duke of Edinburgh Award Scheme:

1   Service (Corps of Canoe Lifeguards)

2   Expeditions

3   Physical Recreation

Canoe building is a choice in the remaining 'Skills' Section.

Service

Bronze level : Pass the Canoe Safety Test
Silver level : Become an Assistant Lifeguard of the Corps of Canoe Lifeguards
Gold level : Become a Lifeguard of the Corps of Canoe Lifeguards

Expeditions

The journey chosen must provide a challenge appropriate to the candidate's ability and experience.
Bronze – 2 days, including one night away, involving at least 4 hours paddling per day.
Silver – 3 days, including two nights away, involving at least 5 hours paddling per day.
Gold – 4 days, including three nights away, involving at least 6 hours paddling per day.

Pre-requisites:
Bronze – hold the BCU 3-Star or Proficiency Test Certificate
Silver and Gold – hold the Proficiency Test and satisfy the assessor as to competence to undertake the planned journey.

Suitable rivers are listed on the Touring in Great Britain notes supplied by BCU Headquarters. Silver and Gold level expeditions can be on sheltered coastal waters. A number of other requirements and recommendations pertain, which are related to normal safety procedures. For Canoeists Code of Conduct and Water Safety Code see Appendix IV and chapter 4.

Physical Recreation

Candidates must participate for a minimum of six weeks, and obtain the required number of points reflecting both participation and improvement:
Bronze – 24 points
Silver – 30 points
Gold – 36 points

Participation

Two points are earned for each weekly training session of one hour attended. (Not more than two points per week, or four per alternate weekend may be gained through participation).

Standard

The balance of points required may be gained as follows:

Points	6	12	18	24
Star Tests	1 Star	2 Star	3 Star	4 Star
or Proficiency Tests			Proficiency	Advanced
or Competition – % of Winner's time (Racing, Marathon, Slalom or WW Racing)	150%	140%	130%	120%
Devizes – Westminster, Junior Class over 19's must compete in Senior event	For each stage completed		Full completion of course	

Tests are not retrospective. Standards gained before entry cannot be counted. The candidate must work for the next grade. It is essential that *improvement* is shown. Full information is contained within the new Handbook, obtainable from 5 Prince of Wales Terrace, London W8 5PG. The Director of Coaching will be happy to offer guidance where specific problems are encountered.

THE SCOUT ASSOCIATION

Because of the amount of canoeing that takes place within the Scout movement and consequent requirement for the BCU to supply information and advice, and for instructors to train and test its members, a substantial association fee is paid. This entitles Warranted Scout leaders – that is not individual scouts, unless they are members – to take BCU tests at the reduced fee, and to obtain publications and supplies at member rates.

The Scout Association has adopted a grading system for water, and instituted a Charge Certificate Scheme. There is also an Authorising Charge Certificate system. Both are based on BCU tests and awards, and are related to the water grading system.

Throughout the country, Water Activities Committees are responsible for grading the various stretches of water in the area under their jurisdiction, and for satisfying themselves as to the competence of a leader who applies for an Authorising Charge Certificate. In particular, they are concerned:

1   as to whether he is 'a suitable person to hold a Charge Certificate, and that he fully understands the responsibilities it carries and the limits of his authority'; and

2   'that he has a knowledge of the waters for which the certificate is required – he must appreciate the local hazards and limits of operation'.

The grading system which has been adopted is as follows:

Class A
Open sea more than 3 miles* from the shore, and other dangerous waters close inshore; inland water BCU Grade IV and above.

---

*The grading system devised by the Scout movement has to cater for all types of boating. For practical purposes insofar as canoeing is concerned, an arbitrary 1-3 or more miles is probably less helpful than the Open Water definition in Appendix III.

Class B3
The sea up to 3 miles off the shore, but excluding more dangerous waters close inshore; busy commercial parts; exposed parts of estuaries; inland water BCU Grade III.

Class B2
The sea up to 1 mile off the shore, but excluding more dangerous waters close inshore; more sheltered parts of estuaries; large inland lakes and lochs; inland waters BCU Grade II.

Class B1
Sheltered inland waters and other sheltered waters where currents and tides create no real danger.

Class C
Public boating ponds, etc; some canals and other 'safe' inland waters.

	Charge Certificate	Authorising Charge Certificate
Class A Waters	BCU Advanced Inland or Advanced Sea Proficiency	BCU Inland SI and Advanced Proficiency or BCU Sea SI & Advanced Sea
Class B3 Waters	BCU Inland Proficiency or Sea Proficiency	BCU Inland SI or Sea SI
Class B2 Waters	BCU Inland Proficiency or 3 Star Test or BCU Inland Proficiency or 3 Star Test and tidal knowledge	BCU Instructor
Class B1 Waters	BCU 1 Star	BCU Inland Trainee Instructor or BCU Sea Trainee Instructor

THE GIRL GUIDES ASSOCIATION

The Girl Guides Association has a grading system for water, similar to that of the Scout Association, based upon the difficulties and hazards. Responsibility for grading rests upon the assistant advisers (boating) in the counties, with regional consultants carrying out a co-ordinating role. Liaison with Scout water activities committees is encouraged.

A series of progressive tests for canoeists, similar to the BCU Star Tests, are administered by the Association. The Star Tests give exemption from parts of the Girl Guides Association syllabus. Guidance concerning swimming ability, clothing, and the requirements for the wearing of personal flotation aids, is given in the Association's handbook.

All craft owned by, or on loan to Girl Guide units, must be inspected annually, and after major repairs or heavy usage, to ensure sea worthiness. Members contemplating canoeing expeditions should contact the BCU river adviser before making final plans.

THE ST. JOHN AMBULANCE ASSOCIATION AND BRIGADE

Canoeing Proficiency badge

Candidates with no previous experience should pass the BCU 1 Star Test. Those with experience should pass the next highest test above the one they already possess. Where no previous awards are held, the examiner should determine the standard to be gained, after assessing the candidate's ability level.

Appendix III

Check List for the Guidance of Relevant Authorities

INTRODUCTION

1   A person responsible for the training of young people in potentially hazardous pursuits needs:

    a) a sound knowledge of the element in which he or she is operating

    b) a sound knowledge of the possible dangers for beginners being introduced to the activity

    c) sufficient practical competence to handle any problems likely to develop in that situation

2   The safeguards are:

    a) the availability and correct wearing of clothing and lifejackets (or buoyancy aids)

    b) the identification of 'safe' and 'unsafe' areas, conditions and situations.

3   When these principles are applied, the possibility of a serious incident, or a drowning, occurring, is minimal. If it did happen, it would probably occur in circumstances so unusual to be unlegislatable.

4   Problems occur when a tyro is passing from 'novice' to 'proficiency' level. A competent canoe group, with sound background learning and training, should pose no problem. It is when the novice is wanting more excitement or challenge than experience allows them safely to handle, that potential danger really exists. The 'still' water situation looses its appeal – the paddler wants the 'real thing'. Unfortunately the real thing, particularly the sea, does not have the constant predictable state of the sheltered still water situation, and the novice may not have the necessary ability to cope if conditions worsen.

Safeguards still exist, however:

    a) a logged record of the leaders experience

    b) known factors of river grading or sea conditions within rainfalls, or wind strengths which are reasonably predictable: i.e.

      i) a grade II river will stay a grade II river unless it pours with rain for many hours

      ii) an area of sheltered sea in a given wind strength will behave in a known fashion

5   By identifying situations, levels of ability, and areas of operation, it is possible to provide a logical system: one which safeguards the interests of the authority and the students, but gives the leader an understandable progression and a reasonable degree of freedom.

STUDENTS

6   All students undertaking canoeing activities should wear a lifejacket* or a buoyancy aid* the fitting of which should be checked by a suitably qualified leader. Students should be able to swim 50 metres in light clothing.

QUALIFICATIONS

7   For canoeing activities, leaders should be qualified as folows:

a) *To undertake initial training with beginners in designated† sheltered waters:*

Trainee Instructor of the British Canoe Union with Teacher/Leader endorsement.

b) *To undertake canoeing activities on placid (grade 1) water or equivalent sheltered coastal areas only*

Instructor of the British Canoe Union

c) *To undertake proficiency level expeditioning, grade II or above, surfing, or open water canoeing activities*

Senior Instructor of the British Canoe Union

STAFF RATIOS

8   The following staff ratios are suggested as ideal for practical teaching purposes. Instructors and Senior Instructors are, however, trained to recognise when circumstances allow these guidelines to be safely exceeded, or when lower limits should be applied. The person in charge should always be allowed to exercise discretion.

a) For initial training in sheltered water: 1:8

b) For surfing, grade II white water activities 1:6

EXPEDITIONING

9   Open Water ‡

a) The Expedition Leader should be qualified as stated in 7c

---

*The BCU recommendation with regard to personal buoyancy is as follows:

'Lifejackets to BS 3595/81 with inherent buoyancy (min 6 kg inflating to 16 kg) are recommended for sea and open water expeditioning.

Buoyancy aids to SBBNF/79 standards with a minimum inherent buoyancy of 6 kg. are suitable for river canoeing and other situations where close supervision is being exercised.

Buoyancy aids to SBBNF standards (as above) are recommended for rapid river work, surfing, canoe polo, and other situations where a risk of collision is involved'.

† *Designated Areas* 'A sheltered water situation is defined as one so designated by the BCU Regional Coaching Organiser and relevant authority adviser for the purpose. The rating applies from 1 May to 31 October. It implies normal water and weather conditions. The area so determined will normally be a stretch of canal, or similar, small gravel pit or lake, or similar, which is not large enough, or does not have difficult landing areas, to allow for problems to occur should there be a sudden change in conditions. Water classified as 'C' or 'B1' by the Scout Association, should normally prove suitable.

‡ Open Water is defined as the Sea where it is possible to be three miles from land in any direction. For Proficiency Level expeditioning, a simple section of coastline is envisaged. not involving overfalls, tidal races, difficult landings, or open crossings. Forecasts should be for winds not in excess of force 4, with moderate 'summer' conditions prevailing.

b) A ratio of competent canoeists as follows is recommended:
1-4 students: Leader
5-8 students: Leader + 1
9-12 students: Leader + 2
c) 2 parachute rocket flares should be carried by the leader together with the other equipment listed in the BCU Sea Proficiency test syllabus. A spare split paddle on the deck of the leader and his supporters can be a valuable safety aid.
d) Canoes ought to possess maximum buoyancy (single pillar buoyancy should be supplemented). Bow and stern toggles are recommended and adequate spray decks. Deck lines, when fitted, must be taut and not able to foul the cockpit area.
e) Each member of the group should carry all the equipment listed in the BCU Sea Proficiency test syllabus.
f) In addition the following should be available to all:
    i) A waterproof anorak and adequate canoeing clothing
    ii) A brightly coloured crash helmet
    iii) A tow line
    iv) A red hand held flare
g) A spare split paddle, carried in the boat, but easily accessible, by other persons in the group is also suggested.

10 *White Water Grade II*
a) The expedition leader should be qualified as stated in 7.c
b) There should be a ratio of competent canoeists as follows:
1-4 students: Leader
5-8 students: Leader + 1
c) The leader and each member of the group ought to be fully equipped in accordance with the recommendations in the Inland Proficiency Test Syllabus of the BCU. In addition the leader should carry a suitable length of line and a float.

11 *Size of party*
Over-large fleets of canoes on the sea should be avoided. 15 is probably getting towards the maximum size of a party for practical control to be exercised. On rivers, it is better to split groups down into manageable units if this can be achieved while maintaining reasonable staff ratios. Riparian owners and other river users often dislike fleets in excess of 10-12 canoes.

12 *Advanced Level Canoeing*
For leading competent groups on grade III waters or above inland, or sea conditions in excess of the proficiency level definition, ‡(open water) Senior Instructors should hold the Advanced Proficiency Test of the BCU, or be able to show equivalent ability and experience.

ESCORT BOATS

13 There is no 'BCU Policy' on the use of escort boats. A consensus view is that adherence to the precept of the staff being appropriately qualified and experienced, and the proper equipping, training, gradual building up and reinforcement of experience of the students, renders escort boats unnecessary.

Appendix IV

THE CANOEIST'S CODE OF CONDUCT

More and more people are taking to the water. Some do it for recreation; some to earn a living. This code is designed to ensure that canoeists do not come into conflict with any of them. So please observe it at all times.

ON THE RIVER BANK (or beach or lakeside)

1   Obtain permission before using restricted water. Thank those responsible when you leave.

2   Try to avoid overcrowding one site.

3   Park your car sensibly. Avoid overcrowding or obstructing narrow approach roads. Keep off verges. Pay parking fees and use proper car parks.

4   Don't spread yourself and your equipment so that you upset others.

5   Please keep the peace – don't be too noisy.

6   Pick up litter. Close gates. Be careful about fires. Avoid damage to land or crops.

7   Obey special instructions such as National Trust Rules, local bye-laws and regulations about camping and caravaning.

ON THE WATER

1   Keep away from banks from which anglers are fishing.

2   Keep well clear of anglers' tackle, do not loiter in fishing pools, and cause as little disturbance as possible.

3   Keep a sharp look out for fishermen. Comply with any signals they make to indicate whether they wish you to wait for a moment or to pass. Give a hail if you think your approach has been unnoticed.

4   Be particularly careful not to touch anglers' lines.

5   Do not alter course so as to baulk other craft, particularly in narrow waters. Remember that larger boats are less easily manoeuvrable, and that canoes can use much shallower water than other craft.

6   Keep clear of rowing craft – sculls, fours and eights – particularly when racing or serious coaching is taking place. Remember that it is sometimes difficult for rowing craft to see canoes.

GENERAL CODE FOR ALL WATER USERS

1   Avoid damaging banks and shoreline vegetation.

2   Avoid using areas important for wintering wildfowl, nesting birds and spawning fish in the appropriate season.

3   Whenever possible, come ashore from boats only at recognised landing places.

4   Do not trespass on private banks or moorings.

5   Do everything possible to avoid pollution. Do not throw litter or rubbish into the water or leave it lying about on the banks.

6   Obey the general rules of navigation and any local bye-laws, but remember that, even when you have right of way, you have an overriding responsibility to avoid collision.

7   Avoid crossing the bows of oncoming craft at close quarters.

8   Give precedence to others when they are engaged in organised competition.

9   Have special regard for the problems of the inexpert or beginner as you have for the learner driver on the road.

10   A hail is often useful to draw a person's attention to a situation which may result in inconvenience, damage to gear, or a collision; but treat a hail as a friendly warning and not as an insult.

11   Know the signs for the marking of areas used by underwater swimmers and divers.

12   In shallow waters keep well clear of the wading fisherman and leave adequate room both in front and behind him for his cast. Keep well clear when he is playing a fish.

13   Make sure that your craft is safe and that sufficient safety equipment is carried at all times.

14   It is advisable to be in possession, at all times, of a public liability insurance policy.

15   All governing bodies of water sports produce extensive rules for safety and other matters. These should be read and understood before participating in any activity.

Appendix V

Signals for use in Search and Rescue Operations by Canoeists

All signals must be acknowledged by the canoeist. A horn or similar may be needed to attract attention initially.

Red flags with narrow blue diagonal stripe should be operated by the Corps of Canoe Lifeguards signaller on shore. Crash helmets or spray decks may be used in an emergency. Flags used by Surf Life Saving Association lifeguards may be orange with a 4″ diagonal stripe.

The signals on this page are required to be known by Corps of Canoe Lifeguards Assistant Lifeguard, and the complete set at Lifeguard level.

a) Signals from land; *b) signals from canoe*

a) To attract attention

(two hands moved up and down, crossing above head)

b) As above

a) Acknowledging

(one hand raised above head and immediately lowered)
b) As above or paddle held horizontally in both hands and immediately lowered

a) Proceed in direction indicated

(one hand parallel to ground and indicating direction)

b) I am proceeding in direction indicated

a) Remain stationary

(arms held parallel to ground)

b) I am holding my position

a) Come into beach

(one hand held above the head)

b) I am coming ashore

a) Proceed further out

(two hands held above head)

b) I am going further out

a) **Signals from land;** *b)* *signals from canoe*

a) You are in the
   search area now

(one hand waved in a
circular manner above
the head)

b) *Instructions*
   required

a) Investigate
   submerged object

(one hand pointing
down at 45°, the other
pointing the direction)

a) Pick up swimmers

(one hand moved in a
circular motion, and
the other pointing in
their direction)

a) Signals not
   understood

(hand above head and
moved from side to
side)

b) *As above*

a) Assistance no
   longer required

(hands crossed above
head)

b) *As above*

Bibliography

A comprehensive list of books on canoeing was compiled by Brian Skilling for his thesis *British Canoeing Literature 1866-1966* published by University Microfilming Ltd. The University of Birmingham, supported by the Sports Council, has a sports literature service, known as the National Documentation Centre for Sport, Physical Education and Recreation, and publishes regular bulletins.

Detailed here are most of the major British works, and some from North America, with a brief indication of the scope of the book for the modern British section. Many of the older journals will be out of print and a few are now collectors' items. In general the titles of these indicate the nature of the content, which is often an account of a journey. Nine new titles were available, or in the pipeline during 1980-81. A welcome increase.

ARCHIVAL BOOKS

A Canoe Ramble on Thames and Medway; F. Hodges; 1868.
A Canoe Voyage in the Pooion; J. H. Hamilton; 1868.
A Cruise Across Europe; D. Maxwell; 1906.
A Cruise through Scotland; F. Hodges; 1868.
A Thousand Miles in the Rob Roy Canoe; J. A. MacGregor; Sampson Low 1867.
Alone at Sea; H. Lindemann; 1958.
An Englishman in Ireland; R. A. Scott-Jones; 1910.
An Inland Voyage; R. L. Stevenson; Chatto & Windus 1890.
As the Water Flows; E. Barnes; Grant Richards 1920.
Beacon Six; H. Cundy; 1969.
Camping Voyages on German Rivers; A. A. MacDonnell; 1890.
Canoe Errant; Major R. Raven-Hart; John Murray 1935.
Canoe Errant on the Mississippi; Major R. Raven-Hart; Methuen 1938.
Canoe Errant on the Nile; Major R. Raven-Hart; John Murray 1936.
Canoe in Australia; Major R. Raven-Hart; Georgian House 1948.
Canoe to Mandalay; Major R. Raven-Hart; Frederick Muller 1939.
Canoe Touring Abroad; G. Seal; 1969.
Canoe Travelling; W. Baden-Powell; 1895.
Canoeing; B. Jagger; Arco c1965.
Canoeing; W. G. Luscombe & L. J. Bird; A & C Black 1936.
Canoeing; W. G. Luscombe; Philip Allan 1936.
Canoeing; J. D. Hayward; Bell & Sons 1893.
Canoeing; T. H. McCarthy; Pitmans Game and Recreation Series 1940.
Canoeing; P. W. Blandford; Foyles Handbooks 1957.
Canoeing and Camping Adventures in Northern Waters; R. C. Anderson; Gilbert Wood 1910.
Canoeing Complete; Skilling and Sutcliffe; Nicholas Kaye 1966.
Canoeing down the Rhone; J. Wilson; Chapman & Hall 1957.
Canoeing for Beginners; Peter Mytton-Davis; Elek Books 1971.
Canoeing in Ireland; Major R. Raven-Hart; Canoe & Small Boat 1938.
Canoeing; P. W. Blandford; Foyles Handbooks 1963.
Canoeing Today; P. W. Blandford; Vawser & Wiles 1964.
Canoeing Waters; P. W. Blandford; Lutterworth 1966.
Canoeing Waters; W. Bliss; Methuen 1934.
Canoeing with Sail and Paddle; J. D. Hayward; 1893.
Canoes and Canoe Sailing; W. Baden-Powell; 1871.

Canoes and Canoeing; P. W. Blandford; Lutterworth Press 1962.
Cockleshell Heroes; C. E. Lucas-Phillips; William Heinemann. 1956; Pan Books 1957.
Cruise in a Cockleshell; A. H. Reed; 1867.
Cruise of the Ringleader Canoe; J. Inwards; 1870.
Down River; G. Boumphrey; Allen & Unwin 1936.
Down the Jordan in a Canoe; R. J. E. Boggis; 1939.
Down the Nile by Canoe; A. Davy; 1958.
Down the Orinoco in a Canoe; S. P. Trian; 1902.
Elements of Canoeing; A. V. S. Pulling; Prakken Publishing Co. 1933.
Ethiopian Adventure; H. Ritlinger; 1959.
Exploration of the Arroux; P. G. Hamerton; 1867.
4,000 Miles of Adventure; A. Davy; Robert Hale 1958.
Gino Watkins; J. M. Scott; Hodder & Stoughton 1935.
God's River Country; M. and B. Ferrier; 1958
How to Build and Manage a Canoe; A. R. Ellis & Beams; Brown Son & Ferguson 1949 vol. 1 text; vol.2 plans.
Joe Lavally and the Paleface; B. Wicksteed; 1948.
Kayak to Cape Wrath; J. L. Henderson; Maclellan 1951.
Kingfisher Abroad; T. Rising; Cape 1938.
Log of the Guerl and Rapid; J. A. Godwin & T. S. George; 1872.
Men, Rivers and Canoes; I. Player; 1964.
Modern Canoeing; Major R. Raven-Hart; 1939.
Modern Canoeing; Charles Sutherland; Faber and Faber 1964.
My Canoe; C. M. Chenu; Eric Partridge 1931.
Nanook of the North; Robert Flaherty; Windmill Books 1971.
Our Canoe Voyage; M. Black; 1876.
Ouse's Silent Tide; C. Frederick; 1921.
Paddles and Politics Down the Danube; P. Bigelow; 1892.
Practical Canoeing; Tiphys; Norie & Wilson 1883.
Quest by Canoe: Glasgow to Skye; A. M. Dunnett; Bell & Sons 1950.
Rapid Rivers; W. Bliss; Witherby 1935.
Starting Canoeing; Russell; Adlard Coles c1960.
Tackle Canoeing This Way; P. W. Blandford; Stanley Paul 1964.
The Book of Canoeing; D. J. Davis; Arthur Baker 1969.
The Book of Canoeing; A. R. Ellis; Brown Son & Ferguson 1935.
The Boys Book of Canoeing; E. Jessup; Dutton & Co. 1926.
The Canoeing Manual; Noel McNaught; Nicholas Kaye 1956.
The Cockleshell in Ireland; A. H. Reed; 1872.
The Commodore's Cruise; G. Heavside; 1871.
The Dangerous River; R. M. Paterson; Allen & Unwin 1954.
The Danube Flows through Fascism; W. Van Til; 1938.
The Heart of England by Waterway; W. Bliss; 1933.
The Heart of Scotland by Waterway; R. A. Downie; Witherby 1934.
The Lonely Land; S. F. Olson; 1961.
The Rob Roy on the Baltic; J. MacGregor; Sampson Low 1872.
The Rob Roy on the Jordan; J. MacGregor; Murray 1869.
The Unknown River; P. G. Hamerton; 1871.
The Waterway to London; Anonymous; 1869.
Three in Norway; J. Arth & W. J. Clutterbuck; 1882.
Two Canoe Gipsies; M. Chater; 1933
Under Sail through Red Devon; R. Cattell; 1937.
Voyage in a Paper Canoe; N. Bishop; 1878.
Water Music; Sir J. Squire; Heinemann 1939.
*Watery Wanderings Mid Western Locks; T. H. Holding; E. Marlborough & Co. 1886.

**A photo-copy reproduction is available from BCU Supplies

You and Your Canoe; O. J. Cock; Ernest Benn 1956.
Your Book of Canoeing; B. Jagger; Faber & Faber 1963.

MODERN BRITISH BOOKS

A Broadland Canoe Club; K. D. Millican; New Horizon 1980. *The story of the development of a club and the range of canoeing available in a remote Norfolk village.*
Beginners Guide to Canoeing; Alan Byde; Pelham Books 1977. *A fairly complete introduction for the beginner written in 1974.*
Better Canoeing; Alan Harber; Kaye & Ward 1973. *Technically good for both kayak and Canadian, main concentration is on the skills leading to white water canoeing. Written 1974.*
Canoe Building in Glass Reinforced Plastic; Alan Byde; Adam & Charles Black 1977. *First published in 1974 the book gives a complete guide to building in grp.*
Canoe Design and Construction; Alan Byde; Pelham Books 1972. *Here the author gives hints/guidance on designing from scratch, building the plug, the mould and the finished boat.*
* *Canoeing;* Dennis Davies; Hodder & Stoughton Teach Yourself Books 1981. *An inexpensive introduction and guide to the sport.*
Canoeing; Peter Little and David English; Puffin Books 1981. *A fun, but fairly accurate introduction to canoeing for younger people.*
* *Canoeing;* John Brailsford and Stephen Baker; Oxford Illustrated Press 1977. *White water canoeing – including wild water racing slalom and surfing – is the subject. An introduction with excellent and numerous photographs.*
Canoeing; Peter Williams; Pelham Books 1977. *Singles and doubles introductory kayak techniques are covered, leading to inland touring. Ample, explicit photographs and drawings.*
* *Canoeing Complete;* Brian Skilling; Kaye & Ward 1980. *The 1980 edition is up to date for racing, wild water racing, surfing, sea canoeing, and construction. It contains useful training schedule for competition.*
* *Canoeing Down Everest;* M. Jones; Hodder & Stoughton 1979. *Written by the inimitable Dr Mike Jones, later drowned on a similar attempt on K2, the full story of a dramatic first in canoeing history is unravelled, revealing a fresh and almost cavalier approach to major expeditioning, capturing the personality of this extraordinary paddler.*
* *Canoeing Skills and Canoe Expedition Technique for Teachers and Leaders.* Sgn Ldr P. F. Williams; Pelham Books 1976; *First published in 1969 the book covers most aspects of introducing youngsters to inland touring in single and double kayaks.*
How to Build a Glassfibre Canoe; Trylon Limited 1979. *Full information on the subject from a major supplier of materials to the canoeist.*
* *Kayak Canoeing; Know the Game Series;* E. P. Publishing 1977. *A precis introduction to the sport, covering most aspects.*
* *Living Canoeing;* Alan Byde; A & C Black 1969. *The first of Alan Byde's books, written in 1969 and revised in 1975, it is recommended by many as a comprehensive survey of, and introduction to, the pastime.*
Science of Surfing; R. Abbott; John Jones Cardiff Ltd 1972. *This publication is written for board surfers, but gives probably the cheapest comprehensive study of surfing waveology and method available in Britain.*
* *Sea Canoeing;* Derek Hutchinson; A & C Black 1979. *The second edition appeared in 1979 as a result of the resurgence of major sea expeditioning by British paddlers. Completely devoted to sea kayaking, the book explores the rationale, as well as the practicalities, of this fast developing sport.*
* *Sea Touring;* John Ramwell; J. Ramwell 1978. *As the author himself states; 'an informative manual for sea canoeists!'*
* *Start Canoeing;* Anne Williams & Debbie Piercey; Stanley Paul 1980. *A profusely illustrated and well photographed introduction to the sport with a sea canoeing bias. Very detailed diagrams show the equipment and skills described.*

---

*Available from BCU Supplies

The Complete Book of Canoeing and Kayaking; Gordon Richards; B. T. Batsford Ltd 1981. *A difficult title to live up to. The photographs are good and quite numerous.*
The Spur Book of Wild Water Canoeing; F. Barlow; Spurbooks 1978. *A useful publication that won't break the bank.*
* *Wild Water Canoeing;* R. Steidle; E. P. Publishing 1977. *Translated from the German edition in 1976, this is probably the most comprehensive pictorial breakdown of general white water skills available to date.*

TECHNICAL HANDBOOKS

The following books are written for the budding serious competitor and give advice on technique and training methods for the discipline.
* *Slalom Handbook;* Peter King; BCU Slalom Committee 1983
* *Wild Water Racing Handbook;* David Llewellyn; BCU Wild Water Racing Committee 1980.
* *To Win the Worlds;* Bill Endicott; Reese Press, Baltimore, USA 1980.

TRAINING AND OTHER BCU MANUALS

* *Canoe Building – Glass Fibre*
* *Canoe Building – Soft Skin.*
* *Canoeing for Schools and Youth Groups.*
  Corps of Canoe Lifeguards Training Manual. Sections of the Manual and this Handbook are also available as separate booklets. Send sae for current list and prices.

RIVER GUIDES

* *Guide to the Waterways of the British Isles;* British Canoe Union. *This is the only full guide to the waterways of Britain written from a canoeist's point of view, giving itineraries for every significant river. Regretfully the itineraries have not been updated since 1961 and the situation is now complicated by the current access problems. Reprinted in 1980 it is still very useful in locating rivers and giving factual information as to their practical canoeability. For information on the current legal or licensing situation on a given waterway reference must be made to the BCU river advisory service.*
* *North Wales White Water;* Jim Hargreaves, Barry Storry; Cascade Press 1981. *Good itineraries for the white water rivers of North Wales and the Menai Straits. The mention of rivers and sites does not imply a right of access.*
  A Guide to Scottish Rivers; Scottish Canoe Association 1981. *Visitors to Scotland should contact the SCA, 18 Ainslie Place, Edinburgh before canoeing on Scottish rivers.*
* *Other maps and guides are available, and are being added to, such as: River Wye Map, Guide; River Severn Map; Canoeists Map of UK Rivers and Beaches; Broadlands Map; River Thames Map – Lechlade to Richmond; French Rivers Notes; Austria and Bavaria White Water Guide, canoe touring in East Anglia and other regional guides. Send sae to BCU Supplies for current list and prices.*

NAVIGATION AND WEATHER FORECASTING

The following books are recommended for this subject.
* *Coastal Navigation;* G. G. Watkins; Butler & Tanner 1977.
* *Exercises in Coastal Navigation;* G. W. White; Stanford Maritime Ltd. 1980.
  Weather Forecasting for Sailors; Frank Singleton; Hodder & Stoughton 1981.

---

*Available from BCU Supplies

SOME BOOKS FROM NORTH AMERICA

The following are published in USA unless otherwise stated. 'Canoeing' means that the subject is open or decked Canadians.

Basic River Canoeing; Robert E. McNair, American Camping Association Inc. 1972.
Boat Builders Manual; Charles Walbridge; American Canoe Association.
* *Canoeing;* American Red Cross; 1977. *This is the comprehensive handbook on open Canadian canoeing.*
Canoeing with the Cree; Eric Savareid; Minnesota Historical Society 1968 (Reprint of 1935 edition).
From Start to Finish; George P. Sipos; 1965.
Fundamentals of Kayaking; Jay Evans; Ledyard Canoe Club 1964.
Kayaking; the new Whitewater Sport for Everyone; R. R. Anderson and J. Evans; 'American Canoe Association'.
Man and the Sea; Philip Banbury; Book Club Associates 1975.
On the River; Walter Magnes Teller; Rutgers University Press 1976.
Pole, Paddle, Portage; Bill Riviere; Van Nostrand Reinhold 1974.
River of the Sacred Monkey; D. Krustev; Wilderness Holidays 1970.
Rushton and His Times in American Canoeing; Atwood Manley; Syracuse University Press 1978.
† *Sea Kayaking;* John Dowd; Douglas & MacIntyre, Vancouver, 1981.
Survival of the Bark Canoe; John McPhee; Straus and Girox 1975.
The Canoe and White Water – from Essential to Sport; C S Franks; University of Toronto Press 1977.
The Canoe Campers Handbook; Roy Bearse; Winchester Press 1974.
The Canoe Campers Handbook; Roy Bearse; Winchester Press 1974.
The Complete Wilderness Paddler; J. W. Davidson and J. Rugge; Alfred Knopf 1976.
The Path of The Paddle; Bill Mason; Van Nostrand Reinhold 1980. *A superb, comprehensive book of the open canoe.*
The Sound of White Water; Hugh Fosburgh; Belmont Books 1971.
The Starship and the Canoe; K. Brower; Holt Rinehart and Winston 1978.
To the Arctic by Canoe; C. Stuart Houston; McGill Queens University 1974.
* *White Water – (Running the Wild Rivers of North America);* Bart Jackson; Walker & Co 1979. *A beautifully produced guide with good colour and black and white photography.*
* *White Water Handbook for Canoe and Kayak;* Appalachian Mountain Club 1981.
White Water Racing, Eric Evans and J. Burton; Burton Nantahala Outdoor Centre 1980.

CLASSICAL WORKS

The Bark Canoes and Skin Boats of North America; Adney and Chapelle; Smithsonian Institute, United States National Museum Bulletin No 230 1964.
British Coracles and Irish Curraghs; James Hornell; Society for Nautical Research.
Nunaga: Ten years of Eskimo Life; Duncan Pryde; MacGibbon & Kee 1972.
The Eskimos; Birket-Smith; Methuen 1959.
The Exploration of the Colorado River and its Canyons; John Wesley Powell; Dover 1895.

MAGAZINES

* *Beach Break* – BCU Surf Committee
* *Canoe Focus* – BCU house Journal *(free to members)*
Canoeing – Ocean Publications
Canoeist – Stuart Fisher
* *Ceufad* – Welsh Canoe Association *(free to WCA members)*
* *Feedback* – BCU Slalom Committee
* *SCAN* – Scottish Canoeing Association *(free to SCA members)*

---

* Available from BCU Supplies   † Available from the Long River Canoeist Club

Index

Including annotated glossary of terms not defined in the text

DOs and DON'Ts
for Canoeists

6 Do keep away from weirs. They are DANGEROUS.
7 Do ask about local conditions. Tides, currents, rapids and weather changes can all be dangerous.
8 Don't have slack decklines, loose ropes or gear in the cockpit. They are dangerous in an emergency.
9 Don't wear wellington boots or heavy clothes. You can't swim in boots and jackets.
10 Do provide bouyancy...airbags in the boat and a life-jacket for yourself.